Filibusters an

The story of William Walker and
His associates

William O. Scroggs

Alpha Editions

This edition published in 2019

ISBN : 9789389247695

Design and Setting By
Alpha Editions
email - alphaedis@gmail.com

FILIBUSTERS AND FINANCIERS

THE STORY OF WILLIAM WALKER AND HIS ASSOCIATES

BY

WILLIAM O. SCROGGS, Ph.D.

PROFESSOR OF ECONOMICS AND SOCIOLOGY IN
THE LOUISIANA STATE UNIVERSITY

New York
THE MACMILLAN COMPANY
1916

Norwood Press
J. S. Cushing Co. — Berwick & Smith Co.
Norwood, Mass., U.S.A.

PREFACE

WHEN the writer of these pages first began to study the filibustering activities of William Walker and his associates, he
did so with no intention of producing a book. As he continued his investigations, however, he became convinced that
this subject deserved more attention from the historian than
it had yet received, and he therefore determined to write the
full story of those filibustering movements which are so closely
interwoven with the life of William Walker, and at the same
time to give the events thus narrated their proper setting in
the whole field of American history.

The accounts of Walker's various enterprises appearing in
general works on American history are always meagre, and
in many cases are actually misleading. The usual explanations
of his motives are much too simple. The forces underlying
filibusterism were in fact exceedingly varied and complex, and
to describe them requires the telling of a long but interesting
story. The part played in Walker's career and in Central
American politics by American financiers and captains of industry; the designs of Walker upon Cuba; his utter repudiation of the annexation of his conquests to the United States;
the appeals of Central American governments to the leading
European powers for deliverance from the filibusters; the
thinly veiled machinations of Great Britain, Spain, and France
against the American adventurers — these are some of the facts,
hitherto overlooked or ignored, which it is here sought to set
forth in their true light. Some of the results of this investigation have already appeared in print. (See the *American
Historical Review* for July, 1905, and the *Mississippi Valley
Historical Review* for September, 1914.)

In making acknowledgment to those who have assisted him in the preparation of this work the author feels that he is indebted most of all to two of his former instructors, Professor George Petrie, of the Alabama Polytechnic Institute, and Professor Albert Bushnell Hart, of Harvard University. Professor Petrie first aroused his interest in the filibustering movement and directed his earliest investigations, and Professor Hart trained and aided him in his further research. Professor Andrew C. McLaughlin, while Director of the Bureau of Historical Research of the Carnegie Institution, aided him very materially in the investigation of manuscript sources in the archives of the State and Navy departments at Washington. Others who have been of much assistance in giving advice or furnishing materials are Professor St. George L. Sioussat, of Vanderbilt University; Lieutenant Campbell B. Hodges, of the United States Army; and Mr. Antonio Guell, of the Louisiana State University, a nephew of two of Walker's greatest opponents, President Mora and General Cañas of Costa Rica. To General John McGrath, of Baton Rouge, La., a veteran of Walker's first Nicaraguan expedition, the author is indebted for the courtesy of a number of pleasant interviews, which have given him a clearer insight into the motives and aspirations of the adventurers in Central America. He is also greatly obligated to Mr. Robert Lusk, of Nashville, Tenn., for the loan of a scrapbook compiled by Major John P. Heiss, one of Walker's friends and supporters. The author also desires to return acknowledgment of the many courtesies extended to him by officials in charge of the archives of the State and Navy departments and by the staff in the reading room of the Library of Congress. To his colleagues, Professors Walter L. Fleming and Milledge L. Bonham, Jr., who have kindly read the manuscript and offered many valuable criticisms, he feels especially indebted.

CONTENTS

LIST OF MAPS

FILIBUSTERS AND FINANCIERS

CHAPTER I

WHY MEN WENT A-FILIBUSTERING

THERE is a proverb current among Frenchmen to the effect that "the appetite comes with eating," and in the case of the land hunger of the American people the truth of this assertion seems well established. As soon as they set foot on American soil the colonists from Europe were compelled to wrest their lands from the savages, many of whom resisted the invaders to the death. Nature as well as the natives had to be subdued. Road and field were cleared with axe and spade; pioneers built their log cabins far in the wilderness, and, like the advance guard of a marching army, kept always ahead of the main body of westward-moving settlers. There was no arrest of this westward progress till the pioneer stood on the shores of the Pacific. In 1803 the boundary was moved from the Mississippi to the Rockies, and the next generation saw it extended from the Rockies to the sea. A whole continent had been won, but the land hunger seemed keener than ever. The appetite had increased with the eating.

Now that the red man was a negligible factor, and the mysteries of the great interior of the continent had been revealed, adventurous men began to look beyond the borders of the United States for the activities their natures seemed to demand. Natural selection had operated to produce a distinctive type of American, whose whole philosophy of conduct may be summed up in the phrase "go ahead." One of the leading exponents of this idea had indeed prefaced the injunction to go ahead with a monition that one should first be sure that he was right, but to the average American in the first half of the nineteenth century such cautioning was entirely superfluous. He was always sure that he was right. This belief of the Americans in their own excellence was one of the things which most impressed and puzzled the foreign visitor. Success in the struggle for existence in the New World had produced unbounded egotism and self-confidence. Every vigorous boy passes through such a stage as he approaches adolescence. To other members of his family and to his neighbours he seems something of a bully. In this period other nations entertained a similar opinion of Young America. All the world regarded this country as a braggart and a bully, and the estimate was not entirely unjust. It is consoling, however, to record that our faults, numerous as they were, were symptoms of youth and superabundant health rather than signs of senile degeneracy.

Under such conditions it was natural that Americans should believe that their great republic was eventually to dominate both continents of the Western Hemisphere, and to such an idea they applied the very expressive term "manifest destiny." To them it was inconceivable that the rapid growth of past decades should not continue. There was no reason why it should terminate with the acquisition of California, when to the southward there lay the fairest portions of the earth cumbered with a discordant and retrograding people. Was it not our duty to plant a new population and a new government in these lands, even as Moses and the Israelites of old had dispossessed the heathen Canaanites? To Young America the answer was obvious. "It is the fate of America ever 'to go ahead,'" wrote a Californian in 1854. "She is like the rod of Aaron that became a serpent and swallowed up the other rods. So will America conquer or annex all lands. That is her 'manifest destiny.' Only give her time for the process.

To swallow up every few years a province as large as most kingdoms of Europe is her present rate of progress. Sometimes she purchases the mighty morsel, sometimes she forms it out of waste territory by the natural increase of her own people, sometimes she annexes, and sometimes she conquers it." This writer did not seek to defend such a policy on any grounds of abstract morality. "America (that is the true title of our country) secures the spoils won to her hand, however dishonestly they have come. That is only her destiny, and perhaps she is not so blamable as a nation in bearing it willingly. One may profit by the treason, yet hate the traitor. Let the distant monarch of the lands beyond the great lakes and the tawny people of the far South look to it. America must round her territories by the sea." [1]

The phenomenon of filibustering was a natural outgrowth of such ideas. When Americans gathered their scant stock of goods, assembled in small bands, shouldered their guns, and set out toward the West or Southwest, they were not seeking solely for sordid wealth, but were prompted in part by a desire to move in a broader field, to occupy a larger stage, and have a better opportunity to " go ahead." They were filled with the idea of the bigness of their country, and desired to act on a scale commensurate with its greatness. Some of their ideas and manners impress us to-day as being wonderfully exaggerated. Even their humour was mainly a form of grotesque exaggeration. This type of American was an unsocialized product, but his lack of social ideals was offset by an aggressive individualism, which in this period yielded increasing returns. If such men chanced to direct their energies toward the American wilderness, they were called pioneers. If, on the other hand, they happened to direct their attention toward another nation, whose sovereignty was formally recognized by their own, they were called filibusters.

The term "filibuster" was originally one of opprobrium, and its

---

[1] Soulé, Gihon, and Nisbet, *Annals of San Francisco*, 476. (New York, 1855.)

use in the fifties was much resented by those to whom it was applied, inasmuch as it was regarded as synonymous with pirate or buccaneer.   In this volume the word is used in no such offensive sense, but is employed to designate those adventurers who, during the decade preceding the Civil War, were engaged in fitting out and conducting under private initiative armed expeditions from the United States against other nations with which this country was at peace.   Whether the persons engaged in such activities were pirates or patriots, they shall be designated here as filibusters, and the use of this term implies *per se* neither condemnation nor commendation.[1]

In its final analysis filibustering may be described, in the phraseology of Herbert Spencer, as a process of equilibration of energy. Whenever a superior or more energetic people are brought into contact with an inferior or less energetic group, a process of equilibration between the two groups necessarily occurs.   This equilibrative movement is always some kind of conflict, and in its primitive aspect we call it the struggle for existence.   This conflict may assume many forms, varying from the complete annihilation to the "benevolent assimilation" of the weak by the strong. Viewed in this broad way, filibustering is but a part of that movement common to all periods of history, wherein we see human hordes, prompted by wanderlust, land hunger, pressure of population, religious zeal, or what not, move out from their ancestral dominions and despoil some weaker peoples of their fields and flocks and homes.   When the nomadic barbarian dispossessed the savage huntsman and converted his hunting ground into a cattle range, he was the predecessor of the modern filibuster.   And the Angles, Saxons, and Jutes, who left their gloomy northern peninsula for Britain's sunnier clime and made their name for Briton a synonym

---

[1] Etymologically, the word *filibuster* is a variant of freebooter (Dutch *vrijbuiter*), and was first widely used to designate the pirates who plundered the Spanish colonies of the West Indies in the seventeenth century.   Hence originally filibuster = freebooter = free + booty = a plunderer.

for slave, were they not true filibusters? And were not the de-
scendants of these freebooters themselves the victims of another
filibustering raid led by Duke William of Normandy, who was
also of filibustering antecedents? From the point of view of the
American aborigine even the Pilgrims and Puritans were filibusters.

The American people in 1850 possessed superabundant energy.
They had conquered a continent, and they sighed for other lands
to conquer. The "splendid isolation" in which they had been
reared had failed to produce that sense of international obligations
which undoubtedly would have developed if they had been near
neighbours of other strong peoples; and for half a century they had
been taking the lands next to theirs in whatever way seemed most
convenient. Louisiana they bought; West Florida and Texas
they got mainly by filibustering; and California they got by conquest. The moral distinction between public and private pillage
of the territory of a weaker nation was but vaguely drawn. All
that was required of the filibuster was success. If he succeeded,
he was a hero and a patriot; if he failed, he was a reprobate. It is
rather doubtful if we have advanced very far from this idea even in
the twentieth century. A close relation always exists between our
ideas of international morality and our material interests.

Following the treaty of Guadalupe-Hidalgo American expansionists found the prospects remote for further land-grabbing by
governmental activity. Already the British government had
refused to be impressed by the bluster of "fifty-four forty or
fight," and had compelled an avowedly expansionist administration to compromise its territorial claims in the Northwest. It
was known too that Great Britain was jealously watching for any
suspicious movement of the United States in the Caribbean, and
had already taken steps to forestall us in that region. But even
if the American government were temporarily impotent, the expansionists were as active as ever. Private initiative would find
a way where President and cabinet were helpless. The United

States, therefore, in 1850 was a fertile field for filibusterism, and a
contemporary French observer declared this to be almost a national
institution of the American people.[1]

These filibustering propensities were somewhat stronger in the
Southern States than in other parts of the Union. Southern civilization, as is well known, was more militant than that of the North.
The slavery régime made it so. Southern men also clung more
tenaciously than their Northern brethren to the traditions and
customs of their forefathers; the ideals of an earlier age still prevailed. Men still resorted to the code duello in the defence of
their honour and the honour of their women. Others might
laugh at their ideals of chivalry, but they accepted them in all
sincerity. Prosaic industrialism had not yet invaded this region,
and its youth looked upon life from a more romantic point of
view than is possible in these days of factories and skyscrapers.
It is not to be inferred, however, that the typical young Southerner
was a convivial cavalier or a troubadour twanging his guitar and
writing sentimental verses to his lady. Southern life has always
been marked by a large amount of Puritanical austerity, and such
austerity is by no means incompatible with militancy, as witnesseth
Oliver Cromwell or Stonewall Jackson.

It was natural, then, that many of the foremost filibusters, such
as Quitman, Walker, and Crabb, should be Southern men, and
that their activities and aspirations should evoke strong sympathy
in the South. But there was still another reason for the Southern
attitude toward filibustering. It was the desire for the further expansion of slave territory. The men who actually joined the filibustering expeditions were by no means the zealous apostles of
slavery propagandism that some writers have depicted, but many
of their abettors were men of that type. The wastefulness of
the slavery system necessitated the constant accession of virgin

---

[1] "Il y est presque une institution nationale." Auguste Nicaise, *Les Flibustiers
Américains*, 32. (Paris, 1860.)

lands. Without these the "peculiar institution" would be doomed, and the South would be compelled to undergo a social and industrial revolution the outcome of which no one could foresee. This problem also had its political phases. By common consent Congress had followed the practice of admitting new States in pairs, one slave and the other free, with the object of preserving the balance of power in the Senate between the two sections of the Union. It had become evident, however, that without further expansion southward the equilibrium of the Union would eventually be destroyed, as the South was being outstripped in population by the rapidly growing North. Without this carefully maintained balance between the free and slave States the dissolution of the Union seemed to many Southern leaders inevitable. Such an idea played a part in the acquisition of Texas, and was most probably responsible for the provision, in the joint resolution admitting that State, that its territory might be subdivided into not more than four additional States.

The gaining of Texas by the South was somewhat offset by the results of the Mexican War, which had proven to be to the advantage of the North, and had failed to restore the equilibrium between the sections. Covetous eyes, therefore, were cast southward towards Cuba, Mexico, and Central America.

Some historians have regarded this desire for slavery extension as the fundamental motive actuating all American filibusters; but, as subsequent chapters will reveal, the real explanation of the activities of these men is by no means such a simple one. When William Walker, for instance, had among his ranking officers men like Charles Frederick Henningsen, the European soldier of fortune, Domingo de Goicouria, the Cuban "liberator," Bruno von Natzmer, a Prussian cavalry officer, Frank Anderson, of New York, and Charles W. Doubleday, of Ohio; when he was induced to go to Nicaragua by Byron Cole, a New Englander; and when his enterprise was first chronicled and he himself greatly

lauded by another New Englander, William V. Wells, a grandson
of Samuel Adams, it was evident that such an undertaking appealed
to many besides the slavery propagandists.   The filibustering
spirit was in the air, and the daring enterprises seemed to enlist
the sympathies in nearly equal degree of California pioneers, Texas
plainsmen, political exiles from Europe, Southern slavery advo-
cates, and Northern devotees of manifest destiny.   A goodly
portion of Walker's recruits were drawn from human derelicts of
all sorts and conditions in New York, San Francisco, and New
Orleans, the ports whence steamers voyaged to the coveted goal
of the filibusters.

It is the purpose of this work to show that the raids on Latin
America between 1850 and 1860 were not mere accidents, but are
vital facts of history, symptomatic in a high degree of the American
spirit of that decade.   Indeed, they were as irrepressible as the conflict which came in 1861, and which in its outcome so altered the
character of American society as to reduce filibustering to the
status of a lost art.

The story of these ventures naturally centres in the career of
William Walker, rightly designated as the greatest of the American
filibusters.

CHAPTER II

The Early Life of William Walker

Our knowledge of the early life of William Walker is somewhat fragmentary. His father, James Walker, was a Scotchman who settled in Nashville, Tennessee, in 1820, and was for a time engaged in mercantile business but later became president of a local concern known as the Commercial Insurance Company. James Walker married Mary Norvell of Kentucky, and from this union there were four children, William, Norvell, James, and Alice. William, the eldest, was born May 8, 1824. His two brothers were later to follow him to Nicaragua, without, however, adding additional lustre to the family name, as Norvell proved to be incompetent, insubordinate, and dissipated, and James succumbed to the cholera soon after joining his two older brothers on the isthmus. The sister, Alice, married a gentleman of Louisville, Kentucky, by the name of Richardson.

In his boyhood days William gave no indication of being a coming soldier of fortune. Indeed, he impressed the neighbours of his family as being rather effeminate and firmly tied to the maternal apron-strings. Those who knew him well, however, did not regard him as a prig. As he grew up his mother became an invalid, and he usually spent his mornings by her side, reading aloud for her diversion and comfort. "He was very intelligent and as refined in his feelings as a girl," says Miss Jane H. Thomas, a friend of the family. "I used often to go to see his mother and always found him entertaining her in some way." [1] Death deprived this mother

[1] Jane H. Thomas, *Old Days in Nashville, Tennessee*, 78–79. (Nashville, 1897.)

9

of both the joy and the sorrow that she would have experienced from the vicissitudes of her son's later career. James Walker, the father, lived in Nashville until after the Civil War, but spent his last years in Louisville, where he died in 1874.

At school, it was said, William was not a very satisfactory pupil. Though of bright mind and studious habits, he found the schoolroom galling to his restless nature, but in spite of this handicap he easily fulfilled all the requirements of both school and college, and in 1838, when only fourteen years of age, he was graduated from the University of Nashville. Most American colleges of that period were little more than the modern academy or high school, and the fact that Walker received his diploma from this institution at what is now the high school age might give an impression that he received only the equivalent of a secondary education. An examination of the entrance requirements and curriculum, however, shows that the students of the University of Nashville received a fairly thorough cultural and practical education. The subjects then required for admission comprised "the Grammar, including prosody, of the Greek and Latin tongues, with Mair's *Introduction*, and such other elementary books as are usually taught in respectable Grammar Schools; Cæsar's Commentaries, Virgil, Cicero's Orations, Greek Testament, and Dalzel's *Collectanea Græca Minora*, or with other Greek and Latin authors, equivalent to these; and also with English Grammar, Arithmetic, and Geography." The studies prescribed for undergraduates included algebra, geometry, trigonometry, descriptive and analytical geometry, conic sections, calculus, mensuration, surveying, navigation, mechanics, astronomy, chemistry, mineralogy, geology, experimental philosophy, natural history, Roman and Grecian antiquities, Greek and Latin classics, rhetoric and belles-lettres, history, mental and moral philosophy, logic, political economy, international and constitutional law, composition, criticism and oratory, natural theology, Christian evidences, and the Bible.

As compared with present-day collegiate courses, the student received only a smattering of many of these subjects, excepting, perhaps, those that were strictly classical; but there is little doubt that the instruction afforded Walker and his fellow-students provided about as good a foundation for culture and civic usefulness as could be obtained in that day. Great emphasis was laid on moral training. Prayers were offered in the chapel twice a day, and attendance was compulsory. At the beginning of each meal in the dining-hall the students stood while a blessing was pronounced; at its close they again arose and stood while thanks were offered. Church attendance was required, and the study of the Bible, natural theology, and evidences of Christianity was prescribed for Sunday. Attendance upon balls, horse-races, cock-fights, and theatres was forbidden, and students were denied the luxuries of dogs, horses, carriages, and servants. They were allowed "to learn music, fencing, and other accomplishments" not taught at the University only by written request of parent or guardian. Every evening, after prayers in chapel, at least two students were required to deliver orations, their speeches being made in rotation, with the Seniors producing original compositions. The hours of study were from sunrise to breakfast, from nine to twelve o'clock, from two to five, and, in the winter, from eight till bedtime. During these periods it was against the rules for the student to leave his room except to attend classes.[1]

Under such an environment, Puritanical in its austerity, was educated the man whom statesmen and diplomats of three continents were later to denounce as a freebooter and pirate. His rearing, moreover, was different in no material respect from that of countless other Southern youths, and those novelists and literary historians who have pictured the typical young Southerner as bred like the seventeenth-century cavalier would do well to revise their references.

[1] *Laws of the University of Nashville*, 1840.

Walker graduated in a class of twenty, two of whom entered the ministry.[1] Being then at the most impressionable age, he shortly professed religion and became a member of the Christian (Disciples') Church. It was his parents' desire that he too should enter the ministry, a profession for which he seemed by disposition and character to be well adapted; but his inclinations led him to the study of medicine, and in accordance with the custom of the times he began a course of reading in the office of a Dr. Jennings preparatory to entering a medical college. He next entered the medical department of the University of Pennsylvania, and in 1843 received from that institution the degree of M.D. It was peculiarly appropriate that Walker, whose striking eyes were later to gain him the title of "the grey-eyed man of destiny," should have chosen "The Iris" for the subject of his graduating essay. As will be seen later, the resurrection of an old Indian legend in Central America caused the brilliant grey of his eyes to become one of Walker's greatest physical assets.

Walker's parents were determined that he should enjoy every educational advantage, and provision was made for the completion of his medical studies in Europe. Immediately, therefore, after receiving his degree from the University of Pennsylvania Walker went to Paris and remained a year there in the study of medicine. He then spent over a year visiting the interesting cities of Europe and gaining a fair knowledge of several of the continental languages.

When he returned to Nashville in 1845, he had barely attained his majority, and yet there were few men of his community who had enjoyed such opportunities for education, culture, and professional training. One of his friends, also a later soldier of fortune, declared him "the most accomplished surgeon that ever visited the city," and this was probably no exaggeration so far as theoretical training was concerned. For some reason, however, the practice

[1] *Catalogue of Officers and Graduates of the University of Nashville*, 1850.

of medicine proved to be not to his liking, and he announced his intention of studying law. He began his readings in the law office of Edwin H. Ewing, of Nashville, but his native city was not destined to see the display of his legal abilities, for a few months later he removed to New Orleans. This change of residence necessitated further study, as Louisiana did not follow the English common law like the other American States, but maintained a legal system based upon the Code Napoleon. In due time he was admitted to the bar and displayed his shingle at 48 Canal Street. Here his career as an attorney was quite brief and almost briefless. The natural reserve of his manner prevented his making many intimate friends, and any legal talent he might have had was unrecognized.[1] Despairing of success as a lawyer, he turned to journalism, and in the winter of 1848 became one of the editors and proprietors of the New Orleans *Crescent*. He was associated in this work with J. C. Larue and W. F. Wilson. The tone of this journal was very conservative, and several hot-headed editors of Mississippi and South Carolina referred to it as a "Yankee paper." In its editorial columns it heaped ridicule upon the filibustering designs then directed against Cuba, and these articles were later attributed to none other than Walker. Partly because of its conservatism the *Crescent* soon fell on hard lines, and after it was sold out in the autumn of 1849 Walker had to look elsewhere for employment.[2]

During his sojourn in New Orleans Walker made two acquaintances that were destined to play a part in his later career. His legal and journalistic duties brought him into frequent contact with the clerk of the United States Circuit Court, a young Virginian named Edmund Randolph, a grandson of the statesman of that

[1] The New Orleans *Delta*, July 27, 1856, quotes a former reporter of the *Crescent*, connected with that paper when Walker was editor, as saying that Walker was very silent and very kind, with the look of a man bent upon a hard course of study, and nearly always poring over some book.

[2] New Orleans *Picayune*, Dec. 22, 1853.

name. The two became fast friends and were to meet again in
San Francisco. There Randolph was to be the one man among
men to whose advice Walker would lend an ear; and, as the sequel
showed, no one was to wield a greater influence, either for good or
for ill, over Walker's destiny than he. The second acquaintance is
interesting because it gives us a glimpse of the sentimental side of
Walker's nature. There was in New Orleans a young lady by the
name of Helen Martin for whom the doctor-lawyer-editor developed a very warm attachment. The details of the romance are
somewhat conflicting. According to one account, they met in
Nashville shortly after Walker's return from Europe, and she was
the magnet that drew the embryonic lawyer to start his legal career
in New Orleans. Another version is that they met for the first
time in New Orleans while Walker was still busy mastering the intricacies of the Louisiana civil law. Though well educated and of
engaging personality, the young woman had suffered one great
misfortune: she had been born deaf. To his many other accomplishments Walker now added the sign language of deaf mutes,
and proceeded to press his suit. One story has it that his love was
not returned; another, that his affection was reciprocated, but that
a misunderstanding caused an estrangement; and still another,
that they were happy in their love and had actually fixed the date
for the wedding.

It matters little which of these statements is true, for the
outcome, so far as Walker was concerned, was the same. The city
was scourged by one of its visitations of yellow fever, and Helen
Martin was an early victim. This terrible disappointment was
said by his friends to have produced a noticeable change in the
character of Walker. His naturally serious demeanour became
even more melancholy, but in place of the former studious habits
there came a daring ambition and a reckless disregard of life.[1]

---

[1] Many accounts of this romance were published after Walker became famous
in Nicaragua. See, for example, the New York *Daily News*, Feb. 28, 1856.

Every adventurous spirit in 1849 heard the call of California, and Walker was no exception to the rule. With no further ties to hold him in New Orleans he joined the great caravan then moving westward in quest of the Golden Fleece, and in June, 1850, he arrived in San Francisco. Before leaving New Orleans, however, he showed something of the fire that smouldered under a quiet exterior by seeking out one of the editors of *La Patria*, a tri-weekly Spanish-American paper, and giving him a severe flogging on account of the publication of an article at which he took personal offence.[1]

In San Francisco journalism again engaged Walker's energies, and he became one of the editors of the *Daily Herald*. Within a few months, as a result of a controversy with the district judge, Levi Parsons, he found himself a popular hero. The city for some time had been suffering from an epidemic of crime and lawlessness, and the newspapers had loudly criticised the authorities for their failure to bring offenders to justice. Judges themselves came in for their share of the censure, and Judge Parsons, waxing wroth at the attacks upon the bench, laid the matter before the grand jury, taking occasion to denounce the press as a nuisance. But the grand jury ignored the suggestion, and the editors, emboldened by this evidence that public sentiment was on their side, returned to the attack with renewed vigour. The severest of these criticisms came from the pen of Walker and appeared in the *Herald* under the title "The Press a Nuisance." As a result, a few days later Walker was haled before Parsons' court, adjudged guilty of contempt and fined to the amount of five hundred dollars. Walker the lawyer was now attorney for Walker the editor; he denied the judge's jurisdiction, refused to pay the fine, and went to jail. The whole San Francisco press immediately raised a clamour, declar-

---

[1] Wheeler Scrapbook no. 5, p. 59 (one of a collection of scrapbooks in the Library of Congress, compiled by J. H. Wheeler, minister to Nicaragua while Walker was in that country).

ing that the people were being robbed of the palladium of their liberties; and the free and unterrified pioneers were quick to respond. A mass meeting was held on the plaza on March 9, 1851, with several thousand citizens in attendance. Resolutions were quickly adopted approving Walker's conduct, calling on Parsons to resign his seat, and asking the local representatives in the legislature to initiate impeachment proceedings. After adjourning, the citizens marched in a body to the jail and made Walker a visit of sympathy.

Habeas corpus proceedings were next instituted before a judge of the superior court, who held that Parsons might institute a suit for libel, but that his punishment for the contempt alleged in a newspaper statement was inconsistent with the freedom of the press and a violation of the Constitution. Walker was thereupon set free. He at once presented a memorial to the legislature, and the committee to which it was referred recommended on March 26 that Parsons should be impeached. A special committee was then appointed to investigate the charges, and upon its reporting insufficient grounds for impeachment the case was ended.[1] Had Walker possessed anything like personal magnetism, he might have made of this episode the foundation of a successful career in California politics. He was indeed not without political ambition, but in the prime requisites of a successful politician he was woefully lacking.

Even the stirring scenes in San Francisco in the early fifties did not long satisfy this restless spirit, and shortly after the Parsons affair Walker removed to the newly incorporated and rapidly growing town of Marysville. Here in 1851 and 1852 he was a partner of Henry P. Watkins in the practice of law. Marysville, like any other young Western community, was a place of open-hearted, democratic hospitality, but Walker, with his usual indifference, held himself aloof and made confidants of none. His law partner,

---

[1] Soulé, Gihon, and Nisbet, *Annals of San Francisco*, 322 f.; Louisville *Times*, Jan. 15, 1856.

however, was a better "mixer," and the firm of the two W's enjoyed some practice.[1] One of Walker's colleagues at the Marysville bar was Stephen J. Field, later to sit on the Supreme bench of both California and the United States. In recording his recollections of Walker in 1877 the justice states that "he was a brilliant speaker, and possessed a sharp but not a very profound intellect. He often perplexed both court and jury with his subtleties, but seldom convinced either."[2]

Walker had hardly settled in Marysville before rumours began to circulate that strange schemes for the colonization and conquest of portions of Mexico were brewing in San Francisco among the French element of that city. These rumours were not without foundation, as the following chapter will show. It was from these French adventurers that Walker received his impetus to abandon the practice of law and try his talents in still another field, and one which seemed to offer greater rewards for his ambition than the quiet pursuits of doctor, lawyer, or journalist.[3]

[1] H. S. Hoblitzell, *Early Historical Sketch of the City of Marysville and Yuba County*, 9. (Marysville, 1876.)

[2] S. J. Field, *Personal Reminiscences of Early Days in California*, 97. (Privately printed, 1893.)

[3] In connection with this sketch of Walker's early life it may be well to call attention to a curious story concerning his origin which was circulated in Paris during the autumn of 1858. It seems that some ten years before this date an aide-de-camp of the Duke de Nemours had been ostracized and compelled to leave France for cheating at cards in a game with certain noted personages. He was reported to have gone to Mexico. In 1858 a girl mistress who had followed him returned to Paris, and the stories she told of her lover were distorted into a statement that the French exile was none other than William Walker, then contending that he was the lawful president of Nicaragua. For a short time this absurd story gained wide credence in Paris. *Harper's Weekly*, II., 775.

CHAPTER III

WHILE the immigrant Frenchmen were developing their schemes of Mexican colonization, other men of California were already going a-filibustering into Latin America. Indeed, some Pacific pioneers took to this business with the proverbial aptitude of the duckling for water. In 1845 President Juan José Flores resigned the presidency of Ecuador to avoid further trouble from a revolution then brewing in his country, and spent nearly all his remaining years in Europe and the United States, watching for a chance to regain his lost power. The friends of the exiled president saw in the heterogeneous population of San Francisco good material for an armed expedition to restore Flores to his ungrateful country. In 1850 some two hundred and fifty adventurous souls were persuaded to join in this enterprise. The moving American spirit in this exploit was an Alabamian by the name of "Alex" Bell, whom we may designate — until some one finds an earlier one — as the first of the Californian filibusters. In the forties Bell had been a steamboat captain on the Tombigbee River in Alabama, but having little business ability, he was exploited by swindlers and fell into financial difficulties. Becoming dissatisfied at the irregular pay which resulted from their employer's monetary embarrassment, his crew one day went on a strike, whereupon Bell under some pretext induced them to go into the hold of the steamboat, and after battening down the hatches secured another crew, and proceeded down the river. When the boat reached Mobile, the miserable strikers were nearly dead of starvation, having had no food for several days. Finding that the Mobile authorities

18

were disposed to invoke the rigour of the law against him, Bell stood
not on the order of his going, but turned his face toward Texas,
where he joined the army of Zachary Taylor and served as a spy
throughout the Mexican War. When peace was concluded, he
proceeded overland to California in quest of further adventure
and found it with the organization of the Ecuadorian expedition in
San Francisco in 1850.

The filibusters left San Francisco in 1851. At Panama many
friends of Flores and other Spanish-American adventurers joined
them. On reaching the coast of Ecuador they landed, captured
Guayaquil, and marched on Quito. The fact that the Americans
had a separate camp from the rest of Flores' supporters seems to
indicate that the two elements were already objects of mutual
suspicion, and one morning the Americans awoke to find themselves surrounded by their Latin allies, who were strongly protected by entrenchments and barricades. Blood had proved
thicker than water. The rival factions had effected a reconciliation and had now united to get rid of the newcomers. The latter
were informed that they would be disarmed and sent home,
but after being marched back to Guayaquil they received free
passage only as far as Panama, where they were left to shift for
themselves. A number straggled back to California, among them
their leader, Alex Bell, who died in San Francisco in 1859.[1]

In this period every tenth man that one met in California was
a Frenchman, and this nationality constituted a very peculiar
and at the same time an important element of the population.
While Irish, Germans, and Mexicans contributed a labouring
population, fitted for life on the ranch or in the mines, the French
contributed an urban element, including all sorts and conditions
of men, from the noble marquis to the humblest peasant. Many
of these had left their native country because of the political

[1] This account is taken from Horace Bell's *Reminiscences of a Ranger in Southern
California*, 203 ff. (Los Angeles, 1881.)

troubles of 1848, and a large proportion of them had received excellent military training. After the gold discoveries the French were among the earliest to reach the Pacific coast, as there was a large number of them in the near-by Spanish-American countries and the Pacific islands. French wines, brandies, canned goods, and preserved fruits brought good prices in the mining regions, and vessels laden with such cargoes afforded an available means of reaching the gold fields.[1] Free tickets to California were offered in Paris as lottery prizes, and the advertisement of such prizes served as a further stimulus to emigration. Some five hundred persons actually drew such tickets,[2] and came to the Pacific coast to seek their fortunes. The lot of these immigrants was unduly hard. Slow to become assimilated, and having no desire for naturalization, they herded to themselves, while British, Germans, and Scandinavians became rapidly Americanized. The French complained, not without cause, that the Americans were more kindly disposed toward these other nationalities, but they were themselves partly to blame. Refusing to become citizens, they had little influence with the authorities, with the result that ruffians drove them from their mining claims, and there were few chances for them to gain a livelihood in a frontier town like San Francisco. They formed, therefore, a clannish and sorely discontented element of the population, and were fine material for exploitation by some of their adventurous countrymen. In due time several of these exploiters appeared on the scene.

In the same year in which Walker reached San Francisco there arrived two French noblemen, the Marquis Charles de Pindray and Count Gaston Raoul de Raousset-Boulbon. These men were not made for our era. In Middle Ages they would undoubtedly have passed for peerless knights, but the verdict of these more prosaic times denounces them as prodigal sons who had wasted their sub-

---

[1] Daniel Lévy, *Les Français en Californie*, 107 (San Francisco, 1884); Soulé, Gihon, and Nisbet, *Annals of San Francisco*, 461–5.

[2] John S. Hittell, *San Francisco*, 185–7. (San Francisco, 1878.)

stance in riotous living and had then gone forth into a far country. De Pindray was born of a noble family of Poitou, and is described as being handsome, eloquent, full of courage and energy, with the strength of a giant and a skill at handling weapons which gained him a great reputation in France as a duellist, and had brought him all too many victims. Such virile qualities gave him an incontestable advantage in affairs with the gentler sex, and he was by no means remiss in his gallantries. But when this gay cavalier arrived in San Francisco from a journey over the plains, he was quite penniless, and for a time was hard put to it to get his daily sustenance. Thanks to his excellent marksmanship, he was enabled to eke out a living by supplying the market with bear meat and other game, but his chivalrous nature rebelled at this butcher's business, and he began to cast about in his mind for some achievement more in keeping with his noble breeding. In his discontented compatriots he found material to his hand for a somewhat venturesome undertaking in Mexico. The Mexican government had issued a call for volunteers against the Apache Indians, who were committing depredations in the mining regions of Sonora. In return for their services these volunteers were to receive a grant of valuable lands, which they were supposed to colonize. It seems to have been the purpose of the government to plant settlements which would serve as a buffer between the Indians of the Sonoran desert and the Mexican villages in the more habitable regions. De Pindray made the tavern of his countryman Paul Niquet his headquarters, and in a very short time had raised a company of volunteers and had secured sufficient funds to provide a ship. As the Mexicans had not yet recovered from the sting of their defeat by the United States, they had stipulated that Americans should be excluded, and the adventurers were all Frenchmen. While his plans were maturing De Pindray is said to have approached Count Raousset-Boulbon and invited him to join the enterprise. The latter declined, as he was at that moment concocting a similar scheme of his own in which he would not have to share the glory and rewards with another.

On November 21, 1851, the adventurers set sail from San Francisco and landed at Guaymas, Sonora, the chief Mexican port on the Pacific, on the day after Christmas. They were joyfully received by the natives, who greeted them with volleys of musketry, to which they would have added salvos of artillery if only they had had the guns. Mexican merchants vied with one another in entertaining the newcomers, and their stay at Guaymas was a continual round of merrymaking. The authorities furnished provisions, horses, mules, and munitions of war and promised to pay the men for their services. De Pindray's compatriots now numbered one hundred and fifty, and a number of natives also joined the expedition. Proceeding to Arispe, De Pindray received further assurances of good-will from Cuvillas, the governor, and from General Miguel Blanco, the captain-general of the province, and then began his march across the desert, whose only inhabitants were those nimble-legged demons, the Apaches. The mines of Arizona were the Frenchmen's objective point, but thither they were destined never to arrive. The task was greater than they had supposed; friction developed between De Pindray and his men, and ill-feeling arose between the Mexicans and French. Finally their leader fell ill, and in May, 1852, the expedition halted. At the Mexican village of Rayon De Pindray one day was found dead with a bullet wound in his head. Whether as a result of illness and disappointment he took his own life, or whether he was assassinated by one of his discontented followers, no one knows. The survivors made their way out of the desert as best they could, and on their way they met a new expedition under the leadership of none other than Count Raousset-Boulbon.[1]

[1] Lévy, *Les Français en Californie*, 146-8; Charles de Lambertie, *Le Drame de la Sonora*, 207-56 (Paris, 1856); Hittell, *History of California*, III., 727-45.

On March 4, 1852, some three months after the departure of De Pindray, and ten weeks before the sailing of Raousset-Boulbon, a second French expedition left San Francisco for Sonora. This was directed by Lepine de Sigondis, an agent of one of the many companies formed in Paris to exploit the gold placers of California. The enterprise was devoid of military features, and the sixty or more men who went to Sonora made a fruitless effort to found a colony and disbanded. The idea of French colonies to serve as a buffer against further American expansion was much favoured by the Mexican authorities.[1]

Count Raousset-Boulbon, the leader of the third expedition to Sonora, was born at Avignon on December 2, 1817. Reared without a mother, he grew up headstrong and turbulent, these qualities being aggravated by the severity of a father who failed to understand him. As he was of small physical proportions, his youthful nickname of *Petit Loup* (Little Wolf) well describes him.[2] He was nevertheless energetic, courageous, clever, and well educated. In his make-up there was a streak of idealism, and he was not devoid of personal magnetism. These qualities were somewhat offset, however, by his fondness for pleasure, and when he became possessed of his inheritance, he quickly cast it to the winds. In 1845 he went to Algeria and served in the campaign in Kabylia under General Bugeaud. After his return to Paris he aspired to a political career, set up a newspaper to promote his cause, and was an extreme liberal in his views, as the name of his journal, *La Liberté*, indicates. A novel entitled *Une Conversion* and a few scraps of his poetry still remain as evidences of his versatility.[3] As a result of his prodigality he found himself,

[1] Lévy, *Les Français en Californie*, 148.
[2] Du Roure, *Généalogie de la Maison de Raousset*. (Paris, 1906.)
[3] The following verse, composed perhaps on the eve of his departure from Paris, is one of his literary relics :

> Mon cœur, en désesperé
> Court la pretentaine,
> Qui peut savoir si j'irai

in 1850, without money and without friends, and he then determined to seek fortune anew in California. On August 22, 1850, he reached San Francisco, making the journey as a steerage passenger on an English steamer.[1] This ruined nobleman now tried his hand at several different jobs and strove industriously to make an honest living. Until wharves were built in the harbour he stuck to the work of a lighterman, and then became by turn a cattle dealer, miner, fisherman, and, like the Marquis de Pindray, a hunter. In none of these callings did he achieve success, but his red flannel shirt and cowhide boots could not conceal the fact that he was above the common order of men, and his associates unconsciously looked upon him as a leader. Large numbers of his compatriots, like himself, had seen the seamy side of life and had been tried in the fierce fires of adversity. From among these he could pick a group who were ready to engage in any undertaking, it mattered not how desperate, if only it promised to improve their fortunes.

The Count, like De Pindray, was attracted by stories of the rich Sonoran mines. The output from these, so the story went, had once been considerable, but in late years they had been abandoned on account of the murderous incursions of the Apaches. Raousset-Boulbon then evolved a mining and colonization scheme, in which M. Patrice Dillon, the French consul at San Francisco, became deeply interested, and at Dillon's suggestion he took the precaution to visit Mexico City and secure favourable consideration by the government. Here, after much labour, in which he

Jusqu'à la trentaine ?
Mais que l'avenir soit gai
Ou qu'on me fusille —
Baisez-moi, Camille, ô gué !
Baisez-moi, Camille !

His novel, *Une Conversion*, is a description of his own conversion from an aristocrat into a democrat. He represents his life at the time of the writing as a calm after the storm.

[1] Lévy, *Les Français en Californie*, 107.

was warmly seconded by the French minister, M. Levasseur, he
effected the organization of a company styling itself *La Restauradora*, and in February, 1852, obtained for it the concession
of the gold and silver mines of Arizona in the province of Sonora.
In April he secured the services of the banking house of Jecker,
Torre and Company as underwriters for the enterprise, and then
engaged to bring 150 men to Guaymas as soon as possible and with
them to explore the region known as Arizona and to take possession of all mineral lands in the name of the company. The expedition was to be organized on a military basis in order to clear
the region of Indians. The Restauradora was to bear the expenses
of the expedition and to share with Raousset-Boulbon and his
followers one-half the lands, mines, and placers of which they took
possession. Both the French minister and the governor of Sonora
were financially interested in the company.

Having completed these arrangements, Raousset-Boulbon hurried back to San Francisco, opened a recruiting office, and sent
agents out to the mines. The consul Dillon loudly voiced his
approval, and the force was raised without difficulty. They
sailed for Guaymas on May 19, 1852, and landed twelve days
later. Their welcome was as noisy as that previously accorded to
De Pindray. In the meantime, however, a new company with
which many high Mexican officials were concerned and which had
the backing of the San Francisco banking house of Bolton and
Barron, had been organized as a rival of the Restauradora; and
while the populace of the little town were profuse in their greetings
the local authorities showed a coolness which foreboded ill. It
was especially unfortunate that General Blanco, the captain-
general of Sonora, whose word was law, had been won over in the
interest of the rival company. On May 1, while the French expedition was in preparation, he had issued a decree which was designed ostensibly to promote colonization, but which contained
several stipulations that in American political parlance would be

called "jokers." Among other inducements to the stranger to
come to Sonora, the decree declared that every colonist would
become a citizen of Mexico, but it also added that he would renounce his allegiance to his former government, obey the authorities, enlist in the militia, and give a tithe of the produce of every
harvest to the church, education, and public works.[1] The wily
captain-general knew well enough that these stipulations could be
made a source of endless embarrassment to the French who engaged in the service of the Restauradora.

After their arrival at Guaymas Raousset-Boulbon and his
followers were compelled to remain there for a month, owing to
Blanco's refusal first on one pretext and then on another to give
them permission to go into the interior. Enforced idleness and
an unhealthful climate began to show its effects on the men, and
they also consumed a large share of the supplies that were to maintain them in the desert. Finally they received permission to
depart, but only by a difficult and indirect route which was twice
as long as the way generally followed. The Count ignored the
stipulation as to direction and started over the shortest road. On
the first night out the native muleteers deserted, taking with them
as much plunder as they could carry. In August the French
finally reached the pueblo of Santa Anna, a few days' journey
from their claim, and here they were overtaken by a courier from
Blanco with orders to the leader to cease his advance and to
report in person to the captain-general at Arispe, over one hundred
miles distant. Raousset-Boulbon started to the capital, and on
his way encountered the eighty survivors of De Pindray's ill-
fated venture. He now decided to return with these to his command and sent two of his officers to Blanco in his stead. On
rejoining his followers he had some difficulty in persuading them
to wait for Blanco's message before proceeding to their claim.
The officers brought back an ultimatum which laid down three

---

[1] *Alta California*, April 29, 1854.

courses of conduct from which the men might choose: first, they might renounce their nationality, become Mexican citizens, and serve as soldiers subject to Blanco's orders; secondly, they might take out letters of safety, to be procured from Mexico City, which would give them the right to explore but not to take possession of any mines, and incidentally would involve another delay of several months; thirdly, Raousset might reduce his company to fifty men and with a Mexican responsible for them they might proceed on their way as labourers in the service of the Restauradora — provided, of course, that the Apaches offered no serious objections. After receiving this ultimatum Raousset called together his men, announced the conditions, and told them that they could take their choice. Blanco's propositions were received with shouts of derision. The men were told that if any wished to leave they could draw their supplies and do so, but not one spoke of going. The captain-general was therefore notified by the Count that the provisions of the ultimatum were personal matters in which each must speak for himself; that the leader could not speak for his men, but as to himself he rejected the provisions *in toto*. To this Blanco replied that such an answer made the Frenchmen armed enemies of the government, and both parties then prepared for hostilities. To gain the support of the natives, Raousset began to pose as the champion of Sonoran independence. The idea of organizing a rebellion seems to have been hitherto foreign to his thoughts. In true Spanish-American style, both sides now issued their pronunciamientos, Blanco trying to induce the Frenchmen to desert by promising protection to all who should do so, and Raousset urging the natives to enlist under the banner of free Sonora. Such a banner he raised on the 21st of September. On October 14 hostilities began with an attack by Raousset upon Hermosillo, a city of about 12,000 inhabitants, guarded by 1200 soldiers with cannon behind adobe walls. The French numbered only 243, and by all the rules of warfare they should have been soundly beaten. Luck was on their side that day, however, and they stormed and took the town with ease, Blanco himself narrowly escaping capture. This victory brought no tangible advantage, as the native population gradually slipped away rather than render allegiance to new masters. Raousset and a number of his officers were ill, and they now had on hand also a number of wounded. Raousset and his men seemed desirous above all else to get out of the interior and proposed to the new governor of Sonora, Gandara, to evacuate Hermosillo if they would be permitted to go unmolested to Guaymas. Raousset was to release his prisoners, and the Mexicans in return were to care for the wounded that he was compelled to leave behind. After holding the town only twelve days the French withdrew and took the road to Guaymas. At the outskirts of this town Blanco met the Count, but the two came to no definite understanding, as the latter on that same day became critically ill and left his men to make such an agreement with the authorities as they could. Five months previously they had been fêted and cheered by the people of this town, but now there was not a peon so poor as to do them reverence. The captain-general caused them to sign an agreement to obey the laws and respect the authority of the country, which was virtually equivalent to their disbandment, and he then provided the means for any who so desired to return to the United States. Most of them departed in December, but a few chose to remain. Raousset, who had not signed the agreement, went to Mazatlan in Sinaloa, where he slowly recuperated and was finally summoned back to San Francisco by Dillon.[1]

On returning to San Francisco he received a great ovation. The Californians of that day had a great admiration for the man who "did things." The Count was like all others who have been infected with the filibustering fever; the disease is incurable; hard-

[1] Lambertie, *Le Drame de la Sonora*, 80–9; Hittell, *California*, III., 731–9,

ships and suffering seem only to aggravate the symptoms. He
made no secret of his plans to return. "Je ne plus vivre sans la
Sonore," he said.[1] Walker and his law partner, Henry P. Watkins,
made him a visit and offered a proposal of coöperation; but
Raousset declined to associate with Americans in any venture in
Mexico, where these people were so cordially detested. A series
of revolutions had brought to the head of the Mexican republic
Antonio Lopez de Santa Anna, and Levasseur had notified Dillon
that the prospects were now good for establishing a French colony
in Mexico. Raousset therefore made a second trip to Mexico
City, arriving in June, 1853. Santa Anna seemed well disposed,
and made a contract by which the Count was to bring 500 Frenchmen into Sonora to serve as a garrison against the Apaches with
a stipulated monthly pay. Shortly afterwards he revoked this
contract and proposed that Raousset should become a naturalized
Mexican and join his army. The latter rejected this in great
indignation and both flew into a rage. Raousset then fled for
his life, and Santa Anna proclaimed him an outlaw.[2]

When the Count returned to San Francisco he found that the
Americans who had previously offered to join him were engaged
in preparations for an independent expedition under the leadership of William Walker. There seems to have been no feeling
of rivalry or jealousy between the two filibustering parties.
Raousset, though refusing to affiliate with the Americans, apparently had a friendly interest in Walker's plans. The preparations of others caused the fever to rage all the more fiercely in
the Frenchman's veins, and he determined to return to Sonora,
whether Santa Anna approved of his coming or not. Frenchmen
of means were appealed to and at first seemed favourably disposed. A report, however, that Mexico had sold Sonora to the
United States gained credence in California as a result of the

[1] Hittell, California, III., 739–40.
[2] Lambertie, Le Drame de la Sonora, 99–102.

Gadsden negotiations, and though the Count protested that such could not be true its effect on his enterprise was paralyzing. Public interest now became centred in the activities of Walker and his associates, and for a time the Frenchman passed into something like an eclipse. Walker's enterprise, however, was to revive Raousset's chances of returning to Sonora in a most unexpected manner, as will be explained in a later chapter.

CHAPTER IV

THE RAID ON LOWER CALIFORNIA

ACCORDING to Walker, the idea of founding an American colony in Sonora had its origin with several men of Auburn, in Placer County, California, early in 1852.[1] They paid the expenses of two of their number — one of them being Frederic Emory, of whom more is to be told later — to visit Guaymas and undertake to secure a grant of land near Arispe, in return for which the grantees were to protect the frontier from the Indians. The agents arrived at a very inauspicious moment, as Raousset-Boulbon had just made his contract through the agency of the Restauradora, and their mission was fruitless. After Count Raousset and General Blanco had had their unpleasantness and the French had finally agreed to leave the country, the American enterprisers took fresh courage and revived the Auburn scheme. Walker and his former partner, Henry P. Watkins, were this time selected as agents, and they sailed for Guaymas in June, 1853. They received anything but a cordial welcome. The prefect of the town refused at first to honour the passport which Walker had taken the precaution to secure from the Mexican consul before leaving San Francisco and subjected them to a long examination. The American consul warmly espoused Walker's cause, and a somewhat acrid correspondence between him and the Mexican officials followed, consuming time but accomplishing nothing. Finding the Mexicans so ill-disposed, the visitors made preparations to return to California. After they had boarded a vessel, word came from Governor Gandara to the prefect to permit them to visit him at the capital, but they were now satisfied that

[1] Walker, *War in Nicaragua*, 19. (Mobile, 1860.)

they could not rely upon the government's good faith, and they returned to San Francisco much disgusted. A report was even circulated in that city that the government had offered a reward for Walker dead or alive.[1]

Mr. T. Robinson Warren, an American traveller temporarily residing in Guaymas during the summer of 1853, saw a great deal of Walker and tells us that he was greatly impressed with his astuteness and determined character. He found him "insanely confident of success," and yet evincing such an extreme degree of caution as almost to disarm the Mexicans themselves of suspicion before he left them. Just how the adventurer impressed this unprejudiced observer is interesting enough to justify quoting at some length:

"His appearance was anything else than a military chieftain. Below the medium height, and very slim, I should hardly imagine him to weigh over a hundred pounds. His hair light and towy, while his almost white eyebrows and lashes concealed a seemingly pupilless, grey, cold eye, and his face was a mass of yellow freckles, the whole expression very heavy. His dress was scarcely less remarkable than his person. His head was surmounted by a huge white fur hat, whose long knap waved with the breeze, which, together with a very ill-made, short-waisted blue coat, with gilt buttons, and a pair of grey, strapless pantaloons, made up the ensemble of as unprepossessing-looking a person as one would meet in a day's walk. I will leave you to imagine the figure he cut in Guaymas with the thermometer at 100°, when every one else was arrayed in white. Indeed half the dread which the Mexicans had of filibusters vanished when they saw this their Grand Sachem — such an insignificant-looking specimen. But any one who estimated Mr. Walker by his personal appearance made a great mistake. Extremely taciturn, he would sit for an hour in company without opening his lips; but once interested he ar-

[1] *Alta California*, Sept. 12, 1853.

rested your attention with the first word he uttered, and as he proceeded, you felt convinced that he was no ordinary person. To a few confidential friends he was most enthusiastic upon the subject of his darling project, but outside of those immediately interested he never mentioned the topic." [1]

Though balked in their designs at Guaymas, Walker and his associates did not abandon their plans. Walker says that he saw and heard enough while there to convince him that a very small body of Americans could hold the frontier and protect the Sonorans from the Indians, and that this would be an act of humanity, whether it met the approval of the Mexican government or not. As if in further justification of his conduct, he adds that several women at Guaymas urged him to return to the United States at once and bring down enough men to protect them from the Apaches. Like Adam of old, he was glad to shift what responsibility he could upon the shoulders of some Eve. Whether exaggerated or not, the reports of terrible Apache outrages were a source of alarm in Sonora and were generally credited in California. San Francisco newspapers above all suspicion of filibustering proclivities, such as the *Alta California*, were filled with these stories. The issue of this journal for September 15, 1853, gives an account of eighty murders by Indians in one week, and it declares editorially that Sonora must become totally depopulated if aid is not soon rendered from some foreign quarter. "How long," it said, "the unhappy and defenceless people of Sonora will be subject to their present troubles it is difficult to determine. They cannot protect themselves and the government cannot protect them. Their only hope is in a war and the occupation of their territory by United States troops." [2] The reports were not without foundation, and may have been literally true.

[1] T. Robinson Warren, *Dust and Foam; or, Three Oceans and Two Continents*, 212–13. (New York, 1858.)

[2] It is very significant that this editorial appeared a few days after the return of Walker and Watkins to the United States. *Alta California*, Sept. 15, 1853.

Warren, who spent many months in Sonora at this time, has much to say of the desolation of the country since the independence of Mexico, and attributes this to the incompetence of the government and its neglect of the northern Mexican states. Over its most fertile plains one could ride for a hundred miles and see no sign of human beings — only abandoned ranches, uninhabited villages, and a few wild horses and cattle, remnants of the droves that had escaped the marauders.[1]

Coupled with these stories of Indian outrages were reports of fabulous mineral wealth, and especially of silver deposits which could be worked with very little expense. The effect was naturally to arouse the interest of speculators as well as of adventurers in any movement directed toward Sonora. Some weeks before Walker and Watkins visited Guaymas, bonds of the "Republic of Sonora" were issued and offered for sale in San Francisco, and these securities show, better than any other available evidence, the real designs of the promoters of the expedition. The grant of lands which they hoped to secure from the authorities was to be made only a means of effecting a peaceable entrance, and after they had once established themselves they purposed to overthrow the existing government and proclaim the independence of Sonora. It is more than probable that Gandara had seen through their duplicity, and during their stay at Guaymas he fought them with their own weapons. Certain it is that if the Mexican consul at San Francisco had ever seen one of the bonds of the "Republic" he would have notified his government of the real motives of the Americans.[2] The Mexican grant would have saved the filibusters

[1] T. Robinson Warren, *op. cit.*, 183–4; 201–2.

[2] Copy of a Bond issued May 1, 1853.

$500   *Independence Loan* $500

The Independence Loan Fund has received of   the sum of $500, and the Republic of Sonora will issue to him or his assigns a land warrant for one square league of land, to be located on the public domain of said Republic.

Signed this first day of May,

WM. WALKER,

Colonel of the Independence Regiment.

From *Alta California*, Dec. 1, 1853.

from annoyance by the Federal authorities in San Francisco and assured them of no molestation on landing in northern Mexico. In other words, it would have given to the expedition the stamp of legitimacy.

During Walker's absence the preparations for the undertaking were not suspended, and after his return in September, 1853, they were pushed to a conclusion. The lack of papers from the Sonoran governor, to indicate that the undertaking was for peaceable colonization and had the approval of his government, now proved a serious handicap. At about midnight on September 30 a detachment of troops acting under the orders of General Ethan Allen Hitchcock seized the brig *Arrow*, which for several days had been receiving a suspicious cargo. In its hold were found a quantity of cartridges, cooking kettles, and other camp outfit. Many of the boxes containing this equipment were marked "Col. Stevenson's Regiment." It was noted, too, that arrangements had been made in the galley to prepare food at sea for an unusually large number of men.

Hitchcock turned the vessel over to the United States marshal. Walker went before a judge of the Superior court and secured a writ of replevin, alleging that the vessel had been seized and held without legal warrant. In issuing the writ the judge gave an opinion to the effect that the vessel could not be held without being libelled. At this juncture Hitchcock took the vessel again in his charge and placed a Major Andrews aboard with fourteen soldiers. When the sheriff appeared to serve the writ, the major ordered him off with threats of violence. Whatever may have been his motives, Hitchcock's methods were pretty sure to involve him in difficulties with the court, and, as was to be expected, he was ordered on October 8 to show cause why he should not be adjudged guilty of contempt. Walker at the same time filed a complaint of trespass against Hitchcock and R. P. Hammond, the collector of the port, and laid claim to damages accruing from the seizure of the vessel. It is interesting to note that one of the attorneys for Walker was Edmund Randolph, the friend of his New Orleans days. The vessel was ordered released, and the court took the matter of contempt under advisement.[1] Suspicion was next directed toward the brig *Caroline*, which on October 15 took clearance papers for Guaymas. At about one o'clock on the morning of the 16th officers seized a quantity of ammunition as it was being taken on board, but, perhaps profiting by their experience with the *Arrow*, they made no attempt to seize the ship. Shortly thereafter the *Caroline* weighed anchor and stood out to sea. Hurrying her departure so as to escape further interference, she left behind a number of disappointed filibusters as well as the ammunition which had been seized.[2] On board the vessel were forty-five men under the leadership of William — now Colonel — Walker, once doctor, lawyer, and editor, now soldier of fortune and filibuster.

Although the ultimate goal of Walker and the First Independent Battalion, as his men were called, was Sonora, they were as yet too few in numbers to attempt an invasion. Their leader had the prudence to profit by the troubles of De Pindray and Raousset-Boulbon and keep away from Guaymas. He determined, therefore, to establish himself in Lower California and after receiving reinforcements to reduce this State to submission and make it the base of his operations against Sonora. He seems, however, to have left the details of this plan to work themselves out; for his frequent changes of base after his landing can be accounted for in no other way. On October 28 the *Caroline* touched at Cape San Lucas and thence proceeded to La Paz, where the expeditionists landed on November 3, made a prisoner of the governor, hauled down the Mexican flag and replaced it with the flag of the independent Republic of Lower California. All this consumed

---

[1] *Alta California*, Oct. 2, 9, 11, 1853 ; Soulé, *Annals of San Francisco*, 474–80.
[2] *Alta California*, Oct. 18, 1853.

perhaps one half of an hour. Meanwhile Walker picked up the weapon with which he was most skilled — the pen — and indited his first proclamation; namely, "The Republic of Lower California is hereby declared free, sovereign, and independent, and all allegiance to the Republic of Mexico is forever renounced." By this decree of twenty-three words a new republic was supposed to be born into the world and to take its place at the council board of the nations. Walker at once entered upon his duties as "President." The terrible earnestness of the man makes the situation all the more comical. Four days later two more decrees were issued; one, of nine words, established freedom of trade with all the world; the second declared the Civil Code and the Code of Practice of the State of Louisiana to be "the rule of decision and the law of the land, in all the courts of the Republic to be hereafter organized." [1] To this latter decree some of Walker's critics attached a sinister significance, claiming that he was merely accomplishing by indirection what he feared to do openly and above board; namely, open his new republic to African slavery. [2] Since Louisiana was a slave State, they say, the promulgation of its legal system in Lower California could have been for no other conceivable purpose than to set up there the peculiar institution. They fail to observe, however, that the legal systems of Mexico and of Louisiana had a common origin and were in many respects similar, and that inasmuch as Walker was well versed in the civil code of Louisiana he was introducing into his government a body of law with which both he and the natives would be familiar. Had Walker maintained himself in Lower California he would undoubtedly have considered the question of slavery extension and in all probability would have favoured it, but those who see such a motive in his decree of November 7 are merely reading the future events into his present acts.

Finding La Paz unsuitable for his seat of government, Walker

[1] *Alta California*, Dec. 8, 1853.   [2] Hittell, *History of California*, III., 763.

remained there only three days and then embarked for San Lucas, taking with him Espanoza, the captive governor, and the archives of the province. At this juncture a vessel entered the harbour bringing a Colonel Robollero, the new governor who was to succeed Espanoza. He was likewise taken prisoner and brought aboard the *Caroline*. Before hoisting sail, six men were sent ashore to gather wood, and were fired upon by the natives. This precipitated the first fighting of the expedition. Walker landed with thirty men, and there was some discharging of firearms for an hour and a half; after this the filibusters withdrew to the ship, claiming a great victory, which was also claimed in equal degree by the Mexicans.[1]

On November 8 Walker reached San Lucas. A Mexican revenue cutter cruising off the Cape offered no resistance. On landing they found the place incapable of sustaining any considerable force and the next day the men reëmbarked and proceeded to Ensenada, about one hundred miles south of San Diego, California, and on the Pacific side of the peninsula. For some time this remained the filibuster headquarters, as the place could be defended from attack by the Mexicans and was a convenient point at which to await reinforcements.

The affair at La Paz was advertised in California as a great victory, "releasing Lower California from the tyrannous yoke of declining Mexico and establishing a new republic." [2] As soon as the news reached San Francisco a recruiting office was opened and the flag of the new republic was hoisted at the corner of Kearny and Sacramento streets. There was no excitement, the news being taken as a matter of course. It was very plain that public sentiment was on the side of the adventurers.[3] On the

---

[1] The filibuster version may be found in the *Alta California*, Dec. 8, 1853; the unfavourable version, later in reaching the United States, may be found in the same journal for Jan. 3, 1854.

[2] The San Diego correspondent of *Alta California*, Dec. 8, 1853.

[3] Bell, *Reminiscences of a Ranger*, 212; *Alta California*, Dec. 10, 1853.

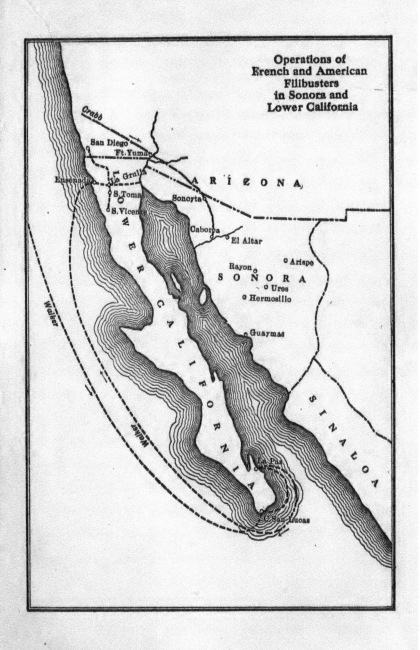

very day after the news of La Paz was received a meeting was held at one of the engine houses of the fire department and about fifty more men volunteered. Seekers after gold who had failed in their quest, and scores of others who had found fortune as fickle in the West as elsewhere, were now anxious to try their luck again in Lower California, feeling that if their lot were not bettered it at least could be no worse. The chances of fame and fortune were indeed remote, but at any rate they would have adventure and excitement. General Hitchcock, who previously had shown so much hostility, had been detailed elsewhere, and his successor, General John E. Wool, had not yet arrived. The civil authorities were indifferent. Securities of the new republic were offered for sale at ten cents on the dollar.[1] Within five days the new expedition was ready, and on the night of December 13, 230 men put to sea in the bark *Anita*, under the leadership of Watkins.[2] They joined Walker at Ensenada. During his period of enforced waiting the President, if we may believe the reports inspired from his headquarters, had placed the new government on a firm and sure basis. He now had a cabinet, consisting of Secretaries of State, War, and Navy, and a military and naval organization. Frederic Emory, the Secretary of State, in the absence of pressing business in the department of foreign affairs, was despatched to the great neighbouring republic of the North to secure further enlistments and contributions for the cause, and there he became involved in difficulties with the Federal authorities, as will appear later. Charles H. Gilman, the ranking military officer, with the title

[1] Soulé, Gihon, and Nisbet, *Annals of San Francisco*, 479.

[2] The scenes attending the departure of the *Anita* are graphically described in William V. Wells, *Walker's Expedition to Nicaragua*, 30-2. (New York, 1856.) Many of the recruits had celebrated their departure by too generous libations of liquor, and in spite of the efforts of their leaders to maintain silence and secrecy, so as to prevent any governmental interference at the eleventh hour, they sang and cheered to their hearts' content, but without arousing the attention of the authorities. As a result of their departure, says Soulé, the San Francisco annalist, "the recorder's court at San Francisco had much less daily business, and the city was happily purged of the old squad of rowdies and loafers."

of captain of battalion, was destined to lose a leg in the service, and in spite of his sufferings and of this great handicap he was among the first to join Walker two years later in Nicaragua.[1] On November 30 Walker issued an address to the people of the United States, giving his reasons for the course he had taken. It was, he said, "due the nationality which has most jealously guarded the independence of American States to declare why another Republic is created on the immediate confines of the great Union." He declared that the peninsula, being isolated geographically from the rest of Mexico, had been woefully neglected, and that in order "to develop the resources of Lower California, and to effect a proper social organization therein, it was necessary to make it independent."[2] The spectacle of a man still in his twenties, with some twoscore social misfits as his entire support, solemnly explaining to twenty-five million people why he had seen fit to create a new nation on their borders, needs the pen of a Cervantes to do it full justice. But still more surprising things were to follow.

While awaiting reinforcements at Ensenada, Walker was attacked by Mexicans, and for several days his company was closely besieged in an adobe house where they had taken refuge. At length, early on the morning of December 14, a sortie was planned which Walker proposed to lead himself, and called for volunteers. His men, however, dissuaded him from taking the risk, and the command then fell upon Crocker, who made the attack with twenty men and drove the besiegers away. In this attack Lieutenant McKibbin was killed, and the house was named Fort

---

[1] The full roster of officials was as follows: William Walker, President; Frederic Emory, Secretary of State; John M. Jarnigan, Secretary of War; Howard H. Snow, Secretary of the Navy; Charles H. Gilman, captain of battalion; John McKibbin, first lieutenant; Timothy Crocker, second lieutenant; Samuel Buland, third lieutenant; Wm. P. Mann, captain of the navy; A. Williams, first lieutenant of the navy; John Grundall, second lieutenant of the navy.

One man in every four was thus a cabinet official or a commissioned officer.

[2] Wells, *Walker's Expedition*, 245.

McKibbin in his honour. During the siege the *Caroline* weighed anchor and sailed away for no known reason, and in her hold she carried off most of the remaining provisions. It is possible that the two captive governors on board may have won over the crew and sailed southward to liberty. On the 28th the *Anita* arrived with the long-expected reinforcements, but she brought only men and arms and no food.[1] As a result, there were over two hundred additional mouths to be fed from Walker's already dwindling stores. There was no alternative but to begin foraging on the country, and the attack of a fortnight previous was easily made an excuse for living off the enemy.

On the 29th Walker despatched sixty-five men to attack a noted Mexican outlaw named Melendrez, who had stationed himself in the neighbouring village of San Tomas, and after driving him away they seized a large number of horses and cattle, on the ground that these, being the property of the outlaw, had already been declared confiscated by the government.[2] The filibusters were now reduced to a diet of beef and corn, and discontent and desertions naturally followed. Watkins returned immediately to the United States to seek further aid, and the desertions were for a time counterbalanced by new arrivals.[3]

It was not Walker's intention to remain upon the desolate peninsula a day longer than was necessary, as Sonora had all along been his real objective. He now believed that he was strong enough to undertake his real work and began his preparations for a march to Sonora by way of the Colorado River. Such property

[1] In this party of recruits was one woman, a Mrs. Chapman, the wife of one of Walker's captains. She rendered much service in looking after the sick and wounded.

[2] *Alta California*, Jan. 10, 1854.

[3] Some of these, however, encountered on their way deserters returning from Lower California, and the gloomy stories of the latter caused many a would-be filibuster to turn back. On January 26 no fewer than one hundred and twenty-five of them left San Francisco on the steamer *Goliah* for San Diego. From this town the recruits made their way to join Walker as best they could. *Alta California*, Jan. 27 and Feb. 4, 1854.

of the unfriendly rancheros in the neighbourhood as could serve
his purposes was confiscated. Cattle were slaughtered and beef
was dried for the march; wild horses were broken for the men, and
the men were also broken to the horses.[1] Then followed the most
Quixotic of all his decrees, four of them, all bearing the date of
January 18, 1854. By these he annexed Sonora to his Republic
of Lower California, changed the name of his country to the
Republic of Sonora, divided it into the two States of Sonora and
Lower California, and defined their boundaries. All decrees of
a general nature previously issued under the Republic of Lower
California were declared in force as decrees of the Republic of
Sonora. Walker therefore became president of Sonora, and
Watkins was his vice-president. To practical Americans with
their keen sense of humour the comedy of these pronunciamientos
was delicious. "He [Walker] is a veritable Napoleon," said the
editor of one newspaper, "of whom it may be said, as of the
mighty Corsican, 'he disposes of courts and crowns and camps as
mere titulary dignitaries of the chess board.' Santa Anna must
feel obliged to the new president that he has not annexed any
more of his territory than Sonora. It would have been just as
cheap and easy to have annexed the whole of Mexico at once, and
would have saved the trouble of making future proclamations."
The incident reminded this writer of the petty prince of a handful of Ethiopians described in the pages of Mungo Park. After
filling himself with camel's milk and hominy, that sable potentate
ordered his prime minister to go out and give a loud blast on his
horn and announce that all the world might go to dinner. This
for a long time had been regarded as the climax of the ridiculous,
but Walker had surpassed Prince Gumbo.[2]

The discontent of Walker's men increased with inactivity and
poor food until a number of them were on the verge of mutiny.
Finally an order which he issued depriving the company of Cap-

[1] *Alta California*, Jan. 31, 1854.   [2] *Ibid.*, Jan. 30, 1854.

tain Davidson of a number of horses which they had picked up brought matters to a crisis. These men thought that they were entitled to their mounts and resented seeing them taken away and given to others. The murmurings became so serious that the leader assembled the men and addressed them, and at the end of his speech announced his intention of exacting from them an oath of allegiance. Some fifty men refused to take the oath, the majority of them being members of Davidson's company. These were requested to leave camp within two hours, and after filling their pockets with corn they took their guns and started on foot in the direction of San Diego. An officer rushed after them and told them that they must leave their arms behind. They ignored him, however, and he drew his pistol, whereupon they flourished their weapons and dared him to fire. The officer next summoned the guard and ordered them to fire on the deserters. They refused to do so, or even to remain in ranks. Some of the hot-headed supporters of Walker now aimed a loaded field-piece at the retreating party and Walker had difficulty in restraining them. He himself now started after the men with a squad of his loyal followers, overtook them, and spoke to them very kindly, urging them to go back and get some rations and to leave their guns behind, as they were badly needed. Two men gave up their rifles and several sullenly smashed theirs on the rocks. The deserters then went on their way to San Diego, where they received a free passage on the steamer to San Francisco.[1]

Desertions, wounds, and sickness now reduced Walker's effective force to one hundred and thirty men. A Mexican brig-of-war blockaded the mouth of the harbour to prevent further reinforcements, and on February 11 the United States ship-of-war *Portsmouth* arrived in the harbour, and its officers visited Walker at his quarters. This visit seems to have boded no good to the filibuster cause; for Walker at once hastened his departure, spiking

[1] *Alta California*, Feb. 4, 1854.

and burying all his guns but one, which he took with him, and leaving behind eight sick and wounded men, who were taken care of by Captain Dornin of the *Portsmouth* and carried to San Diego.[1]

The filibusters left Ensenada on February 13, reached the village of San Tomas on the 16th, and on the 17th proceeded to San Vicente. Here for the first time Walker tried to exercise something like political control over the natives. He summoned a "convention" of the Mexicans in the vicinity on the 28th, and on that day sixty-two of them attended. The delegates were received with full military honours, which were undoubtedly intended for something more than mere ceremony. After these formalities the oath of allegiance was administered; the delegates volunteering to do this, according to the filibuster version, and being compelled to do so by threats, if we may believe Walker's enemies. At any rate the ceremony of oath-taking was made as impressive as circumstances would permit. A table was secured and placed in an open space. In front of this were placed two flags of the Republic of Sonora crossing each other in such a way as to form a kind of arch. The president and his cabinet and staff officers stood on one side of the table and "a member of the Judiciary" — a department apparently created for the occasion — and an interpreter on the other. Each native came up, gave his name, took the oath, and then passed under the flags in token of his submission. When the last man had taken the oath the field-piece was fired, the soldiers cheered, and several Germans who had brought their musical instruments from California attempted a few martial airs. On the following day a paper was promulgated entitled the "Declaration or Representation of the Inhabitants of the State of Lower California, of the Republic of Sonora, to his Excellency the President." Ostensibly, it was a result of the deliberations of the "convention." It states that the delegates have assembled voluntarily, is full of praise for

[1] *Alta California*, Feb. 22, 1854.

Walker and the conduct of his men, and declares that the signers
will serve him faithfully unto death. Every sentence of the
"Declaration" refutes its genuineness. It was inspired, if not
actually written, by Walker himself, and is carefully worded with
a view to contradicting in the United States the unfavourable
reports of his treatment of the natives. Even if there were no
other reason to doubt the authenticity of the document, the last
sentence alone lets the cat out of the bag. "We request of your
Excellency that the provisions we have on hand, and may receive
in the future, be subject to your orders when the requisitions
are properly signed by your commissary, which requisitions will
always be cheerfully complied with, confident that we will be
reimbursed hereafter." [1] Verily, the belief of the filibuster leader
in the gullibility of the American people must have been great,
if he supposed that they would be taken in by such barefaced
trickery. While such deception gained Walker no friends, it
seems to have done him no particular harm. Indeed, this and
all other facts indicating that he was in a desperate situation
served only to arouse sympathy at home for the Americans in
distress.

The president of Sonora was still far from his intended destination. Governmental interference in San Francisco had
stopped all hope of further reinforcements, and with desertions
and increasing native hostility he was growing weaker every
day. Still his camp was not a band of unorganized rabble; the
leader was a strict disciplinarian, and punctilious in matters of
military etiquette to an exasperating degree. To men who had
never known the meaning of discipline or self-control this restraint
was especially galling and was one cause of the numerous desertions. An incident which illustrates the severity of his rule occurred just two days after the San Vicente convention. Four of
his men were charged with organizing a party to desert, where-

[1] *Alta California*, March 15, 1854.

upon Walker ordered the two leaders shot and the other two flogged and driven from his camp.[1] At length, on March 20 the journey toward Sonora was begun. A small force of twenty men was left at San Vicente to hold the barracks, and with one hundred men and a drove of cattle Walker turned eastward and began the march across the rugged trails of the Sierras to the Colorado River. The journey occupied two weeks, the distance being about two hundred miles as the crow flies. In the mountains they lost some of their cattle, and treacherous Indian guides carried off still more.[2] After much suffering the men arrived at the Colorado about six miles above its mouth. Here the river was so wide, swift, and deep that it was impossible to convey the cattle across. The men crossed on rafts, but such cattle as they attempted to swim were drowned. They were at last in Sonora, but the country before them seemed as uninviting as the one they had just left behind. The men had received no clothing since leaving San Francisco, and were now in rags. Walker himself had only one dilapidated boot. To go forward without their beef was impossible; to remain where they were meant starvation. The nearest point at which relief might be obtained was Fort Yuma, some seventy miles up the river and just over the American boundary. About fifty men deserted and betook themselves there. The expedition had now disintegrated. The men seemed particularly to resent Walker's standing upon his dignity in such an extremity, and his apparent lack of sensibility to their sufferings. He was unable to let them forget that he was still their commander and president.[3]

After three days in Sonora Walker and the remnant of his

[1] *Alta California*, March 15, 1854.

[2] Arthur W. North, in *Camp and Camino in Lower California*, 53–4 (N. Y., 1910), gives the route pursued by Walker to the Colorado. As he got his information from Indians in this region over fifty years later, his account must be handled with great caution. This is especially necessary when it is observed that the author's whole story of Walker in Lower California is full of inaccuracies.

[3] *Alta California*, April 26, 1854.

followers recrossed the river and began retracing their steps to San Vicente, mainly because there was no other course open to them. Arriving there on April 17, they found that the garrison which they had left behind had been attacked and wiped out by Melendrez. That leader now appeared on the outskirts of the town, where his men shouted insults at the filibusters and trailed a captured flag of the Republic in the dust. From this time till the final surrender of Walker to officers of the United States army, Melendrez and his followers constantly harassed the men without risking a serious encounter. The Mexican sent Walker a note under a flag of truce offering him freedom to leave the country unmolested if the men would lay down their arms. As Walker had no idea of relying on Mexican promises, he tore up the note and drove the messenger from his quarters.

Melendrez was making it too unpleasant for the remaining handful of filibusters, and they turned their faces toward the American border. As they retreated mounted Mexicans circled continually around them and made life still more miserable for the dejected men. As they neared the boundary Melendrez notified them that they would not be allowed to cross unless they first disarmed. Walker sent word that if Melendrez wanted their arms he must come and take them. The Mexican leader also notified Major J. McKinstry, commanding the post at San Diego, of his intention to capture Walker, and received word that the American government would interfere in no way. The news of Walker's approach drew many spectators out from San Diego, and they posted themselves on a hill to see the fighting. Melendrez interposed himself between Walker and the boundary as if to block the way, but Walker on approaching the position ordered his "advance guard" to charge, and as they rushed forward with a cheer the Mexicans put spurs to their horses and galloped away. Walker met Major McKinstry and Captain H. S. Burton at the boundary, where he and his men surrendered and agreed

E

on their parole of honour to go to San Francisco and report to General John E. Wool, charged with violating the neutrality laws of the United States. Thirty-three men besides Walker signed the parole, being all that were left with the leader at the end of his career as President of Sonora. Walker surrendered on his thirtieth birthday, May 8, 1854. A week later the entire party were in San Francisco awaiting the action of the Federal authorities.[1]

The sober judgment of history must condemn the whole affair in Lower California as an inexcusable raid upon an unoffending people. The high moral ground upon which Walker bases his defence — that the dictates of humanity are superior to the law of nations — was later to be used against him to his own injury. It is needless, moreover, to inquire into the merits of his contention that he engaged in the undertaking for the defense of the helpless Sonorans against marauding Indians, although it is not improbable that Walker succeeded in convincing himself that this was true. Of the two evils the Sonorans would very probably have preferred Indians to filibusters.

It is easy enough to point out the strategical blunders of the expedition. Attempting to invade a hostile country with only forty-five men; having no definite plan of campaign, sailing for Guaymas, but landing at La Paz, then doubling back to Ensenada, and from there straggling back and forth from village to village, next starting toward Sonora over a desert route whose difficulties were unknown, and finally retracing his steps along the same weary way on account of meeting with an impassable physical barrier — such errors show only too plainly that Walker was devoid of many of the essential qualities of leadership. On the other hand, we must bear in mind the enormous difficulties with which he had to contend. His untamed men had to be broken to the work like wild horses; his resources were woefully slender,

[1] *Alta California*, May 16, 1854; Wells, *Walker's Expedition*, 276.

and aid and support from home were uncertain and irregular at best. Many joined the enterprise in search of adventure or virgin mines. As they found neither of these, but only irksome camp life in an almost desolate country, it is not surprising that they deserted at the first opportunity. And the desertions were not due to lack of discipline but to too much of it. That Walker after this failure did not become an object of ridicule was due to his manifestation of personal bravery. A man who could face such dangers without flinching and never for a moment lose his dignity and composure was bound to challenge the admiration of the pioneer Californians, and they made him a hero.

One other question now remains to be considered. How far was Walker influenced in this undertaking by a desire for the expansion of slavery? If we may believe some writers this slavery extension idea was the foundation stone of the whole scheme.[1] Every intelligent American citizen was fully aware that territorial expansion southward at this time would in all probability be followed by slavery extension, and adopting a *post hoc ergo propter hoc* line of reasoning a number of recent writers have assumed that all expansionist activities to the south of the American republic were prompted and directed by slavery propagandists. Reasoning from such a premise, they have naturally concluded that Walker was an agent or tool of this group of partizans. One writer indeed has gone so far as to assert that Walker left New Orleans and went to California for no other purpose than to enlarge the domain of slavery.[2] In support of their assumptions they allege, first, that Walker got his idea from the movement against Cuba, which was centred in New Orleans during his residence there; secondly, that he had the support of the slavery element in Washington, as is attested by the fact that General Hitchcock was relieved from his duties

[1] See, for instance, a letter in *Alta California*, Dec. 24, 1853.
[2] Auguste Nicaise, *Les Flibustiers Américains*. (Paris, 1860.)

as commander of the department of the Pacific by Jefferson
Davis, the Secretary of War, immediately after his interference
with the departure of the *Arrow;* and thirdly, that one of Walker's first political acts in Lower California was to declare in force
the laws of Louisiana, a slave State. The first of these allegations has been refuted in an earlier chapter, in which it was shown
that Walker, while a New Orleans editor, had opposed the filibustering movement against Cuba. The second is more serious,
implying a widespread conspiracy on the part of the slavery
element to wrest portions of territory from Mexico for their own
aggrandizement, and assuming some subtle connection between
the unprepossessing Marysville lawyer and a high official in the
President's cabinet. On this point, fortunately, we have the aid
of General Hitchcock's diary. On December 16, 1853, two months
after the affair of the *Arrow,* he records: "The mail to-day brings
a letter of approval of my work from the new Secretary of War.
Previous order confirmed. I am specially designated to command the Department of the Pacific according to my brevet
rank — certainly complimentary, considering that there are
many officers of the army who rank me and yet are without
department commands. . . . I have applied for leave of absence to go to the East, by way of China, India, etc."[1]   On
February 2, 1854, Hitchcock records in his diary that he is to be
relieved by General Wool, and alleges as the reason the fact of
his close friendship for General Scott, to whom Pierce and Davis
were hostile. There is never a hint that his opposition to Walker
was in any way connected with his removal from the head of the
department of the Pacific. Moreover, if such had been the case,
Davis would have at least taken the precaution of supplanting
him with some officer more likely to favour filibustering than
was General John E. Wool. The latter, as the next chapter will

---

[1] *Fifty Years in Camp and Field: Diary of Major-General Ethan Allen Hitchcock,*
edited by W. A. Croffutt, 405. (New York, 1909.)

show, went to far greater extremes than Hitchcock in making life burdensome for the filibusters.

If Walker really went to Lower California in the interests of the slavery party, we should naturally expect the Southern journals to champion his cause. The New Orleans *True Delta* of December 27, 1853, refers, however, to "the freebooters under 'President Walker,'" and the *Picayune* of January 15, 1854, declares Walker's followers are "rash young men" and his expedition "a rash and desperate undertaking, and if . . . they escape back with their lives it will be fortunate for them that they were unable to get farther."

All evidence goes to show that the Sonoran enterprise was the result of no concerted movement of Southern men to enlarge the bounds of slavery. Had such been the case, it would have come nearer meeting with success. There is less reason for assuming that Walker was at this time the agent of slavery propagandists than there is for believing that De Pindray and Raousset-Boulbon were agents of Louis Napoleon.

CHAPTER V

The Filibusters before the Courts

JANUARY 9, 1854, was an evil day for the French and American filibusters on the Pacific coast, for it was on this date that Secretary Jefferson Davis assigned to the command of the Department of the Pacific Brevet Major General John E. Wool.[1] On the day following this assignment Wool wrote to Davis asking for his views concerning the course that should be pursued toward expeditions against Lower California, which, according to the latest advices, were then attracting much attention in San Francisco. Davis replied on the 12th, stating that there would devolve upon Wool "the duty of maintaining our international obligations, by preventing unlawful expeditions against the territories of foreign powers. Confidence is felt that you will, to the utmost of your ability, use all proper means to detect the fitting out of armed expeditions against countries with which the United States are at peace, and will zealously coöperate with the civil authorities in maintaining the neutrality laws."[2]

Wool arrived in San Francisco on February 14 and at once gave his attention to breaking up filibustering. On March 1 he notified Davis that he had arrested Watkins and had thereby broken up Walker's recruiting rendezvous. He also stated that he was close on the trail of Count Raousset, whom he regarded as one of Walker's assistants. On the 15th he reported the arrest at San Diego of Frederic Emory, Walker's Secretary of State, and

---

[1] House Ex. Doc., no. 88, 35 Cong., 1 Sess., 5.   [2] *Ibid.*, 6.

several others of his adherents.[1] Among the others were Major
Baird, Captain Davidson, and Dr. Hoge, Walker's surgeon.[2]

On March 1 a Federal grand jury returned true bills against
Watkins, Davidson, and Baird, and the trial of Watkins began on
the 20th. The attorneys for the defence were Edmund Randolph
and Henry S. Foote, a former governor of Mississippi. The
evidence tended to show that Watkins had taken the leading part
in fitting out the *Anita* and enlisting recruits for reinforcing
Walker; that the ship carried arms and ammunition; that the
men drilled regularly while at sea; and that Watkins was in command during the voyage and brought the ship back after landing
the men at Ensenada. In his speech for the defence Randolph
took the ground that Watkins had committed no hostile act against
Mexico until he had left the jurisdiction of the United States.
His only hostility while in the United States had consisted in *thinking*, and he could not be tried for what he *did*, as it was done in
Mexico. Foote's argument for the defence consisted of an attempt
to prove the neutrality laws unconstitutional. The Federal district attorney, Mr. S. W. Inge,[3] in summing up for the government,
dwelt upon the fact that the defence had made no attempt to
answer the testimony of any of the witnesses for the prosecution;
he explained wherein the expedition was a violation of the law, and
then sought to work on the prejudices of the jurors, several of whom
were prominent business men, by declaring that successful filibustering would be a positive injury to the city and State by draw-
ing off the population and depreciating property values. Judge
Hoffman's charge to the jury was not at all favourable to the
accused. They were to pay no attention, he said, to the question
of the constitutionality of the neutrality laws; that point had
already been settled by the highest court in the land. "I do not

---

[1] House Ex. Doc., no. 88, 35 Cong., 1 Sess., 10, 19. Emory was arrested on the
8th. *Alta California*, March 15, 1854.

[2] *Alta California*, March 3, 1854.

[3] Inge was a Southerner, a native of Alabama.

desire the conviction or the acquittal, but I do know that in this case, for the honour and credit of the nation and government, it is of great importance that the verdict shall be according to the law and evidence, and without any regard to the majority of the remarks addressed to you by the counsel." [1] After five hours of deliberation the jury declared Watkins guilty, but recommended him to the mercy of the court. A fine of $1500 was imposed by Judge Hoffman, who made the penalty light, he said, as he regarded the law vindicated by the conviction. "It will astonish the pious people on the Atlantic," said the *Alta California*, "to learn that San Francisco has done what New York and New Orleans failed, discreditably failed, to do." [2]

The case of Captain Davidson came up a week later, but the district attorney entered a *nolle prosequi*, stating that he had been unable to get enough evidence to satisfy a jury. A week later Frederic Emory, Walker's Secretary of State, was arraigned and plead guilty. He was fined $1500, like Watkins. [3] On the following day the United States marshal was ordered by the court to take Watkins and Emory into custody until their fines had been paid, but he reported that they could not be found in the city. The next day, however, they were found and brought before Judge Hoffman. They declared that they were unable to pay the fine but would do so as soon as they could. Hoffman promised to release them if they would take the oath of insolvency in due form, but when they declined to do this the court took the matter under advisement, and there it ended.

With the arrest and conviction of Walker's two chief abettors, the downfall of the Republic of Sonora seemed only a matter of a few weeks, and interest in his enterprise waned. At the same time Raousset-Boulbon, whom we have seen fleeing before the

---

[1] Ogden Hoffman, the presiding judge, was appointed from New York and was under thirty years of age when he took his place on the Federal bench.

[2] *Alta California*, March 24, 1854.　　　[3] *Ibid.*, April 4 and 11, 1854.

wrath of Santa Anna, again came into the foreground. Just as the
Count was beginning to despair of ever again reaching Sonora, his
chances were suddenly brightened in a very surprising manner
through the instrumentality of Walker and his companions. The
invasion of Lower California by an armed band of Americans convinced Santa Anna that he was between the devil and the deep
sea, and that he must choose between French and American filibusters. Of the two evils he chose the former, and authorized Luis
Del Valle, the Mexican consul at San Francisco, to send three
thousand Frenchmen to Guaymas without delay. Del Valle
naturally consulted Dillon, the French consul, and the latter at
once sent for his filibustering compatriot, Count Raousset. To the
dejected adventurer this was a most unexpected windfall, and he
and Dillon busied themselves with enlisting recruits. Nearly
eight hundred of them enrolled at the office of the Mexican consul,
who had advertised for a thousand men on March 12, and a British
ship, the *Challenge*, was chartered to take them to Guaymas. Just
at the moment when Raousset's prospects seemed brightest the
Federal government again bared its arm and dashed his plans to
the ground. On March 23, at the instance of General Wool, the
Challenge was held up by the collector of the port on the technical
ground that she was carrying more passengers than the law allowed.
This law had been constantly violated by every shipowner, and its
sudden invocation at this moment was merely a convenient pretext.[1] Six days later the vessel was libelled, and the Mexican consul was placed under arrest upon the affidavit of two Frenchmen,
Cavallier and Chauviteau, who had made a contract with Del
Valle to carry the men to Mexico at forty-two dollars a head. It
was commonly believed that the government had promised these
men to release the vessel if they would appear against the consul,
and much colour is given to this statement by the fact that the

---

[1] The *Challenge* was authorized to carry only 250 passengers, but there were
nearly 800 on her list. *Alta California*, March 23, 1854.

vessel was released and suffered to depart unmolested on April 2 with 350 men.[1] On April 5 the Mexican consul was indicted by a Federal grand jury for violation of the neutrality laws, and when his case came up a few days later his counsel demurred to the jurisdiction of the court,[2] but were overruled. The trial received considerably more importance when Del Valle's attorneys subpœnaed the French consul as a witness for the defence. The government's lawyers would have been glad to call him as a witness for the prosecution, but a treaty with France, of February 23, 1853, stipulated that the consuls of the two countries should be immune from compulsory process. The government's attorneys, therefore, merely invited him to appear, but he declined. The attorneys for Del Valle now claimed for their client the constitutional right of an accused to be confronted by witnesses, and the court upheld their argument, declaring that treaties must yield to the constitution. A subpœna was then issued for Dillon, and on April 25 the United States marshal proceeded to the French consulate to serve the order of the court. He found the house surrounded by nearly two thousand excited Frenchmen. After some discussion Dillon consented to accompany the marshal to the court, after making a formal protest, and as they left the house the throng outside made a move as if to rescue their countryman. The consul coolly restrained them, however, but thanked them for their sympathy and told them that he would do his duty. Reaching the courtroom, he again made a formal protest and declared that he would stand on his rights and answer no questions. The question of whether Dillon was in contempt was reserved by the court for

[1] *Alta California*, April 3 and May 1, 1854. Wool later stated on oath, at the trial of Dillon, that he permitted the departure of the *Challenge* only on the French consul's pledging his honour and that of his nation that the men aboard were merely colonists. *Alta California*, May 25, 1854.

[2] They held that the constitution of the United States made the Supreme Court the court of original jurisdiction in all cases affecting consuls. District Attorney Inge, however, argued that jurisdiction over consular cases was fixed by an act of 1789, and the court adopted his view.

later decision, and he was allowed to return to his consulate. The crowd was still there and he made a speech urging them to be calm and assuring them that the American people would permit no injustice and that his government was amply able to protect its agents in the discharge of their duties. He concluded by asking them to return to their homes and to do their best to promote good relations with their American neighbours. Dillon now hauled down the tricolour over the consulate as a sign of a violation of his treaty rights, and refused to act longer as consul until instructed by his government. But as he was also consul for Sardinia he continued to act in that capacity and incidentally to look after French interests. On April 26 the court announced that it would not construe Dillon's action as a case of contempt, and the next day Judge Hoffman announced that he had erred in issuing the subpœna, as the consul was immune from coercion, and that his attitude in maintaining his treaty rights was proper.[1]

Meanwhile the trial of the Mexican consul proceeded. Del Valle was a quiet, elderly gentleman who had been in San Francisco but a short time, and had been doing only what he had seen others do. He had acted so openly that it is doubtful if he was aware of any violation of the law. The evidence tended strongly to show that he had been made a tool by Dillon. The latter had frequently avowed himself in public as opposed to Raousset's undertakings and had published a card in the *Echo du Pacifique*, a French newspaper of San Francisco, stating that his government viewed such undertakings with displeasure. Some one had suggested to Del Valle that the surest way to break up the schemes of Raousset would be to induce as many of the latter's followers as possible to join this new enterprise, as they would in this way be weaned away from their old leader. Dillon readily approved this proposal,

---

[1] This clause of the treaty was later interpreted by the two governments to mean that the consuls must always give evidence unless a disability existed. House Ex. Doc., 88, 35 Cong., 1 Sess., 134.

ostensibly because it would break up forays that might disturb the harmonious relations between his country and Mexico, but really because it would enable the Count to place his men in Sonora free of all cost, and their leader could join them later.[1]

The defence tried to make two points: first that Del Valle's expedition was really an antidote to filibustering, inasmuch as it designed to thwart the plans of Raousset; and secondly, that even if it did violate the neutrality law, that law was unconstitutional. In his charge to the jury, Judge Hoffman, as in the Watkins case, affirmed his belief in the constitutionality of the law and was not especially favourable to the accused. After fifteen minutes' deliberation the jury returned a verdict of guilty, with a recommendation to the "kindest consideration and mercy." [2] Sentence was deferred till May 29, when District Attorney Inge asked that no further proceedings be taken, as the purpose had been to get the facts before the public and this had been achieved.

Enough evidence had been secured at this trial to implicate Dillon, and on May 15 an indictment was returned against him for violation of the neutrality laws. The case came to trial on the 23d. His counsel read his protest against the proceedings, and after this was received as a complaint the trial proceeded. The government attempted to prove that the accused was the real offender in the violations for which the Mexican consul had been indicted. Walker and Watkins were both summoned to tell what they knew of the relations between Dillon and Raousset. Both refused to testify on the ground that they would incriminate themselves, though Watkins admitted that he had been present at conversations

---

[1] General Wool never had any doubt of the good understanding between Dillon and Raousset, and was convinced also that as soon as the latter reached Mexico he would join forces with Walker. Dillon had told Wool at one time that the Frenchmen enlisted by Del Valle would become Mexican citizens and join the Mexican army; in a second letter he assured him that they were all red republicans and revolutionists, and would never fight for Santa Anna. House Ex. Doc., 88, 35 Cong., 1 Sess., 95–6.

[2] *Alta California*, April 2, 6, 11, 13, 14, 25, 26, 27, 28.

between Walker and the Count. Edmund Randolph, Walker's best friend, was summoned by the defence and testified in Dillon's behalf.[1] The jury, after deliberating for six hours, reported a disagreement, ten standing for conviction and two for acquittal. A few days later the district attorney entered a *nolle prosequi*, and the complaint was dismissed.[2] Californians regarded the whole proceeding against the consuls as a piece of political claptrap designed to arouse American chauvinism and promote the political prospects of General Wool, who was then thought to have presidential aspirations.[3] Colonel E. D. Baker, an able attorney who volunteered his services in Dillon's behalf, in addressing the jury asked why the district attorney allowed Walker to go away in broad daylight, and after he had failed and filibustering had become unpopular he should turn against foreigners. The *Alta California* declared editorially that it was no horror of filibusterism that prompted these indictments, but a desire for notoriety or a pat on the back from some big man in Washington, or a chance to ride into power as a result of the storm they were expected to raise.[4]

On the very day on which Dillon's case came to trial, Count Raousset-Boulbon, the real cause of this commotion, embarked on a small schooner with eight companions and a good supply of munitions of war and stole away by night to join the Frenchmen who had sailed some weeks earlier in the *Challenge*. His going was perhaps a good thing for Dillon's cause, as he might have given damaging testimony, and it is certain that had he remained many days longer in California he would have been arrested by Wool. After suffering shipwreck on the island of Santa Margarita, off the coast of Lower California, and enduring many other mishaps, he

[1] Hittell in his *History of California* says that the arrest of the consuls was effected by the slavery party, who desired Sonora for themselves. Evidence, however, shows this view to be erroneous. Randolph was an ardent slavery man, friendly to Raousset, and a witness in favour of Dillon.

[2] *Alta California*, April, May, 1854; Soulé, *Annals of San Francisco*, 531-35.

[3] Lévy, *Les Français en California*, 148-55.

[4] *Alta California*, May 27, 1854.

landed near Guaymas late in June, and betook himself secretly into the town by night. Only a small number of the Frenchmen who had preceded him were willing to join in his plan to seize Guaymas, fortify himself there, and wait for reinforcements from California. Disappointed in his countrymen, he next tried to win over Yañez, the commander of the garrison, urging that they both join a revolution then brewing against Santa Anna. The wily Mexican feigned much interest, but did this only to make Raousset reveal his plans and to gain time in which to strengthen himself for an attack on the Frenchman. Perceiving that he was duped, the Count sent Yañez an ultimatum, demanding two pieces of artillery for the French for their protection and three Guaymas merchants as hostages. This was of course rejected. The French for some time had been spoiling for a fight, and their leader could now restrain them no longer. He therefore drew up all the French battalion that had joined his side and made them a ringing address. "We shall have the victory of Guaymas as a pendant to the victory of Hermosillo," he said, and his men responded with cries of "Vive la France." An attack was now made on the barracks, where the Mexicans were stationed in great force with artillery and with adobe walls for their defence. The attacking party received a withering fire and were about to fall back, when Raousset put himself at their head and ordered a charge. Only a score dared follow. He seemed to be seeking death; bullets cut his hat and clothing; even bayonets tore his flannel shirt, but they did him no harm. With so few to follow he withdrew. In the streets he rallied some half a hundred men and called in vain for another attack. They all with one consent began to make excuse; the principal reason being that they had no ammunition. Some started for the French consulate, and the rest, badly demoralized, followed like sheep. Last of all came their erstwhile leader. The *émeute* lasted about three hours and resulted in the death of some sixty men, the losses being about equal on both sides. Sixty

French were wounded and about twice as many Mexicans. Joseph Calvo, the vice-consul, promised protection to all who took refuge under his flag, but hesitated for some time before extending this to include Raousset. The latter was given every chance to flee, but refused, claiming the protection of the French flag. He and his followers were placed under arrest, and on August 10 he was tried before a war tribunal for inciting conspiracy and rebellion. His men were called as witnesses, and with a single exception they tried to save themselves by turning against their leader. The vice-consul denied that he had ever promised him protection, and Raousset was condemned to die. Early on the morning of the 12th he met death by the fusillade — a fate that overtook so many other filibuster leaders. His followers were pardoned. Some returned to California, and others went to South America or remained in Mexico.[1]

As soon as this news reached California Consul Dillon published a long letter purporting to have been written by Raousset on May 19, 1854, on the eve of his departure for Guaymas.[2] The letter absolves Dillon of all complicity in the adventurer's plans, and one cannot help wondering why it was not produced at the consul's trial. The fact that it was brought to light only after the death of its alleged author militates strongly against its authenticity.

The matter of the consul's compulsory attendance as a witness naturally led to an exchange of notes between the governments at Paris and Washington. The American government declared its regret "that any occurrences should have disturbed, even for a moment, the good understanding of the two countries," and expressed a desire to make full reparation.[3] It was agreed that the first French ship of war that entered the harbour of San Francisco should receive a salute of twenty-one guns, but it was not until

[1] Lambertie, *Le Drame de la Sonora*, 102–6; Hittell, *California*, III., 741–55.
[2] *Alta California*, Sept. 24, 1854.
[3] House Ex. Doc., 88, 35 Cong., 1 Sess., 134–5.

November 30, 1855, that an opportunity to make these formal amends presented itself. At two o'clock on the afternoon of this day the French warship *Embuscade*, which had entered the harbour and anchored near the American frigate *Independence*, received a salute of twenty-one guns from this vessel and also from the garrison at the Presidio. At the same time the tricolour was again hoisted over the French consulate for the first time in eighteen months. The French population had been notified beforehand and had gathered *en masse* before the consulate. With the hoisting of their national emblem they became almost delirious in their enthusiasm. Dillon made them a speech full of unctuous flattery for the United States in general and for California in particular. This was followed by a reception at the consulate to which many leading citizens, including Judge Hoffman himself, came to extend their congratulations. With the termination of this happy incident French filibustering in California became a matter of history.

The interest of the diplomatic representatives of France in these plans of Mexican colonization was made the basis for a report that Louis Napoleon was quietly sanctioning the expeditions.[1] It was believed that the French government would quickly have supported any of these ventures if they had proved successful. The aid later accorded to Maximilian by this same ruler refreshed men's memories of the earlier French enterprises and tended to confirm their suspicions that an ambitious monarch was behind them all.

In the midst of the trial of Dillon the grand jury brought in an indictment against William Walker and his Secretaries of War and Navy, John M. Jarnigan and Howard A. Snow. Walker was arraigned on June 2, and plead "not guilty," stating that the expedition was organized on a military basis only after it had left the United States.[2] Edmund Randolph appeared as Walker's

---

[1] Such a view was expressed by the New York *Herald*, Aug. 4, 1856.
[2] *Alta California*, May 27 and June 3, 1854.

attorney. Walker was not arrested after his indictment, being regarded as still on parole, but after his arraignment he was placed under bond. Owing to the absence, first, of Frederic Emory, a material witness, and later also of Judge Hoffman, in the East, the case did not come to trial till October.[1] Randolph and Benham, Walker's attorneys, resorted to the same tactics employed in the trial of Del Valle and insisted upon the summoning of Dillon. This Judge J. S. K. Ogier [2] refused to do, but invited Dillon to appear and testify if he saw fit. The consul replied that he was prevented by "urgent reasons beyond his control" from accepting the invitation, but intimated his willingness to submit an affidavit affirming his entire ignorance of all circumstances calculated to militate in favour of or against the accused. The trial then began. It is interesting to note that the first witness for the government was Henry A. Crabb, a native of Nashville and schoolmate of Walker's. He was now a prominent Whig politician and member of the State Senate. His appearance on the stand brought out no material facts, and the event is here referred to because Crabb was later to invade Mexico and follow in Walker's footsteps.

Walker acted as one of the attorneys in his own defence, and in introducing his witnesses he said : "In defence of the charges against me, gentlemen of the jury, I shall introduce evidence to show that at the time of leaving this port, my intention was to proceed to Guaymas and thence by land to the frontiers, and I shall also prove that it was only after we had got to sea and beyond the territory of the United States that this intention was changed, so as to land at La Paz ; and previously to this it was not my intention to proceed and land there in a hostile manner." The arguments of the counsel were along the same lines followed in the trial of Watkins. Benham attacked the constitutionality of the neutrality laws and

[1] *Alta California*, June 7 and Oct. 16, 1854.

[2] Judge J. S. K. Ogier was from South Carolina, but had lived in New Orleans for a time before migrating to California.

F

declared that if the invasion were an assault upon the people of Mexico it should be punished by Mexico. If Walker had first conceived at sea the idea of making war on Mexico the jury could not touch a hair on his head. While Benham was speaking Consul Dillon and Admiral Despointes, in command of the visiting French squadron, entered and took seats within the bar. Randolph, who followed Benham, made skilful use of this incident, stating that the consul's refusal to testify, though he was able to attend the trial, had deprived the defendant of his constitutional rights. Walker's speech in his own defence was naturally of especial interest. None of the Frenchmen, he said, who had gone to Mexico had been prosecuted. Why, then, should the government turn on him? He related certain incidents of his visit to Guaymas, stated that the people had invited him to return and that he had planned to do so. Owing to governmental interference, however, he found himself at sea with only forty-five men, and with so few followers he was compelled to land in a sparsely settled region and protect himself with some sort of flag. The only thing that had supported him and his men in the terrible march across the desert was their consciousness that right and humanity were on their side. He had hoped to emulate the Pilgrim Fathers by rescuing Sonora from the savages and making it the abode of civilization. District Attorney Inge ridiculed the humane purposes of the filibusters, but argued that even if they were going to Mexico to protect the inhabitants against Indians their expedition was a distinct violation of the law. He affirmed the constitutionality of the law and cited the conviction of Watkins and Emory as precedents. Judge Ogier's charge was practically identical with Judge Hoffman's in the previous cases, except that he undertook first to summarize the evidence. This brought an objection from Walker, who declared that the constitution of California forbade judges to charge on the facts. Ogier stated that this applied only to State courts. At the end of the charge Walker gave notice of a number

of exceptions. The jury was out only eight minutes and returned
a verdict of not guilty.[1]

With the acquittal of the chief of the filibusters the government
dropped the cases against the less important participants. It
had shot its last bolt and had little to show for its trouble.
Wondrous indeed were the works of these juries. They had convicted the guileless Mexican consul, whose chief offence had been
to allow himself to be made a catspaw by others; they had dis-
agreed over Dillon, who was the high-priest of the French filibusters;
they had convicted Watkins, an agent of Walker, and had then
acquitted that agent's principal!

As to General Wool, the prime mover in the arrests of consuls
and adventurers, he of course got no thanks from the filibusters,
and he received no praise from their opponents. The latter thought
that he was playing politics. Jefferson Davis, while happy to
note Wool's "cordial coöperation in the views of the [war] department," hinted strongly that he should not usurp the functions of
civil officers by originating arrests and prosecutions for mis-
demeanours.[2] The Washington *Union*, the administration organ,

[1] *Alta California*, Oct. 19–20, 1854.
[2] House Ex. Doc., 88, 35 Cong., 1 Sess., p. 52. Wool regarded this as a censure of
his course and wrote a lengthy explanation and defence. To this Davis replied on
Aug. 18, 1854. "It is not necessary to argue whether your construction of them
[your instructions] is sustained by their letter. It is sufficient to the department to
presume that the interpretation you originally put on them was sincere, and that
you acted in accordance with that interpretation; but when you received my letter
of the 14th of April, stating to you the construction that the department designed
you to place on your instructions, you should have been content to act in conformity thereto. Doubtful questions may arise in regard to the powers vested in
the President to enforce our neutrality laws, and the extent to which he may devolve
authority for that purpose upon military officers. These laws have not yet received, in all points, a full judicial consideration. But it is understood from the
language of the Supreme Court that the President may authorize a general in command to use his command directly against violators of these laws, and without the
interposition of the civil authorities. But the court were also of the opinion that
this 'high and delicate power' ought only to be exercised when, 'by the ordinary
process or exercise of civil authority, the purpose of the law cannot be effectuated,'
and when military or naval force is necessary to ensure the execution of the laws."
Ibid., 98–100.

also criticised Wool for giving his whole attention to local and civil duties in the harbour of San Francisco, while people were being massacred in the outer settlements by the Indians.[1] Full of resentment at such criticism, Wool, like Achilles, sulked in his tent, and subsequent filibustering expeditions were allowed to depart unmolested. This attitude of the departmental commander was not without its effect on Walker's later career in Nicaragua.

[1] *Alta California,* Dec. 24, 1854.

CHAPTER VI

WALKER AS A CALIFORNIA POLITICIAN

AFTER Walker's return to California he did not regard himself as having been expatriated by becoming president of Sonora, but resumed his status as a citizen of Marysville and at once took an active interest in local politics, championing the cause of David C. Broderick, an ardent Democrat but a strong anti-slavery man. Broderick was regarded as the leader of the "regular" faction of the party in California and rallied around him all who were opposed to the domination of Southern men in the party councils. The anti-Broderick faction were designated by their opponents as the "custom-house party," on account of the large share of Federal offices that fell to them, and they were under the leadership of Senator Gwin, formerly of Mississippi.[1] If the various characterizations of Walker as the apostle of slavery were true, we should find him enrolling under the banners of the Gwin faction, and the fact that he is found in the opposing camp is at least significant. There was at this time, however, no sharp sectional alignment in California politics, and many Southerners were zealous supporters of Broderick the free-soiler, while Northern men were among his bitterest foes.[1] Edmund Randolph, Walker's friend, though an ardent pro-slavery man, was also a supporter of Broderick.

On July 18, 1854, the Democratic State convention met at Sacramento, and "Mr. Walker of Yuba" was one of the most prominent

---

[1] So many of the decayed Virginia gentry were provided with Federal offices at Gwin's disposal that the San Francisco custom house was jocularly referred to as the "Virginia poor house."

[2] Jeremiah Lynch, *Life of David C. Broderick*, 81. (New York, 1911.)

delegates. The members assembled in the Baptist church, and each faction, ignoring the presence of the other, chose its own presiding officer and organized for its work. The two presiding officers sat side by side, put motions, ruled on points of order, and appointed committees without regard to each other's existence. This of course created terrific confusion, but as neither side would yield an inch the turmoil continued throughout the day. In the afternoon Walker, as a Broderick man, took the floor to make a speech and began to voice the free-soil sentiments of his leader. At this some hostile delegate shouted denunciation of free-soilers and abolitionists and precipitated still further uproar. During the confusion a pistol was accidentally discharged by some nervous delegate, who was handling his weapon in his belt so as to be ready for any emergency, and in the panic that followed many delegates leaped from the windows, but no one was injured. When quiet was restored, Walker resumed speaking, but the anti-Broderick forces hooted him into silence. The convention then dispersed, to meet the next day in separate halls, and the Broderick faction appointed a committee of compromise and conciliation. Walker was made chairman of the committee, and with his fellow members repaired to the meeting place of the other faction to bring about a reconciliation. All his overtures were rejected, and one irate member moved that Walker and his committeemen be thrown out of the window. Walker was also chairman of a committee to nominate permanent officers and a member of the committee to draft a platform and prepare an address to the Democracy of the State.[1] These facts show that his short career as a Sonoran filibuster at least had its compensations in a political way, for it is doubtful if a man of his taciturn and retiring disposition would have received any such recognition at so turbulent a convention without the generous advertising he had received from his

---

[1] James O'Meara, *Broderick and Gwin*, 98 f. (San Francisco, 1881); *Alta California*, July 20, 1854.

invasion of Mexico. It is especially interesting at this time to see
Walker denounced as an abolitionist on account of his allegiance
to Broderick. This episode of his career has been overlooked.

The great political question at this time was the Kansas-
Nebraska bill. Walker's attitude on this issue may be seen from
the following contribution appearing over his name in the San
Francisco *Commercial Advertiser*:

"Events are justifying the foresight of the Southern men who
opposed the Nebraska-Kansas bill. The South is regularly 'done
for' in the measure. She has, as many think, violated solemn
promises and binding engagements. And to crown all, she has
lost instead of gaining by the act. The North has thrown the odium
of repeal of the Missouri Compromise on the South and has managed to get control of territory she would not otherwise have
obtained. A few hot-headed and narrow-minded men have persuaded the South into a course she already begins to repent of.
Carried away by the passions of the moment, the slave States
have been blinded to the consequences of the Nebraska-Kansas
measure. It is too late now to repent. The North will have
Kansas before Congress meets in December.

"The consequences of the Nebraska-Kansas bill are only another
illustration of the assertion frequently made by wise and moderate
men from the South to the effect that ultra-slavery men are the
most active and efficient agents abolitionists can have in the
Southern States. The true friends of the South are those who
repudiate the ideas and acts of the South Carolina school and who
believe the true policy of the slave States is conservative and not
aggressive. All agitation of slavery, whether North or South,
only tends to fan the flame of abolitionism and make that formidable which would otherwise be contemptible." [1]

Here we observe the same conservatism for which Walker had
previously been noted while connected with the *Crescent* in New

[1] Copied in the Sacramento *Daily Democratic State Journal* of Aug. 12, 1854.

Orleans. He has only contempt for the radicals on both sides, the slavery propagandists as well as the abolitionists. Walker's views later underwent a radical change in this respect. Circumstances which he could neither foresee nor control were to draw him closer and closer to the extreme position of the Southern party, until finally he was in complete harmony with the most advanced of the secession agitators. Walker's views in 1854 were radically different from those of 1858, but this change has been overlooked by most writers. They have read the motives of the Walker of '58 into the acts of the Walker of '54, and the result has been a distorted picture.

In addition to his political activities, Walker resumed his vocation of journalist. He at first assumed an editorial position on the Sacramento *Democratic State Journal*, a strong Broderick paper, but soon removed to San Francisco, where he became the editor of the *Commercial Advertiser*. One of the proprietors of this paper was a New Englander named Byron Cole, who had developed a keen interest in Nicaragua and succeeded in imparting some of this to Walker. Cole and Walker frequently discussed the condition of the Central American republics, and it was Cole's opinion that Walker should abandon all idea of returning to Sonora and devote his attention to the American colonization of Nicaragua, which was better endowed with natural resources and better situated geographically, and where the prospects of success seemed more favourable. The *Commercial Advertiser* was not a successful venture; Cole sold out his interest in the paper, and upon its suspension Walker resumed his position with the *Democratic State Journal* in Sacramento. In the meantime Cole had sailed for Nicaragua on a mission fraught with great consequences for Walker.

CHAPTER VII

The Increasing Importance of Nicaragua

BYRON COLE was not the only American to become greatly interested in Nicaragua at this time. Since the treaty of Guadalupe-Hidalgo in 1848 Central America had assumed a greatly increased importance in the eyes of the entire United States. The treaty had hardly been signed before gold was discovered in California, and this part of the newly acquired territory underwent a remarkable development which brought to the American government a new problem. In order to maintain the nation's integrity, it was necessary that unbroken communication should be secured between the component parts of the Union; and in the early fifties this was a difficult matter, so far as California was concerned. The great expanse of unoccupied land between the States and the Pacific slope served to divide rather than unite the two sections. The journey across the plains or around Cape Horn was not only long and tedious but also fraught with great dangers, and in the search for a better route the attention of Americans was directed toward the Central American isthmus. Here two possible routes presented themselves, one across the isthmus of Panama and the other through Nicaragua. American enterprise soon made itself felt in both places: in Panama the construction of a railway connecting the ports on the Atlantic and the Pacific was undertaken; in Nicaragua the construction of a canal was contemplated, but when this proved to be not immediately practicable a substitute was devised by placing steamers on the San Juan River and Lake Nicaragua and enabling the passengers to make all but twelve

71

miles of the trans-isthmian journey by water. Both routes were
well patronized, and to and from the gold fields there flowed a
constant stream of wide-awake, energetic travellers. Many of
those who passed through Nicaragua were attracted by the luxuri-
ant vegetation and the magnificent scenery of the country and
could not help noting the scanty use which the natives were making
of such lavish gifts of nature. For the mongrel population they
had little but contempt; and especially was this true of those
Americans who were returning from California, where they had
learned to detest all "greasers." In many instances, too, this scorn
was based on something more than mere race prejudice, as the
constant revolutions caused the traveller no little inconvenience
and made him long for the day when the United States should
interpose a strong arm and establish law and order on the isthmus.
Of this final outcome no American at that time expressed the
slightest doubt, for it was then that the belief in the "manifest
destiny" of the United States was strongest and the land hunger
of its people sharpest. In the past fifty years they had devoured
everything west of the Father of Waters and the appetite had only
increased with the eating.

Another land-hungry power, however, had been looking on with
jealous eyes as the Americans began to take an increasing interest
in Central America. Far-sighted English statesmen had seen that
our war with Mexico would end with great gains of territory on
the Pacific coast, and that this might result in American ascendency
in the Pacific if the United States enjoyed quick and easy communication between its eastern and western parts. Fearing for
her commercial supremacy in the Orient, Great Britain then began
to throw such obstacles as she could in the way of interoceanic
communication for the United States. At this time the only feasible route for a ship canal appeared to be through Nicaragua by
way of the San Juan River and the lake. On February 17, 1848,
therefore, England seized the town and harbour of San Juan del

Norte commanding the mouth of this river, claiming that it lay within the territorial limits of the Mosquito Indians, over whom she was exercising a protectorate. How England came to exercise such a protectorate will be explained in a subsequent chapter. The Mosquito territory had been understood to extend from Cape Gracias á Dios only as far south as the Bluefields Lagoon, and this extension of the claim to the mouth of the San Juan River was regarded in the United States as merely a pretext for preventing the construction of a canal.   There could have been no other reason for this action; for, disregarding its geographic situation, the village of San Juan del Norte was one of the dreariest spots in the world.   Travellers describe it as a mean collection of some fifty or sixty thatched houses, with a population of about three hundred persons of every shade of colour, but consisting mainly of Jamaica negroes with a few native Nicaraguans and an occasional European. A number were fugitives from justice, and very few owned any property or had any visible means of support.   Its sole importance lay in the fact that it was the only Nicaraguan port on the Atlantic and apparently the only available place for the eastern terminus of the future canal.[1]

In the eyes of the Americans the seizure of this port was a palpable violation of the Monroe Doctrine and it led to extensive diplomatic negotiations, which in 1850 were settled for the time being by the Clayton-Bulwer treaty. By this treaty the two powers agreed to join in the construction of a canal through Nicaragua over which neither would seek to obtain exclusive control, and they further declared that neither of them would "assume or exercise dominion over any part of Central America." A few days before the exchange of ratifications, however, Sir

[1] E. G. Squier, *Nicaragua*, pp. 47–50 (New York, 1860); *British State Papers*, XLVI., 868. Laurence Oliphant, the English traveller and newspaper correspondent, gives this contemporary impression: "How extended soever may have been the traveller's experience of dreary localities, Greytown must ever take a prominent place among his most doleful and gloomy reminiscences." *Patriots and Filibusters*, 191. (Edinburgh, 1860.)

Henry Bulwer notified Clayton, the American Secretary of State, that he did not understand the treaty to be renunciatory of any existing British dependencies. Clayton accepted his interpretation, and Great Britain saw fit to maintain not only her protectorate over the Mosquito Coast but also her arbitrary interpretation of the boundaries of this region. San Juan del Norte was consequently made a "free city" and renamed Greytown. It claimed its independence by virtue of a grant from the Mosquito king. All its municipal regulations, port charges, and customs duties were determined by a mayor and council, who were mere creatures of the British consul.[1] The latter was virtually a dictator.

In 1851 this free, sovereign, and independent State of Greytown attempted to collect port duties from the steamers of the Accessory Transit Company, the corporation conveying passengers and freight between the Atlantic and Pacific ports of the United States via Nicaragua. When the company refused to pay, a British vessel fired on the *Prometheus*, one of its steamers. Across the harbour, on a low sandy spit known as Punta Arenas, the company had erected homes for its employees, and wharves, stores and warehouses for equipping its steamers and supplying the wants of its passengers. The council claimed that this property lay within the "city" limits, and the citizens asked that the stores be removed to Greytown, where they could enjoy some of the passengers' trade. The company ignored the request, whereupon a mob crossed the harbour and destroyed some of the property and tore down and trampled the American flag. After this Greytown was boycotted by everyone connected with the Transit Company,[2] and this only increased the ill-feeling. On February 3, 1853, the council passed a resolution ordering the company to remove within five days certain buildings it had just completed and to vacate the entire tract within thirty days, as it was the property of the "city"

[1] Senate Ex. Doc., 8, 33 Cong., 1 Sess.; *American Whig Review*, V., 191.
[2] *British State Papers*, XLII., 207.

and would be needed for its use. The company as usual ignored the demand and appealed for protection to an American man-of-war in the harbour. A boatload of armed men were sent over from Greytown to execute the orders of the council, but on landing they found the property guarded by American marines. Americans who entered the village were thereafter liable at any time to assault or insult by its miserable denizens.[1] Matters went from bad to worse. On May 5, 1854, employees of the company chased across the harbour some thieves who had been pilfering the warehouse and seized one of them just as he was landing in Greytown. A party of men, well armed, came to the rescue, however, and drove the pursuers away. The next day a band of armed men crossed over from Greytown, seized the employee who had attempted to arrest one of the thieves, and carried him back as a prisoner. The company's agent, Joseph Scott, followed and sought to bail the man, but was also arrested.

On May 16 the river steamer *Routh* came down the San Juan River with Mr. Solon Borland, the American minister, on board. On this trip the captain of the boat, named Smith, had an altercation with one of his negro boatmen and shot him. On arriving at Punta Arenas the *Routh* made fast to the ocean steamer *Northern Light* to transfer her passengers, and while this was taking place a native bungo containing about thirty Jamaica negroes pulled alongside and a "marshal" announced his purpose of arresting the captain. The latter procured his gun and made ready to fight. Minister Borland then appeared and told the negroes that the American government had never recognized the right of the Greytown authorities to arrest American citizens, and ordered them to leave. Several negroes rushed for the steamer, brandishing their weapons and using threatening language, but Borland seized a gun and stepping over the railing, told them that if they boarded the vessel it would be at the peril of their lives. This had the

[1] *British State Papers*, XLVII., 1006 ff.

desired effect, and the bungo returned to Greytown. That night
Borland was rowed over to the village to visit the United States
commercial agent, Joseph W. Fabens. During the visit a mob
surrounded the house, and their leader, a negro, declared that
they had come to arrest the American minister. Borland then
attempted to address the mob and was struck and cut in the face
by a broken bottle. He was held a prisoner in the house all night,
and the next morning when a party of men from the *Northern Light*
embarked for his rescue they were fired upon and not allowed to
land. On the second morning the negroes had quieted sufficiently
to permit Borland to return to the steamer. On reaching the United
States he laid his case before Secretary Marcy.

The Secretary, however, found this a perplexing problem. On
the day following the attack on Borland every officer in Greytown
had resigned his position, and the municipality became practically
non-extant. There were no authorities of whom to exact reparation or to inflict punishment upon any individuals who were
responsible for the insults. Many of the ringleaders also found it
expedient to return to Jamaica. The United States man-of-war
Cyane, Commander George H. Hollins, was despatched to Greytown to demand satisfaction. The instructions to Hollins were
necessarily somewhat indefinite; he was to consult with the commercial agent, Fabens, and learn the true condition of affairs; it
was desirable that these people should be taught that the United
States would not tolerate such outrages, but it was also desired
that this should be done without destruction of property and loss
of life. The department, however, would trust much to Hollins's
prudence and good sense.

Fabens in the meantime was instructed by the Department of
State to notify the people of Greytown that his government would
demand payment for the property taken with their connivance and
also protection thereafter for the Accessory Transit Company. As
there was no official government, he addressed the communication

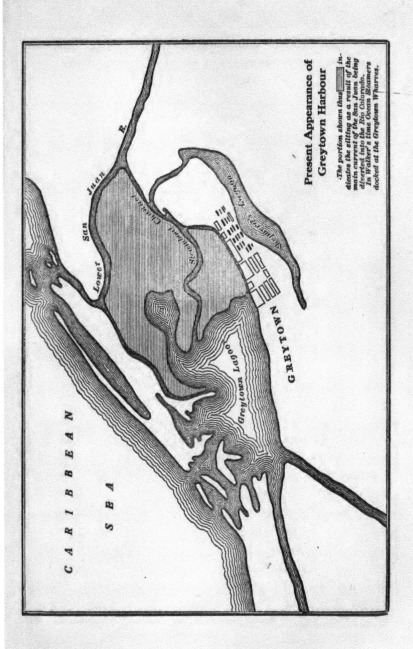

Present Appearance of
Greytown Harbour

The portion shown thus [ ] indicates the silting as a result of the
main current of the San Juan being
diverted into the Rio Colorado.
In Walker's time Ocean Steamers
docked at the Greytown Wharves.

on June 24 "To those now or lately pretending to and exercising authority in San Juan del Norte." On July 11, after a consultation with Hollins, who had just arrived, he repeated the communication and added to it a demand for an apology to Hollins and satisfactory assurances of future good behaviour toward the United States and her functionaries. No attention whatever was paid to Fabens's demands other than insolent rejoinders from a few individuals. The British war schooner *Bermuda* was in the harbour at the time, and this seemed to the population an ample guarantee against molestation by an American officer. There can be little doubt that all the trouble was instigated by the British consul and the ever-present naval officers.

Hollins now had only one of three courses to follow: he must sit still and swallow the insults; or sail away with his mission unaccomplished; or turn his guns on the town. The last seemed the only course that would not detract from his nation's dignity, and on the morning of June 12 he gave notice that if Fabens's demands were not complied with within twenty-four hours he would bombard the town. The British vice-consul and Lieutenant Jolly of H. M. S. *Bermuda* both protested; the latter expressing regret that "the force under my command is so totally inadequate against the *Cyane*, that I can only enter this my protest." Hollins replied that he regretted exceedingly that "the force under your command is not doubly equal that of the *Cyane*." At daylight the next day Hollins sent in a steamer to take away all who would leave, and at nine o'clock the firing began. At four in the afternoon a force was landed to complete the destruction of the town by fire. Practically everything in the wretched place, except the property of a Frenchman who had protested against the inhabitants' misdeeds, was destroyed, but no lives were lost.[1] It was a pitiable spectacle to see a great republic wasting its powder on the miserable huts of these outlaws, while the real offenders

[1] *British State Papers*, XLVI., 859–88.

against its dignity sat quietly by under the protecting folds of the
Union Jack. It was a vicarious punishment. The guns of the
Cyane might with more justice have been turned upon the insti-
gators of all the trouble.

Great Britain maintained its claim to a protectorate over the
Mosquito Coast until 1856.[1] The facts in connection therewith
have been given at length in order to convey some idea of the
resentment that developed in the minds of the American people
as a result of British aggression in Central America. This hostility
to England was not without its effect upon the attitude of large
numbers of Americans toward the entrance of Walker into Nicaragua. When he entered the country the facts just narrated were
still fresh in men's minds, and any movement tending to check
the pretensions of Great Britain on the isthmus was sure to meet
with some favour in all parts of the United States.

In spite of British intrigue and arrogance, American influence
made itself felt in Nicaragua in no small degree. It was the enterprise of the American capitalist, however, and not of the American
diplomat that achieved such a result. The importance of Nicaragua to the United States as a consequence of the Mexican War and
the discovery of gold in California has already been indicated.
With the first rush of adventurers to the gold fields the question
of an interoceanic canal aroused great interest. A prime mover
in the promotion of this canal was Cornelius Vanderbilt, the greatest captain of industry of his time. At this time the Pacific Mail
Steamship Company had a monopoly of the transportation service
via the isthmus, sending its vessels from New York to Aspinwall
and from Panama to San Francisco. A company had been organized in 1850 to construct a railway across the isthmus of Panama,
and after enormous expense and great loss of life the road was

---

[1] For an account of this controversy between Great Britain and the United
States, see I. B. Travis, *History of the Clayton-Bulwer Treaty* (Ann Arbor, 1900);
and L. M. Keasbey, *Nicaragua Canal and the Monroe Doctrine* (New York, 1896).

completed in 1855. While the Panama company was developing its business, Vanderbilt and his associates were busy with plans for a rival route through Nicaragua. In 1849 he with Joseph L. White and Nathaniel J. Wolfe organized the American Atlantic and Pacific Ship Canal Company and secured a charter from the republic of Nicaragua giving the company a right of way through the country and the exclusive right to construct the canal. In 1850 Vanderbilt visited England to secure the coöperation of British capitalists in financing the undertaking, and they agreed to assist in the project if fuller surveys should show that it was practicable. The new surveys were made and indicated that the waters in the lake were insufficient to make the construction feasible. The earlier surveys were shown to have been inaccurate. The scheme for a canal was then abandoned, but Vanderbilt and his associates obtained a new charter for another corporation, styled the Accessory Transit Company, which was "grafted on the body" of the American Atlantic and Pacific Ship Canal Company. This Accessory Transit Company received a right of way between the oceans and the monopoly of navigating the waters of the State by steam. Vanderbilt was president of the company, and he soon made it a formidable competitor of the Panama line. Shortly after returning from England he proceeded to Nicaragua, where for several weeks he directed soundings on the river and lake and satisfied himself that a steamship route from San Juan del Norte to the western shore of Lake Nicaragua was entirely practicable. He had planned at first to make Realejo the Pacific port, but found a new and unnamed harbour at a more convenient point, which became San Juan del Sur. From this point to the lake the distance was only twelve miles, and he planned to connect the lake and the ocean with a macadamized road. After his return home he sent down two small steamboats for the river and a larger boat for the lake. He also despatched three steamers to the Pacific, and was soon ready to carry passengers to and from California. Another

steamer which he had constructed for the lake he was told by his
engineers could never be conveyed up the river on account of the
rapids. Vanderbilt thereupon went to Greytown with the boat
and himself conveyed her over the rapids. New ocean steamers
were built in 1852, and an additional line from New Orleans to
Greytown was inaugurated.[1]

Passengers at Greytown would proceed up the river in boats
of light draft until they reached the lake. There, at a point called
San Carlos, they would transfer to larger steamers provided with
comfortable state-rooms and cross the lake to the town of Virgin
Bay. Next there would be before them a twelve-mile ride by land
to San Juan del Sur, where they would take the steamer for San
Francisco. This ride at first was made on mules over a bridle path
through a very rugged country, and the discomforts were serious,
especially for women and children.[2] In 1854, however, the
macadamized road was completed, and comfortable carriages were
placed upon it. Each of these was painted in the national colours
of Nicaragua, white and blue, and was drawn by four mules. The
vehicles would move in a line of twenty-five at a time, carrying
the passengers of the latest ship to arrive, and being followed by
many wagons conveying freight and baggage.[3] This of itself was
an impressive sight, and the scenery along the route was another
feature.

The new interoceanic route was completed in the face of tre-
mendous difficulties, with no governmental favours and in spite

---

[1] *Harper's Weekly*, III., 146; F. Belly, *À Travers l'Amérique Centrale*, II., 96
(Paris, 1867); Wm. A. Croffutt, *The Vanderbilts and the Story of their Fortune*,
43 ff. (Chicago, 1886.)

[2] Mrs. Alfred Hart, in *Via Nicaragua: A Sketch of Travel* (London, 1887), describes the transit line across Nicaragua when it was first inaugurated. There
was then much hardship, no decent accommodations on the river or lake boats, and
only a bridle-path from Virgin Bay to the Pacific. Three years later, on a second
journey, she found conditions much improved. See also *Memoirs of General
William T. Sherman* (N. Y., 1875), I, 94 f.

[3] H. H. Bancroft, *Chronicles of the Builders of the Commonwealth*, V., 386–95.
(San Francisco, 1891.)

of the opposition of a powerful competitor. As a result of competition the fare between New York and San Francisco was reduced from six hundred to three hundred dollars, and travel by sea between East and West was further stimulated. By the Nicaraguan route the distance was reduced somewhat over five hundred miles, and the average time saved was about two days.[1] When the company was at the height of its prosperity it would transport as many as two thousand Americans through Nicaragua in the course of a single month.

These facts in connection with the history of the Accessory Transit Company have necessarily been given in considerable detail because of the intimate relation of this corporation to the rise and fall of Walker in Nicaragua. The existence of the company drew the attention of the filibusters to Nicaragua; its favouritism is responsible for whatever success they achieved while there, and its hostility compassed their downfall.

[1] E. G. Squier, *Honduras*, 241–250.   (London, 1870.)

CHAPTER VIII

THE SAILING OF "THE IMMORTALS"

IF we are to have a clear understanding of the conditions leading to Walker's invasion of Nicaragua, we must take into consideration the political condition of that country as well as its geographical importance. The five States of Central America declared their independence of Spain in 1821 and in 1824 established a republic modelled after that of the United States. This union maintained a precarious existence, being dissolved in 1826, reestablished in 1829, unsettled by revolutions from 1830 to 1840, abolished, then partly restored in 1851, and at length permanently dissolved in 1852. From 1830 to 1855 the State of Nicaragua suffered from constant revolution.[1]

The people had been brought up under a highly despotic colonial régime, and had never had an opportunity to learn the lessons of self-government. It is doubtful, moreover, whether such a heterogeneous population could have ever developed into a democracy. The total population of Nicaragua in 1850 was estimated at 260,000. One-half of these were of mixed Spanish-Indian descent, a third were pure-blooded Indians, a tenth were whites, and the rest were negroes.[2] The people as a whole were proud, ignorant, and intolerant, and were given to violent factionalism which was based on no real principles. Class feeling played its part and served to aggravate the strife. There were two parties, the Liberal, or democratic, and the Legitimist, or aristocratic. These may once have stood for what each professed to advocate,

[1] H. H. Bancroft, *Central America*, Vol. III., *passim*. (San Francisco, 1887.)
[2] Squier, *Nicaragua*, 648; *Dublin Review*, XLIII., 361.

82

but by 1850 they had degenerated into "ins" and "outs." Sectional jealousies also played a part in the struggles. Granada, the largest city, was the Legitimist stronghold and dominated the southern half of the republic; and it was natural, then, that Granada's rival, the city of Leon, should become the headquarters of the Liberal faction and dominate the politics of the North. When the Liberals were triumphant they transferred the seat of government to Leon; with their downfall Granada would again become the capital. The party which for the time being was triumphant did not stop at victory, but resorted to wholesale proscriptions of its opponents. Neither faction hesitated at confiscation, exile, or assassination, if such seemed likely to strengthen its precarious tenure of power. Opposition to the existing government was dangerous, and since it did not dare show itself in the open it was compelled to compass its ends by methods dark and treasonable. Any one who would change the existing status, even though his motives were the noblest, became perforce a conspirator, mayhap a traitor. During a period of six years Nicaragua had had no fewer than fifteen presidents. Moreover, there was little hope for improvement. In 1855 the old generation which had lived under the restraints of Spanish rule was dying out, and a new generation, reared in an environment of bloodshed and revolution, had come to years of maturity if not of discretion.

The disastrous effects of the constant turmoil made a vivid impression upon all visitors and travellers in the country, and none were quicker to observe the widespread disorder and desolation than the Transit Company's passengers. They beheld deserted fields, abandoned houses, and churches whose walls were marred by shell and bullet as a result of their use as fortresses. On visiting any of the near-by towns while awaiting a steamer they were apt to find the plaza barricaded and a sentry to challenge them at every street corner. Reports of such conditions were carried to the States, and it is not surprising that Nicaragua tempted private adventurers to flock thither in search of fortune and excitement.

As has already been shown, one of the Americans thus interested in Nicaragua was Walker's friend and associate, Byron Cole. On the 15th of August, 1854, Cole sailed on the Transit steamer for San Juan del Sur to see what American enterprise might accomplish in Nicaragua. He was accompanied on this trip by another New Englander, William V. Wells, a grandson of Samuel Adams. Wells was making the trip as the agent of the Honduras Mining and Trading Company, which had received a large grant of land in the department of Olancho and was planning to develop the gold placers on its holdings and promote commercial intercourse between Honduras and the United States. Cole was also interested in the promotion of this enterprise, but his main purpose at present was to look into conditions in Nicaragua.[1] After landing at San Juan del Sur these two Americans proceeded to Leon, where they parted, Wells going on to Honduras, and Cole remaining in Nicaragua.

At this time Nicaragua was in the throes of one of its periodic revolutions, and Leon as usual was the headquarters of the Liberal party, which on this occasion constituted the "outs." A word concerning the native actors in this revolution is necessary. In 1853 a president had died a natural death, and in the election that followed the successful candidate was Fruto Chamorro, the most aggressive of the Legitimists and the head of a very large and influential Granada family. The Leonese naturally could not stomach such a choice; and the new president, seeing their disaffection, banished their more prominent leaders, including his recent opponent for the presidency, Francisco Castellon. Chamorro next sought to make his tenure of office still more secure by calling a constitutional convention, which increased his term from

[1] Wheeler Scrapbook no. 5, pp. 17, 54; Wells, *Walker's Expedition*, 41.

two to four years and in various other ways strengthened the powers of the executive. The new constitution, instead of accomplishing the desired purposes, merely precipitated another revolution, with the result that Castellon and his banished companions, who had taken refuge with the Liberal president of Honduras, General Trinidad Cabañas, returned to Nicaragua, rallied their former supporters, and soon were besieging Chamorro in Granada. The constitution of 1854 was made the pretext for these hostilities. Castellon and his followers avowed their support of the constitution of 1838, styled themselves Democrats, and adopted the red ribbon as their emblem. The Legitimists supported the new constitution and adopted the white ribbon as their party badge.[1] In spite of aid from President Cabañas of Honduras, the struggle went against the Democrats, and in January, 1855, they were compelled to abandon the siege of Granada, which they had conducted in a very desultory fashion for six months, and retreat to Leon. Matters became still worse when Cabañas, who was on the verge of a war with Guatemala, withdrew his contingent of troops and left the Democrats to shift for themselves. Their leaders were left with only one ray of hope. While the revolution was at its height Castellon had made two contracts with Byron Cole, by which he had authorized the latter to bring a detachment of Americans to Nicaragua to take service in the Democratic army. The first of these contracts, made in the autumn of 1854, had authorized Cole to secure three hundred men for military duty and had stipulated regular payment for their services and a grant of land at the end of the campaign. Cole hastened to California and submitted the contract to Walker. The lawyer's eye saw that its language was too bold, and that action under it would constitute a literal vio-

[1] F. Belly, À Travers l'Amérique Centrale, I., 268–73; Blackwood's Magazine, XLII., 317–18; Dublin Review, XLIII., 367; Wells, Walker's Expedition, 314; C. W. Doubleday, Reminiscences of the "Filibuster" War, ch. 3 (New York, 1886); Walker, War in Nicaragua, ch. 1; American Whig Review, VI., 337 ff.

lation of the neutrality laws and involve the participants in endless legal difficulties with the Federal government. He therefore declined to act under it, but suggested to Cole that if he returned to Nicaragua and secured a colonization grant "something might be done with it." [1] Cole thereupon returned to Nicaragua and executed a second contract, which provided for the introduction into Nicaragua of three hundred colonists, who were to have forever the privilege of bearing arms. This document was signed December 29, 1854, and reached Walker at Sacramento early in the following February. Walker now gave up his newspaper work and went to San Francisco, where he busied himself with preparations for his second filibustering expedition.

The times were so propitious for an undertaking of this kind that Nicaragua in all probability would have been invaded by an expedition from California even if Walker had never lived. While Walker was at work on his project in San Francisco he met his old schoolmate Henry Crabb, who had just returned from a visit to the East and who had been contemplating a scheme similar to that which Walker had in mind. This idea had occurred to Crabb while crossing Nicaragua on his way to Cincinnati, and during his visit to the Atlantic States he had succeeded in arousing the interest of Thomas F. Fisher, of New Orleans, and Captain C. C. Hornsby, a Mexican War veteran, in his plans. Hornsby had been sergeant-at-arms in the California legislature when Crabb was a member of that body. These men left New Orleans together in January, 1855, and on their way to Greytown they persuaded Julius De Brissot to join them. All of these but Crabb remained in Nicaragua and undertook to make contracts with the Democratic leaders to engage Americans for service in Nicaragua. Fisher visited General Jerez, the Democratic leader, in his camp at Jalteva, and contracted with him to bring five hundred men to Nicaragua with liberal pay for

[1] Walker, *War in Nicaragua*, 25.

their services in land and money. Hornsby and De Brissot at the same time entered into an agreement with Espinosa, the governor of Rivas, to wrest the control of the San Juan River from the Legitimists. Crabb in the meantime returned to California and there he soon developed political ambitions to such an extent that he lost all personal interest in the Nicaraguan enterprise, and when Fisher arrived, bringing his contract with Jerez, Crabb offered it to Walker. The latter, however, preferred his contract with Castellon and declined the proffer. Meanwhile Hornsby and De Brissot had been worsted in their attempt to seize the stronghold of Castillo Viejo on the San Juan, and they too shortly appeared in San Francisco, where they joined Walker in his enterprise. Fisher later followed suit. Crabb remained only an interested observer, but as will appear later, he himself was eventually to lead an expedition into Sonora.[1]

Four months passed before Walker was able to set forth on his new adventure, and these were months of weary waiting and heart-rending disappointment. His chief difficulties this time were financial rather than legal; for the government seemed indisposed to interfere. Walker presented his contract to District Attorney Inge, who gave an opinion that action under it would not be in violation of the neutrality laws. General Wool, who had proved such a thorn in the side of the Sonoran filibusters, next remained to be consulted, and to Walker's relief the old soldier stated that he had no authority to interfere unless requested to do so by the civil officers.[2]

[1] Jeronimo Perez, *Memorias para la Historia de la Revolucion de Nicaragua y de la Guerra contra los Filibusteros, 1854 a 1857*, pt. 1, 136–7 (Managua, 1857); Walker, *War in Nicaragua*, 24–27.

[2] The accounts of this meeting between Walker and Wool are related by themselves. Between them there is some discrepancy. Wool states that he told Walker that even if the expedition were unlawful he had no authority to interfere until asked to do so by the civil officers, and gives as his reason for so acting the interpretation of his instructions by the Secretary of War. See New York *Times*, July 23, 1857. Walker, however, says that Wool not only promised non-interference but shook hands with him as they parted and wished him success. See

Money was the next consideration, and it was procured in such small amounts that the expedition had to be provided for on a most economical scale. The men accepted for the expedition were a picked lot who had already been tried with fire. Some of them, like Hornsby and Frank P. Anderson, had served through the Mexican War; others, like Achilles Kewen, had followed Lopez in his ill-fated expedition to Cuba; and even Timothy Crocker, who had endured all the hardships of Walker's campaign in Lower California, was still in a filibustering humour and ready for whatever fate had in store for him in Nicaragua. Still another interesting member of this band was a physician, Dr. Alexander Jones, who had recently returned from a very romantic expedition to Coco Island in quest of buried treasure. It seems that one of his patients, whom he had treated successfully, out of gratitude had given the doctor certain papers purporting to reveal the exact spot where some fifteen million dollars of pirate loot had been buried. The gold hunters got only bitter experience for their reward.[1] In making his preparations Walker had the constant aid of Edmund Randolph and Alexander P. Crittenden.[2]

War in Nicaragua, p. 28. Wool's reprimand by Davis has already been referred to in Chapter V.

[1] _Alta California_, Jan. 12, 1855. Such gold hunting expeditions to the island were frequently repeated; one as late as 1912.

[2] Crittenden was a native of Kentucky and a member of the first California legislature in 1850, when he sought unsuccessfully the position of speaker of the House. In 1857 he was a candidate for the United States Senate. After the Civil War he was a law partner of S. M. Wilson, a noted California attorney. He was murdered in 1870 by a woman he was alleged to have wronged. Hittell, _California_, III., 785-7; IV., 90, 202, 515-16.

Edmund Randolph was born in Richmond, Virginia, in 1819. He graduated from William and Mary College, studied law at the University of Virginia, and was admitted to the bar in New Orleans. He served there as clerk of the United States Circuit Court, and in 1849 went to San Francisco. He, like Crittenden, was a member of the first legislature, and the two sought to secure the adoption of the civil code for California in place of the common law. In 1860 he was the candidate of the anti-Lecompton Democrats for the United States Senate. In 1861 he was an ardent Union man until his native State seceded. His sentiments thereupon changed, but he was then mortally ill and died in September of that year. O. T. Shuck, _Bench and Bar in California_, 261 (San Francisco, 1889); Bancroft, _History of California_, VI., 679 n.; Hittell, _California_, II., 806; III., 785; IV., 287-88.

Joseph C. Palmer, of the prominent banking house of Palmer, Cook and Company, proved a friend in need by contributing one thousand dollars. It is also worth noting that Colonel John C. Frémont, who had once crossed the isthmus by way of Nicaragua, likewise manifested much interest.

Walker received one proposal of aid from an unexpected quarter. In Sacramento at this time there was a rival paper to the *Democratic State Journal*, which issued from the press under the name of the *State Tribune*. Its editor was Parker H. French, who had arrived in California about 1852, under very suspicious circumstances. No one in California in those days, however, scrutinized too closely his neighbour's past, and as French was a clever and polished individual, he secured a seat in the legislature. All who had financial dealings with French had cause to regret it, and he soon acquired the reputation of being one of the cleverest rascals on the Pacific coast. Moreover, he was a megalomaniac. It was his morbid desire to do big things that accounted for his presence in California. Constantly devising great enterprises and with his oily tongue easily persuading large numbers of people to enter into his schemes, he lacked the honesty and strength of purpose to carry his plans to a successful conclusion, and usually abandoned the undertaking as soon as he had filched from his associates all the money they were willing to entrust to his care. Between him and Walker there had never been any intimacy. In fact, the paper with which the latter had been connected had attacked French very sharply on more than one occasion,[1] and Walker was somewhat surprised when French approached him with an offer of coöperation. He claimed that he had great influence with C. K. Garrison, the San Francisco manager of the Transit Company, and that he had already interested him in the expedition, as it was bound to affect the situation of the corpo-

[1] In March, 1855, French was accidentally shot in the leg while trying to separate two quarrelling companions in a steamboat bar. A few days after the accident the *State Journal* expressed its gratification that French was recovering *slowly*.

ration in Nicaragua. This was another instance of French's megalomania. Whether or not Garrison were interested, he did not lift a finger in aid of the expedition, though his later relations with Walker, to be presently described, may have been a result of French's suggestions at this time. This meeting between Walker and French was not to be the end of their relations. The latter was to make his appearance in Nicaragua on more than one occasion and to affect the fortunes of the filibuster leader immeasurably for both good and ill.

In the midst of his preparations Walker became engaged in a controversy with a former resident of Sacramento named W. H. Carter, and the quarrel ended in a duel on March 15, fought with pistols at eight paces. Walker was wounded in the foot, and the injury confined him to his room for some time and delayed his preparations for sailing.[1] When he left San Francisco, seven weeks after the affray, the wound still gave him trouble.

To secure a vessel was no easy matter, but at length the *Vesta*, a leaky old brig which had weathered the waves for twenty-nine years, was chartered, and the men and their supplies were placed safely on board. When everything was in readiness for sailing the sheriff appeared with a writ of attachment and seized the vessel for a debt due by its owner. A posse was placed on board to prevent the brig's departure, and the sheriff as a matter of further precaution took away the sails of the vessel. Misfortunes did not come singly. Provisions had been secured from dealers who had agreed to accept Nicaraguan stock in payment. They now changed their minds and demanded cash. Failing to get this, they libelled the vessel, and the United States marshal served the writ and placed a revenue cutter astern of the *Vesta* to prevent her leaving port. With Federal and State officers

[1] *Philadelphia Daily News*, April 9, 1855. B. C. Trueman in his *Field of Honor* (New York, 1884) credits Walker with two additional duels, one fought in New Orleans with an editor named Kennedy and another in San Francisco in January, 1851, with Graham Hicks.

both guarding the ship and with the sails unbent and stored on
shore, the chances of the *Vesta's* departure seemed slim indeed,
and Walker's eventual escape from so many entanglements is
very creditable to his ingenuity and persistence. It happened
that the creditor who had seized the vessel for debt was a warm
friend of Henry Crabb, and this proved a means of friendly approach and of persuasion to release the vessel on easy terms. It
was seen that the merchants who had supplied the vessel with
provisions had libelled it at the instigation of the owner, who
after getting into trouble himself was disposed to make trouble
for others. In his case intimidation was employed and he was
led to believe that the reckless men would make it unsafe for him
if they were compelled to stay in San Francisco much longer.
The libel was therefore dismissed. There was, however, still
more trouble ahead. The sheriff demanded the payment of his
fees, amounting to three hundred dollars, before he would surrender the sails. He was kept in ignorance, however, of the
dismissal of the Federal writ and believing that the revenue cutter
was still guarding the *Vesta* he consented to return the canvas.
Nevertheless he kept a deputy on board to watch for any suspicious movement. After the commander of the revenue cutter
was notified that the brig was no longer to be detained a friendly
officer of that vessel kindly lent Walker the services of its sailors
to bend on the sails. In the meantime the sheriff's deputy had
been enticed into the cabin, and was regaled with liquor and
cigars while the work of bending the sails went silently on.[1]
Shortly after midnight the work was completed, and a steam tug

---

[1] According to the story commonly reported at the time of the *Vesta's* departure,
the deputy was informed, as soon as he entered the cabin, that he would be detained
there for a time as a prisoner, as the vessel was going to sea that night. "There,
sir," Walker is reported to have said in his drawling voice, "are cigars and cham-
pagne; and there are handcuffs and irons. Pray take your choice." The deputy,
who had been a member of the California legislature and was of a somewhat philo-
sophical turn of mind, was not handcuffed. *Harper's Weekly*, I., 332; New York
Herald, June 2, 1855.

came alongside and took the vessel in tow. After towing the *Vesta* outside the Heads, the tug cast her off, and taking the deputy sheriff on board steamed back to port. The *Vesta* spread her sails and stood out to sea, carrying fifty-eight men (afterwards styled "the Immortals") for service in Nicaragua.[1] This was early on the morning of May 4, 1855.

The incidents connected with Walker's departure have been given in what is perhaps tedious detail, but this has been done purposely. The financial difficulties of the expeditionists at this time are ample refutation of a subsequent assertion, frequently repeated, that the whole movement was inaugurated by officials of the Accessory Transit Company. It is inconceivable that that corporation should have undertaken any enterprise on so pitiful a scale.[2]

While the events just narrated were taking place in San Francisco, another movement upon Nicaragua was being planned in the Atlantic States, and the day for its departure had been set for May 7, just three days after the sailing of the *Vesta*. This was the expedition of Colonel Henry L. Kinney, to be described in the following chapter. It was a common supposition at this time that Walker and Kinney had some kind of an understanding and were planning to sail simultaneously and effect a junction at some convenient point in Nicaragua.[3] Such an idea, as will be shown later, was erroneous, but the Kinney enterprise only further substantiates the statement already made, that Nicaragua would have suffered an invasion from the United States whether or no there had ever been a William Walker.

---

[1] The number actually carried was fifty-eight, though the newspaper accounts at the time gave it as fifty-six. For some reason, which it is useless to try to explain, the number reported by the papers became commonly accepted even by the men themselves, who gloried afterward as belonging to the "Fifty-six Immortals."

[2] The New York *Herald*, Nov. 29, 1856, says that the idea of inviting Walker to Nicaragua did not originate with a belligerent faction there, but was "a brilliant idea of the managers and principal agents of the Transit Company."

[3] New York *Herald*, June 6, 1855.

CHAPTER IX

The Mosquito Kingdom and Colonel Kinney

COLONEL KINNEY was acting under a grant which had come to him indirectly from one of the ebon sovereigns of the Kingdom of Mosquitia, and thereby hangs an interesting story. The Mosquito Shore was originally a strip of coast about two hundred miles in length, extending from Cape Gracias á Dios to the Bluefields Lagoon. As it was a low, marshy, and uninviting region, it offered no attractions to the Spanish adventurers of the sixteenth century, who were seeking gold and silver and therefore settled elsewhere. Missionaries visited the region, but the native population was so sparse, and of such inferior intelligence, that they transferred their activities to more promising fields. In the next century the buccaneers found the region useful for their purposes. The much-broken and uncharted shore line, with its numerous islands and streams, enabled them in their light-draft boats easily to avoid pursuit by any vessel of war; and from their hiding places they could readily fall upon any luckless galleon that came their way. Fugitive slaves from the West Indian plantations added a new element to the population, which was further increased by the wreck of a slave-ship on the coast with a large cargo of Africans. A few Jamaican planters also attempted to form settlements and brought over a number of slaves with them.[1] In the course of time, therefore, the natives, always designated as Mosquito Indians, were really an intricate mixture of Indian and negro, with now and then a strain of blood of pirate or of Jamaican planter. The pirates themselves were mainly

[1] Travis, *Clayton-Bulwer Treaty*, 17 ff.; Squier, *Waikna, passim.*

English, and were generally unmolested if they were willing to share a reasonable amount of their booty with the Jamaican governors. Graft is as old as humanity itself.

As the English element was largely in the ascendant, it was inevitable that the idea of annexation should occur, and in 1687 a governor of Jamaica took the initiative in a peculiar way. He caused one of the chiefs to be carried to Jamaica, where he was kindly but somewhat forcibly clad in European garments and designated as King of the Mosquitoes. Solemn coronation ceremonies were arranged for the sable sovereign, but the programme was somewhat upset when the worthy potentate, unappreciative of the greatness thrust upon him, eluded his guardians, divested himself of the superfluous clothing, and ensconced himself in the branches of a tall tree, safe from all pursuit. After many entreaties he came down, and as a sort of ironical concession to the weakness of the white man he accepted a cocked hat and a paper commissioning him as king. The king next was required to place his realms personally under the protection of the British Crown. Half a century was to elapse before the English again interfered. In 1740, while England and Spain were at war, the governor of Jamaica commissioned Robert Hodgson to take possession of the Mosquito Territory and arouse the natives against the Spanish settlements in the vicinity. Hodgson visited the country, raised the British flag, and after filling the chiefs with rum made a kind of treaty with them by which they recognized British suzerainty.

Spain protested at English pretensions on the Mosquito Coast, and after prolonged negotiations the British government in 1786 abandoned its claims. With the downfall of Spanish rule in Central America, however, England again asserted her pretensions to dominion over the Mosquito Indians, and the Sambo Kingdom was revived in great style.[1] One of the chiefs who

[1] The word "Sambo" was applied on the Mosquito coast to individuals of mixed Indian and negro blood. At this time it was frequently written "Zambo."

seemed to possess the desired qualities in greatest degree was taken to Belize, in British Honduras, where emblems of royalty, consisting of "a silver-gilt crown, a sword, and a sceptre of moderate value" were secured to add to the impressiveness of the coronation ceremonies. These modern Warwicks, however, were sorely disappointed in their choice for sovereign, as he combined within himself "the bad qualities of the European and Creole, with the vicious propensities of the Sambo and the capriciousness of the Indian." It was perhaps with great relief that this monarch's sponsors learned in 1824 that he had been killed in a drunken brawl. Two other kings succeeded within the course of a year and gave no better satisfaction, and on April 23, 1825, another, who took the title of Robert Charles Frederick, was crowned with all solemnity at Belize. It is the doings of this monarch with which we are concerned in relating the story of the expedition of Colonel Kinney.

The ceremonies attendant upon the coronation of Robert Charles Frederick have been narrated by an eyewitness, and at the risk of digressing from the main story they will be briefly described, as they afford a striking commentary upon British pretensions in Nicaragua. The coronation took place at the church, following a procession, which began at the court-house. King Robert rode a horse, and wore the uniform of a British major, while his chiefs, who followed him on foot, were supplied with the cast-off scarlet coats of British officers of various ranks and with the trousers of common seamen. On arriving at the church "his Majesty was placed in a chair, near the altar, and the English coronation service was read by the chaplain to the colony, who on this occasion performed the part of the archbishop of Canterbury. When he arrived at this part, 'And all the people said, let the king live forever, long live the king, God save the king!' the vessels of the port, according to a previous signal, fired a salute, and the chiefs rising, cried out, 'Long live King Robert!'

"His Majesty seemed chiefly occupied in admiring his finery, and after his anointing expressed his gratification by repeatedly thrusting his hands through his thick bushy hair and applying his finger to his nose, in this expressive manner indicating his delight at this part of the service.

"Before, however, his chiefs could swear allegiance to their monarch, it was necessary that they profess Christianity; and, accordingly, with shame be it recorded, they were baptized 'in the name of the Father, Son, and Holy Ghost.' They displayed total ignorance of the meaning of this ceremony, and when asked to give their names took the titles of Lord Rodney, Lord Nelson, or some other celebrated officer and seemed grievously disappointed when told that they could only be baptized by simple Christian names.

"After this solemn mockery was concluded, the whole assembly adjourned to a large schoolroom to eat the coronation dinner, when these poor creatures got all intoxicated with rum; a suitable conclusion to a farce as blasphemous and wicked as ever disgraced a Christian country." [1]

British agents on the coast soon found themselves hoist by their own petard. They had made of Robert Charles Frederick a sovereign, and he proceeded in 1838 and 1839, in accordance with his sovereign will and pleasure, to give away sundry portions of his dominions in return for certain barrels of whiskey, bales of bright-hued calicoes, and other coin of the realm. One such grant he made to a London trader, John Sebastian Renwick, on September 20, 1838, bestowing upon him the region between the Patook and Black rivers, now in Honduras, and also permitting him to lay such customs duties and taxes as he saw fit. Then on January 28, 1839, this same sovereign, "in the fourteenth year of our reign," granted to Samuel Shepherd and Peter Shep-

[1] Henry Dunn, *Guatimala, or the United Provinces of Central America*, 25-7. (New York, 1828.)

herd, British subjects,[1] late of the island of Jamaica, another
princely donation, beginning on the south bank of the San Juan
River and running south and east along the seashore, taking in the
Boco del Toro and the Chiriqui Lagoon. When his Majesty's
liberal disposition became known to the traders, they were not
slow to purchase vast estates. In one of these grants the king
gave away all the territory south of the San Juan River to the
boundaries of New Granada (the eastern half of Costa Rica),
and any one who felt so inclined could easily have secured a grant
to any portion of North or South America he desired — provided, of course, he deemed the grant worth the necessary present
of grog.[2]

These various assignments of territory were made necessarily
without the knowledge of the British authorities, and when the
superintendent of Belize, Colonel McDonald, heard of them he
endeavoured to secure their revocation. The traders, however,
were a fearfully determined set of men of whom King Robert
stood in awe, and nothing could induce him to revoke the grants.
He may have feared too the loss of his rum. McDonald then
did the next best thing; he persuaded the king to make his last
will and testament appointing McDonald and others nominated
by him as "Regents" in case the king should die before the
"Crown Prince" attained his majority. Shortly after this King
Robert was considerate enough to die, and McDonald as regent
issued a decree in the name of the boy king, George William
Clarence, revoking the grants. This decree set forth that most
if not all of the cessions of land had been improperly obtained
from the late king without any equivalent return for them, and
that "many of the cessionaries had obtained said cessions from
the late king when he was not in his sound judgment [*i.e.* drunk]
and as said cessions despoil the successor of the late king of ter-

<hr>

[1] While the Shepherds claimed British citizenship, they were natives of Georgia.
[2] *American Whig Review*, V., 202–3.

ritorial jurisdiction in his kingdom and of his hereditary rights . . .
it is necessary and convenient for the security, honour, and welfare
of this kingdom that said cessions be annulled and abolished." [1]

No one need accuse the boy king of lack of filial respect in thus
hinting officially at a moral weakness in his deceased parent;
for no royal hand of ebon hue drafted this document. It was
McDonald's doing, and it is marvellous in our eyes. The youthful king was now entrusted to the care of McDonald's secretary,
Patrick Walker, who became the Johannes Factotum of the kingdom, and was a well-known character along the coast, where he
was usually designated as "Pat" Walker. The Central American
States were meanwhile too much engrossed with their domestic
tribulations to take any note of British aggressions along the
Mosquito Coast. Nicaragua, however, ever since its independence, had asserted its claims to this territory. In 1844 Patrick
Walker served notice on the Nicaraguan government that its
occupation of San Juan and other places along the shore was
without legal right, as this territory lay within the boundaries of
the Mosquito kingdom. Four years later, when war was waging
between Mexico and the United States, the British government
foresaw the results and sought to check as far as possible the inevitable American expansion by seizing the port of San Juan, which
was apparently the key to future interoceanic communication.

Mention has already been made of the Mosquito king's grant
to the two Shepherds. They later associated with themselves
Stanislaus Thomas Haly.[2] For about fifteen years they held the
documents containing the "his ✕ mark" of King Robert Charles
Frederick in a securely locked chest, and naturally disregarded
the decree of revocation of the succeeding sovereign. To them the
decree of one king was as good as that of another. Later grants

---

[1] MS., Department of State, Bureau of Indexes and Archives, Central American
Legations, Notes to Department, II.

[2] *Prospectus of the Central American Company* (Philadelphia, 1855): P. F. Stout,
Nicaragua; Past, Present, and Future, 171–82 (Philadelphia, 1859).

to other traders also fell into the hands of the Shepherds, and when our first minister to Nicaragua, Mr. Ephraim G. Squier, visited Captain Samuel Shepherd at his home in Greytown, in 1850, the veteran trader, then nearly blind, showed him documents conveying the title to about two-thirds of the king's dominions.[1] In their extreme old age the Shepherds tried to dispose of their grants, first, it is said, in England, and finding no buyer there, they succeeded in disposing of them in the United States to Henry L. Kinney and his associates. Kinney was a native of Pennsylvania, but in 1838 he migrated to western Texas, and some years later was one of the founders of the town of Corpus Christi. He had served in the Mexican War, attaining the position of division quartermaster of Texas volunteers, with the rank of major. He had also served several terms in the State legislature and had traded in live stock and speculated in real estate on an extensive scale. His purchase of the Shepherd grant of twenty-two and a half million acres was the greatest of all his land deals, and it is said that he had agreed to pay the grantees half a million dollars for their concession.[2] To carry out his plans, a corporation was organized with an authorized capital of $5,625,000 and was styled the Central American Company.[3] The ostensible objects of the company were to colonize

[1] Squier, *Nicaragua*, 55 ff. Their claims are described by the grantees as "beginning on the south bank of the river San Juan, and running south and east along the seashore, taking in the Boco del Toro and the Chiriqui Lagoon, and running thence up to the rock called King Buppan, adjoining New Granada, and from thence southerly to the ridge of the mountains that divide the two oceans up to the Spanish lines, and thence parallel with the seacoast in a northerly direction, crossing the San Juan, and running thence to where the Bluefields Main River intersects the Spanish lines, thence back by the northern banks of the Bluefields River to Great River and by said river to the sea, and by the seacoast southerly to the mouth of San Juan, including all islands and especially Little Corn Island and the Island of Escuda de Varagua [*sic*]." *Prospectus of the Central American Company*.

[2] Thrall, H. S., *A Pictorial History of Texas*, 579 (St. Louis, 1878). Kinney stood high in the esteem of the Texans, and a county of that State bears his name.

[3] There were twenty-one directors, most of whom resided in New York, Philadelphia, and Washington. The president of the company was James Cooper, of Philadelphia, an ex-Senator of the United States, and the company's solicitor was William B. Mann, then an assistant district attorney of Philadelphia.

the lands and develop the natural resources of the Mosquito kingdom. Two hundred and twenty-five thousand shares of stock were issued with a par value of twenty-five dollars each, and every share was backed with one hundred acres of land and could be exchanged for this amount when presented at the company's office in Greytown. Here, then, was a chance for the emigrant to secure some of the most fertile lands of the tropics for twenty-five cents an acre. The company advertised extensively, opened offices in New York and Philadelphia, and seemed to have no difficulty in developing its plans of colonization. Between the humble beginning of Walker's undertaking and the flourish with which the Kinney enterprise was inaugurated, there was the greatest contrast. No secret was made of the preparations. Kinney even made several trips to Washington, where he had many friends among the politicians, including, it is said, the President of the United States.[1] A notable addition to the company appeared in March, 1855, in the person of Joseph Warren Fabens, the American commercial agent who had figured so prominently in the events preceding the bombardment of Greytown. He had acquired the title to a large tract of land upon the plateau of the Chontales district near Lake Nicaragua, a region much more healthful and richer in natural resources than the Mosquito Coast; and he and Kinney now agreed to pool their interests. The Secretary of State, Mr. William L. Marcy, saw fit, however, to interfere at this juncture by notifying Fabens on

[1] After the failure of Kinney's enterprise, his partner, Joseph W. Fabens, published what purported to be an exposé of the relations between President Pierce and Kinney. He declared that Kinney turned his attention to Central America at Pierce's suggestion, that among Kinney's early associates in the enterprise were Sidney Webster, Pierce's private secretary, and Judge A. O. P. Nicholson, editor of the Washington *Union*, the administration paper, and printer for the House of Representatives. He further stated that he joined forces with Kinney at the earnest solicitation of Webster and Nicholson, who approached him on this subject on the very night he arrived in Washington on his visit from Nicaragua; and that opposition from the administration developed as a result of a quarrel between Kinney and Cushing. Kinney also quarrelled with White, of the Transit Company, which was at first friendly. Wheeler Scrapbook no. 4, p. 176 (Library of Congress).

April 25 that he could no longer hold his position of commercial agent if he joined the Kinney expedition, and when Fabens continued his relations with Kinney Marcy promptly dismissed him.[1] Another important personage who became deeply interested in the movement was Fletcher Webster, a son of the famous orator and at this time surveyor of the port of Boston. The fact that Webster had once been secretary of legation in China under Caleb Cushing, who was now a member of the Pierce cabinet, served to strengthen still further the impression that the movement had the sanction of men high in the nation's counsels. It was even reported that Webster would go to Nicaragua with Kinney.[2]

In New York Kinney chartered the new and speedy steamer *United States*, which had recently broken all records in the run between that city and Havana, and laid his plans to sail on May 7 with between four hundred and five hundred emigrants. His preparations were on a tenfold greater scale than those of Walker in San Francisco, who was at this time sorely hampered by the creditors who had tied up his decayed brig. But Kinney also was destined to encounter opposition. It came in the first place from the Nicaraguan minister at Washington, Señor Marcoleta, who began to discharge his diplomatic pop-gun at the expeditionists, not only through the regular official channels but also through the press. The minister's attacks could not possibly have been inspired by his government, which was then battling for its life with the Democratic faction and was in such a precarious condition as to render the status of Marcoleta himself somewhat ambiguous. The secret of his active opposition was revealed when it became known that his legal adviser in this matter was Joseph L. White, the attorney for the Accessory Transit Company. As the Nicaraguan government had never recognized the Mosquito claims, it would naturally oppose the

[1] New York *Herald*, May 12 and 16, 1855.　　　[2] *Ibid.*, April 21, 1855.

schemes of the Central American Company, which was acting
under grants from the Mosquito king; but it had never done
more than make a formal protest against this encroachment upon
its territory. Marcoleta, however, was now showing surprising
energy in asserting the claims of his republic. Plainly, he was
being used as a catspaw by White. It soon became evident that
the Kinney enterprise had met a deadly foe in the Transit Company. It was to the interest of that corporation that Greytown
be wiped off the map, and it had succeeded in inveigling the
government into doing this bit of dirty work. But it had barely
made itself the absolute master of the port before Kinney appeared
with a proposition to revive the settlement, introduce a more
energetic population, and assert the rights of Greytown to auton-
omy in a more vigorous fashion than ever before. The Central
American Company, if once it got a foothold in Greytown, might
grant special privileges to a rival steamship concern and destroy
the Transit Company's monopoly. It was rumoured, too, that
the Transit Company was maturing a scheme to rebuild Greytown for its own profit. White and his associates, therefore,
determined to thwart the Kinney enterprise at all hazards.

The results of this opposition were quickly apparent. Kinney
was indicted by a Federal grand jury and was arrested on April
27 on a charge of fitting out a military expedition against the
republic of Nicaragua. Five days later, Fabens, who had been
indicted jointly with Kinney, was arrested in Washington and
taken to New York. He and Kinney were released on bail.
Fabens, when arrested, still held his position as United States
commercial agent, and was not removed till a week later. The
trial was set for May 7, and when the case was called John
McKeon, the United States district attorney, declared that the
government was not ready, on account of the absence of material
witnesses, and asked for a postponement. Counsel for the defendants urged that the delay requested by McKeon was only a

scheme to break up the expedition, as the expense of holding the
steamer and feeding several hundred men amounted to more than
two thousand dollars a day, and that unless the case were adju-
dicated at once the expedition would be compelled to disband.
They declared that McKeon had made no special effort to find the
witnesses and could not give their full names, and was merely
seeking to effect an abandonment of the enterprise without going
to the trouble of securing proof of its unlawfulness. The court
ordered the trial to proceed, but McKeon declared himself unwilling to conduct the prosecution without preparation and left
the question of the further disposition of the case to the court.
Kinney and Fabens were then discharged on their own recognizances.

It was next announced that the expedition would sail on the
19th, but on the 14th an indictment was returned against Kinney
in Philadelphia, where he had also been recruiting for his expedition. This necessitated his going to that city for a preliminary hearing, which resulted in his release on a bail of $4500.
His counsel, George M. Dallas, strove hard, but in vain, to have
the bond reduced. At the hearing the Federal district attorney
alleged that Kinney was fitting out an expedition of three hundred
men to go direct from Philadelphia to Greytown, and that he had
freely promised civil and military commissions in order to induce
enlistments.[1] The Philadelphia entanglement caused further
postponement, and during his absence from New York Kinney
was made the defendant in a civil suit brought by two New York
merchants for goods which they had sold him seventeen years
previously, before his migration to Texas.[2] White and Marcoleta
seemed resolved to wear Kinney out with litigation, knowing that
every day's delay involved enormous expense and increasing de-
moralization among his followers. Opponents of the enterprise
even resorted to slander, alleging that the leader would take a

[1] Philadelphia *Daily News*, May 22, 1855. [2] New York *Herald*, May 29, 1855.

beautiful and wealthy young New York woman with him to Nicaragua on a honeymoon journey, when every one of Kinney's acquaintances knew that he had a wife in Texas.[1]

Meanwhile three government steamers and a revenue cutter on May 24 established a close blockade of the steamer *United States*, to prevent Kinney's secret departure. This had been done on orders from Washington issued on the basis of a report that the vessel would leave on the 26th.

The trial of Kinney and Fabens in New York was set again for June 5, and when they failed to appear their recognizances were declared forfeited and warrants were issued for their arrest. They were arrested the next day, and after making satisfactory explanations to the court for their non-appearance were again released on their recognizances, with instructions to appear for trial the following day. Fabens duly appeared on this day and on the next, but Kinney was nowhere to be found. The government on the 8th asked a postponement until both defendants could be arraigned, and this ended the case; for Kinney was then on the high seas.

The story of Kinney's escape may be quickly told. To divert attention from his movements a meeting in his behalf was called to take place on the evening of the 6th at the dock where the *United States* was moored. The moving spirit in the meeting was John Graham, the owner of the blockaded steamer, and also reputed to be a sort of high admiral for the Cuban junta in New York. Graham, it seems, had gained great popularity during the previous winter by his generous donations to the poor. This meeting was to be one of working people, who were summoned to convene and protest against the shabby treatment their benefactor was receiving at the hands of government officials. A large crowd — the newspapers say three thousand — assembled on the pier, where a speaker's platform had been erected near the

[1] *Herald*, May 11 and 18.

steamer. After an organization was effected, a statement was read showing that the government's interference had tied up Graham's business and had caused him to discharge a large number of mechanics. Several speeches were made by friends of Kinney and Graham, after which the meeting was declared adjourned till a later date. A report had been circulated, perhaps designedly, that while the meeting was in progress the steamer would slip her hawsers and go to sea. This drew a larger crowd than would otherwise have appeared. At the very hour of the assembly Kinney and thirteen companions quietly sailed out of the harbour in the schooner *Emma*. The promoters of the meeting may have been innocent tools of shrewder men, but to all appearances it was carefully designed to put the officials on a false scent.[1]

The blockade of the *United States* was not raised when it became known that Kinney had departed, as it was expected that the vessel would follow him with the remainder of his expeditionists. Fabens and Fletcher Webster went to Washington and exerted all their energies to secure the vessel's release, but the administration would listen to none of their pleadings.[2]

The question of Kinney's real motives must next be considered. Was he merely a colonizing agent, as he publicly proclaimed himself to be, or was he an ambitious adventurer seeking to carve a new state out of the chaotic republics of Central America? A letter purporting to be from him to a friend in Texas was published in the Brownsville *Flag* of May 5 and widely copied in other papers. There is no reason for questioning its authenticity. In it Kinney thus summarizes his plans: "It requires but a few hundred Americans, and particularly if Texans, to take control of all that country. I have grants of land, and enough to make a start upon safely and legally. I intend to make a suitable government, and the rest will follow." While the gov-

---

[1] New York *Herald*, June 6, 7, 17, 1855.   [2] *Ibid.*, June 24.

ernment's allegations that Kinney's enterprise was a military expedition against a friendly nation were never proven in a court of law, there was a general belief that this was its character, and all available evidence goes to substantiate it. We must therefore enroll Kinney and his men in the ranks of the Central American filibusters. There was a widespread impression that Kinney and Walker were partners. Later events showed them to be competitors.

The news of Kinney's coming created no excitement among the enervated population of Greytown. The place had been rendered even more desolate by the chastisement administered by Hollins. No one there believed that five hundred white men would long remain in such a God-forsaken region. Bad luck followed Kinney and his thirteen companions on the *Emma*. The schooner was wrecked near Turk's Island, and the party after much suffering finally reached Greytown on an English steamer. But the leader was now a ruined man. He had exhausted his pecuniary resources, and there was not the slightest prospect of further aid from the United States, where the government remained obdurate and the Transit Company continued hostile. Still he did not abandon hope. The disconsolate inhabitants were inclined to accept his leadership, thinking that no change could be for the worse, and at a public meeting on September 6 and 7, 1855, a provisional government was created and Kinney was chosen civil and military governor. A council of five was chosen to advise with him and to draw up a new constitution, which was to be ratified by popular vote. In the meantime the former constitution, modelled on that of the United States, was to serve as the basis for the provisional government. Kinney had brought with him a printing press, which he now set up, and on September 15 issued the first number of his bi-weekly newspaper, *The Central American*. The chief object of the journal was to advertise the resources of the country and attract immigrants.

There is, however, a kind of melancholy humour in the extensive advertisements of Greytown lawyers, merchants, schools, traders, physicians, hotels, and places of amusement, all of which owed their existence to paper, printer's ink, and a vivid imagination.[1] A full roster of civil officers was chosen to coöperate with Governor Kinney. Haly, one of the partners of the Shepherds, became chief judicial magistrate, and Samuel Shepherd, Jr., a member of the council. Other officials were the secretary of the government, captain and collector of the port, attorney-general, postmaster and recorder of deeds, provost marshal, deputy provost marshal, surveyor, constable, and two editors.[2] There were just about as many officers as Kinney had followers. Before his departure Kinney had authorized agents in all parts of the United States to advertise his scheme and solicit emigrants, but no help from this source arrived. British agents, who were responsible for Greytown's pseudo-autonomy, refused to recognize the new provisional government, and the new expedition under Walker had entered Nicaragua from the west, and was meeting with notable success. Kinney's means were exhausted; he himself was ill; and a number of his followers decided to try their fortunes under the rising star of Walker. In spite of reverses Kinney stubbornly held on with the persistence characteristic of all filibusters. His former associate Fabens followed him to Greytown, and toward the end of the year they decided to approach Walker with a proposal of coöperation. This was their last hope, and, as the sequel will show, it was destined to bitter disappointment.

[1] Extracts from Kinney's paper were reproduced in many American newspapers. See, for example, *Alta California*, Nov. 4, 1855.
[2] Stout, *Nicaragua*, 176 f.

CHAPTER X

THE AMERICAN PHALANX

WALKER and Kinney were on the sea and bound for Nicaragua at the same time. The *Vesta* had a rough voyage, but its occupants were more fortunate than Kinney's men in the *Emma* and escaped shipwreck. On the 16th of June, the fifty-eight Americans landed at Realejo, the northernmost port of Nicaragua, and on proceeding to Leon, Walker was gladly welcomed by Castellon, as the fortunes of the Democratic party were then on the wane. The fifty-eight newcomers were designated as the American Phalanx, and their leader received the rank of colonel, a title by which he had been designated ever since his invasion of Lower California. Walker now divided the Phalanx into two companies; Achilles Kewen was appointed lieutenant-colonel, Crocker became major, and Hornsby senior captain. Most of the men became naturalized Nicaraguan citizens, as a simple declaration of intention was the sole requirement of any native-born citizen of an American republic. It was Walker's plan to occupy the Transit road in order that he might recruit his forces from the passengers crossing the isthmus. Accordingly, on June 23 the men reëmbarked on the *Vesta* with one hundred and ten native allies and sailed southward. They landed about eighteen miles north of San Juan del Sur and took the trail toward Rivas, a town some miles north of the Transit and about midway between Virgin Bay and San Juan del Sur. It was necessary for Walker to occupy this town if he intended to control the Transit. The Legitimists had been apprised of his coming, Walker thought through the treachery of General Muñoz,

Castellon's commander-in-chief, who had resented the latter's employment of Americans and at Realejo had thrown many obstacles in the way of their departure. Castellon had promised Walker two hundred natives, and the fact that only about half that number appeared Walker also attributed to the influence of Muñoz.

Rivas was attacked at noon on the 29th. Walker's native troops fled at the first fire, leaving his fifty-five Americans opposed to a force of over five hundred. The *falanginos* took refuge in several houses, where they were surrounded by the enemy and held at bay for four hours. American rifles did fearful execution, but Walker's two ranking officers, Kewen and Crocker, were killed; and three other officers, Anderson, De Brissot, and Doubleday, were wounded. Five of his men were dead and twelve wounded, leaving only thirty-eight to continue the fight against fearful odds. Then the Legitimists conceived the plan of setting fire to the houses in which the men had taken shelter. This necessitated a retreat. The Americans raised a loud shout and sallied forth, while the enemy, somewhat dazed by the sudden offensive movement, waited an attack and allowed the Americans to escape with the loss of only one more man. Five of the wounded were too severely injured to join in the retreat. These were butchered by the natives and their bodies burned. The Legitimists' losses were ten times as great as those of the Americans. But Crocker and Kewen were men whom Walker could never replace. The former had stood by Walker in all the hardships of his campaign in Lower California, and in his cold and undemonstrative way the filibuster leader had come to regard him as almost a brother.[1]

With the survivors of the fight Walker with difficulty made his

[1] In this account of what is usually referred to as "the first battle of Rivas," I have followed Walker's own narrative, which is remarkably accurate and accepted as correct by such a hostile writer as the Costa Rican historian, Dr. Montúfar. See Walker, *War in Nicaragua*, ch. 2; Lorenzo Montúfar, *Walker en Centro-América*, 69–78 (Guatemala, 1887); Wells, *Walker's Expedition*, 51–55.

way to San Juan del Sur, where as they marched through the streets they presented a most unimposing spectacle, some bareheaded, some barefooted, some limping from wounds, and all extremely dirty and hungry. Gloomy as prospects then appeared, there were two men in the town who joined the Phalanx.[1] The *Vesta*, which had been ordered to cruise off the port, was nowhere to be found, and Walker impressed into service a Costa Rican schooner, the *San José*, which had just dropped anchor in the harbour, and set sail for Realejo. The captain of the vessel made the best of the situation, especially after being notified that the vessel might be libelled at Realejo for having recently brought a Guatemalan chieftain, General Guardiola, into Nicaragua for the purpose of aiding the Legitimists against the Democrats. On the way the *Vesta* was overhauled and the men were transferred. Realejo was reached on July 1st, two days after the fight at Rivas.

Walker submitted to Castellon a written report of the events, in which he roundly accused the natives of bad faith, and attributed their treachery to the agency of Muñoz. He demanded an investigation of the conduct of that officer and affirmed that if the general's conduct were not cleared of suspicion the Phalanx would withdraw from the Democratic service. Castellon sent Dr. Livingston, an American, to Walker with explanations and an urgent request to remain. The latter, however, feigned to sulk in his tent, or rather in the cabin of the *Vesta*, and appeared to be ready at any moment to sail away. Such, however, was far from his purpose. His real objects were to give his men a much-needed rest and his wounded time to recover, and also to impress Castellon with the necessity of American aid. After ten days Walker yielded and agreed to take the Phalanx to Leon, the Democratic capital, where the inhabitants were in great fear of an attack by the Legitimists. Horses and ox carts were supplied by the grateful Demo-

---

[1] Walker has sought to perpetuate their memory by giving their names — Peter Burns, an Irishman, and Henry McLeod, a Texan.

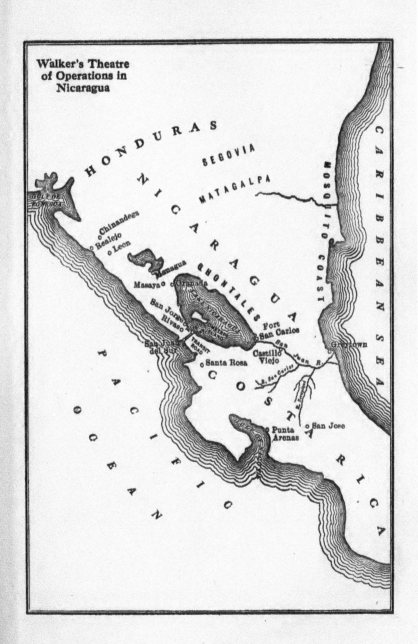

Walker's Theatre
of Operations in
Nicaragua

HONDURAS

GULF OF
FONSECA

SEGOVIA

MATAGALPA

NICARAGUA

CHONTALES

CARIBBEAN SEA

MOSQUITO COAST

o Chinandega
o Realejo
o Leon

Managua
Masaya o o Granada

San Jorge o
Rivas o

TRANSIT
ROAD

San Juan
del Sur

o Santa Rosa

Fort
San Carlos

Castillo
Viejo

San
Juan R.

Greytown

R. San Carlos

R. Sarapiqui

o Punta
Arenas

o San Jose

COSTA RICA

PACIFIC

OCEAN

crats, and the wounded were well cared for in Chinandega. Indeed, for some days the *falanginos* lived on the fat of the land.

On the way to Leon Walker met his old friend Byron Cole. The latter, after sending his contract to Walker, had waited week after week for the coming of the Americans, and at length had abandoned hope and followed Wells to the mining region of Olancho. On hearing of Walker's arrival, he had hastened back to Leon, bringing with him a former Prussian cavalry officer, Bruno von Natzmer, whose knowledge of the language and of the country made him a valuable man to the commander of the Phalanx. These two accessions offset somewhat the loss of tried and trusted followers at Rivas.

After the fears of a Legitimist attack on Leon had subsided Walker proposed a second expedition to the region of the Transit and again he met the opposition of Muñoz, who wished to divide the Americans into squads of ten, distribute them among the native companies, and march on Granada. Seeing that the natives were indisposed to assist him in his plan of campaign, Walker ordered his men to make ready to return to Chinandega, and issued his requisition for horses and ox carts. The requisition was ignored, and three hundred and fifty native soldiers were marched into quarters opposite those of the Phalanx. A clash was momentarily threatened, and Walker served an ultimatum on Castellon to withdraw the troops within an hour or he would regard him as a hostile force and act accordingly. This had the desired effect; the Democratic soldiers were marched away, and the Americans were furnished with horses and carts. On their march they kept a sharp watch for any treacherous movement on the part of their erstwhile friends. Castellon was undoubtedly glad to be free of their presence.

These difficulties foreshadowed the more serious troubles that were to follow. When Walker arrived the Democrats were aware that their cause was lost without his help, and for a time they looked upon the Phalanx as the means of their salvation. But they now perceived that their ideas and Walker's were by no means the same; they hoped to subjugate their rivals by foreign aid; the commander of the Phalanx, as they were soon to learn, was planning to Americanize the country. The full meaning of Walker's coming had not yet been perceived by the Democratic leaders, but it had become apparent that he was not going to waste much time in campaigning solely for their benefit. Walker's objective was the Transit road, where he could enlist recruits. The Democrats were interested only in defending Leon and attacking Granada, where their opponents lay in great force. A campaign along the Transit was about the last thing they would have undertaken. This difference in motives, which so quickly made its appearance, was the fundamental cause of all subsequent hostilities between natives and Americans. While the *falanginos* remained at Chinandega, making such preparations as they could for a campaign in the Meridional department, Byron Cole had tarried in Leon and had used his influence with Castellon in two important matters. Now that Walker and his men were safely beyond the jurisdiction of the United States and the neutrality laws, it was no longer necessary to maintain the pretence of acting under a colonization contract. Cole therefore secured a new grant authorizing Walker to enlist three hundred men for the military service of the State, with pay at the rate of one hundred dollars a month and a grant of five hundred acres of land at the close of the campaign. The second arrangement perfected by Cole had much more far-reaching consequences, though its importance at the time was not very apparent. He secured from Castellon full authority for Walker to adjust all differences between the republic and the Accessory Transit Company. Walker's subsequent relations with this corporation constitute the most important factor in his entire career.

Although Castellon had not authorized the expedition, Walker in the middle of August marched his men to Realejo and placed them aboard the *Vesta*. An Indian named José Maria Valle, who was sub-prefect of Chinandega, had come to admire the Americans as warmly as he hated the Legitimists, and he was therefore persuaded to recruit a force of natives to accompany Walker to the Meridional department. Castellon ordered him to desist, but without avail, and he brought a force of over one hundred and sixty men to Realejo. Walker pretended to be on the point of sailing to Honduras, where a war was waging with Guatemala. The Honduran president, General Trinidad Cabañas, had asked Democratic aid against his enemy in return for his services to Castellon the previous year, and this gave colour to Walker's pretext. He had not the slightest idea, however, of abandoning the Transit; and on August 23, in spite of Castellon's urgent request to return to Leon, he sailed for San Juan del Sur, accompanied by Valle with one hundred and twenty natives. The Indian ally had lost already a fourth of his contingent through desertion and the ravages of the cholera, to which the Americans so far had been immune.

It will be observed that in undertaking this second expedition to the Transit route Walker was acting in direct disobedience to his superior, and in fact was starting a little revolution of his own. It is interesting to note his ready adoption of the revolutionary tactics of the Spanish-American chieftains, and at this we need not be surprised; for he was merely adapting himself to his environment. There was no sovereign power to evoke or compel obedience, and disobedience to a merely titular dignitary could hardly be regarded as treasonable. Nevertheless, it must be noted that in defending his course in later times Walker always asserted with emphasis that he went to Nicaragua at the express invitation of Castellon. This statement implied his recognition of Castellon's authority as supreme director; and his subsequent actions were certainly not consistent with any such assumption. In other words, if he were right in going to Nicaragua only because of an invitation from the supreme director of the Democratic government, he was wrong in sailing for the Transit without permission from the same source.

Shortly after anchoring in the harbour of San Juan del Sur, Walker learned that no less a personage than Parker H. French was in the town en route to San Francisco after a visit to the Legitimist headquarters at Granada. What motives French may have had in visiting that city will never be known. He may have attempted to secure a contract from the Legitimists similar to Cole's, and he at least used this as a pretext for getting into communication with the leaders. Being looked upon as employed in the Legitimists' interests, he was of course debarred from communication with Walker. The clever rascal, however, had himself arrested and carried aboard the *Vesta* as a prisoner. There he explained to Walker that he had gone to Granada merely to spy out the land, and proceeded to relate what he had found. Walker did not make too close an inquiry into his story, but resolved to make the best use of the man that he could and authorized him to return to San Francisco and enlist a company of seventy-five men.

It was reported at San Juan del Sur that the Legitimists were in force at Rivas and that Guardiola, the Guatemalan chieftain, would soon take command. He had been defeated by Muñoz in the North and had fled to Granada. He now swore to revenge himself on the filibusters and drive them into the sea. Not wishing to remain entirely on the defensive or to allow his men to become demoralized by inactivity, Walker marched his force on the night of September 2 the entire length of the Transit road to Virgin Bay. Here on the following morning, while the men were preparing breakfast, they were attacked by six hundred men under Guardiola. He had left Rivas the same night, and on reaching the Transit road at a point where the *falanginos* had passed but a short time before, had started toward Virgin Bay in pursuit. Walker's men had to fight with the lake at their backs, and as

there was no chance of retreat natives and Americans held their
ground and fought well side by side. The result was a victory for
the Democratic force. Not an American was killed, and only two
of their allies. Sixty of the enemy were found dead after the fight
and over a hundred and fifty guns were picked up which they had
thrown away in their flight. During the action Walker was
knocked down by a spent ball, which struck him in the throat,
and a package of Castellon's letters in his coat pocket was cut to
pieces by a bullet. To the surprise of the natives Walker ordered
the wounded of the enemy to be as carefully attended to as his own
men, and none were more amazed than the poor stricken wretches
themselves, who expected to be shot or bayoneted according to
the Nicaraguan custom.

On the afternoon following this engagement the Phalanx marched
back to San Juan del Sur. The news of their success brought additional recruits to their ranks. A report of the victory was forwarded to Castellon, but when the news reached Leon the provisional director was in his death struggles, and an hour later had
breathed his last, a victim of the cholera. Castellon's successor,
Nasario Escoto, thanked the force for the victory and promised
to send what aid he could, but added that the spread of cholera
would make it difficult to secure any voluntary enlistments, the
only kind Walker would consider.

After a month of waiting at San Juan del Sur, during which
time Walker was compelled to levy a military contribution upon
the local merchants for his maintenance, help finally came from
the United States. On the 3d of October a steamer of the Transit
Company arrived from San Francisco bringing thirty-five recruits
under the command of Colonel Charles Gilman, the one-legged
veteran of the Lower California expedition, whose terrible experience in that campaign had failed to cool his filibustering fervour.
With Gilman came also another veteran of that expedition, who
has also appeared before in these pages, Captain George R. David-

son.[1] But the most important arrival on that steamer, so far as Walker's interests were affected, was not these recruits but a Scotchman, Charles J. McDonald.   Gilman introduced McDonald to Walker as the friend of C. K. Garrison, the San Francisco manager of the Accessory Transit Company,[2] and this meeting was pregnant with results for the future of the filibuster cause. To Walker McDonald's arrival was most gratifying, as it seemed to indicate a willingness on the part of a group of financiers to assist the Americans in establishing themselves in Nicaragua.

Fortunes, as well as misfortunes, never come singly. On the same day that Gilman and McDonald arrived there came thirty-five Democratic volunteers from Leon, whom the provisional director, true to his promise, had enlisted for service in the Meridional department. This brought Walker's total strength up to two hundred and fifty men, one hundred and fifty being natives. He was now ready for strong offensive operations.

[1] Charles Gilman was a native of Baltimore who migrated to California and was admitted to the bar of that State in 1852. Davidson was born in Frankfort, Kentucky. He served as a lieutenant in a Kentucky regiment during the Mexican War, and soon thereafter went to California. Both Gilman and Davidson survived in Nicaragua but about two months. New York *Herald*, Jan. 14, 1856.

[2] *War in Nicaragua*, 127.

CHAPTER XI

THE CAPTURE OF GRANADA

ENCOURAGED by the apparent interest shown in his plans by officials of the Transit Company, Walker resolved on a bold stroke, which was one of the few acts of his career that indicated anything like real generalship. As the entire Legitimist force was at Rivas, he knew that they had left Granada, some thirty miles to the north, practically undefended. By marching to Virgin Bay and embarking his men on one of the lake steamers of the Transit Company, he could easily approach the Legitimist capital by water and seize the city before its small garrison were aware of his approach. Accordingly, on October 11 Walker proceeded to Virgin Bay, where he took possession of the Company's steamer *La Virgen*, and the next afternoon he placed his entire force aboard. In the darkness, with her lights extinguished, the *Virgen* steamed past Granada to a point three miles north of the city, where the men disembarked, and at three o'clock on the morning of the 13th began their advance on Granada. They reached the outskirts shortly after daybreak, and in a few minutes the city was theirs. The small garrison, taken entirely by surprise, fired a few shots and fled. Firmly entrenched in the enemy's capital, Walker was now practically master of the State. He set free about a hundred political prisoners, many of whom were in chains, and thereby gained the further good will of the Democrats. At the same time, however, he estranged many of his followers by not allowing them to plunder the hated city or wreak their vengeance on many of the prominent Legitimists.

The next day was Sunday, and Walker and a number of his officers attended eight o'clock mass and listened to a sermon by the curate, Padre Augustin Vijil, who counselled peace and good will toward men. Throughout his career in Central America Walker made special efforts to gain the friendship of the clergy, knowing well the powerful influence of that class in Latin countries; and the reports of his desecrations of holy places, which were circulated by his enemies and apparently believed by some hostile historians, are mere fabrications.[1] On this same day the municipal officers met and drew up resolutions in which they tendered Walker the presidency. Walker naturally declined to accept what they had no right to give and suggested that they tender the place to Corral, the Legitimist commander, with whom he was now anxious to effect a conciliation.[2]

He therefore turned his attention to negotiating for peace, and a commission was despatched to the camp of Corral at Rivas, to urge the termination of hostilities. Mr. John H. Wheeler, the American minister, also agreed to use his good offices and proceeded to Rivas. Corral refused to treat with the native commissioners, and Mr. Wheeler not only failed to see the commander, but was treated with many indignities while there. The Legitimist leader in the meantime sent frequent letters to Walker, indicating a desire to treat with him independently, but to such proposals the commander of the *falanginos* turned a deaf ear.

Certain incidents now occurred which brought Corral to terms. Four days after the capture of Granada the San Francisco steamer arrived at San Juan del Sur bringing Parker H. French and sixty recruits. One member of the party was Birkett D. Fry, a soldier of the Mexican War, to whom French, with his usual maladroitness, had given the title of colonel without authority from Walker or any one else. French was still a megalomaniac. He proposed

[1] See, for example, Bancroft, *Central America*, III., 356 note.
[2] Senate Ex. Doc. 68, 34 Cong., 1 Sess.

a march to Virgin Bay, which was made without mishap, though they were lucky to have escaped an ambush with the enemy so near at hand as Rivas. On reaching Virgin Bay French next proposed that they board a lake steamer and capture Fort San Carlos, which commanded the point where the lake debouches into the San Juan River. The men were placed on board with the passengers, many of whom were women and children. After making a demonstration before the fort they found it too strong to capture with their single brass field piece, and headed the steamer toward Granada. After landing the recruits the steamer returned with the passengers to Virgin Bay, as it would have been folly for it to try to enter the river after its previous threatening approach upon the fort. The passengers, some two hundred and fifty, were then quartered in the company's buildings, and there they were fired upon by a party of Legitimists and several were killed and wounded. To the native the neutral passenger and the hostile filibuster looked very much alike. Moreover, the other lake steamer, bringing passengers up the river from the Atlantic States, was fired on when it approached San Carlos, and a woman and child were killed. Under such circumstances traffic across the isthmus was temporarily suspended, and all the passengers were taken for protection to Granada.[1] French and Fry in their desire to distinguish themselves had caused death and suffering to women and children and had threatened ruin to Walker's prospects by causing the closure of the Transit. Yet Walker was in no position to take them seriously to task. He overlooked their blunders and placed all the blame on the Legitimists, whom he resolved to punish in a typically Nicaraguan fashion. Mateo Mayorga, a cabinet minister under the Legitimist government, who had been

[1] Commodore Paulding to Secretary Dobbin, Dec. 21, 1855, and Jan. 22, 1856, MS., Archives, Navy Department, Home Squadron, I., 98, 116, 120, 121; Minister Wheeler to Secretary Marcy, Oct. 23 and 30, 1855, MS., Department of State, Bureau of Indexes and Archives, Despatches, Nicaragua, II.; Senate Ex. Doc. 68, 34 Cong., 1 Sess., 22–32.

taken prisoner at the capture of Granada and placed on parole in the house of Minister Wheeler, was selected as the object of retaliation, being the most prominent Legitimist in Walker's power, and early on the morning of the 22d, he was led to the plaza and shot. Native Leonese were chosen for this nasty business and seemed well pleased with the opportunity to draw Granadino blood. Walker was proving an apt pupil in the art of Latin-American statecraft.

A French resident of Granada was now sent to Corral at Masaya with the news of Mayorga's execution and of the reasons therefor, and with the further notice that the families of Granada would henceforth be held as hostages subject to the good behaviour of the Legitimists. This had the desired effect. The families of most of Corral's officers were in Granada, and with one consent the latter began to advocate peace. On the morning of the 23d the two commanders met in Granada and drafted a treaty which provided for peace between the warring factions, and a provisional government in which both sides should be represented.[1] Patricio Rivas, an elderly and well-esteemed man with Legitimist leanings but moderate in his politics, was chosen provisional president, Corral became minister of war, and Walker was made commander-in-chief of the army of the republic. White and red party emblems were to be discarded, and in their place all troops were to wear a blue ribbon bearing the words "Nicaragua Independente."[2]

Here again we have evidence of Walker's rapid assimilation to the political methods of his adopted country. He and his opponent in the field negotiate out of existence the governments which they were serving and unite in devising a *tertium quid* to take their place. Neither of the men had any legal right to create a new government and name its president, and Walker states that he treated only as

[1] For text of this treaty see Senate Ex. Doc. 68, 34 Cong., 1 Sess.
[2] Wheeler to Marcy, Oct. 30, 1855, MS., Department of State, Bureau of Indexes and Archives, Despatches, Nicaragua, II.; Walker, *War in Nicaragua*, 125-134; Wells, *Walker's Expedition*, 77-82.

a commanding officer, whose acts were subject to ratification by
his government. Such ratification was duly made, but there was
no legal sanction for it. The new government with Rivas as president was as revolutionary, therefore, as the two which it supplanted
and owed its existence solely to military force. Since the contest
had proven the supremacy of neither party, the legitimacy of
neither of the preëxisting governments had been established.
Had Walker's party completely triumphed, the new government,
to be legal, should have been established in accordance with the
constitution of 1838. Had the Legitimists triumphed, the new
government would have been legal if established in accordance
with the constitution of 1854. None of these things occurred,
and the Walker-Corral treaty therefore was nothing more nor less
than a revolutionary act of compromise.

It was Corral who proposed the treaty and it was he who wrote
it. He clothed it in religious phraseology. The entire document,
save a single clause relating to naturalization suggested by Walker,
was the product of his brain. A week later the two knelt in the
Cathedral before a crucifix and swore on the Holy Gospels to
observe it. But Corral was at that very moment cherishing a
grievance. After signing the treaty on the 23d he had returned
to his headquarters at Masaya and made his preparations to enter
Granada with his men. It was his understanding that Walker was
to disband his Leonese, but when he marched into the city on the
29th he found that the commander had drawn up his whole force
in battle array on the plaza, as though suspecting treachery. This
was enough to excite his anger if he were innocent of any hostile
intent; but the sight of Americans and Leonese both in line
enraged him. Smothering his resentment, he met Walker at the
centre of the plaza, and the two, arm in arm and followed by their
officers, entered the church, where a *Te Deum* was sung. On the
following day they took the oath as already stated. Corral had
evidently hoped, by appearing to be on very friendly terms with

Walker, to arouse resentment against the filibuster leader among the Leonese, who would claim no man as their friend who was intimate with Corral. He disliked the Democrats tenfold more than the Americans, and he was scheming to use the latter to get rid of the former. On the day following the oath the new cabinet was completed. There had been no native Democrats in Granada of sufficient ability to fill a cabinet position, but on this day General Maximo Jerez, the chief of them, arrived from Leon with news that the treaty of the 23d had been duly ratified by the government at Leon, which thereby terminated its existence. Walker at once insisted that Jerez be given the most important remaining position in the cabinet, the Ministry of Relations, declaring that as the chief of one party was Secretary of War, the chief of the other should also have a prominent place in the government. Corral vehemently protested, but Walker's views gained the favour of President Rivas, and prevailed. The Legitimist leader's cup of bitterness was now filled to the brim, and the next day, with the oath of allegiance fresh on his lips, he wrote a letter to Guardiola: "It is necessary that you write to friends to advise them of the danger we are in, and that they work actively. If they delay two months there will not then be time. . . . Nicaragua is lost; lost Honduras, San Salvador and Guatemala, if they let this develop." To Pedro Xatruch, one of the officers, he wrote another letter equally treasonable. The letters fell into Walker's hands, owing to their having been entrusted to a Democratic prisoner at Managua, who received his liberty in advance as a reward for taking them to the Honduran frontier. The ex-prisoner, however, smarting with his wrongs at the hands of the Legitimists, and suspecting that such an extraordinary condition of release meant that mischief was brewing, carried the letters to Granada and gave them to Walker's faithful Indian ally, Valle. The commander-in-chief at once laid the letters before the cabinet in the presence of their author, who admitted his responsibility. As no courts were yet established, Corral was tried by court-martial, the court at his own request being made up of Americans.[1] He was found guilty of conspiracy and treason and sentenced to death, but the members all recommended him to the mercy of the commander-in-chief. Walker now had the choice of three courses: first, to banish the prisoner and thus allow him to marshal the discontented Nicaraguans beyond the border and return to plague the peace of the republic; secondly, to imprison him and allow him to become a centre of plots for his release and of conspiracies against the government; or thirdly, to carry out the sentence of death, horrifying the Legitimists and arousing their resentment for the time being, if not permanently, but at least ridding the government of a dangerous enemy. He decided upon the last course and remained firm in spite of all entreaties. In Granada Corral was immensely popular, and the sympathy for him was well-nigh universal. But Walker had come to see that no milk-and-water methods would suffice for the government of a population like that of Nicaragua. The subsequent history of this and of neighbouring republics has fully demonstrated that the mailed fist is essential to the peace and tranquillity of these regions, and has shown the wisdom of Walker's policy. On November 8, at two o'clock in the afternoon, the idol of the Legitimists was shot. His admirers of course made him a martyr, and gathering round his quivering form, they clipped locks of hair from his head and dipped their handkerchiefs in his blood.[2]

In destroying one great enemy the commander-in-chief had made several thousand lesser ones. This incident is typical of his history in Nicaragua. He not only raised up new foes by destroying old ones, but whenever he gained a new friend he usually also made a new enemy. This will become evident as the story is told

---

[1] Hornsby was president, Fry judge advocate, and French counsel for the accused.

[2] Montúfar, *Walker en Centro América*, 141–46; Walker, *War*, 134–39.

K

He could favour neither political faction in Nicaragua without displeasing the other. What made his cause popular to Americans as a whole was to make him an object of suspicion to the British. He succeeded in gaining support in the Southern States only at the expense of antagonizing his friends in the North. By winning the support of one group of American capitalists he incurred the wrath of a powerful captain of industry, who resolved that he must be destroyed. These were matters beyond the filibuster leader's control. For lack of any better explanation we may as well attribute them to the decrees of fate.

After the death of Corral the office of secretary of war was bestowed upon an ardent Democrat, Buenaventura Selva, and the balance of power between the hostile factions was destroyed. This tended only to increase the discontent of the Legitimists. Their entire force, which had marched into Granada with Corral, had been disbanded on the 4th, the day before Walker discovered their leader's treason. Most of the Democratic troops had also been disbanded, leaving only the Phalanx for the military service of the provisional government. Walker as commander-in-chief was thus the real head of the State, as military force was the sole basis of authority in that condition of society. These were great changes to bring about in the course of a fortnight, and in forcing matters so hastily, Walker showed woeful lack of consideration for the prejudices and susceptibilities of a highly emotional people. He lacked the foresight to perceive that a reaction against such rapid innovations was inevitable. Perhaps the sense of imminent danger, which he seemed to experience from the very moment of his entrance into the Legitimist stronghold, prevented his taking thought for the morrow and caused him to give attention only to present security.

In spite of the fact that Walker's star seemed to be in the ascendant, his situation was indeed critical, and it had not been improved by the treaty of October 23. Peace had only brought

a great influx of unstable natives into Granada whom he had
fought without subduing; and the firing of a single gun might have
precipitated an uprising among them which would have wiped
out the handful of Americans.

Two events, however, seemed to augur well for the future of
the filibuster régime. McDonald, Garrison's agent, had followed
Walker to Granada, and he now proved a friend in need by offering
to help finance the new government. Owing to the constant revolutions the treasury was empty — if indeed it had ever been otherwise — and no government that is bankrupt can long retain respect
at home or abroad. Walker was at first doubtful of McDonald's
authority to go so far as the latter proposed; namely, to advance
to the commander-in-chief the sum of twenty thousand dollars.
Perhaps it seemed too good to be true. McDonald showed
Walker a vaguely worded power of attorney from C. K. Garrison,
empowering him to act as his general agent in Nicaragua; but the
commander, with a lawyer's caution, was still not convinced until
he had made inquiry of Gilman as to the personal relations between
the Transit official and his agent. After satisfying himself as to
McDonald's authority, Walker accepted his proposal. The money
was immediately forthcoming, for McDonald simply extracted
that amount of gold bullion from a shipment in transit from California. He gave the owners of the bullion drafts on Charles
Morgan, the Transit Company's New York manager, for the
value of the amount taken, and these drafts were duly honoured.
It was apparent, then, that the managers of the Transit Company
in New York and in San Francisco had come to an understanding
that Walker was in a position to promote their interests. They
would never have donated twenty thousand dollars as an act of
charity. The loan was well secured, as the Nicaraguan government pledged its redemption out of the annual payments the company made to the State for the enjoyment of its franchise.[1]

[1] Walker, *War in Nicaragua*, 127-28.

Another seemingly auspicious event was the recognition of the new government on November 10 by the American minister, Mr. John H. Wheeler. Just two days before this, however, Secretary Marcy had forwarded instructions to Wheeler to abstain from all intercourse with the new administration until it could show beyond all question that it was the *de facto* government. Wheeler's action, therefore, was premature and contrary to the instructions then on their way to him. When his report of his recognition reached the State Department his action was disavowed and he was reprimanded.[1] Perhaps the only thing that saved Wheeler from dismissal was the fact that he had a warm defender in the cabinet in the person of James C. Dobbin, the Secretary of the Navy. These two men were from North Carolina. There Dobbin had made a two-year fight for the United States Senate against Romulus M. Saunders, and had received Wheeler's support during the protracted deadlock, the latter then being a member of the legislature. Dobbin was now in a position to repay his debt, and on this and other occasions stood between the minister and his chief when the latter's patience was sorely tried by Wheeler's ill-concealed friendliness toward his fellow-countrymen.[2]

The months of October and November, 1855, brought many new experiences to the Granadinos. For a quarter of a century their

---

[1] MS., Dept. of State, Bureau of Indexes and Archives, American States, Instructions, XV., 251 ; House Ex. Doc. 103, 34 Cong., 1 Sess., 35, 39, 51.

[2] John H. Wheeler was born in Murfreesboro, North Carolina, on Aug. 2, 1806. He served in the legislature from 1827 to 1830, was an unsuccessful candidate for Congress in 1830, and was a member of the board of commissioners to adjudicate the French Spoliation Claims from 1831–34. He was superintendent of the mint at Charlotte, North Carolina, from 1837–41, state treasurer, 1841–42, and again a member of the legislature in 1852. He became minister to Nicaragua in 1854, and after his recall lived in Washington till the outbreak of the Civil War. The years 1863–65 were spent in Europe collecting materials for a history of North Carolina. He had already published a history of his State in 1851, but he planned a larger edition. Feeble health, however, interfered with his work and prevented its completion. He was an industrious compiler of scrap books. About twenty of these are in the Library of Congress, and four of them deal with Walker's career in Nicaragua. A clipping in one of them indicates that he had also planned a history of the filibuster movement.— Ashe, *Biographical History of North Carolina*, III., 472.

city had served as a political storm centre, and they had become used to war and war's alarms. They had seen the plaza with comparative regularity barricaded by their friends and besieged and bombarded by their enemies. But now peace seemed to reign supreme. The streets were no longer patrolled by the bare-legged and dark-skinned soldiers clad in dingy white, with officers always on the alert to prevent their deserting the detested duties. Taller men, of fairer hue and heavily bearded, wearing wide-brimmed wool hats, blue flannel shirts, and corduroy or jean trousers tucked into heavy boots, with a brace of pistols and a bowie knife in each belt and a trusty rifle on each right shoulder, were now the masters of Granada. It seemed that a new civilization was about to be engrafted upon the older and decadent one. Six days after the capture of the city Fry arrived with sixty additional recruits. Three of these, being musically inclined, secured a fife and two drums and in the twilight paraded the plaza, playing tunes that were strange to the native ear. The Americans fell in behind the musicians, and the procession marched to the quarters of their leader, who was serenaded with "Yankee Doodle" and "Hail, Columbia." When the music had ceased there were loud calls of "Colonel Walker! Colonel Walker!" The "colonel" appeared. On such occasions a speech is of course inevitable. "Fellow citizens and soldiers," said he, "this is, perhaps, the first time such music has been heard on the plaza of Granada; let us hope that it may be heard through future ages."[1] Thus we see transplanted into the heart of Central America a little scene typical of American life in the great republic of the North. There is hardly a village in the United States that has not at some time or other serenaded its leading citizen and called for a speech.

On the following day, just a week after the capture of the city, another American innovation appeared in the form of a newspaper printed in English and Spanish. This was a weekly journal

[1] *El Nicaraguense*, Oct. 20, 1855.

entitled *El Nicaraguense*, issued every Saturday. The subscription price was ten dollars a year, and each copy sold for twenty cents, payable, presumably, in Nicaraguan scrip. The first issue contains an account of Walker's progress from his leaving San Francisco to his capture of Granada. Two columns are devoted to a description of Nicaragua's resources, and were written evidently for readers in the United States. The second issue gives the latest news concerning the Crimean War. The issue of December 8 has even an original love poem on the first page and chronicles the birth of a young American, who was christened William Walker Wallace. A man who in such a short time could set to work such a civilizing agency as the printing press was something more than the mere bandit or marauder that he has sometimes been called.[1]

Walker's paper was responsible for the soubriquet "Grey-Eyed Man of Destiny," which was frequently applied to him from this time on. In 1850 a Baptist missionary named Frederick Crowe published a book entitled *The Gospel in Central America*. In this he mentioned an old Indian tradition to the effect that the aborigines would some day be delivered from Spanish oppression by a "grey-eyed man." *El Nicaraguense* on December 8 called attention to this tradition, and added: "If we were disposed to believe that the race of prophets did not die with Isaiah and Jeremiah (and why should they?) we could say that this traditionary prophecy has been fulfilled to the letter. 'The Grey-Eyed Man' has come. He has come not as an Attila or a Guardiola, but as a friend to the oppressed and a protector to the helpless and unoffending. The prophecy is deemed by the Indians as fulfilled; for last week we saw in Granada a delegation of them, who rarely visit this city, who desired to see General Walker.

[1] There is an incomplete file of *El Nicaraguense*, containing most of the numbers from Oct. 20, 1855, to Aug. 9, 1856, in the archives of the State Department at Washington.

They were charmed by his gentle reception, and offered to him
their heartfelt thanks for their liberation from oppression and
for the present state of quiet of this country. They laid at his feet
the simple offering of their fruits and fields and hailed him as the
'Grey-Eyed Man' so long and anxiously awaited by their fathers."
Thus the only impressive physical feature of the filibuster leader
was made to serve as proof that his coming was the fulfilment of
prophecy. "The Grey-Eyed Man of Destiny" was twice and
thrice blessed with an enterprising press agent.

In the meantime things had not been going well with Kinney in
Greytown, and he resolved to form, if possible, some sort of offensive and defensive alliance with Walker. Accordingly, Joseph
Fabens and a Captain Swift were despatched to Granada with a
score or more of followers and reached the city the day after the
execution of Corral. Walker greeted them courteously, and after
much circumlocution the "ambassadors" finally broached the object of their mission, a union of the two adventurers for their
reciprocal advantage. There was no hedging in the reply of
Walker: "Tell Governor Kinney, or Colonel Kinney, or Mr.
Kinney, or whatever he chooses to call himself, that if I ever lay
hands on him on Nicaraguan soil I shall surely hang him." Visions
of the fate of Corral and of Mayorga rose before the excited imag-
inations of the "ambassadors"; they decided that it would not be
healthy to return to Greytown, and the entire delegation then and
there deserted Kinney and enrolled under the rising star of Walker.[1]
El Nicaraguense now heaped ridicule upon the governor of Greytown, whom it contemptuously designated as "Farmer Kinney."
There were two reasons why Walker should oppose Kinney. In
the first place, the Nicaraguan government had never recognized
the legal existence of the Mosquito kingdom, which was the foundation of all Kinney's claims. In the second place, Walker had
gained the favour of the Accessory Transit Company, whereas

[1] Wheeler Scrapbook no. 5, p. 59; New York *Herald*, Jan. 30, 1856.

Kinney and the company were breathing fearful threats against each other.

In spite of the defection of Fabens, Swift, and many more of his followers, Kinney persisted in remaining at Greytown and asserting his claims to the whole of the Shepherd-Haly grant. On the 8th of February, 1856, Rivas, the provisional president, at Walker's instigation, issued a decree declaring the right of Nicaragua to the territory called Mosquito to be incontestable and the claims of Kinney to be null and void and an attempt against the integrity of Central America.[1] Some of Walker's men were personal friends of Kinney and sought to use their good offices to effect a mutual understanding between the two. Carlos Thomas, Walker's treasurer-general, and Colonel Fisher, who has already been referred to, visited Greytown and urged Kinney to see Walker in person, Thomas pledging his life for Kinney's security. The latter thought this practically an official invitation, and reached Granada unannounced on February 11, as fate would have it, just three days after the issue of the proclamation mentioned above. Kinney, who had thought Walker in a conciliatory mood, was therefore greatly surprised at the status of affairs on his arrival. Walker was equally surprised at Kinney's coming, but received him courteously, probably thinking that he was ready to surrender and follow the example of Fabens. The governor of Greytown proposed to recognize the military authority of Walker over the Mosquito kingdom if the latter would recognize Kinney's civil government. This was equivalent to a proposition that Walker should use his forces to protect Kinney in his possessions and receive nothing in return. The commander-in-chief cited the recent decree to the effect that the territory belonged to Nicaragua. Kinney retorted that the land was his by purchase; that a hundred thousand dollars had already been spent in connection with the

[1] New York *Herald*, Feb. 29, 1856, contains the decree copied from *El Nicaraguense* of Feb. 16.

grant, and that he would not surrender it until legal means had been employed to determine the title. Walker announced that the government determined such questions for itself, and inquired whether Kinney was in a position to render any service to the Rivas administration. The latter stated that he could bring a large number of immigrants, negotiate a loan, and use his political influence to secure recognition of the new government by the United States. The two then parted, with the understanding that they were to consult further on the next day. Before they met again, however, Kinney committed an egregious blunder. He met Rivas and some of his cabinet and explained his colonizing schemes to them, affirming, it is said, that one colonist was worth five soldiers, and that an overgrown army, such as Walker was accumulating, would devour the substance of the country. Busy tongues carried this conversation to Walker, and when Kinney called upon him to learn his decision as to the propositions of the previous day, he met with a cold reception. The commander-in-chief told his visitor that he desired no further communication with him, as he had been using very improper language in discussing government matters, and added, as he left the room, that he had ordered Kinney's arrest. Shortly afterwards he was placed under arrest on a charge of treason, and Walker would undoubtedly have carried out his previous threat to hang him if he had not been notified of the condition under which Kinney had come to Granada. Kinney was therefore released and sent away under a special escort. The passport which Walker furnished him was couched in very insulting language.[1]

[1] The New York *Herald* produced what purported to be a copy: —

Feb. 14, 1856.

Mr. Theo J. Martin will be allowed to pass freely from this place to San Juan del Norte. No authority will place any impediment in his way.

Mr. H. L. Kinney goes in charge of Mr. Martin to San Juan.

William Walker,
General in Chief of the Army of Nicaragua.

All but the last sentence of the passport is in the usual form.

Like most of Walker's acts, his treatment of Kinney made him more enemies than friends. Among American politicians of influence Kinney had many warm friends, and they resented Walker's conduct. Even Franklin Pierce is said to have shared this feeling.[1] The rest of Kinney's career may be briefly told. For some months after the events just narrated he managed to vegetate in Greytown, but finally surrendered his governorship and departed sick and penniless. In 1857 he managed to interest some English Mormons in his grant, and one of their agents agreed to buy one-half of the territory. On the strength of this agreement he borrowed a sum of money from some Panama merchants, and with several companions sailed to Greytown, where he landed on April 19, 1858. They attempted to take possession of the government, but were arrested and placed in the guard-house. Captain C. H. Kennedy, of the United States ship *Jamestown*, then intervened in their behalf, and received the prisoners aboard his vessel after they had given their solemn promise in writing not to return to Greytown except with peaceful intentions toward the local authorities. Kinney then went to Aspinwall, and from there took passage to the United States. In the autumn of this year he was back in Texas, where some of his friends were trying to persuade him to become a candidate for governor. In 1861 he was shot and killed in Matamoros, where he had become involved in the quarrels between the Rohos and the Crinolinos.[2]

[1] New York *Herald*, Feb. 29, 1856; Jamison, *With Walker in Nicaragua*, 126.
[2] Wheeler Scrapbook no. 4, p. 305; New York *Herald*, May 31, 1858; *British State Papers*, XLVIII., 661–2; *Harper's Weekly*, II., 678 (Oct. 23, 1858); Thrall, *Pictorial History of Texas*, 579.

CHAPTER XII

FILIBUSTERS AND FINANCIERS

IT has already been shown that the Transit Company had allowed Walker to use one of its steamers to capture Granada and shortly thereafter had advanced the new government the sum of twenty thousand dollars in gold. Having observed this manifestation of its good intentions, the commander-in-chief, whose situation was still extremely critical, wrote to Crittenden, urging him to make some arrangement with Garrison for sending five hundred Americans to Nicaragua as soon as possible on his company's steamers. In doing this, Walker naturally avoided consulting Rivas and his cabinet. Garrison received the proposal kindly, and every steamer to San Juan del Sur brought its quota of recruits, practically all of whom were carried at the company's expense. At length, in December, 1855, Garrison sent his son, accompanied by Edmund Randolph and C. J. McDonald, to Granada to make arrangements with Walker for securing some return for the assistance rendered; for it must not be supposed that such a practical, self-made business man as the San Francisco manager had been acting from altruistic motives. With young Garrison, as an earnest of his father's friendly attitude, came a hundred more recruits, who, as usual, received free passage. Randolph now revealed to Walker the agreement which Crittenden had made with Garrison, whereby the American forces were to be recruited. The Transit Company, he explained, had failed to fulfil its obligations to the State and had forfeited its right to corporate existence. It was proposed, therefore, that Walker should secure the annulment of its charter and obtain a new

133

concession for the benefit of Garrison and the New York manager, Charles Morgan, whom Garrison proposed to associate with himself.[1] In return for this favour Morgan and Garrison were to transport to Nicaragua free of charge any and every person who cared to go. The why and the wherefore of the visit of McDonald and of the loan of twenty thousand dollars in October now becomes readily apparent. Garrison was doing this at the expense of the company but for his own personal benefit.

It was generally known in the United States during the autumn of 1855 that the Transit Company was rendering Walker valuable services, and the prevailing opinion was that the expedition had been fitted out by the officials of this corporation in the hope of introducing a stable element into Nicaragua and thus putting an end to the revolutions that were so injurious to the company's interests.[2] It has already been shown, however,

[1] Charles Morgan and Cornelius K. Garrison were associated as partners in the San Francisco banking firm of Garrison, Morgan, Rolston and Fretz, and were prominent American captains of industry in the middle of the nineteenth century. Morgan was born at Clinton, Connecticut, April 21, 1795. At fourteen he was a grocer's clerk in New York; later he began the importation of tropical fruits and thus became interested in shipping. He started the first steamer between New York and Charleston, and in 1836 inaugurated a line from New Orleans to Galveston, even before Texas had gained her independence. This is the germ of the well-known "Morgan Line" of to-day. See L. E. Staunton, *Dedication of the Morgan School Building* (New York, 1873) ; and N. H. Morgan, *Morgan Genealogy* (Hartford, 1869).

Cornelius K. Garrison, like his associate Morgan, was a self-made man, born March 1, 1809, near West Point, New York. He worked on river boats when a boy and later became a builder of steamboats. For a time he was connected with several transportation enterprises on the Mississippi River. After the gold fever began he opened a bank in Panama, and in 1853 went to San Francisco and became manager of the Accessory Transit Company. In October of this year he was chosen mayor of the city. After accumulating a fortune in the West, he returned to New York City in 1859 and retained his interest in the steamship business. See O. T. Shuck, *Representative Men of the Pacific Coast*, 143–64 (San Francisco, 1870) ; Bancroft, *California*, VI., 766 n.

[2] The Philadelphia *American and Gazette*, Nov. 15, 1855, contained the following editorial: "Walker, it seems, represents a more substantial organization than a mere band of filibusters. In fact, it is generally asserted and believed that his expedition was projected, supported and maintained by the Transit Company. That corporation has a capital of three million dollars. His expedition looks too well organized and supplied with munitions, money and men to be based on his own

that this idea was erroneous. The real explanation of the favours shown Walker involves a sketch of certain stock manipu-
lations on Wall Street and of the previous relations of the company with the Nicaraguan government. For many months the
stock of the Accessory Transit Company had served as a football
on the New York exchange. Cornelius Vanderbilt, the first
president, had retired from this position in 1853, on the eve of
departing for his famous tour of Europe, and was succeeded by
Charles Morgan. During Vanderbilt's absence Morgan and Garrison had manipulated the business so as to make large sums
out of stock fluctuations and incidentally to occasion considerable
financial losses to Vanderbilt, who was then abroad and unable
to help himself. After Vanderbilt's return he is said to have
sworn to get revenge. "I won't sue you," he is quoted as saying
to his rivals, "for the law is too slow. I will ruin you." [1] At
once there began a struggle for control of the company, with the
odds in favour of Vanderbilt. But there was another factor to
be reckoned with, and that was the republic of Nicaragua. The
corporation was a creature of that government, and in return for
its right to exist as a legal person it owed certain duties to the
State. When the company received its first charter in 1849, it
agreed to pay annually the sum of ten thousand dollars until the
canal had been completed; and for the exclusive right of navigating the interior waters and opening a line of transit it agreed
to pay ten per cent of the profits accruing from its trans-isthmian

efforts. The company undoubtedly sent arms to Nicaragua, which fell very suspi-
ciously into Walker's hands, and the transit steamers were yielded to him with a
facility which is singular, in view of the small force he commanded."

On December 14, 1855, Attorney-General Cushing wrote as follows to S. W.
Inge and Pacificus Ord, the United States attorneys at San Francisco and Monterey, respectively: "I am directed by the President to address you further on the
subject of the illegal military enterprises against the State of Nicaragua, which have
been, and, as it appears, still continue to be carried on from the ports of California.
. . . Suggestion has been made of some complicity of the Nicaragua Transit Company in these acts, and that point may be entitled to your consideration." Senate
Ex. Doc. 68, 34 Cong., 1 Sess., 11.

[1] Croffut, *The Vanderbilts and the Story of Their Fortune*, 43 f.

traffic. From 1849 to 1855 inclusive the corporation had paid regularly the annual dues of ten thousand dollars, but it had never seen fit to pay any of the ten per cent quota of profits, for the stated reason that no profits had accrued. Against this assertion the Nicaraguan government had no recourse, as the company's methods of bookkeeping gave the State nothing on which to base a claim. The number of passengers and the shipments of freight and specie were known to be very large, but the officials were careful to keep no records in the country that would enable the government to prepare a balance sheet.[1] Expenditures for permanent improvements, such as a pier at Virgin Bay, were said to have come out of current receipts. It was also alleged that the company had fixed a low rate for conveying passengers through Nicaragua with the distinct purpose of eliminating profits and had made its ocean rates high enough to secure an ample return on both its marine and trans-isthmian business.[2] Just a week before Walker landed in Nicaragua the Legitimist government had appointed two agents to proceed to New York and attempt to settle the claim by negotiation or arbitration. The Nicaraguan agents, perhaps without any definite idea of what was due the State, claimed thirty-five thousand dollars. The company offered to settle for thirty thousand, thus admitting that it had avoided the payment of its just dues; but the offer was rejected. Both sides then agreed to refer the matter to special commissioners for arbitration. The company, however, did all it could to delay matters, and before the commissioners could begin their work the Nicaraguan government changed hands, Walker having taken possession of the capital. This caused further proceedings toward adjusting the controversy to be abandoned.[3]

[1] MS., Dept. of State, Bureau of Indexes and Archives, Despatches, Nicaraguan Legation, II.

[2] New York *Herald*, March 31, 1856.

[3] Cornelius Vanderbilt to Secretary Marcy, Senate Ex. Doc. 68, 34 Cong., 1 Sess., p. 11.

This was the situation when Morgan and Garrison began to court the favour of Walker. Seeing that they were about to be ousted from the control of the company, they proposed to use Walker and checkmate their powerful rival. Their plan was simple; the filibuster commander, by virtue of his authority, was to use the government's claim against the Transit Company as a ground for annulling its charter and confiscating its property, while Morgan and Garrison, in return for the aid they had given and were to give to Walker, were to receive the property of the defunct corporation and a charter constituting them a new company for doing a transportation business within the territory of Nicaragua. Such was the plot which had germinated in the brains of unscrupulous captains of industry seeking to thwart the designs of an equally unscrupulous rival. When the scheme was broached to Walker he had no alternative but to become a party to the transaction. To refuse meant no more recruits or supplies from the States; it meant defeat and probably death. To accept meant growing strength, victory, glory, the realization of his fondest ambitions. "We have the power and have helped you; you have the power, now help us," was virtually the ultimatum of the steamship managers. Walker consented with no qualms of conscience. His legal training enabled him to find justification in law for every step of the procedure.

About two weeks before Walker had received this proposal from Garrison's representatives he had secured the appointment of a minister to represent the Rivas government at Washington. This minister was none other than the rascally Parker H. French; and Walker gives as the chief reason for the appointment of such a dubious character his desire to get the trouble-maker out of Nicaragua. He was too much in French's debt to dismiss him, and the undoubted ability and wiliness of that individual seemed to suggest that his talents might serve the most useful purpose if diverted into the devious channels of diplomacy. Among other

duties French was instructed to present again the claim of the
Nicaraguan government against the Accessory Transit Company.
The arbitration of this claim, it will be recalled, had been prevented by Walker's invasion of the country. As Morgan was now
the manager, French found it an easy matter to make tentative
arrangements for a settlement. It was agreed that, pending a
determination of the exact amount due the government, the
company should carry emigrants to Nicaragua at twenty dollars
per passenger — a rate much lower than the usual fare — and
that the amount due the company for their transportation should
be charged to the State and later deducted from whatever sum
the company might be found to owe the government. Vanderbilt
and other prominent stockholders did not at first suspect Morgan's real designs; they knew only of the controversy between
Nicaragua and their company and thought it advisable to grant
French's request as a means of conciliating those in power, especially as their own seemed to be the weaker side of the case.
They accepted the plan with the stipulation that the men should
go as emigrants and not in military bands. As a result, therefore, of French's arrangement recruits began to reach Walker from
the Atlantic States, and in two and a half months the company
transported about a thousand "emigrants" to Nicaragua.[1]

This arrangement between French and Morgan had hardly
been completed before Randolph, young Garrison, and McDonald arrived in Granada, as previously stated. Randolph and
Walker were the closest of friends, and it was an easy matter for the
former to convince the commander-in-chief — if indeed he needed
any convincing — that the Accessory Transit Company had forfeited its right to corporate life. The two then worked out the
details of a new charter for the benefit of Morgan and Garrison.
As soon as the plans were completed Garrison went to New York
to secure their approval by Charles Morgan, while McDonald

[1] Senate Ex. Doc. 68, 34 Cong., 1 Sess., pp. 120–121.

returned to San Francisco to obtain the ratification of the elder Garrison. Until these two returned to Granada Walker and Randolph merely bided their time. The visit of the well-known San Francisco attorney to Walker was noted in his home city, and it was commonly reported that the object of his mission was to assist Walker in drafting a constitution for the new government.[1] This idea was perhaps suggested merely by the fact that Walker's friend bore the name of one of the fathers of the American constitution.

Meanwhile recruiting for Nicaragua was conducted openly and extensively in San Francisco, New York, and New Orleans. After it became generally known in California that passengers would be carried to Nicaragua free of charge there were more volunteers in San Francisco than could be accommodated, and the departure of a Transit steamer was sometimes accompanied by much disorder and rioting on the part of those who were forcibly left behind.[2] In New York and New Orleans advertisements were placed in the newspapers to attract volunteers.[3]

This activity brought forth protests from Señores Molina and

[1] Wheeler Scrapbook no. 5, p. 61.

[2] The *Alta California*, Dec. 6, 1855, notes that there were 400 passengers anxious to leave for Nicaragua, but only 150 could be taken on the last steamer. On the 10th it notes that E. J. C. Kewen, a brother of Achilles Kewen killed in the first engagement at Rivas, was trying to secure one of the idle steamers in the harbour to take recruits to Nicaragua. On the 21st it reports the sailing of the *Cortez*, with 350 passengers, 124 of them being Nicaraguan emigrants. Twenty-five had smuggled themselves on board without tickets and were marched off. Garrison himself inspected the vessel to see that the law was not violated.

[3] In December, 1855, the following harmless-looking advertisement appeared in the journals of New York: "Wanted. — Ten or fifteen young men to go a short distance out of the city. Single men preferred. Apply at 347 Broadway, corner of Leonard Street, room 12, between hours of ten and four. Passage paid."

The notice in the New Orleans papers was more explicit: "Nicaragua. — The Government of Nicaragua is desirous of having its lands settled and cultivated by an industrious class of people, and offers as an inducement to emigrants, a donation of Two Hundred and Fifty Acres of Land for single persons, and One Hundred Acres additional to persons of family. Steamers leave New Orleans for San Juan on the 11th and 26th of each month. The fare is now reduced to less than half the former rates. The undersigned will be happy to give information to those who are desirous of emigrating. Thos. F. Fisher, 16 Royal St."

L

Irisarri, the ministers from Costa Rica and from Guatemala and San Salvador respectively. The latter complained of the indifference of the officials toward filibustering, and the former accused the Transit Company of having conspired to overthrow the Legitimist government, which had threatened it with a lawsuit; and he expressed the hope that since he had named the culprits the American government would call them to account.[1] A week after the protest of Irisarri President Pierce issued a proclamation warning all persons against participating in any way in the fitting out of expeditions to Nicaragua, and stating that those who went, whether organized or unorganized, to take part in the military operations in that country should forfeit the protection of the United States government. He urged all good citizens to discountenance such disreputable and criminal undertakings and charged all civil and military authorities to maintain the authority and enforce the laws of the United States.[2]

Attorney-General Cushing also addressed a circular letter on the same date to the district attorneys in the principal ports of the United States, stating that his department had received information of unlawful enlistments for Nicaragua and urging these officials to take measures to detect and defeat such enterprises and to notify the President if there should be occasion for the exercise of his authority. John McKeon, the district attorney at New York, replied that he had no information of any filibustering movement there, but about a week later he reported that Parker H. French was then engaged in recruiting. About the same time the Federal attorney at New Orleans notified the collector of the port to keep a sharp lookout on the steamer *General Scott*. Cushing on the 14th sent additional instructions to S. W. Inge, the district attorney at San Francisco, asking him to

[1] MS., Department of State, Central American Republic, Notes, 1849-51 Central American Legations, Notes, 1844-57.
[2] *Messages and Papers of the Presidents*, V., 388-89.

investigate the reports of the complicity of the Transit Company
in the recruiting activities.[1] All reports seemed to indicate that
a great exodus to Nicaragua was about to begin, and the government was taking such steps as it could to nip it in the bud. Events
soon showed, however, that the government could do practically
nothing in the face of a public opinion favourable to the emigrants.

The first serious attempt to enforce the neutrality laws was
made in New York City by District Attorney McKeon. On the
22d of December, about ten days after French's arrival, rumours
reached McKeon that there would be a rendezvous of Nicaraguan
recruits that evening and that they would sail on the 24th on the
Transit Company's steamer *Northern Light*. McKeon himself
went to the designated place of meeting and found a number of
prospective recruits there but not the leaders, who had evidently
scented trouble and stayed away. As a result, there was no meeting, and the "emigrants" were a rather disappointed lot; but
not more so than the district attorney. He now betook himself
to the headquarters of Joseph L. White, the attorney and one of
the directors of the company, and also to the apartments of French
in the St. Nicholas Hotel. He made many threats, but was
treated very disdainfully by both. He shouted at French that
he would seize every vessel of the Transit Company and break up
the line, whereupon the latter replied very coolly: "My country is poor, to be sure; but if you will let us know when you are
going to sell those vessels we shall probably buy them in." Mc-
Keon demanded certain information; French handed him paper
and ink and requested that he submit his questions in writing, as
the conversation was important. The attorney then lost his
temper and shouted that he would do no such thing, as he did
not recognize French as minister from Nicaragua. "I did not
ask you to do that; and it is quite immaterial whether you recognize me or not. Address your queries, if you please, then, to Par-

[1] Senate Ex. Doc. 68, 34 Cong., 1 Sess., 11.

ker H. French as an individual, and I must insist on your writing them." McKeon then stated that he had undoubted proof of French's criminality. The latter retorted that if this were so the attorney should have brought along a warrant, but since he had neglected that duty he (French) would waive that formality and submit to arrest without it.[1] McKeon then left in anger, and the next morning ordered the customs officers to refuse a clearance to the *Northern Light*, as there was reason to believe that she would sail the following day with several hundred recruits for the service of Walker. Through some blunder a clearance was given to the *Northern Light* and refused to another of the company's vessels instead, and on the scheduled hour the steamer put to sea almost under the nose of the district attorney. A revenue cutter was sent down the bay in pursuit and stopped the steamer by sending a solid shot across her bows. An investigation showed that there were on board about two hundred steerage passengers who from their unkempt appearance suggested recruits for Nicaragua. A number of these were placed under arrest, among them being Joseph R. Male, the editor of *El Nicaraguense*, who had gone to New York to purchase printing supplies. On being questioned, some of the recruits gave the details of a rather unique enlistment. Several nights before the steamer was to leave a rendezvous was held, and every man who avowed his intention of going to Nicaragua received a common black pantaloons button, which was to be an "open sesame" to the ship. Each man was told to hand his button to an officer as he went aboard, and to receive a passenger ticket in return.[2]

While the *Northern Light* was detained she was searched for arms, and when none were found she was allowed to proceed, though a revenue cutter accompanied her down the bay to make sure that no men or munitions of war were taken aboard before the vessel reached the high seas. The government's intervention

<hr>

[1] New York *Herald*, Dec. 24, 1855.   [2] New York *Tribune*, Dec. 25, 1855.

had at least one effect. It interfered with the schedules and kept the passengers from California waiting for two and a half days for this steamer at Greytown, where they were supposed to find it ready and waiting to take them to New York.

On December 26 a United States commissioner issued a warrant for the arrest of French, charging him with violation of the neutrality laws. French claimed exemption on the ground of his diplomatic character, and the puzzled district attorney applied for advice to the attorney-general. Cushing replied that the American government had not recognized French as the lawful representative of Nicaragua, and that the extension of any diplomatic privileges to him would be a matter of mere courtesy and not of right. The district attorney was further directed to notify French, on the authority of the President, that no legal process would issue against him if he would leave the country within a reasonable time.[1] French made no haste to leave, and on January 15 he and his secretary, Daniel H. Dillingham, were indicted by a Federal grand jury. With them were indicted nine persons taken from the *Northern Light*. The charge against all of them was violation of the neutrality laws. It had also become known that an official attached to the office of the United States marshal had been sent aboard the steamer to prevent her departure and had served papers on the captain, E. L. Tinkelpaugh, and the engineer, Gilbert Fowler. The *Northern Light* had started to sea anyhow with the process-server on board. This incident led to the indictment on January 18 of the captain and engineer, and along with them of Joseph L. White, who was alleged to be jointly responsible, for interfering with an officer in the discharge of his duty. Their trial took place some months later; the case against the engineer was dropped on account of a flaw in the indictment, and White and Tinkelpaugh were acquitted.[2]

[1] Senate Ex. Doc. 68, 34 Cong., 1 Sess.
[2] New York *Herald*, May 9 and 13, 1856.

Another of the company's steamers, the *Star of the West*, was to
sail on the 9th of January. Shortly before the hour of departure
the authorities went aboard and made a thorough search of the
vessel, arresting five men. There were a large number on board
with tickets for Greytown, but they all declared that they were
labourers employed to work on a new pier which the company
was building at Virgin Bay. This explanation was accepted,
and they were not molested. One of the passengers was James
E. Kerrigan, an ex-councilman of New York, who was taking a
company of twenty-eight vagabonds from the fourth and sixth
wards. The officials gave him no trouble. Kerrigan's company
was designed to be part of a New York regiment, which it was
planned to recruit for Nicaragua. Associated with him in raising
the company were two Mexican War veterans, Thomas L. Bailey
and Henry Dusenbury. Expecting excitement, a large crowd
gathered on the pier at the hour of the steamer's departure, and
while the search was going on they hooted and jeered the officials.
When the steamer left the dock, only fifteen minutes after the
scheduled time, Kerrigan appeared on the paddle box and was
loudly cheered. There were also groans and hisses for Pierce.[1]

On January 24 the *Northern Light* was due to sail again.
A diligent search revealed nothing, but one passenger, an eighteen-
year-old boy, was arrested at the request of his father. He had
a ticket when arrested, but managed to slip it into the hands of
another would-be filibuster on the dock, and Walker probably got
his recruit anyway. The youth was taken to the district attorney's office, but no effort would make him divulge the name
of the man who had given him the ticket, and he indignantly
avowed his determination to go "anyhow, some time or other."
When asked why he wished to go, he replied, "For fun."[2] Fruitless as this search appeared, there were about one hundred filibus-

---

[1] New York *Tribune*, Jan. 30, 1856; New York *Herald*, Jan. 10 and 30, 1856.
[2] New York *Herald*, Jan. 25, 1856.

ters on board. Some of these, on their way out, organized the
"Young America Pioneer Club," whose purpose was to provide
a club and reading-rooms and to do everything possible for the
interests of the members after they reached Granada.

The impotence of the government is easily explained. There
were always on the steamers, besides the recruits for Walker,
large numbers of passengers bound to California or the East, as
the case might be, on their legitimate business. There was no
way of distinguishing between these and the filibusters, as no
man on board would admit that he belonged to the latter class.
Every man had a ticket and claimed to be a regular passenger,
and only when positive evidence had been obtained against
them before their embarkation were individuals arrested on the
steamers.

District Attorney McKeon protested to White against the
company's repeated flaunting of the neutrality laws.   This
brought from the Transit attorney an insolent rejoinder: the
company was "a corporate body, created by the law of Nicaragua," and was compelled to recognize the government that was
in power in that country; the conduct of the corporation would
never be influenced by the government of the United States, nor
did the district attorney's "grandiloquent boasting" that he
would break up its business have any terrors for it.[1] White was
described by one journal as having "a wonderful itching pro-
pensity for notoriety," and was accused of egging on the crowds
which jeered and hissed the officials engaged in searching the
steamers.[2] In defence of the company's course toward Walker
he gave to the press several letters addressed to himself from persons in Nicaragua. The general tenor of these was that the lives
and property of Americans in that country would be unsafe
without Walker's presence, and that the Transit Company would

[1] Wheeler Scrapbook no. 2, p. 46; New York *Tribune*, December 25, 1855.
[2] New Orleans *Commercial Bulletin*, Jan. 4, 1856.

suffer as much as any individual if the filibuster were overthrown.[1]
White little suspected that the men whose cause he now so vocif-
erously championed were engaged at that very moment in digging
a pit into which the Accessory Transit Company was soon to fall.
Feeling sure of his position, he had sneeringly defied the American
government, not dreaming that within three months he would be
appealing to this same government for protection against the
men he had befriended.   Nevertheless, White and French for the
time being rode a high horse, and McKeon received little or no
sympathy in his efforts to prevent filibustering in New York.
In fact, the more vigorously he prosecuted the Transit Company,
which had never before enjoyed even a slight measure of public
esteem, the more it seemed to grow in popular favour.   And as a
large part of the recruits belonged to the floating element of the
slums and river front, there was not the slightest objection from
anyone to their leaving town.   Why should the government try
to prevent a free citizen's going and coming as he pleased if he
did not interfere with the rights of his neighbours?   Did not
Nicaragua have a right to invite colonists to settle within her
borders, and did not Americans have the right to accept the invitation if they wished?   Is England operating behind the scenes
in this mysterious pantomime?   Such were a few of the questions
which American citizens were disposed to ask.   Forty years of
isolation from foreign politics and only weakling republics for our
neighbours, had operated to reduce our sense of international
obligations almost to the vanishing point.

As to French, he became a popular hero in spite of himself.
He could now indulge his grandiose delusions to his heart's content.   After his indictment by the grand jury he scorned to claim
exemption from arrest, as he had done on a previous occasion;
for he now felt that public sentiment was active in his behalf and
that the indictment was really an asset.   On the afternoon that

[1] Wheeler Scrapbook no. 5, p. 9b.

the bill was returned against him a deputy marshal proceeded
to the "Legation" at the hotel, notified him that he was under
arrest, and ordered him to report on the following morning to the
United States marshal. But the government had no idea of
creating any further sympathy for French than he then enjoyed,
and as soon as the blunder was discovered the same deputy was
sent back to the hotel post haste with notice to French that the
order for his arrest had been countermanded. Thereat French
was grievously disappointed, for he had already resolved to pose
as a martyr. He now waived all claim of exemption and demanded an immediate trial. The district attorney demurred;
French's lawyers then went before the United States Circuit
Court and sought to compel McKeon to put the case on the
docket. The court stated, however, that it had no authority to
order the district attorney to prosecute a case, and there the
matter ended.[1] In this matter the government, it must be admitted, came out second best. Had French been let severely
alone the public would soon have estimated him at his real worth
and also have let him severely alone. As it was, the Nicaraguan
movement got an immense amount of free advertising and a
large amount of public sympathy thrown into the bargain. As
in the case of the prosecution in California a year previously, the
vigilance of the prosecutors was regarded as due to no horror of
filibustering or excessive regard for the rights of a weak neighbour.
Commenting on the trials of certain filibusters a short time after
these events, *Harper's Weekly* declared them "all a farce kept
up for form's sake."[2] The New York *Atlas* exclaimed, "When
will this child's play cease? Like India rubber, North American
filibusters jump higher every time they are stricken down; and
all such opposition recently made to their movements, by the
instructions of the President and his cabinet, only increases their
numbers and emboldens them to cling more tenaciously to their

<hr>

[1] New York *Herald* and *Sun*, Jan. 18, 1856.   [2] Vol. I., p. 103.

enterprise." [1] The Cincinnati *Columbian* denounced the governmental interference as "a sop thrown to the British." [2] The New York *Times*, too, declared that the Transit Company had a real grievance in the damage to its business that would necessarily follow from the government's searching its steamers before sailing and firing across their course after they had gotten under way. It was unreasonable, it said, to demand that the company ignore Walker's government, which was a fixed fact, Marcy's laboured arguments to the contrary notwithstanding. [3] McKeon's strenuous activities seemed to be an occasion for mirth, as the following bit of doggerel, inspired by the *Northern Light* affair, will indicate:

"The officer a warrant had to search the vessel through;
From deck to keel, from stem to stern, he must his duty do.
Beneath her coal, within her berths, were articles of war,
Between her sheets were rogues and thieves, and lawless men a score.
Her traffic was against the State, her boilers full of treason.
In fact, for her detention he gave most urgent reason.
And White agreed she should lay to and undergo the fuss.
McKeon rose, he took his leave, they parted with a cuss.

"The morning dawned, from stern to stern, from deck to keel they mussed
    her,
Arrested every man on board as a rabid filibuster.
Some searched about, some watched aloft that none ashore should pass;
They overhauled the coal below, and found beneath it — gas.
They searched each hole, each nook and crack, barrel, box, and trunk,
And found at last an appetite for biscuits, ale and junk.

"Must every ship that helps the poor to plenty's foreign soil
Be treated like a slave, her freight a lawless spoil?
The Eagle bold that guards our shore is clothed in Freedom's mail;
Her strongest pinion proudly fills each vessel's swelling sail.
She spreads her wings upon the bow and steers the *Northern Light*,
Who, though her acts are counted black, her agency is White." [4]

[1] Jan. 20, 1856.   [2] Wheeler Scrapbook no. 5, p. 52.
[3] Feb. 7, 1856; also Wheeler Scrapbook no. 5, p. 81.
[4] Wheeler Scrapbook no. 5, p. 72.

There is every indication that during the month of January, 1856, public sentiment was running strongly in Walker's favour. Federal authorities therefore fulminated in vain. It was only in New York that any serious effort was made to prevent the departure of the expeditionists. In San Francisco the government had shot its last bolt when it prosecuted, without results, Watkins, Emory, Walker, and the two consuls in 1854. District Attorney Inge now told Attorney-General Cushing that he could obtain no evidence that would justify the seizure of a vessel. Though many persons had gone to Nicaragua to aid Walker, they had gone without visible arms and without organization, some avowing their purpose of settling as peaceful immigrants, others with through tickets to New York and claiming to be regular passengers.[1] In New Orleans a similar favourable sentiment prevailed. There in April 208 men embarked to the strains of a so-called Nicaraguan band, and the newspapers announced their departure beforehand. In May, 1856, Señor Molina complained to Marcy that not one of the filibusters arrested by the government had been convicted.[2] Verily the mountain had laboured, and there was not even a mouse to console it for its pain.

This happened to be a case, however, in which it was the government's turn to laugh last. We have left Randolph and Walker in Granada awaiting the return of their emissaries to Morgan and Garrison. Young Garrison, whom they had sent to New York, was there during some of the recruiting episodes just described, and after securing Morgan's consent to the arrangements he returned to Granada. McDonald's mission to the elder Garrison was equally successful. Walker and Randolph now decided that the time had arrived to spring the trap. With much painstaking, therefore, they drew up a decree of revocation setting forth the

[1] Senate Ex. Doc. 68, 34 Cong., 1 Sess.
[2] MS., Dept. of State, Bureau of Indexes and Archives, notes, Central America, I.

shortcomings of the company; it had agreed to build a canal, or, if that proved impracticable, a railroad or a rail and carriage road; it had agreed to pay ten per cent of its annual net profits to the State, and had done none of these things. Walker says that this decree was to state the causes so that the whole world might judge, and that it was drawn with exceeding care. For these shortcomings the charter of the company was revoked, a commission was appointed to determine the exact amount of its indebtedness to the State, and the property was ordered to be seized and held subject to the commissioners' directions. The Nicaraguans had never cherished kindly feelings toward the Transit officials, and it was with undisguised pleasure that Rivas, who had been kept in ignorance of the scheme, attached his signature, on February 18, to the decree of revocation. There are indications too that he was already becoming alarmed at the great influx of armed Americans and was glad that the company which was responsible for their coming was to be broken asunder. But on the following day the joy of the provisional president was transmuted into fear; for Walker brought him a second decree, which bestowed a new charter upon Edmund Randolph and his associates. Rivas was thinking that he had rid the country of the hated corporation, and here it was proposed to grant even greater privileges upon a strange man whom he had seen in close communication with the commander-in-chief for many weeks. In most matters Walker had found the provisional president a pliant tool, but the latter now showed unwonted firmness, and declared that his signature to such a document would mean "a sale of the country." It was not till many of the privileges granted by the decree were stricken out that Rivas would sign it, and even then he did so with reluctance.[1] Although these decrees were

[1] *El Nicaraguense*, Feb. 23, 1856; Senate Executive Document 194, 47 Cong., 1 Sess., 103–04; New York *Tribune*, May 14–15, 1856; Wells, *Walker's Expedition*, 203–20; Walker, *War in Nicaragua*, 152–5.

signed on February 18 and 19, their publication was delayed
somewhat in order to give the grantees of the new charter as much
time as practicable to prepare for business before the steamers
of the old company should be withdrawn. This delay proved
more advantageous than Walker had expected; for nine days
after the decree had been signed two hundred and fifty recruits
under the Cuban "liberator," Domingo de Goicouria, left New
Orleans for service in Nicaragua, their passage having been paid
with drafts on Vanderbilt, who had ousted Morgan and become
president of the Company early in February. Had the decree
been published the day it was signed, Vanderbilt would have
received the news before these men embarked and would have
prevented their departure. "As it was," says Walker, "the
price of these passages was so much secured by the State on the
indebtedness due the corporation." [1] Morgan thus knew of the
annulment of the charter of the Accessory Transit Company before the news reached Vanderbilt, and he must have derived no
little satisfaction from seeing his rival, who a few weeks before had
forced him from the presidency, now spending his company's
good money in aid of the man who had already duped him.

Walker in this way repaid the favours he had been receiving
from the company's two managers. He had acted partly from
a feeling of obligation and partly from a feeling of necessity.
Without the opportune aid from this source his expedition would
long ago have ended in failure. To Morgan and Garrison he
owed most of his present success, and he had placed them in a
position where they could aid him still more and enable him to
reach the goal of his ambitions. But unfortunately for his cause,
he had at the same time raised up a terrible enemy in the person
of Vanderbilt. He could not foresee, of course, when he entered
into the scheme suggested by Randolph, that Vanderbilt was
soon to come to the head of the company and lend his assistance

[1] *War in Nicaragua*, 156.

as Morgan had done. It would have paid him to cast his fortunes with the stronger party, and when the plans were made Walker probably thought that he was doing so, for Morgan and Garrison then represented the "ins," while Vanderbilt was an "out." Even as Walker and Randolph worked on the new charter the tables were turned in Wall Street, and they found, when it was too late, that they really had cast their fortunes with the "outs." Vanderbilt was able to influence the filibusters' fortunes, for good or ill, tenfold more effectively than his rivals, and from the day that he was tricked things were in a bad way for the Americans in Nicaragua.

When the news of the transaction reached Vanderbilt he was greatly enraged. On March 17, and again on March 26, he addressed long letters to Secretary Marcy, urging that the government intervene and protect the property of American citizens in Nicaragua. But it was now the government's turn to laugh. There was small comfort from the State Department for a corporation that a few weeks before had sneered at the neutrality laws and defied the government's officers. Vanderbilt could not shift the blame of aiding Walker on the shoulders of Charles Morgan, as his correspondence shows that he tried to do, for Marcy knew that both men were tarred with the same brush. The government had been told by White that it had nothing to do with this company, which took into consideration only the State of Nicaragua. Newspapers now hurled this back into the teeth of Vanderbilt and White, and jocularly referred them to Nicaragua for relief.

On Wall Street the news of Walker's action created amazement. Financiers at first refused to believe the report, but it was sufficient to cause a panic among the company's stockholders, who rushed to see who could get out first. The stocks had been slowly advancing ever since the new government in Nicaragua had appeared firmly established. On January 1, 1856, they were quoted at 18; on February 14 at 23¼; on March 13, the day before the news reached the Street, the closing price was 22½. On the next day five thousand shares were sold and the price fell to 19¼; on the 18th it fell to 13, and during the preceding four days fifteen thousand shares had changed hands. Men in the Street suspected the real reason for Walker's action, but knowing Vanderbilt's power they could hardly believe the filibuster leader foolhardy enough to match strength with him. The financial editor of the *Herald* declared that Wall Street regarded Walker as a fool and a knave. "The great mass of the American people sympathize deeply with the present government of Nicaragua and will regret to find that its gallant head has perilled its hitherto bright prospects. It will be seen that it is in Mr. Vanderbilt's power to kill off the new government by opening another route and thus cutting off Walker's communications with San Francisco and New York." [1]

Vanderbilt immediately announced the withdrawal of the company's ocean steamers, and as Morgan was not yet ready with his new line the interests of Walker were at once put in jeopardy. For six weeks there were no steamers for Nicaraguan ports, and the filibusters received no reinforcements or supplies. Garrison did try to keep the steamers running from San Francisco to San Juan del Sur after Vanderbilt had withdrawn the vessels from the Atlantic. His scheme was thwarted, however, for Vanderbilt sent an agent from Panama with orders to intercept any of the company's steamers headed for the Nicaraguan port and order them to Panama, where they were to transfer their passengers to the Atlantic by rail. This was done in the case of two steamers, and the Transit for the time being was closed. [2]

At length, on April 8, the *Orizaba*, the first Morgan and Garrison steamer, was ready to sail from New York for Greytown. She was in the command of Captain Tinkelpaugh, who, as com-

[1] New York *Herald*, March 15 and 17, 1856. [2] Wheeler Scrapbook no. 4, 161.

mander of the old company's *Northern Light*, had already carried many a recruit to Walker and at this time was still under a Federal indictment for interfering with a deputy marshal on board the latter vessel. A report that the government would seize the vessel brought a large crowd to the pier. Nothing happened till the lines were being cast off, when the assistant district attorney rushed on board with a warrant for the arrest of nine filibusters. The steamer had reached the middle of the river before the officers were aware that he was on board. The anchor was dropped and the vessel was detained an hour while a search was made for the culprits. Only three could be identified as the men wanted, and these were taken ashore while the *Orizaba* went its way. As usual, the sympathies of the crowd on the dock were not with the government.

It is not surprising to note that one of the passengers on this steamer was an agent in the pay of Vanderbilt, by the name of Hosea Birdsall. He was going to Greytown with instructions to seize all the Transit property at that place, as well as any river boats that might arrive, and thus prevent the recruits from going into the interior. In case the recruits attempted to take forcible possession of the boats, Birdsall was instructed to ask any British war-vessel in the harbour — one was always there — to assist him in protecting American property. He was given to understand that it was his mission to secure the coöperation of the British navy in preventing the recruits from going into the interior so as to accomplish Walker's ultimate downfall. It was especially desirable to prevent the reinforcement of the filibusters at this time, as they were at war with Costa Rica.

After anchoring in the harbour at Greytown the *Orizaba* began to transfer her 480 passengers to the river steamboat *Wheeler*, when word came from Captain Tarleton, in command of H. M. S. *Eurydice*, that this must stop, and that the passengers must be taken back on the steamer and the river boat hauled off.

Tinkelpaugh at once went to Tarleton to find out what such orders meant. The British officer asserted that he had received word from Birdsall that there were five hundred men on board on their way to Walker, and that he would not allow them to go up the river. Tinkelpaugh protested that 420 of them had tickets for San Francisco and none had tickets for the interior, and that he had insufficient provisions on board to permit their being returned to the United States. The British officer then said Tinkelpaugh must take them to Aspinwall, but the latter declared that also impossible. Tarleton then announced his determination to examine the ship's way-bill before making a definite decision. Accordingly, he boarded the *Orizaba*, went to the purser's office, looked over the way-bill, and questioned a number of the passengers. Apparently finding Birdsall's statements unsubstantiated, he allowed the passengers to disembark. Beyond causing an American vessel to be searched by a British warship and creating a little delay and much annoyance, the mission of the Vanderbilt agent was fruitless.[1]

The old financier, however, was not yet through with his plans for revenge. Indeed, this was only the beginning of his fight on his rivals. Through another emissary he entered into negotiations with Rivas, with the object of producing disagreement between the president and the commander-in-chief,[2] and the work of this agent may have been partly responsible for the breach that came a few months later. Vanderbilt also brought suit in September, 1856, in the courts of New York State against Garrison in the sum of $500,000 for alleged defalcations while in the service of the company; among the defalcations alleged being the de-

[1] Commodore Paulding to Secretary Dobbin, MS., Archives Navy Dept., Home Squadron, I., 202; Senate Ex. Doc. 68, 34 Cong., 1 Sess., 152-4.

[2] Joseph L. White testified to this fact under oath in a lawsuit in which the old Transit Company was involved in October, 1856. He declined to give any particulars, stating that if Walker knew who the go-between was the man would be shot. Walker suspected something of this sort, but never detected the traitor in his camp. See New York *Herald*, Oct. 17 and 19, 1856.

M

frauding of the corporation of the passage money due from a large
number of men sent from San Francisco to Nicaragua.[1] In December he also instituted suit in the United States Circuit Court
in the name of the Transit Company against Morgan, Garrison,
and Walker in the sum of $1,000,000, alleging trespass, conversion,
and disposal of the company's goods, and fraudulent conspiracy
to interrupt and molest the corporation in the discharge of its
lawful business.[2] Subsequent chapters will reveal other efforts
of his to destroy the alliance between the filibusters and his rivals
in Wall Street.

Walker had appointed a commission, consisting of Cleto Mayorga, E. J. C. Kewen,[3] and George F. Alder, to ascertain the
amount of the company's indebtedness to the State. They made
their report early in August. As the bookkeeping had not been
done in Nicaragua, the commissioners were compelled to rely on
private records and the testimony of the company's employees.
They came to the conclusion that there was an average of two
thousand passengers per month over the Transit, each paying

[1] Wheeler Scrapbook no. 4, 133, 136; New York *Herald*, Sept. 5, 1856.

[2] New York *Herald*, Dec. 22, 1856. A number of other suits grew out of
Walker's decrees of Feb. 18 and 19. In New York the steamers were placed in the
hands of Vanderbilt as trustee, and a number of stockholders sued in order to get a
receiver to wind up the business of the company and distribute its assets. Vanderbilt resisted, alleging that the decrees had no validity as they were not issued by any
lawful authority. The New York Supreme Court on November 3 declared the
decrees valid, as issued by the *de facto* government, and the annulment an historic
fact, regardless of any considerations of justice. The Atlantic steamers were placed
in the hands of a receiver and ordered sold. In California the attorney-general of the
State brought suit for the possession of the Pacific steamers, alleging that the
Transit Company, a legal person, died intestate on February 18 and that its
property in San Francisco therefore escheated to the State. New York *Herald*,
July 16, Oct. 14, Nov. 4, Dec. 1, 2, 1856; Wheeler Scrapbook no. 4, 159b, 173.

[3] E. J. C. Kewen was a brother of Achilles Kewen, one of the original fifty-six,
who lost his life at Rivas. He had been the editor of a paper in Columbus, Miss.,
and a practising lawyer in St. Louis, Mo., before 1849, when he migrated to California. In 1851 he ran for Congress on the Whig ticket, but was defeated. Walker's
capture of Granada induced him to migrate to Nicaragua, and he became financial
agent of the Republic. He decided with the other commissioners that the Transit
Company was heavily indebted to the government, but advised against the extreme
measures taken. He later went to Augusta, Ga., which he made his headquarters
for recruiting for Nicaragua. Shuck, *Representative Men*, 341–59.

thirty-five dollars for his passage across the isthmus. The monthly receipts from passengers thus amounted to $70,000. The aggregate specie shipments amounted to $34,719,982, which at the rate of one-half of one per cent of their value, brought in a revenue of $4890 per month. The receipts for carrying freight brought the monthly gross earnings to $79,000. The legitimate expenses were estimated at $21,000, leaving a net profit of $58,000 per month, or $696,000 per annum. Of this amount the State was entitled to ten per cent, or $69,600 per annum, from August, 1851, to March, 1856. To this amount the commissioners added interest at six per cent per annum, and, as the company had no representative on hand [1] to prove that the annual payments of $10,000 had been made, these were also added, bringing the total sum due the State to $412,589.16.[2] These figures are of course absurd. Vanderbilt in his complaint to Marcy stated that the value of the confiscated property was between $700,000 and $1,000,000; and it is inconceivable that such an investment should have yielded a net profit of $696,000, or from seventy to ninety-nine per cent a year. Yet such was the finding of the commission. It is also improbable that the Nicaraguan commissioners appointed a year previously should have offered to settle the claim for thirty-five thousand dollars when over ten times that amount was due the State. In making the report Walker's commission frequently found it necessary to use its imagination, and in this respect it seems to have excelled. As soon as the report had been submitted, all the property of the old company in Nicaragua was sold to Morgan and Garrison. They had received bonds for their previous advances to the government, and they now exchanged these for the property of the Accessory Transit Company.[3]

[1] The commissioners had gone through the farce of summoning agents of the company to appear.

[2] Wheeler to Marcy, Aug. 2, 1856, MS., Department of State, Bureau of Indexes and Archives, Despatches, Nicaragua, II.

[3] The Transit *privileges*, which had been bestowed by decree upon Randolph and his associates in February were offered for sale to Vanderbilt in June by Morgan

This is the way that Walker paid his debt to his financial patrons. The new steamship line was now in operation, and recruits were pouring in. To all appearances the filibuster régime was firmly established, but as a matter of fact it had dug for itself a pit as deep as Avernus.

and Randolph, but the financier declared that his duty was to protect the stock-holders of the old company and refused to consider the offer. Morgan and Garrison appear to have purchased Randolph's interest shortly thereafter, and then in August, as above stated, they secured the physical property as well as the franchise. Major J. P. Heiss's Scrapbook, in possession of Mr. Robert Lusk, of Nashville, Tenn.; New York *Herald*, Sept. 7, 1856.

CHAPTER XIII

FILIBUSTER DIPLOMACY AND POLITICS

AFTER securing peace in Nicaragua and strengthening his position by constant accessions of recruits, Walker next gave his attention to the problem of securing formal recognition of the Rivas administration by other governments. Shortly after the treaty of October 23 communications were sent to the other Central American States, giving the terms of the treaty and expressing the desire of the republic of Nicaragua for harmony and fraternity with its neighbours. Official notice was taken of this only by San Salvador. On November 22, 1855, Señor Enrique Hojos, the minister of foreign affairs for that republic, notified the Nicaraguan government that it was very gratifying to find that its people were at last to have a prospect of enjoying tranquillity and of consolidating the happiness and prosperity of their State.[1]

In San Salvador the Democratic party was then in the ascendant, and it naturally favoured the success of the corresponding element in Nicaragua. The Salvadorian journal, *El Rol*, published by Democratic leaders, had applauded the downfall of Granada and expressed great admiration for Walker, whom it hailed as the successor of Morazán.[2] Honduras also had been liberal or democratic in its sympathies. Its president, General Trinidad

[1] Montúfar, 186.
[2] The New York *Herald* of March 30, 1856, contains a translation of a long article in the issue of *El Rol* for January 2, defending Walker and his followers from certain aspersions of the Conservatives. It ends with the declaration, "This much decried invasion of Nicaragua by the North Americans is but an invective and a calumny of the aristocratic party."

Cabañas, had been a devoted friend and disciple of Morazán, and was an ardent advocate of a Central American union. But the views of Cabañas were very distasteful to Carrera, the president of Guatemala, who was a stanch advocate of particularism, or what Americans would call States' rights, and he made war on Honduras, defeating Cabañas and compelling him to flee for safety to San Salvador. Cabañas now looked to Nicaragua for aid in regaining his lost power, and a few weeks after the capture of Granada Walker invited him to come to that city and make his plea in person. The commander-in-chief, on hearing of his approach, sent Hornsby to meet him, and on December 3 received him with every mark of consideration. During the late civil war Cabañas had aided the Democrats in many ways, even to the extent of sending them a detachment of his own troops. He had sheltered Castellon and Jerez when they fled from Chamorro, and had furnished them the means to return and start the revolution which had resulted in the coming of Walker to Nicaragua. He felt, therefore, that he could ask this aid as a matter of right and not merely as a favour. Jerez, now minister of relations, was strongly in favour of taking up Cabañas' cause, as he owed the ex-president a deep debt of gratitude. Walker, of course, had not come to Nicaragua to exhaust his strength in fighting out the quarrels of native chiefs, and was therefore opposed to the suggestion. He gave as his reason the fact that an invasion of Honduras would be seized upon by his enemies as proof that he meditated a war of conquest. This excuse seemed to satisfy Rivas, who postponed giving any definite answer till Cabañas had gone to Leon, and then sent him word that aid would be denied. Upon hearing this Jerez, the foremost Democrat in the country, resigned his place in the cabinet. Selva followed soon after when Walker gave office to a Legitimist. The filibuster thus began to alienate the Democrats as he had previously alienated the Legitimists. Nearly every important act gained him new enemies. Cabañas, bitterly disappointed, returned to San Salvador, which was the only State inclined to act favourably toward Walker, and began an active agitation against the American invaders. He aroused the Liberals with a hostile manifesto against Walker, and the government sent a commissioner, Colonel Justo Padilla, with letters asking why the American forces were being increased and urging that further immigration be stopped. The commissioner arrived simultaneously with the two hundred and fifty men sent by Vanderbilt from New Orleans, and these were drawn up so as to show their numbers to the best advantage when Padilla visited Walker in his quarters.[1] There was only one minister left in the Rivas cabinet; he was Fermin Ferrer, a faithful adherent of Walker, and was now designated as minister-general. Ferrer explained to Padilla that the increase of enlistments was due to the hostility shown toward the Rivas government by the neighbouring republics, and especially by Costa Rica. The envoy stood for a time on the plaza and gazed at the recruits as they marched to their quarters. Then shaking his head, he exclaimed "Muchos soldados," and walked thoughtfully away.[2]

The republic of Costa Rica was the stronghold of the conservative party of Central America, and many of the most prominent Legitimists had taken refuge there after the capture of Granada. The *Boletin Oficial*, the organ of the administration, bitterly attacked the new régime in Nicaragua, and the president, Juan Rafael Mora, not only ignored the circular address sent by Rivas to the various republics, but on November 20, less than a month after the conclusion of peace in Nicaragua, he issued a high-flown proclamation, declaring that the peace of his country was in danger. "A band of adventurers," said he, "the scum of all the

---

[1] Montúfar, 187–207; Walker, *War in Nicaragua*, 159–65; 179–80; New York *Herald*, Apr. 4, 13, 1856.
[2] New York *Herald*, April 13, 1856.

earth, repudiated by the justice of the American Union, not succeeding in satisfying their voracity where they now are, are planning to invade Costa Rica and seek in our wives and daughters,
our houses and lands, satisfaction for their fierce passions, food
for their unbridled appetites. Is it necessary to picture the
terrible evils which may come from our coolly awaiting so barbarous an invasion? No, you understand them; you well know
what may be expected from adventurers fleeing from their own
country; you know your duty. Be on your guard, then, Costa
Ricans! Do not cease your noble labours, but make ready your
arms!" [1]

Walker quickly saw the need of doing something to conciliate
this republic. Accordingly, on January 17, 1856, he sent a personal letter to President Mora, in which he disavowed any hostile intentions toward Central America, declaring that he had
come to Nicaragua for the purpose of maintaining order and good
government, and expressing "a fervent desire for peace and good
understanding between the sister republics of Costa Rica and
Nicaragua." [2] In February Rivas went a step farther and appointed a special commissioner to Costa Rica in the person of
Louis Schlessinger, a German Jew, who had come to Nicaragua
with high recommendations and was one of the few men in Walker's service who had a thorough knowledge of Spanish. Schlessinger was one of the passengers on the *Northern Light* on December
24 for whom the government had issued a warrant. While the
officers were searching for him he had managed to swap clothes
with a sailor and to remove his beard. Appearing on deck in an
oilskin jacket and sou'wester, he was safe from detection.[3] With
Schlessinger were sent an American officer, Captain W. A. Sutter,
and a prominent Legitimist, Manuel Arguëllo. It was thought

---

[1] Joaquin B. Calvo, *La Campaña Nacional Contra los Filibusteros en 1856 y
1857*, 8. (San José, 1909.)

[2] Montúfar, 204–06.   [3] New York *Herald*, Jan. 14, 1856.

that the latter's presence would do something toward reconciling
the Legitimist refugees in Costa Rica to the changes at home.
Schlessinger was instructed to seek to counteract the false impressions concerning the Rivas-Walker government and to protest
against the machinations of the Legitimist *émigrés*. The commissioner encountered only hostility. He and Sutter were ordered
to leave the country immediately, while Arguëllo remained and
later joined the Costa Rican army.[1] The filibuster régime, as
was now seen, had no friends in the neighbouring States.

In Nicaragua alone was Walker able to secure anything more
than momentary sympathy from the natives. From the beginning the clergy there were inclined to take his side. Being men of
peace by nature and profession, they had no heart for civil commotion, and had been compelled to sit as silent spectators while
the belligerents used their churches as fortresses and battered and
barricaded these holy places. Shortly after Walker entered
Granada he was hailed by the curate of the parish, Padre Augustin
Vijil, as "Angel tutelar, estrella del norte" (Guardian angel, star
of the North). Shortly thereafter the vicar capitular of the
bishopric, José Hilario Herdocia, sent him his congratulations
upon restoring peace in Nicaragua, and Walker wrote him in
reply: "It is very satisfactory to me to know that the existing
government is approved by the authority of the Church. Without
the aid of religious ideas and teachers there can be no good government. In God I put my trust for the success of the cause in
which I am engaged and for the establishment of the principles
which I invoke. Without His aid all human efforts are vain, but
with His divine help a few can triumph over a legion."[2] The
influence of the clergy had its effect mainly upon the conservative
element and caused numbers of them to become reconciled to the
new order of affairs. The clergy were also instrumental in reconciling the Indians to Walker's coming. Their dislike of the

strangers was due to race prejudice, and in the district of
Matagalpa they rose against the new government. Against
them Walker sent no soldiers, but despatched to them a priest.
The labours of the churchman pacified them. Perez, who is a
bitter partizan, says that the Legitimist party would have upheld
Walker if he had guaranteed their lives and property. But
that writer forgets that the leader of this party was conspiring to
overthrow Walker at the very moment he was swearing on the
Holy Evangelists to uphold him. The native writers do not seem
to think that the obligations of the Americans and the Nicaraguans
were reciprocal. The Democrats at first looked upon Walker as
the means of their salvation, but they could never feel satisfied
that his aims and theirs were identical, and gradually began to
distrust him. Both sides, however, for a time preferred to see a
foreigner in power rather than a native enemy. According to
Perez himself, during the civil war many families had gone as
refugees into the districts of Chontales, Matagalpa, and Segovia,
which were somewhat removed from the theatre of hostilities,
and whenever they saw a squad of soldiers coming into the neighbourhood they hoped that they were Americans, because these
were less disliked than hostile fellow-countrymen.[1]

Strange to relate, Walker's relations with the clergy and church
have been more distorted than any other phase of his history.
Sir William Gore Ouseley, the British envoy to Central America
in 1859, wrote to Lord Malmesbury that Walker desecrated the
churches, dressed his men in the priests' vestments, and paro-
died the elevation of the host.[2] Such stories were not believed
by any but foreigners, and the attitude of the native priesthood
is a sufficient refutation.[3]

[1] See also Montúfar, 172.   [2] *British State Papers*, L., 216.
[3] The first of Walker's fifty-three "Articles of war by which the army of the
Republic of Nicaragua shall be governed" read as follows :
"Article 1. It is earnestly recommended to all officers and soldiers to attend
divine worship, and any officer or soldier who shall in any way behave with impro-

This friendliness of the clergy Parker H. French, while minister of hacienda (public credit), sought to turn to financial account, and he asked the vicar Herdocia to lend him the funds of the parish of Granada to aid in carrying on the work of pacifying the country. The churchman consented, and French secured 963 ounces of fine silver bullion.[1]

It was partly on account of this rapacity manifested by French that Walker decided to send him out of the country. Before the treaty of October 23 the Legitimist government was represented at Washington by Señor Marcoleta. With the signing of the treaty Marcoleta's government apparently ceased to exist by common consent of all parties. The Legitimist president, Estrada, escaped from Granada at the time of its capture, however, and later issued a manifesto claiming that Corral in negotiating the treaty had exceeded his powers, and that the agreement was therefore null and void. He denounced the provisional government as unlawful, and those serving it in any capacity as traitors. He also set up in the district of Segovia what he claimed to be the only lawful government in Nicaragua. Marcoleta therefore remained at his post in Washington, claiming to represent the government of Estrada.[2] This gave the Pierce administration a hard nut to crack. The State Department could not recognize the legitimacy of the Estrada government, which was obviously a paper affair. On the other hand, to sever relations with Marcoleta would be everywhere interpreted as an encouragement to the American invasion of Nicaragua; and this was what the administration was most desirous to avoid, especially as such a proceeding would be equivalent to waving a red rag in the face

priety in any place of divine worship shall be punished according to his offence by sentence of a court martial."

[1] Perez, *Memorias*, pt. 2, p. 6. Perez says that the silver came from the frontal of the great Altar of Mercy and from the hall of the Virgin of Mercy in the vicar's own church.

[2] MS., Department of State, Bureau of Indexes and Archives, Notes, Central American Legations, II.; Senate Ex. Doc. 68, 34 Cong., 1 Sess., 145-7.

of England. Marcoleta therefore held on, and everyone won-
dered to whom he sent his despatches and from whom he received
his instructions. The Rivas government had already revoked
Marcoleta's commission, but the State Department could not
take official cognizance of this without recognizing the validity of
that government.

Such was the situation when Walker determined to get rid of
French by sending him to the United States as the representative
of Nicaragua. From what has already been said concerning
that individual it will appear that a more unhappy choice for
such a position could hardly have been made. The reasons
which Walker gives for his selection of French were written after
French had proved his unfitness. It is more than probable that
Walker was ignorant of the worst traits in the man's character,
as well as of his previous history, at the time the appointment
was made. It is hardly conceivable, otherwise, that he would
have sent a man to represent his government who would then
have been wearing felon's stripes if he had received his just dues.
Still there is no reason to doubt that Walker was largely actuated
in the appointment by the desire to get rid of French, and he
probably thought that the qualities which the man exhibited in
Nicaragua would have to be suppressed in a different environment.
Walker blundered not only in sending a man of French's character and past record, but also in sending a former citizen of the
United States. Common sense should have dictated the selection
of an intelligent native.

French arrived in Washington in December, 1855, and on the
19th addressed Marcy, requesting an interview preliminary to
presenting his credentials as minister from Nicaragua. Two
days later Marcy replied that "those who were instrumental in
overthrowing the government of Nicaragua were not citizens
belonging to it," nor had those citizens, so far as known, "freely
expressed their approval of or acquiescence in the condition of

political affairs in Nicaragua." When it appeared that the new government had the support of its citizens the United States would undertake to establish diplomatic relations with it.[1]

Marcoleta still hung on. On New Year's day he appeared at the President's reception at the White House along with the other members of the diplomatic corps, and it was observed that many foreign representatives made it a point to pay him attention. This was a delicate way to administer a slap at "manifest destiny."[2] It is not surprising, too, that a minister without a recognized government, but received on an equal footing with well accredited diplomats, should have aroused a great deal of interest. It was commonly reported that for his past services Marcoleta had never received a cent of salary. "The generosity of this gentleman in serving a government which could not pay is only equalled by his piety in continuing to serve it after it is dead," said the New York *Herald;* "he continues with a constancy and disinterestedness unparalleled in the annals of diplomacy to represent its spirit long after the body is dead and buried."[3] Marcoleta was finally disposed of by being informed orally and unofficially that the government which he claimed to represent was no longer in existence and that the only party claiming political control in Nicaragua had repudiated any connection with him.

Receiving likewise no encouragement at Washington, French proceeded to New York a sadder but not, as it proved, a wiser man; for a few days later he became involved in the controversy with McKeon over recruiting, as described in the preceding chapter. The attitude of the administration in rejecting French was to many a matter of surprise. The American press, with a few exceptions, had been sympathetic with the Nicaraguan venture, and was much disposed to criticise Marcy's action. Some even imputed personal animosity on the part of Pierce toward Walker

[1] House Ex. Doc. 103, 34 Cong., 1 Sess., 57, 75.
[2] New York *Sun*, Jan. 3, 1856. [3] New York *Herald*, Jan. 12, 1856.

because the latter the year before had championed the cause of Broderick, the anti-administration candidate for the Senate in California.[1] Others intimated that Walker's treatment of Kinney was responsible, pointing out that Sidney Webster, Pierce's private secretary, and Caleb Cushing, the Attorney-General, had once been interested in the Central American Company, and would naturally use their influence against Walker, because he denied the validity of this company's land claims.[2] French and Fabens — the latter just having arrived in New York as a colonization agent — were responsible for these insinuations; the former had received so much notice from the public during the McKeon controversy that his head was completely turned. Friends of the administration now retaliated by laying bare some of the shady monetary transactions of French in the past. Especial stress was laid on a report of the Senate Committee on Military Affairs, which had been made only a year previously, and which showed up the would-be diplomat in very ugly colours.[3] The report stated that in 1850, when French was leading a caravan of emigrants over his widely advertised new route to California, he reached the army post at San Antonio and there applied for supplies. The War Department at that time authorized army posts to sell supplies to western emigrants if the state of their commissary permitted, and French was allowed to purchase about two thousand dollars' worth of government stores. The purchase was made on the strength of a letter of credit from the banking house of Howland and Aspinwall of New York City. This later proved to be a forgery. Several merchants of San Antonio were duped at the same time. The resurrection of this

---

[1] It is interesting to note that Pierce's refusal to receive French was attributed by members of the Know-Nothing party to the catering of the Democratic party to the foreign Catholic vote. See William G. Brownlow, *Americanism Contrasted with Foreignism, Romanism, and Bogus Democracy*, 99–100 (Nashville, 1856). My attention was directed to this by Professor St. George L. Sioussat.

[2] Wheeler Scrapbook no. 5, pp. 17, 53; New York *Herald*, Jan. 23, 1856.

[3] See Senate Report 455, 33 Cong., 2 Sess.

report produced a great revulsion of feeling, and was as heavy a blow to the cause of Walker as it was a revenge for the much criticised adminstration.[1]

Never did popular hero take so quick a tumble. When the press learned that the man whom they had urged the government to honour was no better than a thief their former sympathy was turned to disgust. French was now called "a panfish become very like a whale," "von big tam humbug," and other things equally as complimentary.[2] "In bitterness of spirit," said the New York *Mercury*, "let us exclaim, with Sir Harcourt Courtly, 'will nobody take this man away?'"[3] While expressing no admiration for Walker's minister, a number of journals still maintained that his official capacity should be recognized. "It is not Captain French, of questionable antecedents, who solicits the ear of our government," said one, "but the agent of a sovereign power."[4] "Worse men than Colonel French have been received as ministers, and eminently bad men, morally, hold high places in the governments with which we maintain friendly relations," said another. "International morals are not so pure that there need be any squeamishness in admitting Colonel French to the diplomatic circle."[5]

French persisted in his efforts to obtain recognition, and on February 5 met a second refusal.[6] Walker, on hearing of French's rejection, caused Rivas to revoke the powers of his minister and to suspend diplomatic relations with Wheeler at Granada until the American government should see fit to change its attitude.[7] In the issue of *El Nicaraguense* for January 12 he discussed the matter of Marcy's attitude in a very remarkable editorial, which

---

[1] For fuller accounts of French's rascality, consult William Miles, *Journal of the Sufferings and Hardships of Captain Parker H. French's Overland Expedition*. (Chambersburg, 1851); and Bell, *Reminiscences of a Ranger*, 261–5.

[2] Wheeler Scrapbook no. 5, p. 46.   [3] New York *Mercury*, Jan. 27, 1856.

[4] New York *Times*, Jan. 26, 1856.   [5] New York *Sun*, Jan. 15, 1856.

[6] House Ex. Doc. 103, 34 Cong., 1 Sess., 76.

[7] Senate Ex. Doc. 68, 34 Cong., 1 Sess.

the New York *Times* pronounced "well-written, high-toned, and with reasoning sustained to a high degree of ability." In this article Walker reminds Marcy that American independence was won with the aid of Lafayette, DeKalb, and Steuben, who, according to the views of the Secretary of State, must have been filibusters. Then, turning to the matter of French's having been a former citizen of the United States, he cites the fact that George III. had received John Adams, a former British subject, as minister from the United States as soon as peace was made. The reading of this editorial reminds us of Justice Field's characterization of Walker as a Marysville lawyer; his arguments are ingenious, but not convincing.

The most important result of French's rejection was seen in its effect upon the other Central American governments. It was hard for them to believe, after lately witnessing the outcome of the Mexican War and seeing now the apparent helplessness of American officials in preventing recruiting, that the invasion of Nicaragua was not sanctioned unofficially by the administration. Marcy's letter declaring that the present government of Nicaragua was not the creature of its citizens and not yet existing with their full consent was therefore loudly heralded in every quarter of Central America and strengthened the hands of those who were meditating Walker's destruction.[1]

After his decline in public esteem in New York French left the city for New Orleans, and there sailed for Greytown in company with a large body of recruits. On reporting to Walker he met with a cold reception, and was told that his further connection with the Nicaraguan government was not desired. French then departed the country, and on reaching New Orleans pretended to be entrusted with business negotiations for Walker's government.[2] On the 28th of April he and Pierre Soulé addressed a public meeting in New Orleans called to enlist sympathy in be-

---

[1] Montúfar, 163–4.   [2] *Ibid.* 163; New York *Herald*, April 4 and 25, 1856.

half of the Americans in Nicaragua.[1] He next proceeded to New
York, where he tried to interest Vanderbilt in some new steamship venture, and also planned to publish a booklet on the natural
resources of his adopted country. He delivered several lectures
on Nicaragua in various cities and still avowed his loyalty to
Walker, though he made no denial of the rupture which had been
reported between himself and his chief. When reports of his
conduct reached Nicaragua, *El Nicaraguense* paid its official
respects to the ex-filibuster, declaring that "he has no connection
whatever with this government; and, as evidence of this, we are
warranted in saying that he is at present engaged in doing the
administration all the injury his genius is capable of. . . . Fortunately, he can do no material damage." [2] This announcement
was widely copied in American papers, and French's candle for
the time being was snuffed out.

During the spring of 1856, as the time for the national con-
ventions of the political parties approached and the discussion of
party issues and presidential candidates waxed warm, it became
evident that the attitude of the administration toward the Nicaraguan movement would become a factor in determining the
action of the Democratic convention. Meetings began to be held
in all the principal cities, at which prominent politicians expressed
their sympathies with the cause of Walker. It began to be predicted that the hostility shown by the Pierce administration would
help defeat him for renomination, as the Democratic platform
would probably sanction what the Americans were doing in Central
America. Pierce and his advisers were accused also of catering
too much to England, and the refusal to recognize Walker was
cited as one instance of this.

Walker was now aware of the political pressure being brought
to bear upon Pierce, and the time seemed favourable for a second

---

[1] Montgomery *Advertiser and Gazette*, May 3, 1856.
[2] *El Nicaraguense* of April 26, quoted in New York *Herald*, June 2, 1856.

N

effort to obtain recognition. Profiting by his former mistake, he now chose a representative to whom no personal objections could be offered. Father Augustin Vijil, the curate of Granada, who had shown his friendship for the Americans on more than one occasion, was selected to represent the Rivas government near the United States. A contemporary Latin-American, not all friendly, describes the priest as endowed with splendid memory and intellect, graceful delivery, unctuous, penetrating voice, and massive physique. Deeply versed in Holy Writ, and renowned as an orator, he was often referred to as the "Bossuet of Nicaragua."[1] He had not always worn the cloth, but had once been a practising lawyer in Granada. Like so many of his fellow-countrymen, he had become involved in political difficulties and had incurred banishment from his native soil. After taking holy orders, however, he was able to return to the familiar scenes of his early days under the protection of the Church. It is said that he aspired to the episcopal chair at Granada, but had been balked in his ambition by Chamorro, who used his influence in behalf of a Guatemalan churchman named Piñol. This was given to explain the padre's devotion to the Democratic cause.[2]

On May 14 Vijil presented his credentials at Washington and was formally received as minister from Nicaragua. On the following day Pierce submitted a message to Congress, giving his reasons for receiving a representative of William Walker. The interests of the United States, he said, demanded that some government be recognized, and as the Rivas-Walker government was the only one in existence there was no choice but to recognize it.[3] The President's line of argument did not carry conviction to the

[1] Montúfar, 427-8.

[2] Perez, *Memorias*, pt. 2, 69. Padre Vijil is said not to have abandoned his legal practice after taking orders, but to have shown equal diligence "for fees and fervour, briefs and beads, courts and confessional, cross-examination and the cross." Wheeler Scrapbook no. 4, 178.

[3] *Messages and Papers of the Presidents*, V., 368-74.

opponents of the Nicaraguan movement. They claimed that
the administration could really have found a better excuse for
rejecting Vijil than it had for turning away French. In the case
of the latter it was chiefly a question as to whether Walker's was
a government *de jure*, whereas, when Vijil was received, all the
neighbouring states were showing hostility, Costa Rica was
actually making war on the filibusters, and the native Nicaraguans
were growing daily more disaffected. It was now a question, they
said, whether Vijil even represented a *de facto* government.[1]
They naturally held that the administration was actuated by
political motives, believing that the recognition of the Nicaraguan
government would be a strong factor in securing the renomination
of Pierce at the Cincinnati Convention. There is no doubt that
the reception of Vijil at this time had its political aspects, though
these had not the importance which enemies of Pierce and of the
Rivas-Walker government ascribed to them.

On May 23 a public meeting was held in New York City to
celebrate the recognition of the Nicaraguan government. Its
chief significance lay not so much in the size and enthusiasm of
the audience as in the fact that men high in the councils of the
Democratic party made this an occasion to align themselves in
favour of the Walker enterprise. Many who could not attend
sent letters expressing their sympathy with the cause. Especially
significant was a letter from Lewis Cass, of Michigan, then regarded as one of the leading candidates for the party's nomination.
"I am free to confess," he stated, "that the heroic effort of our
countrymen in Nicaragua excites my admiration, while it engages
all my solicitude. I am not to be deterred from the expression
of these feelings by sneers, or reproaches, or hard words. He who
does not sympathize with such an enterprise has little in common
with me. The difficulties which General Walker has encountered
and overcome will place his name high on the roll of the distin-

---

[1] *Cong. Globe*, 34 Cong., 1 Sess., 1227–8.

guished men of his age. . . . Our countrymen will plant there
the seeds of our institutions, and God grant that they may grow
up into an abundant harvest of industry, enterprise, and prosperity. A new day, I hope, is opening upon the States of Central
America." Cass ended his letter by paying his respects to that
bête noir of his, Great Britain. Another who sent a letter of
sympathy was Thomas Francis Meagher, the Irish patriot. Among
those who addressed the meeting were Rodman Price, then governor of New Jersey, E. A. Pollard, the journalist and traveller,
and Isaiah Rynders, the Tammany leader. Banners were displayed bearing the inscriptions, "Enlargement of the Bounds of
Liberty" and "No British interference on the American Continent."[1]

On June 2 the Democratic convention assembled in Cincinnati.
Pierce was the choice of the Southern delegates, and had no doubt
strengthened himself with them by his change of attitude toward
Walker. The Northern wing of the party, however, favoured
James Buchanan, and on the seventeenth ballot he was nominated.
This was not a defeat for the friends of Walker, for the platform
upon which Buchanan was nominated declared that, "in view of
so commanding an interest, the people of the United States cannot
but sympathize with the efforts which are being made by the
people of Central America to regenerate that portion of the
continent which covers the passage across the interoceanic isthmus." This, of course, was only a slightly veiled way of expressing sympathy with Walker.

In the meantime Padre Vijil's diplomatic experience was not
one of unalloyed happiness. Most of the diplomatic corps refused to recognize him in his official capacity. Molina, *chargé
d'affaires* for Costa Rica, and Irisarri, representing Guatemala and
San Salvador, protested vigorously to Marcy against his reception. The latter was unusually bold, affirming that as the recog-

[1] New York *Times*, May 24, 1856.

nition occurred when Walker was on the point of being overthrown
it could be regarded only as a means of securing the triumph of
the American invaders, who were threatening to lord it over all
other Central American republics, and "over Mexico, Cuba, and
the isthmus of Panama, leaving the task of extending their dominions as far as Tierra del Fuego to a later date."[1]   Even Marcoleta, who represented no government at all, filed a protest.[2]
Peru and New Granada later followed suit. The latter republic
feared that inasmuch as it too afforded a transit across the isthmus
it might soon suffer the fate of Nicaragua.[3] In the Chilean
Chamber of Deputies a member moved that the government
intervene against the Americans in Nicaragua. The ill-feeling
of the Latin-American representatives culminated in a meeting
in Washington at which they drew up a formal treaty of alliance
and sent it to their governments *sub spe rati*.[4] English and Spanish influences were undoubtedly behind these activities. Spain
was fearful that Walker's success in Nicaragua would lead to her
losing Cuba, and her fears were well founded.

Vijil was also snubbed and insulted by his fellow-clergymen in
America. In passing through Baltimore he paid a visit to the
archbishop. The latter is said to have remarked, "And you are
Father Vijil? Is it possible that a Catholic priest should come
to this country to labour against his church and his native land?"
The poor padre was so abashed at his cold reception that in his
hurry to leave he forgot his hat.[5] Vijil remained at his post only
until June 23.[6] Leaving John P. Heiss[7] to act as *chargé d'affaires,*

[1] Irisarri to Marcy, May 19, 1856, MS., Department of State, Bureau of Indexes
and Archives, Notes, Central American Legations, I.
[2] Text in Montúfar, 453-7.   [3] *British State Papers*, XLVII., 790-92.
[4] Text in *Ibid.*, 465-8.
[5] Gámez, *Historia de Nicaragua*, 648 (Managua, 1889) ; Perez, *Memorias*, 70.
[6] MS., Department of State, Bureau of Indexes and Archives, Central American
Legations, Notes, II.
[7] John P. Heiss had formerly been one of the proprietors of the New Orleans *Delta*.
He had been sent to Nicaragua by Marcy as a special agent of the government to
report upon the state of affairs in that country. After his return to the United

he returned to Nicaragua and made a report of his mission to Walker, who was then president. It is rather significant that he soon thereafter asked for his passports and left for New Granada, where he assumed charge of a church.[1]

States he warmly espoused the filibuster cause and served as a kind of "go-between" for Walker and American politicians.

[1] Montúfar, 661-2.

CHAPTER XIV

Costa Rica Wars on Walker

THE Democratic partizans in Nicaragua had no more bitter enemy, perhaps, than Señor Luis Molina, the Costa Rican *chargé d'affaires* at Washington. He had been driven from Nicaragua by these selfsame partizans, and the memory of his ill-treatment still rankled. His brother Felipe had served his government long and well as minister to the United States and had become dean of the diplomatic corps at Washington. Having been educated in Philadephia, he well understood the intricacies of American politics and kept his government well informed of the designs of the devotees of manifest destiny. At his death Felipe Molina was succeeded by his brother and understudy, the anti-Democratic Luis. The despatches of the latter to his home government must have been exceedingly pessimistic if their tone were in harmony with his notes to Marcy. Some of his protests have already been referred to or quoted. On December 6, 1855, in a communication to Marcy, he referred to Walker's enterprise as "a great crime, complex and multiform, which was hatched and set on foot within the territory of the United States and continued without interruption in a foreign land by North American citizens, with means and assistance and to a certain extent with the moral force of the nation, against the existence of peaceable and friendly states." If the adventurers "are disowned by the government to-day, they hope, not without cause, to be received with open arms to-morrow, arrayed in holiday attire for annexation, and to be exalted, their booty being legitimatized." A fortnight later,

177

in a second communication, he called Walker's adventurers "the dregs of European refuse Americanized." [1] Similar communications were going to his home government, where their substance was reproduced, with variations, in the *Boletin Oficial*.

The president of Costa Rica, Juan Rafael Mora, also showed active hostility to the filibusters from the very beginning. He had governed the country since 1850, and it had enjoyed profound peace. He was a plain, unassuming merchant of pleasant address and great popularity, and when elevated to the presidency was scarcely thirty-six years of age. He had just been reëlected when he heard that Walker had captured Granada. There had been jealousy and ill-feeling between the two republics, and Mora might have pursued a hands-off policy. But there were three good reasons why Costa Rica should look with alarm upon the filibustering movement in Nicaragua. In the first place, the Conservative element strongly predominated and was naturally opposed to the coming of an armed force to aid the Liberal faction in a neighbouring republic. After the treaty of October 23 large numbers of irreconcilable Legitimists fled to Costa Rica and found a ready asylum. Their stories of the misdeeds of the Americans increased the resentment of the people against the invaders. In the second place, Costa Rica had enjoyed a larger measure of political tranquillity than its neighbours, and as a result had developed a stronger sentiment of nationalism. It therefore resented a movement that might lead to the Americanization of any part of the isthmus, believing that this would be a preliminary step to the loss of its own nationality. Finally, Costa Rica had conceived an ambitious design to get the Transit route for itself by taking advantage of the turbulence in Nicaragua and seizing more territory along the San Juan River. It was therefore a grievous disappointment when this region practically fell into the hands

---

[1] MS., Department of State, Bureau of Indexes and Archives, Central American Legations.

of the Americans. The continuous anti-American propaganda carried on in Costa Rica encouraged many a disaffected Nicaraguan to follow the early Legitimist refugees and emigrate thither.

Walker made special efforts to conciliate this republic, as already shown. His selection of Schlessinger, who was still a stranger to him, for such an important mission did not speak well for his discretion; but the result would have been the same, it mattered not whom he chose, as the commissioners were turned back as soon as they reached Punta Arenas, the Pacific port of Costa Rica. Mora called an extraordinary session of his Congress, which authorized him on February 27 to take up arms *for the republic of Nicaragua*, defend its people from the filibusters, and expel the invaders from Central American soil. He was empowered to act alone or in conjunction with the other republics. The president at once issued a call for nine thousand men and took steps to levy a forced contribution of 100,000 pesos.[1] He also declared war on the filibusters, taking care to stipulate that Costa Rica was not fighting Nicaragua. Thirty-three Germans resident in the country signed an address expressing their sympathy and offering their services. In general, the war seems to have had the approval of the foreign residents.

Mora notified the American consul at San José that as the Transit Company's steamers were used for the transportation of "bandits," he had ordered a suspension of the traffic on the river and lake, and any persons attempting to cross the isthmus would do so at their peril. He also announced that he intended to shoot any of Walker's men that fell into his hands. As it happened, no steamers brought passengers while Mora was in the country, and

---

[1] This was not called a forced contribution, but as the amounts to be advanced were apportioned among the various provinces and were to be collected by the provincial governor with the aid of five citizens appointed by him, and as citizens with property of less amount than a house and a thousand pesos were declared exempt, it seems that the contributions were by no means voluntary. See Montúfar, 219–222.

he had no opportunity to carry out that part of his threat. As soon as Marcy was notified of this paper blockade of the river and lake he instructed the American consul to notify the Costa Rican government that the United States would not recognize it, and that Costa Rica must observe the rules of civilized warfare and inflict no barbarities on Walker's men, even though they might be guilty of a misdemeanour by leaving their own country.[1] Mora took personal command, leaving the government in the hands of the vice-president, and mobilized his forces at San José on March 3.[2] To facilitate enlistments, he decreed that all who enrolled, from sergeants down, should be exempt from legal process or foreclosure for debts or contracts assumed before enlisting until one month after the close of the campaign. Rivas retaliated on March 11 by declaring war against Costa Rica. Walker also issued an address, stating that he had been invited to Nicaragua by the Democratic party, and that he and his men had steadily struggled to carry out the principles for which the revolution of 1854 was undertaken; that he had held in check his Democratic friends and had sought to conciliate their opponents; that the provisional government had sought to establish friendly relations with other republics and its advances had been repelled with scorn; that the Legitimists in Nicaragua had sought to undermine the provisional government by giving aid and encouragement to its enemies outside the republic; and that nothing was left for the Americans but to offer eternal hostility to Servile [3] governments throughout Central America. He concluded the address by ordering the troops to assume and wear the red ribbon of the Democrats.[4] This last step was taken on account of the conduct of the Legitimists, but it was virtually a declaration of

---

[1] Senate Ex. Doc. 68, 34 Cong., 1 Sess.　　　　[2] Montúfar, 224–47.

[3] The Servile party in other states corresponded to the Legitimist party in Nicaragua.

[4] MS., Department of State, Bureau of Indexes and Archives, Despatches, Nicaragua, II.; El Nicaraguense, March 15, 1856; Walker, War in Nicaragua, 180–1.

civil war in Nicaragua, and made the Americans again the champions of a party rather than of a united government. It also set the entire Central American household against the man who had declared eternal warfare on the dominant party in these republics.

On March 4 the vanguard of the Costa Rican invaders set out from San José, commanded by General José Joaquin Mora, a brother of the president. While President Mora had fulminated against the employment of foreigners in the military service of Nicaragua, he had no scruples against utilizing them in his own army, and they were most efficient allies. A Frenchman by the name of Marie, who despised everything American and had used a vitriolic pen in attacking the filibusters in the *Boletin Oficial*, accompanied Mora to the front as sub-secretary of foreign affairs. An officer of Zouaves, Lieutenant-Colonel Barillier, rendered invaluable service in the field. Spanish agents also made themselves useful, not so much on account of friendliness to their kinsmen as out of resentment at American expansion, which they feared would end in their country's loss of Cuba.[1] The Costa Ricans marched to Punta Arenas and crossed the Gulf of Nicoya in boats, a number of which were supplied by the captain of a French merchant vessel in the harbour. Mora also sent a detachment of men down the Serapiqui River, a southern tributary of the San Juan, with the purpose of dislodging a small American force at Hipp's Point, where the two streams unite. These troops had been intercepting the Costa Rican mails, which went to San José by that route, and had enabled Walker to learn some interesting facts concerning Costa Rica's foreign relations. It was also the purpose of this expedition after seizing the Point, to prevent the steamers going up the river and thus make effective the paper blockade which Mora had proclaimed. The Costa Ricans attacked the Americans at Hipp's Point on April 10 and though they were repulsed and

[1] Montúfar, 259–62.

the Americans retained the post they reported a great victory, which was duly celebrated at home.[1]

When hostilities began Walker had an effective fighting force of about six hundred Americans. The last recruits sent by the old Transit Company arrived on March 9, just two days before the declaration of war, under the command of Domingo de Goicouria, a Cuban patriot, who had joined Walker after the latter had agreed to aid in the Americanization of Cuba when his work in Nicaragua was finished. It was to be six weeks before additional reinforcements were to come on the steamers of Morgan and Garrison. The cholera, too, had attacked the forces in Granada and had carried off some of the best officers, among them Gilman and Davidson, who had served under Walker in Lower California. To obtain the support of the Democrats, Walker not only assumed the red ribbon, but also consented to the transfer of the capital to Leon. Prominent Democrats now renewed their allegiance. Jerez, who had withdrawn from the cabinet after the refusal of Walker to aid Cabañas, became minister of war, and two other Democrats received cabinet appointments.[2] To avoid the delays in public business which would ensue from the seat of government being in the North while hostilities were carried on in the South, Fermin Ferrer was left in Granada with authority to transact all business in the Oriental and Meridional departments. This really created two governments. On arriving at Leon, Rivas issued a proclamation stating that his object in coming north was to be nearer the governments of Honduras, Salvador, and Guatemala, with whom he desired to cultivate friendly relations. This is strangely inconsistent with Walker's address, in which he declared eternal enmity to the Servile governments of Central America. Walker shrewdly suspected that the plan to make Leon

[1] Montúfar, 309–12.
[2] MS., Department of State, Bureau of Indexes and Archives, Despatches, Nicaragua, II.

the capital was prompted largely by a desire to split the country and weaken his hold upon it. On the 12th Walker despatched a battalion of four companies into Guanacaste to meet the threatened invasion. Schlessinger was put in command of the expedition, partly as a balm to his wounded feelings, and partly because Walker thought that his resentment at his ill-treatment as commissioner would make him fight more strenuously. Of these four companies, one consisted entirely of Frenchmen and another of Germans. Most of the command consisted of raw recruits that had arrived only three days previously, and few of these knew aught of military service. Walker says that Schlessinger was the only officer who could address every man in his own language, and that this was an additional reason for his choice as commander. There was also a reason, which he does not give, for his selection of such raw soldiers for the march. His other men were enervated by climate, fever, dysentery, cholera, and dissipation, and he desired to use his recruits for the arduous march before their strength was wasted in the same manner. The outcome, however, was disastrous. Schlessinger was no military leader. On the march he used no advance guard and took no precautions. His battalion was little more than a rabble. On March 20, after he had crossed the frontier and proceeded about thirty miles southward, Schlessinger was suddenly attacked by the advance guard of the Costa Rican army at the hacienda of Santa Rosa. The attack took him by surprise; the Germans beat a hasty retreat, the French soon followed, and the American officers tried in vain to hold the men in line and repel the enemy's advance. In five minutes, however, the entire command, headed by Schlessinger, was in a complete rout. Their leader was later courtmartialed for cowardice and condemned to be shot, but effected his escape. The loss to Walker was about a hundred men. When the main body of his army reached Santa Rosa, Mora executed his previous threats and ordered all the prisoners to be courtmartialed and shot, including even the wounded.[1] He had carried a printing press with him, and now used it to publish a decree that all filibusters taken with arms in their hands should be shot, but that all who had not used their arms against Costa Rica and would surrender of their own free will should be pardoned.[2] This was published in English, French, German, and Spanish, and appended to the decree, as a stern warning, was a list of the prisoners taken and shot at Santa Rosa.[3] The fugitives from the engagement came straggling into Virgin Bay, and it was several weeks before the last of them arrived, as many lost their way.[4] Their stories caused the men to grow very despondent. Walker himself was ill with fever and suffering from a severe swelling in his face, when the first news of this reverse reached him, and a letter which he wrote to Senator Weller of California at this time shows that he, too, was in greatly depressed spirits.[5] Among the Americans not connected with the government there was almost a stampede to return to the United States. This also had its bad effect on the morale of the troops. Walker decided to move his entire force from Granada to Rivas. This would enable him

[1] *War in Nicaragua*, 182–6.

[2] State Department, Bureau of Indexes and Archives. The Nicaraguan Despatches, MS. Vol. II., contain a copy of this, *Boletin del Ejercito Republica de Costa Rica*, dated March 27, 1856.

[3] One of the prisoners proved to be a newspaper correspondent for the New Orleans *Delta*, Philip E. Toothey. He had been wounded, though not participating in the skirmish, and on satisfying his captors that he was not a soldier his life was spared. New York *Herald*, May 1, 1856.

[4] About forty of Schlessinger's men reached Greytown in terrible destitution, and caused great alarm among the poor villagers, who had little to give them but were compelled by the threats of the desperate fellows to give them food. The natives appealed to Captain Tarleton of H. M. S. *Eurydice* for protection. A collection was taken to pay the men's passage out of the country and Tarleton himself subscribed. MS., Navy Department, Archives, Home Squadron, II., 199.

[5] "So far," he wrote, "we have great moral odds against us. The Government to which we looked for aid and comfort has treated us with disdain. There has been no Government to encourage us, and bid us 'God speed!' Nothing but our own sense of the justice of the cause we are engaged in, and of its importance to the country of our birth, has enabled us to struggle on as far as we have come." *Cong. Globe*, 34 Cong., 1 Sess., 1070–2.

better to protect the Transit, which was apparently Mora's objective, and would also have a good effect upon the native Nicaraguans, who on seeing him advancing to meet the enemy might not think that the Santa Rosa affair was a serious reverse. At Rivas Walker reorganized the broken companies that were straggling in from their first skirmish and decided to have no more companies of other nationalities. All French and German recruits were therefore mustered out of service. Some four hundred of his troops were well drilled and disciplined; the remainder had little or no military equipment. Many fugitives from Santa Rosa had thrown away their guns, and some arrived minus hats and shoes. Altogether, it was not an inspiring sight to see five hundred men, with no immediate prospects of reinforcement from the States, on account of Morgan and Garrison's tardiness in handling the Transit business, preparing to meet an invasion of four thousand, who probably would be welcomed and aided by the native population. News came from President Rivas of a general movement among the other States to unite with Costa Rica. The general depression caused many officers to indulge in a prolonged carouse, which was damaging to discipline. Among those remiss in this particular was Walker's brother Norvell, a captain. Walker reduced him to ranks, and the punishment had a good effect. On March 30, just after arriving in Rivas, Walker had the men paraded in the plaza and made them a very frank and pointed talk. He told them of their peril, and urged this as a necessity for proper behaviour. Not a government in the world was friendly to them. Those whom they had benefited had betrayed them; they stood alone, with nothing to rely upon but the justice of their cause. The speech was short and without rhetorical effect, but it seemed to raise a new spirit in the men.[1]

Mora meanwhile pressed on toward the frontier until he heard of Walker's arrival at Rivas. He then stopped, and was watching

[1] *War in Nicaragua*, 186–8; New York *Herald*, May 9, 1856.

his adversary at a distance when Walker, who could get no trust-worthy information from the natives and knew nothing of the size of the Costa Rican force, decided to return to Granada. He was moved to this course by the news he had received from the provisional president at Leon, who was frightened at the daily reports of a northern invasion. These plans of an invasion by the northern States were only the recoil from Walker's ill-con-sidered proclamation of war against all the Servile governments of Central America. His departure from Rivas in the face of the enemy looked like a blunder also, and General Goicouria requested to be left there with a small detachment to watch and worry the enemy. He was abruptly told to mind his business. Rivas was thus abandoned after only six days' occupation. The men were embarked on a lake steamer and carried to the head of the San Juan River, so as to create an impression that they were either leaving the country or contemplating a counter-movement on Costa Rica. The enemy accepted the former view, and made no effort to restrain their departure. After reaching the river Walker turned back to Granada, while the Costa Ricans, thinking that they now had complete possession, stationed themselves on the Transit road and occupied Rivas. On reaching Virgin Bay they surrounded the building of the Transit Company, murdered nine of · its employees, plundered their bodies, ransacked the warehouse, and burned the company's new pier, declaring death to all Americans.[1]

On reaching Granada Walker heard of the advance of Mora and also found letters from Leon awaiting him stating that the fears of an invasion in the North had quieted. He at once then prepared to march on Rivas direct from Granada. On the way he met a detachment of natives he had left at Rivas as a garrison. Their leader had deserted to Mora, but they had followed a Cuban

---

[1] Senate Ex. Doc. 68, 34 Cong., 1 Sess. For this attack by Costa Ricans on American persons and property the United States demanded reparation.

who remained faithful to Walker. The total strength of the force
was now nearly six hundred. At eight o'clock on the morning
of April 11 they reached their objective and began the attack
upon the town. The Costa Ricans were not expecting an attack,
though they knew of Walker's approach, and were taken by surprise. Walker's men entered the town from four different directions, and rushing through the streets, captured the plaza and the
surrounding houses. Then they discovered that they were surrounded by superior numbers protected behind adobe walls. In
other words, they captured the centre of the town while the
enemy was off his guard, but now that he was alert they found
that their first success had placed them in an awkward predicament. Without artillery they could never dislodge the Costa
Ricans from the surrounding houses, and, consequently they
were in a situation where they could neither advance nor retreat.
From the roofs of buildings the natives poured a galling fire upon
any of Walker's men who exposed themselves. The latter, seeing
that they were in the position of the Cossack who had caught a
Tartar, became depressed and could not be made to charge
through the streets in the direction of Mora's headquarters, as
Walker desired. His officers exposed themselves recklessly, and
the mortality among them was heavy. American rifles, too, were
not idle, and two hundred Costa Ricans were killed and four hundred wounded. Walker's losses in killed and wounded amounted
to one hundred and twenty.

By noon the firing lulled. The Costa Ricans set fire to some of
the buildings around the plaza which were occupied by the Americans and kept up a desultory firing which prevented communication between the various houses in which the filibusters were
sheltered. After nightfall Walker gathered his wounded in a
church on the plaza and placed near the altar those too seriously
disabled to be taken away. Horses were brought for those not
dangerously wounded, and at midnight the whole command

o

silently withdrew from the town, protected by darkness and the exhaustion of their enemy. When morning dawned the Costa Ricans were still ignorant of the departure of the invaders. Walker's brother Norvell had fallen asleep in the tower of the church, and his companions had stolen away so quietly that he was not awakened. Great was his surprise to find himself alone, but he managed to pass through the town unmolested, as the enemy were still sheltering themselves from the dreaded rifles, and he overtook the rear-guard some miles from Rivas.[1] When the Costa Ricans finally discovered that the enemy had gone they entered the church and bayoneted the wounded near the altar. They also shot seventeen prisoners.[2]

The campaign so far had shown that Walker possessed personal bravery but no generalship. Abandoning Rivas in the face of the enemy, he allowed them to seize the Transit road and destroy for the time being his means of communication, not to mention their massacre of inoffensive Americans at Virgin Bay. After allowing them to ensconce themselves in force at the town which he should have held against them, he marched his men fifty miles and attacked the enemy in numbers five times as great as his own and sheltered behind adobe walls. The attack was made, too, with only rifles and revolvers. While he inflicted losses five times as great as those he suffered, every man he lost counted much more

[1] *War in Nicaragua*, 197–203; Montúfar, 325–30.
[2] This is frankly stated by Walker's most hostile critic. See Perez, *Memorias*, pt. 2, p. 48. Mora, too, in his official report, admits putting the wounded to the bayonet. See Montúfar, 331. The battle gave immortality to a Costa Rican common soldier by the name of Juan Santamaria. In the height of the conflict General Cañas called for a volunteer to set fire to a building where some well-sheltered Americans were giving much trouble. Though the attempt meant almost certain death, Santamaria responded, shouting to his companions not to forget his mother. Seizing a torch, he started at a run and applied it to the eaves. A bullet disabled his right arm, but he took the torch in his left hand and continued his work till another shot felled him to the ground. His countrymen have commemorated his heroism with a public monument. See *Las Fiestas del 15 de Setiembre de 1895 Celebrados con Motivo de la inauguración del Monumento Nacional Erigido en San José á los Héroes del 56 y del 57*, 28. (San José, 1897.)

than did the loss of a Costa Rican. He was lucky to have extricated himself from such a difficult position.

But while Walker was not a good general, Mora was not even a soldier. He not only allowed himself to be surprised, but after checking and repelling the attack he did not know how to pursue the retreating foe.[1] Instead, he remained at Rivas, which was an unwholesome town at best, and did not even have enough knowledge of sanitation to bury or burn the putrefying bodies, which were thrown indiscriminately into public wells, poisoning both the air and the water. On the 15th he sent home an account of a glorious victory, but at the same time forbade any of his soldiers to write letters home. "All the time," he said in his official report, "prisoners, wounded and unwounded, are coming in. Up to to-day seventeen have been shot. In brief, our loss, counting the mortally wounded, will not exceed one hundred and ten men, including the officers; that of the enemy not less than two hundred, including those we have shot." He also stated that Walker's forces were from twelve hundred to thirteen hundred men, while his own were about the same or somewhat less on account of the detached bodies used to garrison Virgin Bay and San Juan del Sur.[2] Strange to relate, after stating his losses as being so small, he goes on to explain that he did not pursue Walker because his men were exhausted, and it was necessary to give his attention to his wounded. He thus refutes himself with his own words.

In spite of bombastic reports of a great victory and the ban on letters from the soldiers, the news of Mora's great losses sifted through and caused more apprehension than would have ensued if the people had been told the truth. Dr. Lorenzo Montúfar,

---

[1] Perez says, "Mora abounded in patriotism and in noble ambition, but he was no soldier." Trans. from *Memorias*, pt. 2, 49. Montúfar (p. 331) agrees, saying that if military capacity existed in Central America in that period it was not found among the soldiers. Mora is characterized by him as no soldier, but a patriotic and popular merchant.

[2] Montúfar, 325-7.

the Costa Rican historian, was then employed in the office of the *Boletin Oficial*, and relates from his own observations how that journal gradually broke the news to the people.[1]

Cholera soon appeared at Rivas and proved more effective in thinning the ranks of the Costa Ricans than the most accurate American riflemen. The insanitary conditions already described aided in the spread of the malady. The mortality was frightful; news came, too, that the people at home were about to break into a rebellion against Mora. As the news gradually reached them of the real losses on April 11 their rejoicing over a victory was turned into sorrow for the fallen. The war had burdened them heavily, and a revolution was brewing. Mora hurried back to San José and left his brother-in-law, General José Maria Cañas, in charge of the troops. But the rigours of the pestilence continued without abatement, and Cañas made immediate preparations to abandon the stricken town and hasten home with such as were still well and strong. And now a wonderful thing happened. Those who had cried no quarter were compelled to ask it. Cañas sent Walker a courteous note asking his attention for the sick that he was compelled to leave behind. It was strange indeed that the Costa Ricans, who had put wounded men to the bayonet and shot their prisoners, should now ask favours of the man they had proclaimed a bandit. "In regard for the truth," says the unfriendly Perez, "we must say that Walker treated with humanity the soldiers that were commended to him." [2] No American, of course, is surprised that Walker obeyed the dictates of simple humanity in this instance, but he is surprised that Cañas should expect a "pirate" and "freebooter" to heap coals of fire upon an enemy's head. The march of Cañas homeward was a trail of death. To reduce contagion, the army was broken into small

---

[1] Montúfar, 342–5.
[2] "En honor de la verdad debemos decir que Walker trato con humanidad á los soldados que le fueron recomendados." *Memorias*, pt. 2, p. 51.

groups, but they spread the infection throughout the country they traversed. Over five hundred bodies were interred on the beach at San Juan del Sur, where the waves and tides soon exposed the gruesome remains; and for many months afterward whitening skeletons lined the shore and glistened in the sun.[1] By the middle of May the last of the survivors of the army that had set out for Nicaragua on March 3 was back at home. The pestilence continued. The vice-president of Costa Rica fell a victim, and it was estimated that it claimed the lives of between ten and twelve thousand people.[2] The bishop ordered the clergy to recite the prayer *Pro tempore pestilentiæ*, but piety was unavailing against the plague.

The cholera now became more virulent also in the American camp, though the Americans showed less susceptibility to the malady than the natives. The losses from war and disease were counterbalanced to some extent by the arrival of an Atlantic steamer bringing passengers and two hundred recruits under the leadership of Hornsby, who had been absent for some time in the United States. Unfortunately, Morgan and Garrison had not yet installed their Pacific service, and the passengers from the East were compelled to remain a month in Nicaragua. They observed the ravages of plague and fever, and some of them succumbed thereto. The others, on reaching California, gave such dismal accounts of Walker's situation that numbers refrained from emigrating to Nicaragua, and his cause was seriously injured. Among the last recruits was Walker's youngest brother James, who was promoted to a captaincy. His career as a soldier was short, however, as he soon succumbed to the cholera.

During the invasion the Legitimists in Chontales and Segovia had arisen against the provisional government, but these disturb-

---

[1] Jamison, *With Walker in Nicaragua*, 89.
[2] Belly, *À Travers l'Amérique Centrale*, I., 284.

ances were easily quelled. Goicouria with a company of Rangers scoured the hills of Chontales, and Valle, Walker's old Indian ally, who had been made governor of Segovia, stamped out the opposition there. Some Legitimists in the Meridional department had joined the invaders, and Walker squared accounts with them also. On the surface the country was now completely pacified. Walker removed his troops from Granada, which was now a hotbed of fever and cholera, and quartered them at Virgin Bay. Cholera appeared there also, but the place was more healthful than the old capital. Detachments of men were sent into every corner of the department to create confidence in the strength of the government.

The war was now a thing of the past, and the advantages seemed to be entirely with Walker. His losses had been compensated by reinforcements; the enemy had retired and was in no position to return to the attack. The only immediate foes to be dreaded were fever and cholera. There were two things, however, that caused Walker much anxiety. Randolph, who since the revocation of the Transit Company's charter had been detained at Realejo by a serious illness, was now able to make the journey to New York, and in passing through Virgin Bay he told Walker that there was mischief brewing at Leon, whither the capital had been removed.

The other cause of anxiety was less immediate, but was a source of grave concern. As soon as Costa Rica declared war, Walker had caused the English mail for San José to be intercepted at Hipp's Point as it passed up the San Juan River. In this way he secured a letter from E. Wallerstein, the Costa Rican consul-general at London, acquainting his government with the willingness of the British War Department to sell arms to Costa Rica, leaving it for the latter to decide when they should be paid for. There was also a private letter from Wallerstein to Mora saying, "When I was telling Lord Clarendon Costa Rica had already an army of eight hundred men on the frontiers, he was much pleased, and said that was a right step; and I am persuaded my having made that intimation is the reason for their giving us the muskets."[1]

We know more about this matter to-day than Walker had any chance of knowing. On January 5 the Costa Rican consul asked for arms for Guatemala, and on January 12 asked on behalf of his own country for two thousand muskets "required for the purpose of arming the population for the security of the country against aggression." These muskets were to be paid for "at the earliest practicable period consistently with the exertions which Costa Rica is now making." Both requests were granted, and the consul was allowed his choice of two patterns of smooth-bore weapons. He then wrote to the superintendent of the royal small arms factory at Enfield for advice as to the better type. The latter replied March 4, 1856, stating that as "the troops under Mr. Walker, against whom you may have to defend yourselves, are probably armed, either wholly or in part, with rifles, I should be wrong in counselling you to select any but rifled arms, and I think Her Majesty's Government would not object to my selecting the required number of smooth-bored muskets; and I could arrange for their being rifled and sighted, which operations, including such repairs as may be necessary, would amount to 16s. each arm." This sympathetic officer, Lieutenant-Colonel M. H. Dixon, also recommended that the consul purchase a million rounds of ammunition, with caps, bayonet scabbards, and all other necessary equipment from the British government's stores. On March 18 the War Department formally approved Dixon's recommendation that two thousand muskets be rifled for the Costa Rican government.[2] The British government had a right, of course, to sell arms to

[1] Walker, *War in Nicaragua*, 174–5.; MS., State Department, Bureau of Indexes and Archives, Despatches, Nicaragua, II.

[2] *British State Papers*, XLVI., 784–5; 794, 796, 803.

another government, but the story as revealed by the correspondence indicates its decided hostility to Walker. Indeed, on April
25 a member of the House of Commons asked Lord Palmerston
if it were true, as reported, that the government intended to send
troops into Costa Rica to operate against Walker. Palmerston
replied in the negative.[1]

Costa Rica's relations with England in this period were not
confined to requests for arms. Wallerstein, on December 22,
1855, notified Clarendon of the invasion of Nicaragua by Walker
and Kinney, calling attention to the importance of the Central
American isthmus to Great Britain, and stating that Costa Rica
was defenceless and had incurred the hostility of the United
States on account of its British leanings. "May I not venture,"
he concludes, "to solicit that Great Britain shall adopt effectual
measures, founded upon some great international principle, which
may extend the countenance and protection of the powerful allies
in Europe — more particularly of the great maritime States —
to youthful and comparatively weak countries and territories,
against the system of unprincipled aggression which is calculated
to retard, if not to ruin their career as civilized nations, and
has become intolerable?" A week later Palmerston received a
similar request from Joaquin Bernardo Calvo, the Costa Rican
minister of foreign affairs, who in specific terms asked that the
alliance of England and France should "not be confined solely to
the liberation of Turkey, but will reach wherever it is necessary
to defend right against might, or innocence against injustice."
Calvo also asked that a British war vessel should be placed in the
Gulf of Nicoya to prevent an invasion of Costa Rica from the
Pacific. The government consented to this, shrewdly stipulat-
ing, however, that the cruiser would visit the coast to protect
British interests. For this Wallerstein returned the thanks
of his government, adding "the hope and expectation . . .

[1] *Hansard's Debates*, 3d Series, CXLI, 1536-9.

that the interests of Costa Rica will be included in this protectorate." [1]

It is hard to repel the idea that British jealousy was a stumbling-block in the path of civilization at this time as much in the Caribbean as in the Crimea.

---

[1] *British State Papers*, XLVI., 786, 789, 797.

CHAPTER XV

WALKER BECOMES PRESIDENT

AT the same time that the capital was transferred from Granada to Leon, steps were taken to bring an end to the provisional government and to restore the political machinery as it was provided for in the constitution of 1838. An election, therefore, was ordered to be held on Sunday, April 13, to choose a president, senators, and members of Congress.[1] The election was conducted on this and several succeeding Sundays, but only in those places not disturbed by the Costa Ricans. The vote for president was distributed among Rivas, Jerez, and Salazar, but as the returns were very incomplete the election was not regarded as valid. The Democratic leaders, however, now objected to another election, though they had favoured this one. A number of them thought that the results of the ballots already cast should stand, and that the other districts, such as Chontales and Segovia, where there had been no voting, should now be allowed to express their choice. The reason for this change of attitude is readily explained. If their plan were carried out, the choice of a president would fall upon one of the three named. If a new election were held, the choice would probably be Walker. The result of the Costa Rican invasion and the threatened invasion by other States convinced many that Walker was a fit person to head the government in its crisis; but the real reason of Walker's strength as a candidate was that the people of the South felt that any of the three Democrats named above would, if chosen, remove the capital

[1] MS., Department of State, Bureau of Indexes and Archives, Despatches, Nicaragua, II.

196

permanently to Leon. Granadinos therefore were urgent for a
new election, and Walker was their candidate. On June 4
Walker went to Leon, where he was joyfully received by the people
as their deliverer. A great feast was prepared in his honour;
women of every age and rank gathered in the courtyard of the
house where he was quartered, and thanked him for protecting
their homes. Musicians came and in improvised songs sang the
praises of American valour. News soon arrived of the reception
of Vijil at Washington and of the arrival at Granada of one hundred and eighty more recruits.[1]

The commander-in-chief urged that Rivas order a new election
while the State was still quiet and before the threatened northern
invasion interfered with public order. Whether this was a real
or feigned reason of Walker's, it is difficult to say. The news of
Vijil's recognition and of more recruits so strengthened Walker's
position that Rivas acceded to his request, and on June 10 ordered an immediate election. The next day Walker left Leon
for Granada, escorted by his company of Rangers. President
Rivas and a number of officials accompanied him some distance
from the city, and when they separated Rivas embraced the
commander very affectionately. Jerez, the minister of war, remained behind, and had shown signs of disaffection. Trouble
at once broke out between him and the German officer, Bruno
Von Natzmer, whom Walker had left in Leon with his company
of the Rifles. A few native troops were stationed as a garrison in the towers of the cathedral. Natzmer ordered these out
and placed his Rifles there. Jerez, on hearing of this, countermanded Natzmer's order and told him to return to his regular quarters. The officer refused to obey without first consulting his commander-in-chief. This caused the native officials to
become greatly excited, and Natzmer created further alarm when
he put a squad of his soldiers in charge of a place called *El*

[1] *War in Nicaragua*, 216–20.

Principal, which contained the arms and munitions of the city. The rumour then spread that Rivas and Jerez were to be arrested, along with other leading Democrats, and the president and his minister of war at once fled the city, taking the road to Chinandega. The only Democrat connected with the government who remained was Walker's faithful adherent, Fermin Ferrer. The Leonese became furiously excited and swarmed in the streets shouting "Death to the Americans!" Natzmer sent for a detachment of men stationed in Chinandega, concentrated his forces in the plaza, and prepared to defend himself. He also sent a courier to overtake Walker with a report of what had occurred. All this took place the very day after Walker's departure and only eight days after the inhabitants had vied with one another in shouting his praises. The mercurial temperament of the Latin-American passes the understanding of the peoples of the North. The real secret of this sudden revulsion was a report that Jerez and his henchmen had sedulously spread, after they had failed to prevent a decree for a new election. They had persuaded the Leonese that Walker intended to remove the capital back to Granada. The fatal jealousy of Leonese and Granadinos was thus at the bottom of the agitation.

For two days after leaving Leon Rivas and Jerez lay hidden in a garden and on June 14 they went to Chinandega and sent a communication to the governments of Guatemala and San Salvador asking their aid in expelling the invaders. Guatemala had already taken the field. Rivas also revoked his decree of the 10th ordering a new election.[1]

In the meantime this news had reached Walker while he was en route to Granada. He at once ordered Natzmer to obey Jerez's order and withdraw from Leon, hoping to deprive the minister of any excuse for offering resistance. He tarried on the way until Natzmer's Rifles joined him and then proceeded to

---

[1] Montúfar, 472–80; *El Nicaraguense*, June 14 and 21, 1856.

Granada. His men had been scattered in small detachments all the way from Leon to Castillo Viejo on the San Juan River, for the purpose of impressing the people with the strength of the provisional government, and he now began to concentrate them at the old Legitimist capital and prepare for emergencies.

This was a typical Latin-American revolution. It had now passed its first stage, that of a factional explosion and the flight of the leaders of the weaker party, and was entering upon the second, that of the bombastic pronunciamientos and counter-pronunciamientos. At this stage Walker took the initiative. On the 20th he issued a decree, drawn up with his lawyer's ingenuity, stating that the powers conferred upon Rivas as provisional president were but a delegation of the powers that had been conferred upon Walker by the government when it commissioned him, soon after his arrival, as "expeditionary general." The idea underlying this statement seemed to be that Rivas owed his position to the two contracting generals who drew up the treaty of October 23; hence the provisional president was the creature and Walker the creator. Furthermore, the decree stated that when Rivas went to Leon in March he had delegated his powers in the South to Walker and Ferrer to maintain order; that he had betrayed his duties in the North by inviting an enemy to invade the country; and that, inasmuch as Walker had solemnly sworn to maintain the safety of the republic, he now declared null and void all acts of Patricio Rivas since the abandonment of his sworn duties on June 12, and appointed Fermin Ferrer provisional president until an election could be held in accordance with the decree of June 10. All who in any way aided or obeyed Rivas were declared traitors to the republic.[1] It is useless to examine the lawfulness of Walker's claim of the right to depose and set up provisional presidents. All the acts were revolutionary, and must be judged by results. Walker's statements were true

[1] *El Nicaraguense*, June 21.

only if he were able to demonstrate that they were matters of fact. Two addresses followed, one to the people of Nicaragua and the other to the army. To the Nicaraguans he stated that Americans had endured pestilence in camp and had poured out their blood on the field of battle in order to consolidate the government and maintain the peace and honour of the State. In return for this they had received only the bare necessities of life, and the officials had excited the people against them. He, therefore, in the name of the people, declared the old government abolished and appointed a new provisional government until the nation could exercise its right to choose its own rulers. To the army he stated that the late government had refused to pay the soldiers and was no longer entitled to their respect; but that the new provisional government would be more mindful of its duties.[1]

Ferrer at once assumed his duties as provisional president, and on the 21st he too issued a proclamation to the inhabitants, declaring that the neighbouring republics, on the pretext of driving out foreigners, aimed merely to dominate Nicaragua. He called the Americans faithful brothers "who, though not born on this soil, have left their homes and crossed the ocean in order to take part in your struggles, fighting for your liberty." The Legitimists were called "those unnatural sons who will not remember that no longer than seven months ago a great revolution was ended in which many of your fathers, brothers, and sons were the victims."[2]

It was now the turn of Rivas to issue a rhetorical counterblast. It came on the 26th. Walker was declared a traitor and deposed from the position "with which the republic had honoured him." All who remained with Walker, whether foreign or native, were also declared traitors, and those who had served him were ordered to sever their connection and submit to the Rivas government, which would receive them into its service if they desired, or they

[1] *El Nicaraguense*, June 21.   [2] New York *Herald*, July 17, 1856.

might remain in the country as Nicaraguans. All Nicaraguans between the ages of fifteen and sixty were ordered to take arms against Walker and his men. He also revoked the powers of Vijil and designated Irisarri, then representing Guatemala and San Salvador, to represent his government also at Washington.

There were now three claimants to the presidency: Estrada in Segovia, who as the successor of Chamorro still claimed to be the lawful ruler; Rivas in Chinandega; and Ferrer in Granada. The decree of the 10th had set the elections on Sunday, June 29. Though annulled by Rivas on the 14th it had been reaffirmed on the 20th by Walker, who at the same time declared all acts of Rivas since the 12th (the day of his flight) null and void. There were thus eight days in which to notify the people of the country of the impending election. It should also be noted that the decree provided for a direct election, which was an innovation in Nicaragua and would require time to be put into practical working order. As the country had neither telegraphs nor railways, and only the most primitive methods of transmitting intelligence, it is unlikely that many of the populace were informed of the political contest except in places like Granada, Rivas, and San Juan del Sur. Moreover, as the people were largely illiterate and without political experience, it is improbable that they could master the details of a new method of choosing an executive on such short notice. The northern districts, too, were in the hands of Walker's enemies, and it is inconceivable that an election could have been held, for instance, in the city of Leon, where Walker and all who obeyed his orders had been proclaimed traitors. These facts are given as showing that a fair and full expression of opinion from the people on the question of the presidency on June 29, 1856, was utterly impracticable. Nevertheless, some sort of an election was held, and Walker was declared to be the successful candidate. The "official" vote, as published in Walker's paper, was as follows: Walker, 15,835; Ferrer, 4,447; Rivas, 867; Salazar, 2,087.

The question of the authenticity of these figures naturally arises. They show a total vote of 23,236 out of a total voting population of 35,000. *El Nicaraguense* declared that the entire people took an interest in the election, and that returns were received from all but a few unimportant precincts. Remarkable as this statement appears, it is still more surprising to learn that "In Leon the struggle was very exciting, the strong Democratic friends of General Walker urging his claims with great enthusiasm, and we are proud to note that though Leon is the chief point of dissatisfaction, owing to the intrigues and falsehoods of the late President and his cabinet, the Democratic candidates still received an almost equal number with the opposition." The vote is given in the paper in tabular form and is arranged by provinces and precincts. The returns from the province of Leon are especially interesting, for the reason that Rivas was there and Walker's men had all withdrawn. Moreover, the order for an election had been annulled by the man in power in Leon. According to the published returns, however, the vote in three towns of this province was as follows:

	WALKER	FERRER	RIVAS	SALAZAR	TOTAL
Leon	789	900	946	1042	3677
Chinandega .	96	147	18	125	386
Realejo . . .	63	68	9	55	195
	948	1115	973	1222	4258

The returns also indicate voting in nineteen precincts in Segovia and in ten in Chontales. "After a tedious delay," said the editor, "the election returns have all been received, and after a still further delay on our part in overlooking a lot of documents and vouchers weighing half a ton, we have been successful in arriving at the votes of the various towns in the different departments." If it took so long to get the returns, one might ask, would it not

have taken an equally long time to have notified the people that
that contest was to be held? The entire story of the election
bears on its face the evidence of mendacity. Indeed, Walker refutes a part of it himself, when he says, "The voting was general
in the Oriental and Meridional Departments; but as D. Patricio
Rivas rescinded his own decree after reaching Chinandega, and
as the Guatemalans had already passed the northern frontier of the
State there were no ballots cast in the Occidental Department." [1]
The Occidental department corresponded roughly with the province of Leon. Either Walker or his editor, therefore, is guilty
of falsehood. It is of course the editor; his excessive zeal caused
him to publish a fictitious story of a keenly contested election in
Leon, whereas not a vote was cast there. Since one part of the
story in *El Nicaraguense* has been proven so palpably false, the
rest of it also falls under grave suspicion.

What Walker's enemies say of the election may now prove
interesting. According to Perez, the holding of a direct election
for president was unconstitutional, and the same was true of votes
given to a soldier in actual service and to a foreigner. He says
that ballot boxes were set up in a few pueblos around Granada
and Rivas, and there the soldiers and other American adventurers,
as well as a few natives, cast their votes for Walker. In Granada
lists were made up for all the departments, and the vote recorded
for them was estimated on the supposed number of votes in each
place, due care being taken that Walker should get a substantial
majority. Even the remotest valleys and hamlets were counted
in, and a number of dead towns, destroyed by fire or abandoned
during past wars, were also included. These lists were placed in
envelopes as if they actually came from the various precincts and
were sent to Ferrer's office, where they were opened and the votes
recorded.[2]

[1] *War in Nicaragua*, 228.

[2] Perez, *Memorias*, pt. 2, 77–8; Montúfar, 489. A returned soldier, in September, 1856, told a representative of the San Francisco *Bulletin* that all the soldiers

P

Walker was declared duly elected, and though the election had no legality, his claim to the office was at least as good as that of his two competitors, Rivas and Estrada. The latter could base his claim only on a decree which he had issued declaring himself the chief executive; the former had been recognized only because he had behind him the support of the arms of Walker.

Ferrer named July 12 as the day for Walker's inauguration. A platform was erected on the plaza and decorated with the flags of Nicaragua, the United States, and France, and with the Lone Star of Cuba. Every effort was employed to make the ceremonies impressive. The inaugural parade began at eleven o'clock. Companies of soldiers, a band of music, the municipal officers, foreign consuls, the general officers and their staffs, Minister Wheeler and his suite, and Ferrer and Walker with the presidential suite passed through the streets to the plaza. Ferrer administered the oath to his successor, and Walker solemnly swore, on bended knee, to govern the free republic of Nicaragua, to maintain its independence and territorial integrity, to do justice in accordance with republican principles, to uphold the laws of God, the true profession of the Gospel, and the religion of the Crucified One. In a eulogistic address Ferrer then placed into Walker's hands the destinies of Nicaragua. Walker followed with his inaugural address, which though rather trite, as such compositions usually are, would have been a creditable performance by any chief executive. He began with an appeal to all good citizens to assist him in conducting the affairs of the government with wisdom and prudence and in maintaining that order which is the first requisite in any well-governed state. The 15th of September, 1821, he

were allowed to vote, and that some voted as often as twenty times, but that this made no difference, for the returns were made up in Granada later just to suit the fancy of those in control of the election. A correspondent of the *Tribune* called attention to the fact that in some cases the majorities which Walker received were over four times the total population. Wheeler Scrapbook no. 4, 155a; New York *Herald*, Oct. 14, 1856.

said, was the beginning of a revolutionary epoch in Nicaragua, and he hoped that this day would mark its end. He next discussed the hostility of the four other Central American States to the new government and declared that they would be powerless to check the march of events in Nicaragua. Most significant, however, were his comments concerning the relations of Nicaragua with the greater nations. It had been commonly supposed in the United States and in Europe that Walker contemplated seeking annexation as soon as he had made his position secure. Only his most intimate friends — and these were few — thought otherwise. His address gives the first public pronouncement of his ultimate purposes with regard to annexation, but the language employed is so general that few, if any, grasped its real significance. "In our relations with the more powerful nations of the world, I hope that they may be led to perceive that although Nicaragua may be comparatively weak, she is yet jealous of her honour and determined to maintain the dignity of her independent sovereignty. Her geographical position and commercial advantages may attract the cupidity of other governments, *either neighbouring or distant*,[1] but I trust that they may yet learn that Nicaragua claims to control her own destiny and does not require other nationalities to make treaties concerning her territory without asking her advice and consent."

Here we have a distinct thrust at England and the United States, who were then wrangling over the interpretation of the Clayton-Bulwer treaty and assuming the right to fix the boundaries of Nicaragua without consulting that republic. But the president's determination to maintain the dignity and sovereignty of his adopted country meant more than this, as the sequel will show. He was dreaming of creating a new federal government, embracing the whole of Central America and including Cuba, while many of his most faithful followers thought that they were

[1] Italics are mine.

working to bring Nicaragua into the family of great States in the North.

Walker delivered his address in English, though he could speak Spanish indifferently well, and as his audience was composed largely of natives, his Cuban aide, Colonel Lainé, followed him and read the address in Spanish and with better rhetorical effect than could be shown by its author. After the reading of the address a presidential salute of twenty-one guns was fired, and the procession headed for the church, where a *Te Deum* wás sung.[1] An inaugural banquet followed the ceremonies. In keeping with Walker's temperate habits only light wines were served, but as there were fifty persons present and fifty-three toasts were drunk, conviviality must not have been lacking. Walker proposed a toast to the President of the United States; Hornsby offered one to "Uncle Billy," at which Walker is said to have laughed heartily — an occurrence so rare as to deserve recording.

Two days later the president announced his cabinet, which he wisely constituted of Latin-Americans. Ferrer, his *fidus Achates*, became secretary of state; Mateo Pineda, equally loyal, was made secretary of war, and Manuel Carracosa secretary of hacienda. It is to be noted, however, that sub-secretaries of state and hacienda were appointed and that these were Americans. The sub-secretary of hacienda was William K. Rogers, and to him it fell to provide the forces with food, clothing, and other equipment. Orders were issued that all his commands were to be respected as if issued by the head of the department, and in executing his duties, which soon came to be mainly foraging and paying in scrip for the supplies thus taken, Rogers came to be regarded as a scourge upon the country. His was a thankless task, but he did the work well.

After providing this machinery of government, Walker next

---

[1] A full account of the inauguration is contained in a supplement to *El Nicaraguense* of July 19.

gave his attention to securing money and inducing immigration. The confiscation and sale of the estates of those who, since the treaty of October 23, had assisted the known enemies of the republic was ordered by a decree of July 16. A board of commissioners was appointed to conduct the seizure of such property. Within ten days after the seizure lists of the property were to be published in *El Nicaraguense* and the owners cited to appear within forty days and show cause why it should not be sold on the account of the State. After notification the property was to be sold to the highest bidder and might be purchased either with cash or with military scrip. A board of appraisers was to fix the value of each parcel offered for sale, and no bid of less than two-thirds of this valuation was to be accepted.[1] This plan afforded a means for redeeming military scrip and thus destroying one evidence of the republic's indebtedness. It also was designed to tempt American investments in the country by offering good lands at an upset price far below their value. The issue of *El Nicaraguense* for September 27 contained a list of confiscated property to be sold on January 1, 1857, on the plaza in Granada. Between forty and fifty farms in the department of Rivas, valued at from three hundred to one thousand dollars each, and over one hundred pieces of other property — houses, stock ranches, cocoa, indigo, sugar and coffee estates, and plantain walks — with a total valuation of $753,000, were advertised.[2] Such proceedings naturally alarmed every property-holder in the State, and in themselves were sufficient to have precipitated another revolution.

There was further legislation designed to be highly advantageous to prospective American landowners. On July 14 a decree was promulgated declaring that "all documents connected with public affairs shall be of equal value, whether written in English

---

[1] *El Nicaraguense*, July 19, 1856.
[2] See also *Dublin Review*, XLIII, 375; *Putnam's Monthly*, IX., 431; and New York *Herald*, Oct. 19, 1856.

or Spanish." This made it possible for all the proceedings of courts and recording of deeds to be made in the English language, and would eventually give Americans a decided advantage over natives in litigation over land titles. Another decree was issued requiring all land titles to be registered within the space of six months. The ostensible reason for this decree was that such titles were in a state of great confusion, due to their never having been registered. The registry system, however, was unknown to the native and very familiar to the American, who thus secured a great advantage. Walker says: "The general tendency of these several decrees was the same. They were intended to place a large portion of the land of the country in the hands of the white race. The military force of the State might, for a time, secure the Republic, but in order that their possession might be permanent, it was requisite for them to hold the land." [1]

On July 31, 1856, Walker decreed a new tariff law, alleging that the former regulations failed to give the desired results from either a commercial or a fiscal point of view. Flour, meats, lard, crockery, potatoes, agricultural implements, books, bells, church organs, baggage and furniture for personal use, and seeds, plants, and animals designed to improve the breeds of the country were placed on the free list. Spirituous liquors and tobacco were subjected to specific duties, and all other commodities to an *ad valorem* duty of twenty per cent. Nicaragua had no infant industries to protect, and the tariff was for revenue only. Three open ports were recognized: Realejo, San Juan del Sur, and Greytown. To avoid international complications, however, the custom-house of the last named port was established in Granada and the goods passing through the port were inspected on their way up the river at Castillo Viejo.[2]

Other sources of income were the receipts from the sale of licenses to general retailers and to manufacturers of aguardiente

---

[1] *War in Nicaragua*, 253–4.   [2] *El Nicaraguense*, Aug. 9, 1856.

(the national alcoholic beverage). The expenses of course were far in excess of the government's income, and current expenses were met by issues of scrip at seven per cent, but later issues bore no interest. The value fluctuated between five and ten cents on the dollar. In addition to scrip, the principal currency seen in Nicaragua at this time consisted of small coin in the form of dimes, half-dimes, and francs. Perhaps three-fourths of the coin was dimes. In trading a distinction was always made between the dollar (*dinero*) and the strong dollar (*dinero fuerto*). The former was the dollar of the country, and passed as the equivalent of eight American dimes; the latter was the equivalent of the American dollar of ten dimes.[1]

August 20, 1856, was a momentous day in Walker's administration, for it was then that the Hon. Pierre Soulé arrived in Granada. Early in June Rivas had issued a decree authorizing

[1] *El Nicaraguense*, May 3, 1856. The following is the form (not a facsimile) in which Walker's scrip was issued:

MILITARY SCRIP	*No. 919* *FIFTY DOLLARS* *$50*		**FIFTY DOLLARS**

No. 919   FIFTY DOLLARS $50

THE REPUBLIC OF NICARAGUA

is indebted to *J. H. Marshall* in the sum of

FIFTY DOLLARS

for military services rendered to the State

In witness whereof we have hereunto set our names and affixed the great seal of the Republic, at the city of Granada, this 30th day of August, 1856.

Wm. Walker
          President of the Republic

F. Ferrer
      Minister of Hacienda

El Nicaraguense Print

Across the face of this paper the names of Rogers, Register, and Alex Jones, Paymaster, were written with a pen.

a loan, to be secured by the public lands of the State.   The ostensible object of Soulé's visit was to secure certain modifications in this decree so as to make the loan practicable.   In this he was successful, for on August 28 a new decree was issued authorizing a loan of $500,000 for twenty years at six per cent, secured by one million acres of public lands.   Messrs. M. Pilcher and S. F. Slatter of New Orleans were constituted agents for negotiating the loan, and arrangements were made for payment of the interest at the Bank of Louisiana.   Pilcher and Slatter were also made agents for the sale of public lands in Nicaragua.   The only bonds that Walker's government ever disposed of were sold through this agency.

But this was by no means the only result of Soulé's visit.   He was of foreign birth, but more Southern than most of the Southerners themselves, and being a man with magnificent visions he managed to impress some of his views upon Walker and to inspire many changes in the latter's programme.   This is seen in a series of decrees issued by Walker during September, 1856.   On the 5th there came a decree against vagrants.   Persons without visible means of support and who refrained for fifteen days from seeking employment were to be adjudged guilty of vagrancy and sentenced to forced labour on public works from one to six months. On the next day came a decree concerning labour contracts.   Any contract made for labour for a term of months or years was declared binding on the parties thereto, and any failure on the part of the labourer to fulfil the terms would render him liable to a sentence to forced labour on public works.

These decrees were a logical outcome of the efforts to secure American investments in Nicaraguan lands.   The lands would be worthless to the new owners unless they could secure labour. It was inconceivable that American landholders in a tropical country should till their own fields.   If the natives would not work, they should be made to work by means of vagrancy and labour-contract laws. The ultimate result would be the establishment of a system of peonage. It would depress the poor native but would regenerate the country economically by the introduction of capital and superior managerial ability. These, however, were not the only available means for the regeneration of the country, and it was doubtful if their utilization alone would effect any considerable change in the existing social and economic order. A more certain supply of labour could be secured only by the reintroduction of African slavery. On the 22d of September, therefore, Walker went a step farther and issued the following decree:

"Article 1. All acts and decrees of the Federal Constituent Assembly, as well as of the Federal Congress, are declared null and void.

"Article 2. Nothing herein contained shall affect rights heretofore vested under the acts and decrees hereby repealed." [1]

The purpose of this curiously worded decree was the reëstablishment of slavery in Nicaragua. It did not actually restore the institution, but prepared the way for it. From 1824 to 1838 Nicaragua had been a member of the federation of Central American States, and upon the dissolution of this union all Federal acts and decrees not inconsistent with the Nicaraguan constitution then adopted were declared to be still in force. Among the acts thus remaining in force was one providing for the abolition of slavery. The decree of September 22 sponged from the slate all the old Federal enactments, but the chief end and aim of the measure was to make slavery no longer unlawful in Nicaragua.

When Walker issued this decree he was confronted with a hostile alliance of the Central American States, and he felt the need of bringing his cause more closely into the sympathies of a large portion of the American people. The reëstablishment of

---

[1] MS., Department of State, Bureau of Indexes and Archives, Despatches, Nicaraguan Legation, II.; *War in Nicaragua*, 235.

slavery, therefore, would secure, in addition to the economic advantages already enumerated, the political advantage resulting from the increasing sympathy and coöperation of the Southern States which the decree would invoke. The South was well pleased with his advances. The object of the decree, he says, was "to bind the Southern States to Nicaragua as if she were one of themselves." [1] This binding, however, was not to be effected by bringing Nicaragua into the Union; for Walker, as will be shown hereafter, did not contemplate annexation to the United States. His slave republic in the tropics would have interests in many respects identical with those of the slave States of the American Union and the two regions would therefore be drawn closely together into something like an *entente cordiale*. In the event that the Union were dissolved — a matter then freely discussed — the *entente cordiale* might be succeeded by a formal alliance with the seceding States.

Walker intended not only to reëstablish slavery, but to revive the African slave trade. In fact, from the very nature of things, the second step was essential to the achievement of the first. Slaves would not be carried to Central America from the Southern States, because the demand for negroes in the Lower South was already greater than the supply. Negroes, therefore, would have to be brought from Africa. Four years later, when Walker wrote the history of his career in Nicaragua, he declared that he expected but little opposition to his plan of reviving the slave trade from either England or France. "The frenzy of the British public against the slave trade," he says, "has exhausted itself, and men have begun to perceive that they were led into error by the benevolent enthusiasm of parsons who knew more about Greek and Hebrew than they did about physiology and political economy, and of middle-aged spinsters, smit with the love of general humanity, though disdaining to fix their affections on any objects

[1] *War in Nicaragua*, 263.

less remote than Africa."[1] He knew too that the French Emperor was desirous of increasing the maritime importance of his empire, and he dreamed of negotiating a treaty that should lead to the employment of French bottoms for bringing "African apprentices" to the ports of Nicaragua, "thus furnishing labour to the latter republic, and increasing the trade of French ships."[2] These dreams bear unmistakable evidence of having been inspired by Soulé. It must be borne in mind, however, that Walker never actually introduced slavery into the country. The decree of September 22 was intended only to prepare the way and give notice to the Southern States that his sympathies were with them, as he and they were contending in a common cause. Before planters and their slaves would come to the country it would have to be pacified; the other hostile Central American States would have to be conquered, or appeased; and the new régime in Nicaragua would have to secure recognition as the government *de facto* and *de jure*. Questions of war and diplomacy therefore took precedence over slavery and other economic problems.[3]

It was of prime importance that Walker should secure the recognition of his government by foreign powers, and especially by the United States. In the case of the latter country his wishes were gratified sooner, perhaps, than he had expected. Shortly after the reception of Vijil in Washington Mr. Marcy ordered Wheeler to establish diplomatic relations with the Nicaraguan government.[4] While these instructions were on their way the government changed hands, and the situation when Wheeler received the communication was entirely different from that contemplated by Marcy when he issued it. This would have caused

[1] *War in Nicaragua*, 270.   [2] *Ibid.*, 269.

[3] Montúfar, whose work embodies the enlightened Central American opinion of Walker, attributes his plan of confiscation, contract labour, and slavery, to American race prejudice; Americans were accustomed to white domination at home and were resolved to extend it to Nicaragua. *Walker en Centro-América*, 597–600.

[4] MS., Department of State, Bureau of Indexes and Archives, American States, Instructions to Ministers, XV., 264–5.

any minister possessing ordinary discretion to wait until his government could be acquainted with the new conditions, but Wheeler was too warm a friend of Walker's to let such an opportunity slip. Walker and Wheeler had been neighbours in Granada, and for a long time they had paid each other daily visits, though diplomatic relations between the United States and Nicaragua at the time were suspended.[1] In this matter the American minister showed weakness and allowed Walker to use him as a tool to give dignity to his venture. Wheeler now loosely interpreted his instructions from Marcy as an order to recognize Walker as president, and on July 17, just five days after the latter's inauguration, Wheeler notified him that Marcy had authorized the recognition of "the existing government in Nicaragua." The 19th was selected as the day for Wheeler's formal reception by the new president, and no pains were spared to make the ceremonies impressive. Ferrer, the secretary of state, accompanied by a band of music and a company of soldiers, proceeded to Wheeler's residence and escorted him through the streets to the executive headquarters. Arriving there, Wheeler delivered a platitudinous oration, but in one particular he broke over the bounds of diplomatic propriety by declaring that "the government of the United States hopes to unite cordially with you in the fixed purpose of preventing any foreign power that may attempt to impede its (Nicaragua's) progress by any interference whatever. The great voice of the nation has spoken. Its words must not be unheeded."[2]

Walker had to choose a new minister to the United States to take the place left vacant by the return of Father Vijil. His choice for the place was Appleton Oaksmith, an American who had been in the country only about three weeks. He had come down on the same steamer on which Father Vijil had made his return trip, and went back on the steamer that followed, having

---

[1] Wheeler Scrapbook no. 4, p. 224.
[2] *El Nicaraguense*, July 26, 1856; Wheeler Scrapbook no. 4, p. 131.

been in Granada itself a little less than a fortnight. There was a reason why he should have been honoured so signally by Walker on such a short acquaintance. He had coöperated with Goicouria in securing aid late in 1855 and early in 1856, and among other things had been the moving spirit in promoting the big Walker meeting in New York City on May 23, which has already been described. He was reputed to have wealth and influence, and it was thought that he could assist in raising a loan for the new government, this being before the arrangements made between Walker and Soulé. Oaksmith was a native of Portland, Maine, had visited Nicaragua in 1850, before the Transit was opened, and had travelled extensively in Central and South America and in Africa and the Orient. On August 15 Oaksmith notified Marcy of his arrival in Washington and presented his credentials from President Walker.[1] Marcy notified him, four weeks later, that owing to the condition of political affairs in Nicaragua the President could not receive him. Oaksmith on September 18 asked for explicit reasons why he was rejected, and was told that if the President deemed it proper to give explanations they would be made only to the government which had asked to have him received.[2] As no explanation could be made to a government which the administration had refused to recognize, the matter was closed.

It will be recalled that Rivas, after declaring Walker deposed from command, had revoked the power of Father Vijil as minister to the United States and designated Antonio José de Irisarri as the representative of his government. Irisarri was already accredited as the minister from Guatemala and San Salvador, but

---

[1] Walker's letter to Pierce accrediting Oaksmith was filled with pious phraseology: "God grant a continuance of a happy harmony between two sister republics linked in the same continental cause. God preserve you, many years for the happiness of your citizens." MS., Department of State, Bureau of Indexes and Archives, Notes, Central American Legations, II.

[2] MS., Department of State, Bureau of Indexes and Archives, Diplomatic Correspondence, Nicaragua, I., 116-7.

Pierce refused to receive him in the additional capacity of representative of Nicaragua. It was uncertain, Marcy informed him on October 28, which party actually possessed civil authority in Nicaragua, or whether either of them was entitled to recognition as the *de facto* government. Recognition would involve a decision as to the merits of the controversy between Rivas and Walker, and this the President did not feel prepared to make.[1] While the Rivas government could make no formal representations to the American government, it published at Leon a protest against Wheeler's recognition of Walker as president and demanded that the American minister be recalled.[2]

Marcy was sorely vexed when he learned that Wheeler had interpreted his instructions to recognize the existing government as an authorization to establish diplomatic relations with Walker, and on September 18 he ordered Wheeler to come home, stating that there was no need of a minister in a country while official relations with it were suspended. Wheeler reached Washington in November and had a long conversation with the Secretary of State, who expressed emphatic disapproval of the minister's conduct during the preceding twelve months. Wheeler's visit to Corral in October, 1855, as an emissary of Walker, his recognition of the Rivas-Walker government in the same month without instructions from the State Department, and his subsequent recognition of Walker as president had practically fixed his fate with Marcy. But even while the letter calling the minister home was en route to Granada there came a despatch from Wheeler announcing Walker's decree with regard to slavery and highly commending it. This proved the proverbial straw that broke the back of the camel, and Marcy ended the conference by expressing his displeasure at this despatch and asking Wheeler to

[1] MS., Department of State, Bureau of Indexes and Archives, Diplomatic Correspondence, Central America, I., 119.
[2] New York *Herald*, Dec. 1, 1856.

resign. This request was several times repeated, but Wheeler did not submit his resignation until March 2, 1857.[1] This was just two days before Marcy retired with the rest of the Pierce administration.

On the same steamer that conveyed Wheeler back to the United States was the faithful Fermin Ferrer, designated as the new minister of Walker to the United States to succeed Oaksmith. The obstinate resistance of Marcy to further relations with the new régime was now so apparent that the friends of Walker advised against the risk of another rebuff, which was bound to strengthen the opposition to his cause in Central America, and Ferrer never presented his credentials. The departure of Wheeler and Ferrer to the United States and of Vijil to New Granada, all in the same month, was a serious loss to Walker.

Walker made another diplomatic venture on August 12 in the appointment of Domingo de Goicouria as minister to the Court of St. James. The minister designate, however, had proceeded no farther than New York before he quarrelled with his chief and severed his relations with the Nicaraguan government. The events leading up to this quarrel and the outcome form an interesting and important part of Walker's history. Goicouria was the son of a well-to-do Cuban merchant, and had lived in England during his early manhood as agent of his father's business. Here he imbibed liberal sympathies, which caused him to be deported to Spain by the captain-general of Cuba. Shortly thereafter he came to the United States, and resided for a time in Mississippi, where he worked with Lopez in planning the liberation of his native land. Lopez made his invasion of Cuba against Goicouria's advice, and the disastrous outcome revealed the soundness of the latter's judgment. In 1853 Goicouria be-

[1] MS., Department of State, Bureau of Indexes and Archives, Nicaragua Legation, II.; American States, Instructions to Ministers, XV., 264-5, 279-82.

came associated with General John A. Quitman in a new expedition planned on a much larger scale, but destined to be still-born. At the time of Walker's invasion of Nicaragua Goicouria was in New York, where he lived in handsome style, and with his amiable, conciliatory manners and plain common sense he won a large number of friends. He was then fifty-six years old and wore a long, flowing grey beard, which he is said to have vowed never to shave until his native country was freed from the Spanish yoke. He did not desire that Cuba should follow the example of the Central American States, but thought that its best interests lay in annexation to the American Union.

Walker's enterprise in Nicaragua especially interested the Cuban patriot, because it seemed to offer an opportunity to invade Cuba from a better vantage point than could be secured in the United States. If the Cuban volunteers could be transported to Nicaragua in the guise of regular passengers on the steamers of the Transit Company, they could be mustered there for an invasion of the island without the interference of that bugbear of all filibusters, the American neutrality laws.

Accordingly, in December, 1855, Goicouria sent an agent to Walker in the person of Captain Francisco Alejandro Lainé, who had himself achieved considerable note as a Cuban "liberator." The filibuster chief listened gladly to Lainé's proposals, and on January 11, 1855, he entered into a written agreement with him by which Walker and Goicouria were to pool interests. The articles of agreement stipulated that the Cuban revolutionists should amalgamate their material resources with those of Walker and aid him in "consolidating the peace and the government of the Republic of Nicaragua." After this was accomplished, Walker was to "assist and coöperate with his person and with his various resources, such as men and others, in the cause of Cuba and in favour of her liberty." [1] Goicouria approved the contract and

[1] Montúfar, 208–9.

prepared at once to go to Nicaragua. He secured two hundred and fifty recruits, mostly foreigners, for Walker's service; and the American financier, Cornelius Vanderbilt, who had recently become president of the Transit Company, agreed to advance the cost of their passage.[1]

It was one of the strange ironies of fate that Vanderbilt authorized Goicouria to draw on him for the transportation of these men just at the time that Walker decided to expel the Vanderbilt interests from Central America. The steamer bearing these recruits and the steamer bringing the news of the revocation of the Transit Company's charter passed each other en route. Goicouria and his men reached Granada on March 9, 1856, and it was with amazement that the Cuban patriot then learned that the filibuster commander had bearded Vanderbilt, a man of terrible vindictiveness and with millions to spend in gratifying his passion for revenge. Goicouria felt that Walker had not only killed the goose that laid the golden egg, but had done even worse by creating a powerful enemy in the person of the owner of the fowl. He remained true to his promise, however, and during the coming weeks gave faithful service in the war with Costa Rica, being commisssioned as a brigadier-general. About fifty other Cuban revolutionists joined Walker's army, and the commander made of them a guard of honour. Lainé became one of Walker's aides-de-camp, with the rank of lieutenant-colonel.[2]

On June 21 Goicouria left Granada for the United States preparatory to going to England, but with instructions first to use his influence in negotiating a loan in the States. He landed at New Orleans on July 13, but seeing no prospects there for the sale of bonds, he delegated the work to two agents and proceeded to New York, where he hoped to find a better market for the Nicaraguan securities. During all this time Goicouria had received no inkling of Walker's final purposes, and before leaving

---

[1] Walker, *War in Nicaragua*, 156, 179.   [2] *Ibid.*, 190-1.

Q

New Orleans he wrote to his chief asking for information concerning the form of government that would eventually be established in Nicaragua, so that he, as Walker's minister, could give proper assurances to the European governments. In doing this he violated none of the official proprieties, but he made the fatal blunder of going farther and giving the filibuster leader some unsought advice as to the form of government that should be inaugurated. He did even more, and criticised the Transit deal with Morgan and Garrison, alleging that they should not receive a monopoly of traffic on the San Juan River and Lake Nicaragua, as this violated the principles of free commerce. He suggested that the grantees should receive only the privileges of handling the transisthmian traffic, for which they should pay in accordance with the passengers and tonnage conveyed, and that the revenues of the government from this source should be pledged as security for the contemplated loan.

On reaching New York and consulting with capitalists there, Goicouria became fully convinced that the loan could not be negotiated so long as Walker had to reckon with Vanderbilt as an enemy. Financiers declared that investments in enterprises which he was antagonizing were extra-hazardous. The final arrangements with Morgan and Garrison for inaugurating their new transportation service between the Atlantic and Pacific ports by way of Nicaragua had not yet been completed, and Randolph was still in New York in consultation with them over the details of the contract when Goicouria arrived. It was commonly reported that Randolph was to be paid handsomely for his part in the deal, and the Cuban idealist was surprised and pained that anyone should use his friendship with Walker for the purpose of making money. He notified Walker that the new grantees could never, from their limited resources, carry out the agreement in any way advantageous to the cause, and he even went to the point of consulting his old patron Vanderbilt to learn whether he were not willing to reëstablish his ships in the Nicaraguan service if his former privileges were restored.

Vanderbilt proved amenable, and offered to advance one hundred thousand dollars the day his first ship should sail for Nicaragua, and to pay a hundred and fifty thousand more during the course of the year. Goicouria was enthusiastic. Here was the chance to secure the funds so greatly needed by the filibuster régime, and at the same time to obtain an adequate transportation service and to convert a dreaded enemy into a friend and patron. For all his labour and pains in this matter, however, the Cuban did not get so much as a "thank you" from his chief. Walker's reply to his proposals was frigid: "You will please not trouble yourself further about the Transit Company. As to anything you say about Mr. Randolph, it is entirely thrown away on me. . . . As the government has given you no powers, you cannot of course promise anything in its behalf." [1]

The filibuster leader thus threw away his last chance to make friends with Vanderbilt and redeem the greatest blunder of his career. Goicouria was old enough to be Walker's father, and had had much greater practical experience in both filibustering and business. Walker could ill afford to ignore his advice, and his rebuff to his envoy had the effect of still further embittering Vanderbilt, who might otherwise have championed his cause. The only commendable feature of this act is Walker's loyalty to his friend Randolph.

The censorious note from his chief caused Goicouria no little chagrin, and shook his confidence in the sagacity of the filibuster. Just at this time Walker's new minister to the United States, Appleton Oaksmith, presented his credentials to Secretary Marcy, who, as previously stated, declined to receive him, as the stability of Walker's government then seemed questionable.[2] Goicouria

[1] New York *Herald*, Nov. 29, 1856.

[2] MS., Department of State, Bureau of Indexes and Archives, Nicaragua, Diplomatic Correspondence, I., 116–7; Central America Legations, Notes to Dept., II.

thought it useless to expect recognition from the hostile British government when the more friendly American government declined to receive a Nicaraguan minister, and therefore notified Walker that he should postpone going to England until some notable success had been achieved in Nicaragua against the coalition of Central American States which had just declared war on the filibuster government. Walker, with the manner of a martinet, always demanded blind obedience to his orders, and was seldom open to suggestions from any one. To him Goicouria's attitude was little less than lese majesty, and he notified the latter that if he would not go on his mission, some one else would be sent in his place.[1]

Certain stories had already been circulating at filibuster headquarters to the effect that the Cuban was an agent in the hire of Vanderbilt. Walker attached no credit to them at the time, but Goicouria's avowed championship of Vanderbilt's schemes now caused him to grow exceedingly suspicious, and he communicated these suspicions to his minister in a very blunt manner. The accusation drew from the Cuban an angry protest. His sole object in seeking to reëstablish relations with the Vanderbilt company, he said, was to raise "abundant pecuniary supplies, so as to enable you to meet your immediate necessities and sustain an American immigration, and also to put a stop to a powerful opposition which already has caused you much difficulty and even loss of reputation." The envoy declared that everything that he had done had been met with reproach and recrimination, and that he had been addressed uncourteously and in a style of authority, whereas he regarded himself as a man of independent character. Moreover, the news of Walker's slavery decree, which had just arrived, compelled him to persevere in his determination not to go to London; for England would never look with favour upon such a retrograde step. "You have shut your eyes to the truth,"

[1] New York *Herald*, Nov. 29, 1856.

declared the angry Cuban, "whether it is that you look upon yourself as divinely infallible, and are determined to pursue your
course at all hazards, or whether it is that a third party has filled
your mind with false suggestions, . . . I cannot now in any way
continue my connection with you."

This quarrel between the filibuster chief and his erstwhile ally
was of course unknown to the general public, and the first inkling
of trouble appeared in Walker's newspaper, *El Nicaraguense*, which
contained a brief statement that Brigadier-General Goicouria had
been dropped from the roll of the Nicaraguan army. In the
United States, where interest in the Nicaraguan situation was now
very keen, this news evoked much comment and speculation in
the newspapers as to the causes of this breach between Walker
and his strongest supporter. Goicouria satisfied the public curi-
osity by publishing a portion of his correspondence with Walker,
the substance of which has been given in the preceding paragraphs.
Friends of Walker now came to his defence and accused Goicouria
of being an agent in the employ of Vanderbilt and of seeking to
compass Walker's destruction.[1] Randolph published a card in
which he said, "In the Transit business Don Domingo de Goicouria is an intruder, with a dishonest and treacherous intent,
and knowing the import of the language I use, I shall remain at
the Washington Hotel, No. 1 Broadway, until one o'clock to-
morrow, and longer if it is the pleasure of Don Domingo de Goicouria." [2] As Randolph was then confined to his bed from an
illness he had contracted during his visit to Nicaragua, there
was of course no duel.

The Cuban, however, had shrewdly withheld his most important letters to and from Walker until the latter's defenders had
exhausted their ammunition in repelling his first attack. He

---

[1] Nicaraguan filibusters and Cuban revolutionists aired their grievances and
washed their dirty linen in the New York newspapers during the latter half of
November, 1856. The *Herald* gives the most attention to this controversy.

[2] New York *Herald*, Nov. 22, 1856.

now published further correspondence that was calculated seriously to embarrass large numbers of Walker's friends in the United States. On August 12, 1856, Walker had instructed his envoy as to the policy he should pursue while minister to Great Britain: "With your versatility, and if I may use the term, adaptability, I expect much to be done in England. You can do more than any American could possibly accomplish, because you can make the British cabinet see that we are not engaged in any scheme for annexation. You can make them see that the only way to cut the expanding and expansive democracy of the North is by a powerful and compact Southern federation, based on military principles." [1] This was a heavy blow to the devotees of "manifest destiny," who had been expecting some day to shake the hand of William Walker as Senator from Nicaragua. But this letter of Walker contained another hard jolt for the ardent expansionists: "Tell —— —— he must send me the news and let me know whether *Cuba must and shall be free, but not for the Yankees.* Oh, no! that fine country is not fit for those barbarous Yankees. What would such a psalm-singing set do in the island?" [2]

One may imagine the shock which these words gave to Goicouria. During the past six months he had regarded his time, means, and energy as expended in an effort eventually to bring Cuba into the American Union, and now he was informed that this fine island was not to be for the Yankees! On the contrary, he was labouring for "a powerful and compact federation, based on military principles." Such language did not augur well for Cuba's real freedom, and it is not surprising that Goicouria severed his connection with Walker in much disgust.[3]

---

[1] New York *Herald*, Nov. 24, 1856; New York *Sun*, Nov. 24, 1856.

[2] *Ibid.* Italics are mine.

[3] In his final communication on this subject Goicouria utterly repudiated Walker with these words: "I therefore denounce Mr. Walker as a man wanting in the first element of every kind of ability, namely, good faith. I denounce him as wanting in ordinary sagacity and discretion. I denounce him as false to the interests as well of Cuba as of the United States."

Americans, and especially those in the North, read Walker's letter concerning Cuba with amazement. They got here a first glimpse of his real plans. Instead of introducing American principles and institutions into the country, he really designed to set up a military despotism entirely at variance with the democracy of the United States and a barrier to its further expansion southward. Hitherto Walker's Northern friends had had visions of Nicaragua's becoming a prosperous State, offering a new market for their manufactures and an inviting field for their capital; and they had looked upon events in that country as the beginning of a movement that eventually would open the entire isthmus to American trade and industrial enterprise, and perhaps would bring this region into the Union. The decree of September 22, 1856, revoking the laws against slavery, had by no means alienated all of Walker's Northern supporters, because such a measure had been taken for granted. In the United States there were few at this time who regarded the tropics as an inviting field for free labour, and many anti-slavery leaders oppposed the Walker enterprise because they deemed the expansion of the domain of slavery an inevitable result of its success. Slavery, many Northerners believed, would follow the American invasion of Nicaragua as naturally as would the English language. But Walker's plan to build up a great State that would be a rival of their own country, with aims and institutions diametrically opposed to theirs, gave his Northern friends pause and soon destroyed all their sympathies with his undertaking.

That the revelation of the filibuster's real motives did not also alienate his Southern supporters is to be explained by the fact that the publication of the Goicouria correspondence followed close on the heels of the decree opening the way for the reëstablishment of slavery. The South was then entering upon the final scene in its long struggle to preserve "the equilibrium of the Union," and was coming to see that it was conducting a losing fight. Southern leaders were beginning to perceive that the existing Territories were most probably destined to become free States, and that the balance of power between the South and the constantly growing North was soon to be destroyed. Those with clear vision foresaw "the irrepressible conflict," and believed that some day the Southern States would be constrained to leave the Union, and that they might possibly form an alliance with the Spanish-American countries to the southward to check possible aggression from the republic of the North. They cared little, therefore, about Walker's repudiation of annexation to a Union that they believed to be short-lived; but they were intensely interested in his plan to create a new slave republic. In the event of secession, a powerful military federation in Central America, with slavery as its cornerstone, would prove a most valuable ally. No man in the South held more advanced ideas along this line than Pierre Soulé, and his visit to Nicaragua in August seems to have had the effect of crystallizing the policy of Walker, so far as Cuba, annexation, and slavery were concerned.[1]

The slight extent to which Walker confided in others as to his real motives is aptly illustrated by the conduct of his officers at a birthday party given August 15, 1856, in honour of Colonel Frank Anderson, one of the "fifty-six" and one of Walker's most trusted officers. The toasts proposed indicate their opinion of Walker's purposes: "To General Walker. May he live to see Nicaragua annexed to the United States." "The American Eagle. May she drop her feathers on Nicaragua." This was only three days after their leader had written to Goicouria repudiating annexation. That he took no advice in sending Goicouria on such an errand to England is also evident. The London *Post*, after the correspondence had been made public in England, was puzzled that Walker should so misjudge the English as to suppose that they would become his partners in further slavery ex-

[1] Montúfar, 562.

tension after they had already expended so many millions to get rid of it.[1]

As has been shown in a previous chapter, shortly after Walker's arrival in Nicaragua the American press proclaimed that he went there in the interests of the Transit Company. Later, when he repealed the restrictions against slavery, some journals of the United States were equally sure that such an act was the whole intent and purpose of his expedition. Yet Walker went to Nicaragua neither as the agent of capitalists nor as the tool of slavery propagandists. It is probably his book, *The War in Nicaragua*, written in 1860, when he was preparing to set out on what proved to be his last filibustering expedition, that has led many historians to regard the establishment of slavery as the chief end of Walker's undertaking, rather than a means of attaining another end.[2] In this book, which appeared on the eve of the Civil War, Walker poses as a would-be saviour of the South. If he succeeded in his proposed effort to regain his place in Central America, it would be with Southern support alone. His strong pro-slavery attitude in one chapter of his book has caused him to be depicted as an almost fanatical apostle of slavery propagandism, the very antithesis of John Brown, the apostle of abolition. As a matter of fact, Walker entertained no very strong views on the slavery question. His pro-slavery arguments in his work reveal no real conviction on the part of their author. They are merely a strong bid for Southern support in his newest scheme. At the end of the chapter the reader feels inclined to exclaim that the writer "doth protest too much." Walker was not descended from a slave-holding ancestry; his editorial work in New Orleans showed him to be conservative on the slavery question; in California he supported Broderick, who

[1] Wheeler Scrapbook no. 4, 180.

[2] Professor L. M. Keasbey, in his *Nicaragua Canal and the Monroe Doctrine*, 246 (New York, 1896), says, after describing the final collapse of Walker's enterprise, "the slavery question was at the bottom of it all!" This is an illustration of the mistaking of a means for an end.

was no friend of the institution, against Gwin, the champion of Southern interests. He even admits in his work that when he published his slavery decree he was unaware of the strong feeling against slavery that had slowly crystallized in the North. He had left the Atlantic States six years previously, and during this time anti-slavery views had come to be taught in Northern schools and preached from Northern pulpits without his knowledge. Even had he known this, he says, his conduct would have been the same, as he issued the decree from a sense of sacred duty. His confession of ignorance of the increasing anti-slavery sentiment is interesting, indicating that he had given very little attention to the slavery question in the United States, at least in the years since 1850, and tending to bear out the preceding statement that Walker was no true apostle of slavery extension.

It is important to note in this connection that a large part of the filibuster's following came from the free States, and thence came also many of his most trusted officers. Byron Cole, the immediate promoter of the expedition, was a New Englander. So were Joseph W. Fabens and Appleton Oaksmith, colonizing and diplomatic agents respectively. Colonel Frank Anderson and Captains O'Keefe, McArdle, DeWitt Clinton, and Williamson were from New York. James C. Jamison, one of Walker's lieutenants, states that he conversed freely of conditions in Nicaragua and of the plans and ambitions of the leaders with such men as Generals Fry, Sanders, Henningsen, Hornsby, and others, and never heard it intimated at any time that slavery was a cause of Walker's going to that country.[1]

What, then, were Walker's real motives? Briefly, he planned to create out of five Central American republics a strong federated State organized and governed on military principles; and after achieving this he aimed to effect the conquest of Cuba. To aid in the work of conquest and in the subsequent "regener-

[1] Jamison, *With Walker in Nicaragua*, 96–102.

ation" of the isthmus and island, he purposed to introduce an American population and to secure to it the possession of the land. Next he proposed to afford the new masters of the soil the privilege of cultivating their lands by slave labour if they so desired. He was doubtful indeed whether any other form of labour were adaptable to the tropics, and was of course not unmindful of the sympathy which his slavery policy would evoke for his cause in the Southern States. Finally, as the capstone of his system, he planned to make the dream of an interoceanic canal come true, and thus to bind his new government to the powerful maritime nations of the world by the strong ties of commerce. It should be added that over this tropical federation Walker himself proposed to play the rôle of dictator. What we have seen him doing so far he regarded as only preparatory to entering upon his really constructive work.

CHAPTER XVI

THE FILIBUSTER ARMY AND NAVY

WALKER's loss of Goicouria, Ferrer, Vijil, and Wheeler was somewhat offset by the arrival in October of Charles Frederick Henningsen with arms and munitions of war. The coming of this famous soldier to Nicaragua infused new life into the filibuster cause. He was made brigadier-general in place of Goicouria and was assigned to the special duty of organizing the artillery and instructing the men in the use of the Minié rifle. Henningsen was a soldier of world renown. Born in England of Swedish parents, he enlisted at seventeen to serve Don Carlos in Navarre and the Basque provinces under the partizan leader, Zumalacarregui. He attained the rank of colonel while still in his teens and soon attracted attention as a writer on military subjects by his *History of the War in Spain*. After being wounded and captured, he was paroled on condition of not serving again during the war, and then entered the Russian army and saw service in Circassia. His report on the Caucasian countries was published by the Russian government. He next repaired to Hungary, only to find the cause of independence lost, and he followed Kossuth to America. He had charge of the first Minié rifles ever constructed in the United States. Literature had also occupied his attention during this period, and he published volumes of personal recollections and on Russian life, and even essayed the rôle of a novelist. All his serious works still have substantial value.

When he came to America Henningsen was still a young man, and proved susceptible to the charms of a Georgia widow whom he met in Washington. She was a woman of means, and her husband might now have beaten his sword into a ploughshare and settled down to a life of leisure on a Southern plantation. But news from Nicaragua aroused his interest. Like the warhorse of old, he sniffed the battle from afar, whence ensued much tugging at the domestic halter. Walker's friends urged him to go, but it did not require much persuasion. Henningsen and his wife were residing at the time in New York and were close friends of the noted capitalist and steamship magnate, George Law. The latter had purchased several thousand United States army muskets, and is said to have offered them to Kossuth. He had caused a large number of these to be converted into Minié rifles, under Henningsen's direction, and when Henningsen decided to go to Nicaragua Law equipped him liberally with rifles, howitzers, and ammunition, and this donation was supplemented by a contribution from Mrs. Henningsen, so that the full value of equipment was estimated at thirty thousand dollars.[1]

The entrance of George Law into the field as another capitalistic promoter of filibustering brings up anew the vexing problem of control of the Transit. Law had a live interest in everything concerning steamships. He had established the first line between New York and Chagres, and for a time had managed a line also between Panama and San Francisco, being a keen competitor of the Pacific Mail Company. He finally bought his competitor's business in the Atlantic and sold to his rival his business in the Pacific. He took an active part in promoting the construction of the Panama railway and also inaugurated a line of steamers between New York and Havana. These facts will explain Law's interest in the events then taking place in Central America. He had watched the quarrel between Vanderbilt and Morgan in New York, and was expecting them to neutralize each other's efforts to control the Nicaraguan Transit. He hoped in the meantime to gain Walker's favour by

[1] *Harper's Weekly*, I., 332, 333; New York *Herald*, June 2, 1856.

sending him liberal contributions of munitions of war, and when
Vanderbilt's opposition had paralyzed Morgan's further efforts
in Walker's behalf, Law would ask for a grant of the Transit
privileges and would have his right-hand man Henningsen there to
intercede in his behalf.   Goicouria, on returning to New York,
was said to have approached Law and asked for a cargo of his guns
for the Nicaraguan service, and his request was about to be granted
when Law discovered that the Cuban was also playing some sort of
a game with Vanderbilt and dropped him.[1] This three-cornered
rivalry for control of the Transit was jocularly referred to by the
press as "the war of the commodores," and it was indeed a fortunate
thing for Walker that a third party entered into the contest, for it
became the means of his developing an arm of his service which
had hitherto been neglected — the artillery.

Henningsen shortly after his arrival organized two companies
of artillery and a company of sappers and miners.   Several of the
artillery officers took great professional pride in their work and
developed much skill with the mortars and howitzers.   Henningsen
also prepared detailed instructions for the use of the new Minié
rifles which he had brought with him from New York, but he had
much to contend with in the languor and indifference of the officers,
many of whom were jealous of his sudden promotion.[2]   His real
worth, however, soon became so apparent that most of the jealous
ones became reconciled, though a few never recovered from their
resentment.

While Walker had some serious defects as a commander, the
fact that he could keep his men faithful without other pay than the
bare means of subsistence and prevent serious murmuring during
months of enforced idleness is ample proof that he possessed some
sort of military ability.   He relied almost wholly upon himself,
rarely seeking advice, and was constantly engaged from six o'clock
in the morning till ten o'clock at night.   His only relaxation while

---

[1] New York *Herald*, Nov. 26–29, 1856.   [2] Walker, *War in Nicaragua*, 301–2.

in Granada was a horseback ride in the afternoon, with an orderly
always following him. All his men yielded ready obedience, and
while they complained at times of his utter indifference to human
suffering, they felt that there was no one else to take his place and
conceded to him absolute authority. In March, 1856, when the
Costa Ricans were advancing to the frontier, Walker, it will be
remembered, lay ill for several days, and his sickness impressed
the men, as nothing else could have done, that his life was indis-
pensable to the cause. After his recovery there was great rejoicing,
and the leader was more appreciated than before.

Throughout the many vicissitudes of his career Walker always
remained quiet and imperturbable. Success never turned his head;
failure never caused him to despair. He was as calm under fire
as ever he was in the sanctum of the editor or the office of the
advocate. His manner was always characterized by extreme
simplicity. His usual garb was a blue frock coat, dark trousers,
and a slouch hat; and on going into action the coat would generally
give way to a flannel shirt. His unimpressive physique was a
constant source of surprise to visitors who had heard of his achieve-
ments but had never before seen the man, and some amusing
blunders are recorded of strangers who were expecting to meet an
entirely different sort of personage and addressed the general in a
condescending tone, deeming him some underling in Walker's
service. In spite of his lack of affectation Walker was a great
stickler for the dignity of his office, and allowed no one to offer
suggestions until his opinion was asked.[1] His sharp retort to
Doubleday, who had lived in Nicaragua for some time before the
filibusters came and had a thorough understanding of the native

---

[1] "Instead of treating us like fellow-soldiers and adventurers in danger," wrote a
deserter under the pen-name of Samuel Absalom, ". . . he bore himself like an
Eastern tyrant, — reserved and haughty, — scarcely saluting when he met us,
mixing not at all, but keeping himself close in his quarters, — some said through
fear, lest some of his own men should shoot him, of which indeed there was great
danger to such a man." *Atlantic Monthly*, IV., 665.

character, and who therefore presumed to offer unsought advice, caused this officer to leave the service and return to the United States. This attitude of the leader, however, is not to be attributed entirely to his being self-opinionated. Most of his officers were young — the average age perhaps not exceeding twenty-five — and the fact that they had come to Nicaragua was evidence in itself that they were impetuous, adventurous, and not oversupplied with discretion. Walker was now in his thirty-third year, and was one of the oldest officers in the service.

There are many stories of Walker's cruelty to his men, but with very few exceptions they emanated from foreigners and deserters. The story most widely circulated was the so-called "Address of the Seven Prisoners," purporting to have been issued May 21, 1856, by seven of his soldiers captured by the Costa Ricans at Santa Rosa. Three of the signers were Germans, one an Englishman, and the other three Americans. One of the Americans was a drummer boy, who later denied any connection with the address, which he said was brought to him by a deserter, and declared that his name had been attached after he had refused to sign it. The address was written by some one skilled in the use of English, expert in forming vindictive phrases, and withal thoroughly familiar with every detail of Walker's career in Nicaragua and with political conditions there and at home. No drummer boy or foreigner, or even a highly intelligent American citizen who had just arrived in the country, could possibly have drafted such a voluminous indictment of the filibuster enterprise. The internal evidence against its authenticity is overwhelming.[1] There is one accusation,

[1] In the address the prisoners are made to declare that as Costa Rican captives they were freer than they had ever been under Walker; that a strict censorship was maintained over all news and that only laudatory statements were allowed to go out of the country. They declared that Walker was no general, statesman, or judge of human nature, but only a most indifferent imitator of Don Quixote. They then proceed to point out seven colossal blunders in support of their assertions: (1) Walker's going to Nicaragua without map, guide, or means of subsistence, and with only fifty-six men; (2) his attempt to amalgamate the two factions; (3) then his

however, of which the filibuster leader must stand condemned. He compelled many who had gone to Nicaragua at their own expense to take their places in his ranks and serve his government, whether they had intended to enlist or not.[1] Others whose term of enlistment had expired were refused passports home, and compelled to continue in the army or starve.[2] Still others, attracted by the glowing descriptions of the country published in the United States, migrated thither with the intention of taking up lands and settling as peaceful colonists. Some of these even carried their families with them. On reaching their destination they were told that they must first serve for a year in the army.[3]

The lack of consideration which characterized Walker's treatment of the natives characterized also his treatment of his own men. The latter did not dispute his authority, and they had no idea of rebelling against the man who was their only hope. But he inspired in them none of the self-sacrificing devotion that characterizes the soldiers of a really great leader. There were some, it is true, who stood by him through nearly all his career, but they were men who enjoyed a life of danger and hardship. It must be remembered, when all is said concerning the tyranny and harshness of the commander, that he was on no holiday outing, but was engaged in a life-and-death struggle against fearful odds; and that his only reliance was in a heterogeneous group of adventurers, many of whom were desperate characters. To have sought to control such men by kindness and moral suasion would have been worse than folly; and it is much to the credit of the quiet little man that he

execution of Corral; (4) his sending of French to the United States as minister; (5) his seizure of the Transit Company's property; (6) his putting Schlessinger in command of the expedition into Costa Rica; (7) his trying to recapture Rivas on April 11 without supplying the soldiers with sufficient ammunition. The address in parts is very abusive. Wheeler Scrapbook no. 4, 149. See also New York *Herald*, Aug. 17, and other papers of this date.

[1] Such was the experience of General John T. McGrath, of Baton Rouge, La., as he related it to the writer. See also Boston *Daily Advertiser*, April 30, 1857; Wheeler Scrapbook no. 4, p. 224.

[2] Wheeler Scrapbook no. 4, 222.   [3] *Ibid.*, 224.

R

could perceive and utilize the only practicable method of discipline, the iron hand. He won no man's affection, but every man's respect.

Perhaps if the Americans had been more successful, Walker's men would have shown less inclination to submit to his exacting discipline. Much of their energy vanished under the enervating effects of the climate; much of what remained was expended in getting food, avoiding danger, and in drunken carousing. They both despised and feared the native, whom they had never really conquered, and were thus held together in a common cause. Had they gained the natives' friendship, mastered their language, obtained ample provisions, and made themselves secure in their position, Walker would have found it exceedingly difficult to maintain his absolute authority.

Climate, disease, and debauchery were the Americans' worst enemies. The energy of the rank and file varied almost inversely with the length of their sojourn in the country. Newly arrived recruits were always eager to go into battle, but were handicapped by lack of military training. The new arrivals after the end of the war with Costa Rica were barely more than sufficient to compensate for the losses from fevers and cholera, although they came by every steamer.

Throughout the latter half of 1856 the work of recruiting forces for Walker in the United States was conducted more openly than before, and with very little of the governmental interference which had been so evident but so ineffectual at the beginning of the year. Although Fermin Ferrer made no effort to secure recognition as Walker's minister, he made a colonization contract on Aug. 15, 1856, with William L. Cazneau, of Texas, for the introduction of one thousand able-bodied colonists of good character into Nicaragua within twelve months. The Nicaraguan government, on its part, was to establish them in settlements of not less than fifty families, and each independent settler was to secure eighty acres of land which might be alienated only after a year's residence

McKeon at New York, when shown the contract, said that he could not recognize such colonization as lawful because the government did not acknowledge Ferrer's official capacity.[1] The reports of impending war with all the Central American States prevented any serious attention being paid to a colonizing scheme of this nature, and those who joined the enterprise and migrated to Nicaragua went mainly in search of adventure.

Walker himself sent a number of his officers to the United States to muster in recruits. S. A. Lockridge had charge of the recruiting in Texas and the Middle West; Walker's brother, Norvell, opened a recruiting office in Nashville, and E. J. C. Kewen made his headquarters in Augusta, Georgia, and conducted his work in Alabama, Mississippi, and Georgia. Walker is reported to have declared that he wanted no more recruits from the purlieus of American cities, but preferred more resourceful and self-reliant men coming from good pioneer stock. These he could secure from California, Missouri, and the Southwest. Charles Morgan agreed to carry Texans free of charge on his steamers from Galveston to New Orleans, and from there to Granada their transportation was also free. Lockridge widely advertised this in the Texas newspapers. In Kansas and Missouri the free trip from New Orleans to Granada was also announced in print, and a Colonel H. T. Titus, noted as a "Border Ruffian," recruited a company of one hundred of his followers, whose services in Kansas were no longer in demand, and started in December for New Orleans by way of the Mississippi. Kewen also raised a force in his territory of over eight hundred men, but these were destined never to leave the country, as the news of the downfall of the filibuster régime arrived before they were ready to embark.[2]

The New Orleans *Picayune* of November 26 announced the departure of Lockridge with 283 men and gave a list of the com-

[1] New York *Herald*, Dec. 25, 1856.
[2] *Ibid.*, Oct. 21, Dec. 5, 7, 9, 1856; Jan. 31, 1857.

panies and their officers, showing that this expedition, contrary to
the general practice, was organized on a military basis before it
left the United States. These were the last recruits to reach
Walker from the Atlantic States.

In December, as Walker's situation in Nicaragua became desperate, for reasons to be shown hereafter, his friends in New York
began to take active measures for his relief. On December 20
a large Walker meeting was held in the Broadway Tabernacle.
General Ward B. Burnett, of the New York Volunteers, presided.
Speeches were made by General Duff Green, Appleton Oaksmith,
Isaiah Rynders, and other sympathizers. A collection of over
thirteen hundred dollars was taken. The St. Nicholas Hotel
offered a hundred barrels of bread and the Metropolitan Hotel five
thousand pounds of bacon.[1] "The gathering," said the *Herald*,
"was not only a respectable one as to numbers, but also in the
character and social position of a large number of the persons
present." On hearing of this activity the administration notified
McKeon to prevent the forwarding of supplies to Walker. "We
don't see what right Pierce, Marcy, or McKeon have to intercept
bread, bacon, and shoes anywhere," said the same paper. "On
the bacon point Vattel is expressly clear, and he is quite as good an
authority as poor Pierce."

The steamer *Tennessee* was to sail on the 24th. Boxes of supplies went to the dock. One was marked:

BREAD

To the care of General William Walker. For our old comrades in
Texas, now in Nicaragua, with the warm sympathy, personal and political, of their former commanders.

THOMAS J. GREEN
WILLIAM L. CAZNEAU

And another:

For my old comrades in the Florida and Mexican Wars.

WARD B. BURNETT.[2]

[1] *Harper's Weekly*, I., 7.   [2] New York *Herald*, Dec. 23, 1856.

On the 24th the steamer *Tennessee* sailed with three hundred recruits and two thousand dollars' worth of provisions. The recruits gathered at the corner of Broadway and Leonard streets and marched to the docks on the East River at the foot of Eighth Street. The steamer had been advertised to sail from the foot of Beach Street, and the crowd, which gathered there, expecting governmental interference and some excitement, was much disappointed. McKeon had two revenue cutters ready for any emergency, but nothing happened. Morgan had called on him shortly before the hour of sailing, and announced that no one would be allowed to board the steamer without a ticket. He also promised to convey no passengers who had signed Cazneau's colonization contract. This seemed to satisfy the government's representative and the steamer put to sea. Cazneau a few days later declared that McKeon's opposition to his colonizing activities had prevented a hundred more passengers from sailing on the *Tennessee*.[1] Shortly after reaching the open sea the steamer met rough weather, and during the storm broke her shaft. She managed to put in at Norfolk, where the recruits disbanded, many returning to New York. Morgan sent the *James Adger* at once to Norfolk to take the men and cargo of the *Tennessee* on to Nicaragua. This vessel also carried forty more men from New York. The *James Adger* missed the recruits in Norfolk, as they had left before her arrival, but the vessel proceeded to Greytown with her forty passengers, among whom were Colonel Frank Anderson, who had been home recuperating from a wound, and General R. C. Wheat, a boyhood companion of Walker and his brothers in Nashville, who had served as military governor of Vera Cruz and obtained the rank of brigadier-general in the Mexican army. He had resigned his Mexican commission to join Walker in Nicaragua. Morgan sent no more steamers from New York.

[1] *Herald*, Dec. 25 and 28, 1856. Cazneau admitted that if his colonists, on entering the country, should find Walker in a critical situation, they might strike one bold blow for his rescue.

While these events were taking place in New York similar scenes were being enacted in New Orleans. There on December 28 two hundred and fifty recruits embarked on the steamer *Texas*. The steamer was detained for some time awaiting the arrival of Titus and his "border ruffians" from Kansas, who were coming down the Mississippi by boat. Thick fogs detained the Kansan, and the *Texas* sailed without him. Fortunately for history, there embarked on this steamer the noted traveller and journalist, Laurence Oliphant, and we have from his pen a graphic description of the men who went to Nicaragua. After they were on the high seas the recruits were divided into five companies. These had been enlisted in different States, and the officers received their rank according to the number of men they had enlisted. The soldiers were to receive a monthly pay of twenty-five dollars in Nicaraguan scrip and a grant of land at the end of their enlistment. There was nothing, the author tells us, to indicate that the men had enlisted from mercenary motives. Some were well-to-do; some were running away from troubles at home; some were merely soldiers of fortune. The predominating motive seemed to be love of excitement and adventure. Almost every nationality was represented, and one company was composed entirely of Germans. "There were Hungarians who had fought at Segedin; Italians who had fought at Novara; Prussians who had gone through the Schleswig-Holstein campaigns; Frenchmen who had fought in Algeria; Englishmen who had been in our own artillery in the Crimea; Americans who had taken part in both the Cuban expeditions; others fresh from Kansas." Some of the officers had already seen service in the Nicaraguan army and were returning from their furloughs. There were a few who had been officers in the United States army, "and were as well-informed, gentleman-like, and agreeable as the officers in that service usually are." Oliphant was especially impressed with the exemplary behaviour of the men; there were no spirituous liquors issued even on New

Year's day. The men drilled and practised guard-mounting every
day and seemed to take to the work instinctively. The officer of
the day wore a sword, but there was otherwise not the semblance
of a uniform, the costume varying from red flannel shirt and boots
to seedy and semi-clerical black broadcloth. The faces were not
ill-favoured, and the Englishman was so well impressed with their
appearance that he failed to lock the door of his stateroom and
thereby was divested of some of his loose property.[1]

The strict discipline noted by Oliphant on board the *Texas* was
characteristic of the filibuster army. Walker ruled with a rod of
iron, and had more trouble with his officers than with his men in
ranks. Many of the former, he says, valued their rank more as
an excuse for indulging their ease than as an incentive to difficult
and arduous duty. There was no recognized uniform, but until
the Americans began to be beset by the Central American alliance
in the autumn of 1856 they were comfortably provided with food
and clothing. General John T. McGrath, who served under Walker
and throughout the Civil War, informed the writer that Walker's
men were much better provided for than were the soldiers of the
Confederacy. The nearest approach to a uniform was a costume
consisting of blue flannel shirt, blue cotton breeches, boots, or
brogan shoes, and wide-brimmed black felt hat. When the force
was best equipped the shirts were marked with the number of the
detachment and the letter of the company. Many of the officers
wore the uniform of their corresponding rank in the United States
army, and a few of the more dressy ones aroused much ridicule by
the way they braved the tropical heat in order to display their
regimentals. One of the officers, a Colonel Watson, brought half
a dozen large trunks from New York filled with such apparel.[2]

The Americans consumed large quantities of bad liquor, and this
rendered them more susceptible to cholera and fevers than they

[1] Laurence Oliphant, *Patriots and Filibusters*, 17 ff.
[2] J. C. Jamison, *With Walker in Nicaragua*, 119. (Columbia, Mo., 1909.)

would have been otherwise. Most of them had acquired the drinking habit before leaving home, and the depressing influence of the climate, the removal of the usual social restraints, and the presence of danger combined to increase the amount of drunkenness. It not infrequently happened that when a detachment of troops found itself in a critical situation the officers would take to hard drinking, whether to fortify their courage or out of sheer desperation it is difficult to say.

One result of the prevalent intemperance was much quarrelling, which frequently ended in duels. Walker himself, it will be recalled, had resorted to the code duello in California, but the frequency of the encounters and the trivial causes from which they originated gave him much concern. For a time, says Jamison, a day that passed without a duel evoked comment.[1] A temperance worker from California, the Rev. Israel S. Diehl, visited Granada in the autumn of 1856, and organized a chapter of the "Sons of Temperance." About fifty men, officers and soldiers, joined and took the pledge, but the organization held no meetings after the departure of its founder, and many of its members backslid.[2] One of Walker's lieutenants, while under the influence of drink, shot a private soldier and a fellow officer. He was court-martialed and sentenced to hang, and wrote a confession, admitting that he had shot five other men in the United States, and attributing all his trouble to "whiskey and a crazy mind." Walker commuted the sentence to shooting.[3]

Before the arrival of Henningsen with George Law's present of Minié guns, only two companies were equipped with the rifle. These were the Rangers (Walker's cavalry), who were also provided with pistols and sabres, and the Rifles. The other infantry companies were armed with the antiquated smooth-bore musket that had been discarded by the United States army, and with old-

---

[1] J. C. Jamison, *With Walker in Nicaragua*, 108.
[2] New York *Herald*, Oct. 19 and Nov. 17, 1856.   [3] *Ibid.*, Oct. 19, 1856.

fashioned Colt's pistols. The officers gave much attention to swordsmanship, in which a number became quite expert; but this was an art of no practical use, as a hand-to-hand conflict with the natives was the thing least likely to occur. At the end of 1856 the Nicaraguan service was in nine divisions: the Rifles; the infantry; the ordnance; the arsenal; the Rangers; the Commissary Rangers; the commissary department; the quartermaster's department; and the civil service.

The Commissary Rangers were made up of picked men under the direction of W. K. Rogers, the sub-secretary of hacienda. The natives called Rogers the "confiscator-general." He and his men were among Walker's firmest supporters; they had no regular drill, but to them fell the disagreeable duty of foraging for corn, cattle, and provender and of paying therefor in worthless scrip. The mounts of the Rangers were generally mules of an indifferent quality.[1]

One party of Rangers was sent into the district of Chontales under the command of Byron Cole to levy a contribution of cattle upon the grazers. Cole, who has been described as "the last advocate of gentleness and conciliation" in Nicaragua,[2] would allow none of his men to enter the houses of the well-to-do for fear that they might be unable to resist a temptation to plunder. A nun, who was a refugee from Granada, had established a small school on the Malacatolla River, and when the Rangers reached this point she entertained them for two days. Cole, however, would not allow them to enter the house, and they slept under the portico. Two months later a second party of these Rangers came along and ransacked the house, taking whatever of value they could find.[3] It was the depredations and excesses of these detached filibusters that aroused much of the native resentment against the Americans. It should be said, moreover, that the natives soon learned to discriminate between the undesirable and the well-bred American troopers.

[1] New York *Times*, March 9 and 30, 1857.
[2] *Ibid.*, May 30, 1857.   [3] *Harper's Weekly*, I., 188–9.

Their animosity was especially keen against Californians and
Texans, terms which they regarded as synonymous with plunder-
ers.[1] For their use of the term "Texan" in such a sense they had
some reason. In July, 1856, a party of about thirty men, styling
themselves "Texas Rangers," arrived in Granada and were permitted to form themselves into a mounted company. They
quickly violated the confidence imposed in them by deserting, and
proved to be only a gang of robbers who had come to Nicaragua
for marauding. They were lucky to have put a considerable distance between themselves and Walker's men before their imposture
was discovered, as the latter would surely have hanged any that
fell into their clutches.[2]

It would hardly be just to omit any reference to the filibuster
army's mascots. When the "fifty-six" first landed at Brito and began their march on Rivas, a common cur dog made friends with the
men and followed them wherever they went. He was christened
"Filibuster." He took part in the capture of Granada, and every
scouting or foraging party of Rangers had his company. When
Goicouria made his visit of pacification to Chontales, "Filibuster"
went along, and fell fighting for his companions' cause in a skirmish
at Juigalpa. When the news reached Granada, some poetic adventurer indited a long poem to the canine's memory, which was
published in *El Nicaraguense:*

> A gaunt and grizzled creature, with harsh and matted hair,
> And eyes like some fierce mountain wolf, just startled from his lair;
> No pet for ladies' parlour, nor watch for lonesome hall;
> But, Ishmaelite of canine life, he seemed the scorn of all.
> Yet strangely, too, he followed us, on march or in the fray;
> He was our constant shadow, at midnight or by day.
> Despite of kicks and curses, not few nor far between,
> Despite of wintry [!] weather, and hunger, too, I ween,
> His conduct ever faithful, again and still again,
> By slow degrees did gain for him the favour of our men.

[1] Conversation with General John T. McGrath.
[2] Wheeler Scrapbook no. 4, p. 155.

*　　*　　*　　*　　*　　*　　*　　*

In Juigalpa's plaza our soldiers met the foe,
And a bullet from their riflemen full soon did lay him low.
He fell. 'Twas in the van he fought; the charge he fearless led,
And died still bravely fighting for the cause he'd often bled.

"Filibuster" was succeeded by another of his species named "Prince," who showed the same fondness for things military.

In September, 1856, Walker changed the flag of the republic. In place of the old design, showing five volcanoes in eruption, he substituted a flag of two blue stripes, with a white stripe between them which was the width of the other two combined. In the centre of the white stripe was placed a red star with five points. When the Rifles bore this standard into battle at Masaya, they had inscribed on it the legend "Five or None," expressing Walker's ultimate design of a conquest and consolidation of all Central America.

A few days after his breach with Rivas Walker seized a Costa Rican schooner, the *San José*, which had entered the harbour of San Juan del Sur flying the American flag. The grounds for the seizure were that the vessel was without papers or a lawful flag. A "court of admiralty" was created to pass upon the case, and the vessel was adjudged condemned and forfeited to the government. She was then equipped with two six-pound guns, rechristened the *Granada*, and placed under the command of Lieutenant Callender Irvine Fayssoux. Men were detailed from the different companies to man the vessel, and Nicaragua was now possessed of a navy. The owner of the schooner was a well-to-do Nicaraguan merchant named Mariano Salazar, a Democrat and one of Walker's stanchest supporters. Salazar had made an American, Gilbert Morton, half owner of the schooner, supposing that this would give him the right to fly the United States flag, and under its protection he had planned to conduct a profitable trade along the west coast during the hostilities in Nicaragua. When Walker spoiled these plans Salazar became his dearest foe.[1]

[1] *War in Nicaragua*, 229–30; Wheeler Scrapbook no. 4, 145, 155, 173.

As soon as Fayssoux was ready for sea, he was ordered to cruise in the neighbourhood of the Bay of Fonseca, where it was suspected that the partizans of Rivas were communicating with Guatemala and San Salvador by boats plying from Tempisque, on the Real River, across the bay to La Union in San Salvador. Walker hoped to intercept some of the correspondence between Rivas and his allies and to prevent reinforcements being sent across the bay. On July 21 the *Granada* with four officers, fifteen seamen, and a carpenter weighed anchor and stood out to sea on her first cruise. Her commander had had an interesting history, and was destined to add a still more interesting chapter to the story of his life. Fayssoux was a native of Missouri, and had served as a midshipman in the navy of the republic of Texas. After Texas disbanded its navy and became a State he joined an expedition to Cuba in 1849, in the steamship *Fanny*, but this enterprise was thwarted by American naval officers. The next year he took part in the Lopez expedition in the *Creole*, and distinguished himself at Cardenas by swimming ashore with a rope between his teeth and thus enabling his companions to effect a landing. In 1851 he again followed Lopez in his ill-fated descent upon Cuba, and in April, 1856, he sailed from New Orleans to try his fortunes in Nicaragua. Walker soon found an opportunity to utilize his services. Like his chief, he was small physically and very taciturn, and equally obstinate in matters affecting the dignity of his position.[1]

An incident which occurred in February, 1857, shows the character of the two men. The British man-of-war *Esk*, under the command of Sir Robert McClure, was in the harbour of San Juan del Sur. Sir Robert sent a subordinate aboard the *Granada* to inquire by what authority she flew a flag unknown to any nation and to order her commander to come aboard the *Esk* and exhibit his commission. Fayssoux replied that his commission was in his cabin, and if compelled to do so he would show it there under pro-

[1] Wheeler Scrapbook no. 4, p. 219; New York *Herald*, Dec. 16, 1856.

test, but he positively refused to go aboard the *Esk* with it, although the officer tried both threats and persuasion. When all means failed, the officer invited him to accompany him in his boat as a friend and visit the *Esk*. Fayssoux replied that he would go in his own boat, and did so a few minutes thereafter. Some days later Sir Robert McClure visited Walker to confer about the removal of some British subjects. The general neither rose nor offered the visitor a seat, but remarked after formal greetings had been exchanged, "I hope you have come to apologize for that affair of the schooner." Sir Robert was too surprised to reply, and Walker continued, " Your conduct, sir, to Captain Fayssoux was unbecoming an Englishman and a British officer. I shall make such a representation of it to your government as will cause an investigation and insure an explanation." An apology was quickly forthcoming.[1]

The establishment of a navy was an event of so much interest at the army headquarters that a portion of the vessel's log was published in Walker's paper.

"Monday, July 21, 1856. At three P.M. the schooner *Granada*, Lieut. Fayssoux, sailed from San Juan del Sur — being the first vessel that ever went to sea as a government vessel — the commencement of the Nicaraguan navy.

"Tuesday, July 22, 1856. Running down the coast towards Fonseca.

"Wednesday, July 23, 1856. Opened the boxes of packed ammunition — found it unfit for use. Made eighty round for the guns; at three P.M. bore away for Tigre Island, about twelve miles distant.

"Thursday, July 24, 1856. Cruising in the Gulf. At two P.M. saw a large number of small craft to the eastward; gave chase. At three P.M. a brig about four miles to windward, showing Chilean colours. At four-thirty captured the sloop *Mana* (French papers), no cargo or passengers. At six a heavy squall from South; double reefed the sails and began to work off the shore." [1]

On July 27 Fayssoux captured a bungo with a large number of passengers, among whom was none other than Salazar, the former owner of the *Granada*. A number of letters were also taken, among them one from Thomas Manning, the British vice-consul at Realejo, to a merchant in San Salvador, in which he expressed great regret that the other States were doing so little to expel the Americans, and declared that they should at least double their present forces in the field. Walker at once revoked Manning's exequatur for "unduly interfering in the interior affairs of the republic." [2] Salazar met the fate which befell all whom Walker deemed guilty of treason, and was shot on the plaza of Granada. His previous Democratic affiliations had made him an object of hatred to the Granadinos, and they hailed his death with as much joy as the Leonese had shown at the death of Corral. Salazar's friends at Leon, on hearing of his capture, arrested an American resident, Dr. Joseph W. Livingston, and sent a courier to Granada with a statement that the American would be held as a hostage for the safety of Salazar. The courier arrived several days after the execution, and Livingston was saved only by the prompt intervention of Minister Wheeler.

[1] *El Nicaraguense*, Aug. 9, 1856.
[2] Wheeler Scrapbook no. 4, 145, 155; *War in Nicaragua*, 236-7.

CHAPTER XVII

"HERE WAS GRANADA"

ON July 12, the very day of Walker's inaugural, the first detachment of troops from San Salvador reached Leon. Six days later Guatemalan troops joined them, bringing the total allied force to 1300 men. To these the Rivas government could add only about five hundred. It will be seen, therefore, that Walker's authority never extended over the district of Leon. In spite of the superior number of troops mobilizing in the North, Walker had very little as yet to fear from them. It fell to Rivas to say who among them should take supreme command, and he named the Salvadorian chief, Ramon Belloso. This naturally angered the Guatemalans, who desired the honour for their commander, General Paredes. So much ill-feeling resulted that there were constant street brawls between the three nationalities, and it finally became necessary to confine the men of each command to separate quarters. Stung by his slighting their leader, the Guatemalans gave to Rivas the nickname of " Patas Arriba " (Topsy Turvy).[1]

The Rivas government had sent a commissioner to Honduras to establish friendly relations also with that republic, but Guardiola, then at the head of that State, would do nothing. He had no quarrel with the man who had refused to aid his old Democratic foe, Cabañas. When, however, he saw President Carrera, of Guatemala, his old friend and ally, enter the field against Walker, he could no longer remain neutral, and on July 7 he issued a proclama-

---

[1] Montúfar, 518 ff. In order that English-speaking readers may appreciate the humour of this nickname, it may be necessary to state that Patricio Rivas, under a Spanish tongue, has a sound very similar to *patas arriba*.

tion stating that Nicaragua had implored the aid of Honduras and
they would make its cause their own, not only on account of the
natural sympathy between the two regions, but also because Honduras would be greatly endangered if Nicaragua once submitted
to a foreign yoke.   On July 20 a force of six hundred Hondurans
began their march to the frontier.[1]

√ On July 18 the governments of Honduras, Guatemala, and San
Salvador entered into a treaty of alliance for the defence of their
sovereignty and independence, recognized Rivas as the provisional
president of Nicaragua, promised him their aid with troops, which
they were to furnish in proportions to be later determined, and
announced their intention of aiding in the suppression of internal
dissensions.   They also invited Costa Rica to join the alliance.[2]
That country had not abandoned the idea of making war on
Walker, though in the face of the ravages of the plague it had for
months been helpless. Its minister of foreign affairs, Joaquin
Bernardo Calvo, in June addressed the government of San Salvador,
expressing a hope that the other Central American republics would
continue the work which Costa Rica had so happily begun.[3]   An
agent of the Spanish government also arrived in Costa Rica and
used his influence to egg on the doughty little republic against the
Americans in Nicaragua.   The fact that Walker had rallied to his
side so many of the Cuban revolutionists had aroused suspicions
at Madrid.   When the plague had spent its force Mora gave his
attention again to affairs in Nicaragua, and in August convened
his Congress to make plans for renewing the war.

Spain was not the only European power to show its interest.
The French corvette *Embuscade* protected the Salvadorian forces
crossing the Bay of Fonseca in bungos from attack by the *Granada*,
which was cruising off the bay.[4]   Early in August an English

[1] Montúfar, 547–8.   [2] *Ibid.*, 550–8.
[3] "Mi gobierno confía en que las fuerzas de Guatemala, el Salvador, y Honduras
concliurán la obra que el inició tan felizmente."   Montúfar, 638.
[4] Montúfar, 549.

squadron, consisting of thirteen ships of war, mounting 268 guns and manned by 2500 men, arrived in the harbour of Greytown.[1]

On August 4, Walker, observing the hostile coalition against him, issued a decree declaring all the ports of Central America, except those used for interoceanic transit, in a state of blockade, and ordered his "navy" to put the decree into effect.[2] Sickness and desertion now were depleting his ranks. Granada had always been an unhealthful place for the Americans, and cholera and typhus were now doing their worst. The fear of disease and the known proximity of the allies were the main causes of desertion, but other causes contributed. Food was growing scarcer. The natives had migrated in large numbers from the vicinity of Granada and Rivas, and the Americans had eaten up most of the available provisions. Few recruits in the United States could be induced to migrate to the tropics in midsummer. The large numbers who had left New York during the preceding December and January were partly impelled by a desire to escape the rigours of a Northern winter. The excitement incident to a political campaign in the United States not improbably distracted attention from the Americans in Nicaragua. The bulk of the filibuster forces occupied Granada; about four hundred were stationed in Masaya, which was strongly fortified, and the Rangers under Waters occupied Managua, the point most advanced toward the enemy. Detachments of Rangers sometimes showed themselves in the vicinity of Leon for the moral effect their presence would have on the allies stationed there.

The condition of the enemy was no better than that of the Americans. Cholera and fever were as virulent at Leon as at Granada. Inactivity, sickness, a high death rate, and constant quarrels during the months of July, August, and part of September almost

---

[1] MS., Department of State, Bureau of Indexes and Archives, Nicaragua Legations, II.

[2] MS., Department of State, Bureau of Indexes and Archives, Notes, Central American Legations, II.; El Nicaraguense, Aug. 9, 1856.

destroyed the morale of the allies, and Walker remained quiet while disease and divisions were working in his favour. Not only was there dissension among the different nationalities, but there were also serious disagreements among the Nicaraguans themselves. The old distrust between Legitimists and Democrats would not die down. Jerez, Walker's former co-labourer and the foremost Democrat, was the man best qualified to be their leader, but Legitimists could not tolerate the idea; neither could Jerez bring his former following to give more than half-hearted support to the campaign, because the movement seemed to be largely of Legitimist inspiration.[1] There was not a really capable leader in the allied camps, and the fourth-rate generals were mutually jealous.

The allies finally began their advance southward on September 18. As they approached Managua the Rangers under Waters fell back on Masaya, and the enemy entered the town unresisted on the 24th. There they remained for a week, apparently hesitating as to the next step. At Masaya, twelve miles north of Granada, four hundred Americans were confronting them behind strong barricades. An American newspaper, the *Masaya Herald*, was published at this place. On October 1 it declared, "Masaya is to-day the Sebastopol of Nicaragua, and we say to our enemies, whatever their number, 'Come on, we are ready to receive you as you deserve.'"[2] Walker at this juncture committed a blunder very like that at the beginning of war with Costa Rica. He ordered the evacuation of Masaya and drew all his forces into Granada.[3] The allies then advanced and posted themselves in the town behind his own fortifications. He then allowed them ten days in which to recuperate and receive reinforcements. They also prevented foraging by Walker's Rangers, and thus caused much inconvenience. It is the story of the operations at Rivas all over again. After allowing the enemy to take the town and secure the protection of barricades and adobe walls, he decided to attack them and regain

[1] Montúfar, 612 ff.   [2] *Ibid.*, 614.   [3] *War in Nicaragua*, 288-9.

the lost position, and on October 11 he set out from Granada with eight hundred men.

Meanwhile the bickerings which had so seriously disturbed the allies at Leon broke out again, with the result that Zavala, in command of the Guatemalans, and Estrada, the former Legitimist president of Nicaragua, withdrew their forces to the neighbouring village of Diriomo. Their departure was no loss, as harmony was restored among those who remained. Masaya was now attacked by Walker in very much the same manner that he had attacked Rivas just six months before. Bit by bit the Americans drove the defenders through the streets in the direction of the plaza, and were on the point of taking it, when an unexpected movement on the part of Estrada and Zavala caused him to abandon the attack and hurry back to Granada. This city was menaced by Estrada and Zavala, who, instead of marching to the support of Belloso as soon as they saw that he was attacked, took the road to Granada, which they expected to find undefended. On the part of able generals such a movement might be attributed to military skill, but in this case Central Americans themselves say it was prompted by a desire to win unshared glory, to which we might add, as another inducement, the prospect of loot. Disappointed in finding a small garrison, consisting mainly of civil employees and inmates of the hospital, which offered a determined resistance, these worthies vented their rage on the helpless non-combatants, committing atrocities which even Walker's hostile critic Perez admits and enumerates. Two American missionaries, D. H. Wheeler and William J. Ferguson, were murdered, and their naked bodies were thrown into the market-place.[1] A six-year-old English boy was shot down as he sat at the dinner table, and a merchant, John B. Lawless, a native of Ireland but a naturalized American citizen, who had lived in Granada for years and had enjoyed the esteem of all factions,

[1] MS., Department of State, Bureau of Indexes and Archives, Despatches, Nicaraguan Legation, II.

was taken from his house and his body riddled with bullets and mutilated with bayonets. The American flag, flying on the house of Minister Wheeler, was fired upon, and insulting epithets were shouted at the minister, who was then lying seriously ill. He might have fared even worse had not a few riflemen been sent for his protection by Colonel Fry. The Americans had taken defensive positions in the various public buildings and had sustained an attack for twenty-four hours before Walker returned and drove out the enemy. Father Rossiter, the chaplain of the army, and John Tabor, editor of *El Nicaraguense*, were among the civilians who helped defend the city. The latter suffered a broken thigh. Padre Vijil was less militant than his brother of the cloth, and took refuge in a swamp as soon as the trouble began. Shortly after the enemy's repulse he came from his hiding place and applied to Walker for a passport to leave the country.

Walker drove the enemy from Granada on October 13, the anniversary of his capture of the city from the Legitimists. The pillaging of the Guatemalans seriously curtailed his supplies. He had lost very few at Masaya, but had suffered rather seriously in his attack on Zavala. His aide-de-camp, Colonel Lainé, the Cuban, lost his way between Masaya and Granada and was taken prisoner. Much ado was made over his capture by the allies, and Zavala at once ordered him to be shot.[1] As soon as this news was verified at Granada, Walker ordered the execution of two Guatemalan prisoners of rank, Lieutenant-Colonel Valderraman and Captain Allende, to show the enemy that he would return two blows for one if they chose to wage warfare of that character. The execution of the two Guatemalans, however, disgusted many of Walker's officers with his service. The two prisoners were cultured gentlemen; they took their captivity philosophically, made themselves companionable with the officers, and won their friendship. Walker's

[1] According to Montúfar, Lainé's last words were: "Los hombres mueren, las ideas quedan." (Men die; their ideas remain.)

men acquiesced when the order for the execution was issued, but their hearts burned within them.

Belloso at Masaya had suffered so heavily from Walker's riflemen that he did not follow the filibuster leader on his withdrawal to Granada. He had sent orders to Zavala at Diriomo to come to his support when the attack began, and was so incensed that the Guatemalan had gone to Granada instead that he refused to lift a finger to aid him against Walker and resolved to let his ally take his medicine alone. There was a serious schism in the camp of the allies, but the prospects were brightened a fortnight later when Costa Rica joined in the contest. On November 1, President Mora, realizing the value of the Transit as "a highway of filibusterism," issued a decree declaring that the war with the "immigrant usurpers" had been renewed, and proclaiming a blockade of the port of San Juan del Sur and the San Juan River as long as hostilities against the invaders continued.[1] On the next day General Cañas set out with the advance guard, with the purpose of occupying the Transit road. On the 7th he occupied San Juan del Sur, which was not garrisoned. Indeed, the only force Walker then had in the entire district of Rivas was the "navy" under Fayssoux.

The invasion by Costa Rica threatened to destroy Walker's line of communications, and made it necessary for him to take a position where he could defend the Transit. His forces were too small to permit their division in the face of superior numbers of the enemy. By the middle of the month the allies at Masaya had been reinforced until they numbered over three thousand. To garrison a large city against these, and at the same time to hold the Transit against the incoming Costa Ricans, was a task beyond the filibusters' strength. Their leader then decided to evacuate Granada and establish himself at Rivas, which Mora himself had converted into a strongly fortified town the previous spring. Fearing, how-

[1] MS., Department of State, Bureau of Indexes and Archives, Notes, Central America, II.

ever, that the allies at Masaya might effect a junction at Rivas with the Costa Ricans and thus forestall him in his plan to hold the Transit, Walker resolved upon a quick attack upon both in succession, so as to conceal his real plans. On November 11 he and Henningsen landed with two hundred and fifty men at Virgin Bay and the next day marched to San Juan del Sur, defeating and scattering the forces under Cañas that opposed their progress, and leaving the Costa Ricans so demoralized that he would have nothing more to fear until they were reinforced. The next morning he marched back to Virgin Bay and that night was again in Granada and planning a second attack on the allies in Masaya. Two days later, with a force of five hundred and sixty, he again took the road to Masaya, and when he had covered about half the distance learned that Jerez had set out for Rivas with seven or eight hundred men. This necessitated his sending two hundred and fifty of his force back to Granada with orders to take the steamer for Virgin Bay and hold the Transit.

√Walker was now left with only three hundred available men, and proposed to attack a force eight times that number behind barricades and adobe walls. With Henningsen in charge of the artillery, however, he had some hopes of success. The attack began on the 15th and lasted through the 17th. The artillery failed to meet expectations, as the fuses were timed too short, and most of the shells exploded in the air. Sappers cut through the walls of one house into another, and as the Americans advanced they set fire to the houses behind them to prevent an attack from the rear. The work was slow, but by the night of the 17th they had reached a point within twenty-five or thirty yards of the enemy's posts on the plaza. To drive the enemy from the town would have required several days more of this kind of fighting; and though the foe was badly shaken, Walker was compelled to abandon the attack. His men had reached the point of physical exhaustion, and fully a third of them were killed or wounded. It was almost impossible to make any of them act as guards, so great was their weariness. On the night of the 17th, therefore, they withdrew and retreated in good order to Granada, the horses and mules conveying a long line of wounded. The allies were ignorant of their departure till the next morning, and then gave themselves up to the celebration of a great victory. Had they pursued the weary foe, Granada might easily have fallen into their hands, and the war would have been at an end. It is with much reason that the native historians bring charges of incompetence against the allied chiefs.[1] Walker and his followers reached Granada early on the 18th, and the very next day began their preparations for evacuating the city.

Granada stood on a plain sloping toward the shores of the lake. Its situation proved one of the most unhealthful in Nicaragua, and yet it was always the favourite residence of the Americans. It was of some strategic importance, as it commanded the lake; but with the steamers in their possession the Americans could easily have maintained this advantage without remaining in Granada. Walker's chief purpose in remaining there seems to have been to secure the moral advantage which his occupation of the old Legitimist capital gave him in the eyes of the natives. In the few weeks preceding his evacuation of the place the mortality among his men became fearful. Sudden change of climate, unwise use of fruits, excessive drinking, poorly prepared food, irregular hours, drenching rains, vermin-infested barracks, and general neglect of hygiene soon made the recruit a ripe subject for typhoid or yellow fever, dysentery, or the cholera. Physicians and drugs were obtained for the service, but the doctors were naturally not the pride of the medical profession, and it would have been impossible at that time to secure an American physician who knew anything of tropical diseases. It is only within recent years that the world has learned to combat the dreaded yellow fever or to check the ravages of typhoid, and it would be grossly unfair to judge

[1] Montúfar says, "Con razón se hacen hasta hoy serios cargos á los jefes aliados."

Walker's surgical staff with the twentieth-century physician as a standard. Yet, when all allowances are made, the hospital service stands convicted of inefficiency that was little less than criminal. Two large buildings were chosen for use as hospitals, and they were rightly called chambers of horrors. One fourth or more of the men would be lying there at a time fighting fever, the filibusters' fiercest foe. There was no clean linen for the sufferers, and they had to lie in their filthy woollen clothes, which had served for months as a uniform by day and as pajamas at night. The cots were never cleaned or fumigated, and a wounded man would probably be assigned to a dingy one upon which some wretch a few hours before had succumbed to fever or cholera. Flies swarmed over festering wounds and transmitted infection from one patient to another. Vermin crawled over the bodies and in the hair of the sufferers. Many cried in vain for water; others were raving with delirium and would sometimes roll from their cots and lie for hours on a filthy floor before being replaced by incompetent attendants. The odor was almost overpowering, even to the strong and well. Worst of all, each day the places gave forth an array of ghastly corpses. It is not remarkable that in the presence of such depressing scenes the Americans were prone to resort to hard drinking, and that to the epidemics of fever and cholera there was added a third — desertion. When conditions were at their worst the daily mortality amounted to two or three per cent of the total American population, and at the time Granada was evacuated the death rate was so high that the surgeons declared that unless there were a change for the better every American in Nicaragua would be dead within six weeks.[1]

When Walker decided to evacuate Granada he ordered all the sick and wounded to be moved to the island of Ometepe. Some two hundred were laid on the decks of one of the lake steamers, which then went to Virgin Bay and received additions to its cargo there. Ometepe was a volcanic island used as an Indian reservation and closed to white men unless the aborigines consented to their entrance.[1] Walker disregarded the Indians' privileges and chose the little village of Muigalpa, on the western side of the island and thirteen miles from the mainland, for his hospital site. The place was only sixteen miles from Rivas, which he had chosen for his new headquarters, and he had planned to be in daily communication with it by way of the village of San Jorge, on the lake shore about three miles from Rivas. When the steamer received its gruesome cargo on November 19 and headed for the island the odor was so fearful that the attendants were driven to the hurricane deck. At the end of the trip several of the sufferers were dead, and a number were dying.

On landing the sick it was necessary to lower them eight feet from the lower deck of the steamer to an iron barge, and this caused many of them intense agony. No provision had been made for their coming. The village was a quarter of a mile inland, and the patients had to be laid on the beach and carried bodily, a few at a time, to the village. The natives fled at the approach of the strangers, and the sick and wounded were placed in the abandoned huts. At midnight the barge made its last trip, bringing ashore the dead and the hospital supplies.

The transfer had been conducted by Rogers, the "confiscator-general," who deserves credit for at least one humane act. On returning to Granada he slipped away quietly, leaving on the island a very resourceful officer, Captain John M. Baldwin, who had planned to rejoin Walker's command. Baldwin of course was indignant when he found that Rogers had left him behind, but at once began to set things in order and look after the sufferers. The half a dozen men who had been carrying the sick to the villages finally collapsed from sheer exhaustion, and twenty-four patients still lay on the sands by the lake. A wood contractor for the steamboats,

[1] Boyle, Frederick, *A Ride Across a Continent*, II., 69–70. (London, 1868.)

who lived on the island, had a soup prepared by two native women who had stayed in the village, and at two o'clock in the morning this was fed to those on the beach.   Then, to add to the misery of these wretches, the rain came, and though they were protected as much as possible by cloaks and blankets they were soaked by the shower, and the next morning several were dead.   Five died also in the huts of the village.   In five days there were thirty-six deaths, and a number, delirious or starving, tottered off into the woods and disappeared.   The sight of these gaunt spectres, crying for food or raving with delirium, filled the natives with terror.   There was not even a spade to bury the dead.   No one thought of separate graves, and a pit for the bodies was dug with a wooden shovel and other improvised implements.   Into this was placed each daily quota of corpses, without the use of bell, book, or bier.[1]   The soil they fain would have made their own served only to enshroud their mouldering bodies.

Three days later the steamer made a second visit to the island, bringing over Colonel Fry and a guard of sixty men, besides a number of officers and doctors.   With them came fifty or sixty American women and children, the families of some German merchants, and a number of native women whose husbands still remained in Walker's service.   The women could give some aid in nursing, but the strongest of the sick and wounded had to be removed from the huts to give the women a place to stay.   Many of the newcomers were so debilitated as only to add to the burdens of the rest.   To increase the misery, on the night of December 1 a party of Indian marauders attacked the village, firing into the huts and causing those who were able to leave to flee in terror out into the darkness.   The Indians, however, were only after a chance to plunder the women's trunks, and after satisfying themselves with looting they retired at daybreak.   Many of the men capable of fighting, and even several officers, disgracefully abandoned the

---

[1] *Harper's Weekly*, I., 200 f.

helpless sick, and women and children, and fled at the first alarm. Some of the fugitives put out for the mainland in canoes, and Walker on a lake steamer picked up a party of these early on the morning of the attack and headed at once for the island. As he drew near, he found the large barge used in landing the passengers on the island adrift on the lake and filled with men, women, and children in a most forlorn condition. These were taken aboard the steamer, and from some of the women Walker heard things that the most stout-hearted men would not have dared utter in his hearing. The sick, wounded, women and children were finally all removed to the mainland and quartered at San Jorge. The spirits of the Americans were much improved by their removal to a more healthful location, and the arrival of eighty recruits from California and two hundred and thirty-five from New Orleans under Lockridge did still more to revive their hopes.[1]

While these events were taking place, Henningsen was engaged in a terrific struggle in Granada. On evacuating the city, Walker felt that to leave it intact would give the allies a strong fortress and all the prestige which he had enjoyed from occupying the Legitimist capital. He therefore resolved that the place should be destroyed, and delegated the work to Henningsen. After sending the sick and wounded to Ometepe, and leaving about three hundred men under Henningsen to carry on the work of destruction, Walker withdrew with the rest of his forces, only two companies of infantry, to Virgin Bay, where he expected Henningsen soon to join him with his ordnance stores and other supplies.

The quarters of the men at Virgin Bay were much worse than at Granada. The food, too, was bad. Masaya, which had been called "the granary of Nicaragua," was in the hands of the enemy, and the foraging in the vicinity of the Transit was very poor. Fever was rife; there was danger of an attack by Cañas and his Costa Ricans, who had recently been reinforced at Rivas by Jerez

[1] *War in Nicaragua*, 331-4.

with a large body of native Nicaraguans; and the spirits of the
handful of soldiers fit for duty were very depressed. News came
from San Juan del Sur on November 23 that Fayssoux had gone
out of the harbour with the *Granada* to engage a Costa Rican brig,
and had blown his vessel up to prevent capture. This only added
to the prevailing gloom. The report was corrected a day later,
however, when it became known that it was the enemy's vessel
that had been blown up, and that Fayssoux had gained a
naval victory. The spirits of the men were then greatly improved, and they spent the day in celebration of the first success
at sea.

The Costa Ricans had recently armed and equipped for war a
brig which they renamed the *Once de Abril* (Eleventh of April) to
commemorate their victory at the second battle of Rivas. They
had planned to use the vessel to convey troops and munitions from
Punta Arenas to San Juan del Sur and to intercept the movements
of the filibuster schooner. The *Once de Abril* had four nine-pound
guns and was manned by 114 men. The *Granada* carried two six-
pound guns and had on board twenty-eight persons, five of whom
were non-combatants.

Fayssoux was at anchor in the harbour of San Juan del Sur on
the afternoon of November 23, when at four o'clock a sail was
sighted off the harbour and he weighed anchor and stood out to
meet the incoming vessel. At six o'clock the two vessels were only
a quarter of a mile apart, and the stranger was displaying Costa
Rican colours. The *Once de Abril* opened the attack with cannon
and muskets and the *Granada* returned the fire. For two hours
the fighting continued. In San Juan del Sur the people gathered
on the beach and watched the flashes from the guns in the gathering
darkness. About eight o'clock there was a broad flash of light followed a few seconds later by a noise like thunder, and the spectators
rightly assumed that one of the vessels had been blown up. As
they waited for news and Fayssoux did not return, they concluded

that he had destroyed his schooner to prevent her capture. They knew that his supply of ammunition was very meagre, and after the engagement had lasted two hours they naturally supposed that the commander was in dire straits and had resorted to desperate measures. They had frequently heard him say that he would never be taken. The surmise grew into a conviction, and the news of the supposed disaster was sent by courier to Walker and his dispirited followers at Virgin Bay.

The next morning, however, the *Granada* was seen coming into port, with no apparent damage, but with decks crowded with men. These were the forty-one survivors from the wreck of the Costa Rican brig, whom Fayssoux had picked up out of the water. A shot from the *Granada* had entered the magazine of the brig, causing an explosion and blowing the vessel almost asunder. The burning hull floated for nearly an hour, but only four men could be rescued from the flames, as Fayssoux had only one boat and could pick up only a few at a time. The others who were saved had leaped into the water. The captain and many of the crew were badly burned, and Walker ordered his surgeons to give them the best of treatment. The rest of the crew received passports to return home — Walker could feed no prisoners — and their account of their good treatment astonished the Costa Ricans, whose ideas of filibusters were derived from the abusive accounts in the government journal. When the captain of the *Once de Abril* finally recovered from his injuries he was placed aboard the steamer for Panama. In the engagement Fayssoux had one man killed, two seriously wounded, and six others slightly injured. The *Granada's* chief damage consisted of bullet holes in her sails, of which the crew counted two hundred and sixty.

As soon as authentic news of the victory reached Walker he issued an order thanking Fayssoux in the name of the republic, promoting him to the rank of captain, and bestowing upon him the estate of "Rosario," near Rivas, in acknowledgment of his impor-

tant services.[1] The naval commander a short time thereafter
visited his chief at Virgin Bay. Walker invited him to dine with
his officers at their rather frugal meal and at dinner offered him
wine. Fayssoux, being a total abstainer, declined, but his fellow-
officers more than made up for his lack of conviviality in toasting
him for his victory.

In the meantime bad news came from Granada. The work of
firing the city proved no simple task. As soon as the men saw that
the town was to be burned they began to look after the safety of
their own belongings and then to plunder. A large amount of
fine liquor was found, which it seemed a pity to destroy, and the
rank and file were soon engaged in a glorious carousal. The allies
at Masaya soon learned that Walker had withdrawn from the
city, leaving only a small garrison behind, and the Nicaraguan
leader Martinez and General Paredes urged an immediate attack.
It was enough, however, for Paredes to propose a plan for Belloso
to object; and two days were spent in wrangling before an advance
was made. On the afternoon of November 24 Henningsen was
attacked from three different quarters at the same time. He concentrated his men in adobe houses around the plaza, but the allies
seized the Guadalupe Church, which stood in the centre of the street
leading from the plaza to the lake, and thus blocked his retreat to
the stone pier where he might have been rescued by one of the
steamers. Moreover, a party of twenty-seven men were on the
wharf handling stores when the attack began, and when the church
was seized they were cut off from their companions in the plaza.
The wharf had been built out of a portion of an old stone fort, the
remains of which were still standing. Behind its crumbling walls
these twenty-seven took their stand and kept the enemy at bay for
two days. Walker approached the shore in the *San Carlos* and
communicated with them by night, sending provisions and ammu-

---

[1] *War in Nicaragua*, 315–8; Wheeler Scrapbook no. 4, 219; New York *Herald*,
Dec. 16 and 31, 1856; Montúfar, 687 ff.

nition. It was necessary to hold the wharf if Henningsen were to be relieved, and the little garrison expressed itself as confident of maintaining the position. But there was a traitor among them. A Venezuelan named Tejada, whom the Americans had found in chains and freed when they took Granada a year before, deserted to the enemy, and revealed to them the small size of the garrison and indicated a means of attacking them in the rear by using one of the Transit Company's barges. The following night the defenders of the wharf were surrounded and destroyed to a man.

Henningsen meanwhile set fire to the buildings in the plaza and captured the Guadalupe Church by storm, though he was hampered at the beginning of the assault by the continued carousals of his men, whom the imminent danger seemed to demoralize still further. Into the church were crowded fighting men, sick and wounded, and women and children. His total fighting force now amounted to two hundred and ten, and in addition there were seventy-one women and children and about ninety wounded.

On November 28 the enemy sent a letter to Henningsen under a flag of truce calling upon him in the name of humanity to surrender, and promising his men protection and passports to leave the country if he complied. Henningsen sent a defiant reply, declining to do so. The allies then repeatedly attempted to storm the church, but the American rifle wrought such terrible execution that they became disheartened, and the officers found it impossible to drive the men to further assaults. Those in the church were now reduced to a diet of horse and mule flesh, with a small allowance of flour and coffee. The insanitary condition of the building beggared description. Nearly four hundred men, women, and children, wounded, sick, and well, were crowded together. From the surrounding streets, where lay the putrefying bodies of the enemies' dead, slain in the assaults on the church, there came a horrible stench. There was no proper food for the sick within the church, and death laid its hand heavily there. Then the cholera came, and proved an enemy tenfold more dreadful than the allies. As soon as the men were seized with this malady they were given heavy doses of opium, and were not allowed to drink water, which was regarded as fatal. The drug drove many to the point of madness, and crying for water they would crawl about over the floor and over the bodies of other victims dead and dying. Sometimes two delirious victims would fall to fighting, grappling and falling over the body of a wounded companion, who would shriek with pain.[1]

√ In the midst of such terrible scenes one figure stood out like a shining light: the church had its Florence Nightingale. She was the wife of an actor named Edward Bingham. With her husband, who had become a helpless invalid, she went to Nicaragua under the promise of free passage and a grant of land, and from the time of her arrival she had helped attend the sick and wounded, and at Guadalupe Church perhaps nursed many a victim to recovery. Her self-denial and courage gained her the warmest gratitude of the soldiers, but she too fell a victim to the dread malady and succumbed within a few hours.[2]

In seventeen days there were one hundred and twenty deaths among the soldiers and non-combatants, not counting those killed in action. The sick were finally removed to some huts connected with the church by a line of adobe breastworks, and conditions then improved.[3] On December 1 the movement toward the lake began. At night the breastworks on either side of the street would be pushed farther, and by day they would be defended against the attacks of the enemy. Thirty men were left in the church to prevent an attack in the rear, and communication between the church

[1] *Harper's Weekly*, I., 71.

[2] Her children perished with her, but her crippled husband survived all the horrors of the siege, and the *San Joaquin Republican* of Feb. 12, 1857, announces his arrival in California. See also *Harper's Weekly*, I., 87.

[3] *War in Nicaragua*, 327–9; Montúfar, 720 ff.; MS. in Wheeler Scrapbook no. 4, 208.

and the advancing party was constantly maintained. Henningsen thus retained a place for retreat in case the advancing barricades should be stormed by the allies. Day after day the enemy sought to cut the communications or to capture the church, but every attack was beaten back with heavy loss. The allies were receiving constant reinforcements, while sickness and wounds were depleting the ranks of the Americans, and food and ammunition were growing scarce in their quarters. But the officers showed great ingenuity in manufacturing solid shot for their six-pounders by making hollows in wet sand with cannon balls, partly filling them with iron slugs, and then pouring in molten lead to hold the mass together.

The besiegers, too, were suffering from fever and cholera, and Paredes, leader of the Guatemalans, succumbed, leaving Zavala as chief in command. From Zavala on December 8 came a second letter to Henningsen, urging him to surrender, and stating that Walker could never aid him, as the last steamers on both sides had brought no recruits. This last statement was totally false. Henningsen sent merely a verbal response, to the effect that he was a soldier and would parley only at the cannon's mouth. Walker during all this time had stood off Granada every day in the steamer *Virgen*, watching for some chance to extricate his men from their perilous situation. The two companies stationed at Virgin Bay could not be withdrawn from that point without allowing the place to fall into the hands of Cañas and Jerez, who had effected a junction at Rivas. This would have given the enemy control of the Transit and have led to the immediate downfall of the filibuster régime.

During the first week in December three hundred recruits arrived from California and New Orleans, and the Americans' prospects brightened perceptibly. The new arrivals were in fine spirits and anxious for a fight. A body of one hundred and sixty, organized into five companies, was then placed in charge of Colonel John Waters, the commander of the Rangers, and on the 11th were

T

embarked on the *Virgen*. All of the following day was spent off the shore at Granada in observation of the enemy's position, and after dark the steamer, with all lights out, moved up to the same spot north of the city where the Americans landed to capture Granada exactly fourteen months before. The men were landed, and Walker returned to the place where the steamer had anchored during the day. Toward midnight the sharp crack of American rifles was heard, followed by the rumble of volleys of musketry from the enemy. The firing then lulled for a time, but soon the rifles cracked again, louder and nearer, giving to the chief the glad news that his trusted leader of the Rangers was driving in the foe. The firing lasted only a few minutes, and then all was silent. Straining their eyes and ears in the direction of the ruined city, the men on the steamer heard a cry from the water as of someone calling for help. A boat was speedily lowered and soon returned bringing a swarthy youth whom Walker in the darkness took to be a native, and began to question in Spanish. To his surprise he was answered in English, and the youth proved to be a Hawaiian lad, "Kanaka John," who had come to Nicaragua with Walker on the *Vesta*. The boy had been for hours in the water, and bore in a bottle a message from Henningsen. It notified Walker of the condition of the besieged and indicated certain signals to be given in case they were to be relieved. The signals were given immediately, but the movements on shore prevented their being observed. The fighting on shore was resumed, and at daybreak Waters had stormed all the barricades of the allies and joined Henningsen, with a loss of over a fourth of his force, fourteen killed and thirty wounded. The way in which he had swept over the barricades in the darkness convinced the enemy that the relieving force was many times greater than was really the case. They therefore immediately abandoned the old fort commanding the pier, and Henningsen seized it and established communications with the steamer. Preparations were begun at once to embark

the survivors of the siege on the *Virgen,* and the enemy offered
no opposition to their withdrawal. As he was departing Henningsen stuck up a lance among the ruins, bearing a strip of rawhide
containing the words "Aquí fué Granada" (Here was Granada).[1]

Of the 421 persons in Granada when the attack began, 124 were
killed or wounded, 120 died, two were captured, and about forty
deserted, bringing the total loss in seventeen days to 286. Of the
total fighting force of 277 available at the beginning of the siege,
124 were either killed or wounded, leaving 153 whom captures and
desertions reduced still further to 111. How many of these were
among the 120 who succumbed to cholera and fever, the statistics
prepared by Henningsen do not show.[2] Of the losses suffered by
the allies we have no reliable data. Henningsen's statement that
they lost between fifteen and sixteen hundred, which he claimed to
base on summaries in the Guatemalan papers, is improbable, as
their total besieging force amounted to not more than three thousand,
and his estimate would mean that they had lost every second man.

The survivors of this memorable siege were carried to San Jorge.
When Cañas and Jerez learned of Henningsen's relief, they hastily
abandoned Rivas, fearing an attack from the artillery now at
Walker's disposal, and joined Belloso at Masaya. The attack on
Granada is not one of the great sieges of history, but few combats
have shown such desperate valour on the part of defenders and such
stubborn resistance against fearful odds. When the besieged were
extricated, Walker was deemed to have accomplished the well-nigh
impossible.

Padre Vijil was at Greytown when word of the burning of
Granada reached him. The old priest was heartbroken at the
news, and walked back and forth wringing his hands and expressing
his bitter regret that he had ever joined with the men who had
alienated his friends and destroyed his property.[3]

[1] *War in Nicaragua,* 318–42; Jamison, *With Walker in Nicaragua,* Ch. 9.
[2] Wheeler Scrapbook no. 4, p. 208. (MS. in Minister Wheeler's handwriting.)
[3] *Harper's Weekly,* April 25, 1857.

CHAPTER XVIII

The Vengeance of Vanderbilt

While Walker's situation still remained critical, his prospects in the middle of December, 1856, were better than at any time since the beginning of the war with the Central American coalition. The enemy had held Masaya at fearful cost, and had been unable to prevent the destruction of Granada or to inflict upon the destroyers the punishment they had planned. Their losses in battle were generally threefold those of the filibusters. They were lacking in leadership, torn with dissensions, scourged with the plague. Cañas and his Costa Ricans were so dispirited after their encounter with Walker on the Transit road on November 11 that a short time thereafter they allowed eighty recruits to land at San Juan del Sur and march past their front to Virgin Bay without molestation, although the newcomers were only one tenth the strength of the force Cañas could have brought against them. The allied forces were almost on the point of disintegration when a new power came to their aid.

Vanderbilt for many months had been in correspondence with the presidents of the Central American republics, urging that they unite against the common enemy.[1] Now that all the governments had taken the field and the filibusters were closely pressed, he perceived that the hour for his revenge had come. In the autumn he sent two agents, an Englishman named William Robert C. Webster and an American named Spencer, to San José to show the Costa Rican government the way to give a death blow to filibusterism. Spencer and Webster reached the capital on November 28,

---

[1] Gámez, *Historia de Nicaragua*, 630-1.

and at once entered into secret consultation with President Mora. The president was enthusiastic over their plans and promised the coöperation of his forces. Vanderbilt knew that an open Transit was the key to Walker's strength, and that if by any means the Costa Ricans could get control of the steamboats on the San Juan River no recruits or supplies could reach the filibusters from the Atlantic ports; and, as passengers could then no longer cross the isthmus, the ocean steamers would be withdrawn, and no further reinforcements would arrive from California. Disease, starvation, and the allies could then be counted upon to effect a speedy collapse of the filibuster régime. Moreover, by blocking the passage of the river, Vanderbilt would not only revenge himself upon Walker, but would have the additional satisfaction of driving his supplanters, Morgan and Garrison, out of business. He then expected that in gratitude for his aid in the extermination of the invaders the Nicaraguan government would grant him a new concession of the Transit route, and his triumph would be complete. Indeed, he felt so sure of the success of his scheme that on Christmas day he published a card in the New York newspapers announcing to the stockholders in the old company that "Present appearances indicate a realization of my hopes that the company will be speedily restored to their rights, franchises, and property upon the isthmus of Nicaragua, which has been so unjustly invaded." [1]

The details of the plan to take the steamers were left entirely to Spencer, who, having served as an engineer on one of the Transit boats, knew their crews personally, and was familiar with all the bends, shoals, and currents of the river. There was no other person who fulfilled these requirements so completely. Mora confided the plan to no one, but called for volunteers for an expedition to the Serapiqui River. The leaders chosen were all foreigners — Captain (later Colonel) Cauty, an English officer, Colonel Barillier, a French Zouave, and Private Spencer, an American desperado.

[1] New York *Herald*, Dec. 25, 1856.

The San Juan River has two important tributaries from the south; the Serapiqui, which joins it at Hipp's Point about thirty-five miles above Greytown; and the San Carlos, which enters the main stream about twenty-seven miles above the Serapiqui. Mora gave out the Serapiqui River as the destination of the expedition for the purpose of concealing its real object, and after the detachment of one hundred and twenty men had set out on the march orders came to the officers to proceed to the Rio San Carlos. Here on December 16 the men embarked in canoes and on rafts and floated into the San Juan, on the banks of which they encamped on the night of December 22, just two miles above Hipp's Point. At the latter spot were a detachment of Americans detailed to guard the river and prevent Costa Ricans from coming down the Serapiqui. They did not dream of an attacking party coming down the San Juan, and were not on their guard. One detachment of Costa Ricans moved to the rear of the Americans on the Point, and placed a sentry in a tall tree to watch their movements. A second party approached them from the front, and at a given signal both detachments fell on them while they were at dinner and killed or captured the entire number. The Americans had posted no sentries, and were some distance from their guns, only four of which were taken from their racks during the melée and only two of which were fired.[1]

The day before this, as one of the river steamers was en route to Greytown, with a number of Walker's officers on board, several men on the boat noted a number of strange rafts at the mouth of the San Carlos River, but no investigation was made, and the party went its way unheeding the danger that was so imminent. Among these officers were Lockridge and Rogers. The former was returning to the United States to continue garnering recruits for Walker,

---

[1] It will be noted that Hipp's Point was captured and the effective blockade of the river begun on the very day that the *Tennessee* left New York with provisions and recruits. See above, p. 239.

while Rogers was en route to Greytown to secure, in his capacity of confiscator-general, the printing outfit brought there by Kinney. Most of the equipment of *El Nicaraguense* had been destroyed in the burning of Granada. Had the officers examined the suspicious-looking objects, the American post at Hipp's Point would have been forewarned, Spencer's plans would have failed, and the history of Nicaragua might now read differently.

After capturing Hipp's Point Spencer left a guard of forty men there and took his prisoners on to Greytown, where he arrived at two o'clock in the morning and seized four river steamers before daylight. The engineers and crews were for the most part willing to continue in service, after Spencer had promised to pay them well. The Costa Rican flag was hoisted over the boats, and they were taken up the San Juan. There was not an American war vessel in the harbour to whom the agent of Morgan and Garrison could appeal for the protection of American property. The American commercial agent, Mr. Cottrell, appealed to the commander of the large British squadron then in the harbour, but that officer declined to interfere, alleging that the property was in dispute betwen two parties, the agent of one of whom authorized the seizure, and he was not prepared to pass upon the merits of the controversy.

In the meantime General José Joaquin Mora, brother of the president and commander-in-chief of the Costa Rican army, had followed Spencer to the San Carlos with a large force, proceeding with much difficulty, as the route was only a trail, overgrown so thickly in places with the rank tropical vegetation that the men had to cut their way through with machetes. As the march lay through an uninhabited region and over a trail too rough for animals, the supplies had to be carried on the backs of men, and six hundred of them were used for this purpose. Mora reached the point of embarkation with eight hundred men, all well armed with Minié guns and fixed ammunition which had been sent

by Vanderbilt. On his return trip up the San Juan Spencer
stopped at the mouth of the San Carlos and sent one of the boats
up this stream to bring down General Mora and his men. As the
steamer approached the landing point a picket of Costa Ricans,
stationed on a raft, were frightened nearly out of their wits by the
strange craft, the like of which they had never seen, and in their
terror plunged into the stream and were drowned. Mora took
command and proceeded up the San Juan to Castillo Viejo, where
he captured two more river steamers. Spencer now took the
steamer used to cross the Toro Rapids, and continuing upstream
found the *Virgen* anchored about thirty miles from the lake awaiting the return of Rogers from Greytown. Concealing his soldiers,
he was able to bring his little craft alongside the lake steamer without arousing the slightest suspicion and easily secured possession.
The next objective was Fort San Carlos, commanding the point
where the lake debouches into the river. On approaching it
Spencer gave the signal that all was well, which had been pre-
arranged months before between the boats and forts and had never
been changed. The commandant, Captain Kruger, at once put
out in a boat, and the garrison all came down to the shore. The
arrival of a steamer was a great event in their monotonous lives.
The Costa Ricans on the *Virgen* were again concealed, and as
Kruger's boat came alongside he called out to Spencer if Rogers
were on board. Receiving an affirmative reply, he boarded the
steamer and was at once told that he was a prisoner. It so happened that Kruger was the only officer at the fort, and his capture
left the post in the command of a sergeant. Spencer compelled
Kruger, under a threat of death, to sign an order to the sergeant
to deliver the post to the English officer, Captain Cauty, and Fort
San Carlos thus fell into the hands of the Costa Ricans without
the firing of a shot.[1]

[1] Wheeler Scrapbook no. 4, 187, 195, 198; New York *Times*, March 9, 1857;
Harper's Weekly, I., 312; *Dublin Review*, XLIII., 382–3.

The San Juan River, from its source to its mouth, was now in the possession of the enemy, but Walker still retained the *San Carlos*, the larger and faster of the lake steamers, and thereby still controlled the lake. Spencer thought it unsafe to venture upon the lake so long as that steamer was in the hands of the filibusters, and he therefore dropped ten miles down the stream in the *Virgen* to await the coming of the other steamer. He had not many days to wait. On January 2, 1857, the steamer from San Francisco arrived at San Juan del Sur with her usual quota of passengers for the Atlantic States. These were duly transported over the Transit road to Virgin Bay and there placed aboard the *San Carlos*. The steamer crossed the lake, and on approaching the fort for which it was named it received the usual signal, given by Cauty's soldiers, that all was well. Seeing nothing to arouse suspicion, it boldly entered the river. It was now caught in a trap, being confronted by a river boat in the charge of Spencer and filled with armed Costa Ricans, and unable to return to the lake without passing under the hostile guns of the fort. Spencer demanded that the steamer surrender. Her captain, a Dane named Ericsson, was anxious to run the gauntlet of the fort and return to Virgin Bay, believing that the Costa Ricans could not damage the boat with their artillery, but a son-in-law of Charles Morgan's, named Harris, who chanced to be one of the passengers, forbade the attempt. The *San Carlos* was then surrendered, and the passengers were sent on to Greytown in one of the river boats. Here they met the recently arrived passengers and recruits who had come on the *James Adger* from New York and on the *Texas* from New Orleans. The eastward-bound passengers were sent home on the *James Adger*, and those bound for California, to the number of two hundred, were taken to Panama at Harris's expense and thence sent on to their destination. To send these to San Francisco cost Morgan and Garrison $25,000 in addition to their usual running expenses.

General Mora, who had been reinforced by the arrival of a rear guard of three hundred, now embarked all his forces, except those needed to hold the posts on the river, on the two lake steamers and took possession of Virgin Bay. He was thus in easy communication with the allies in Masaya, while Walker was cut off entirely from communication with the Caribbean and the United States on the east. Spencer's plans had succeeded in every particular. His master in Wall Street had now only to sit and gloat over the filibusters in their death struggle and over his steamship rivals in their utter confusion. Ten thousand dollars of his money was sent from San José to pay the officers and crew of the captured steamers and secure their loyalty to their new flag and masters. From General Mora came a perfervid address, giving no credit to the author of his success: "The main artery of filibusterism is divided forever. The sword of Costa Rica has severed it." [1] It was not the sword of Costa Rica, but the gold of Vanderbilt and the daring of Spencer that did the work.

The real hero of the San Juan campaign deserves more than passing notice. To all his associates and opponents he was known simply by his family name, and it was only after much research that he was found to bear the full name of Sylvanus H. Spencer. He would tell little of his past, but seemed fond of boasting, after his success on the river, that shortly before this exploit he was only a common workman. [2] He gave as his chief reason for going against

[1] Wheeler Scrapbook no. 4, 177; Perez, *Memorias*, pt. 2, 177. An interesting story, first published twenty years after the events narrated above, and therefore of doubtful authenticity, is told in Gámez, *Historia de Nicaragua*, 669 note. According to this account, Vanderbilt gave a dinner in New York to a number of prominent Spanish Americans, and when his guests, as a result of many toasts, were in a state of great exaltation he announced his purpose of putting an end to the filibusters. When asked how, he sent for Spencer. "Do you think it difficult to capture the steamers in Walker's service?" Vanderbilt asked. "I do not," replied Spencer. "Can you and will you accomplish this undertaking?" "I am at your service." Then, amidst the wonder and silence of his guests, the millionaire wrote a check for $20,000 as his first contribution toward the achievement of Walker's destruction.

[2] According to James Jeffrey Roche, Spencer was a son of John Canfield Spencer, formerly Secretary of War, and was therefore a brother of the only American naval officer ever hanged for mutiny. *Byways of War*, 171.

Walker the fact that he had inherited a large amount of stock in the old Transit Company, and that Walker's revocation of its charter had robbed him of all his property, which he was now trying to recover. As soon as he finished his work he returned to New York, his former home. His cruelty to the Costa Rican soldiers made them glad to be rid of his presence. Shortly after reaching Fort San Carlos General Mora wrote to his brother, the president, not to entrust Spencer with any military commissions, as he knew no tactics and could not manage the men, but to "occupy him in urging the house of Vanderbilt to help us with their influence and materials of war." [1] An attempt is noticeable on the part of a recent Costa Rican writer to belittle the work of Spencer and portray him merely as a guide, while ascribing all the glory of the San Juan campaign to his own countrymen.[2] Earlier Central American historians, however, have begrudged the American none of his laurels.

While Costa Rica held the river and lake, three contingents of recruits for Walker arrived at Greytown, and found themselves deprived of means of transportation into the interior. The first steamer to arrive was the *Texas*, bringing the detachment from New Orleans already described. When the vessel entered the harbour Spencer was there with one of the river boats and a party of Costa Ricans. The recruits were kept concealed below decks, and the rifles and ammunition were unpacked in preparation for seizing Spencer's boat at night. The plan was frustrated, however, by Captain Cockburn of H. M. S. *Cossack*, who came aboard the *Texas* and stated that while he was neutral in the matter of the Transit dispute between two different parties of Americans, he would allow no bloodshed or destruction of property in waters under British

---

[1] *Harper's Weekly*, I., 71, 199; New York *Times*, March 30, 1857; Wheeler Scrapbook no. 4, 210.

[2] Señor Manuel Carazo Peralta, in the introduction to his translation of Roche's *Story of the Filibusters* (San José, 1908), says that the only American who took part in the campaign was Spencer, "que hacía oficios de guía."

protection. Spencer meanwhile had taken alarm and moved his boat into the shallow water upstream where the Americans could not follow.[1]

Among those now detained at Greytown as a result of Spencer's activities were many of Walker's best officers. Colonel Frank P. Anderson, of "the original fifty-six," was returning from a furlough granted him pending his recovery from a wounded arm. While at his home in Brooklyn his admirers had given a banquet in his honour and presented him with a sword. On the boat with him was Charles W. Doubleday, who was in Nicaragua when Walker first arrived, and soon joined the Phalanx. He had rendered valuable service on account of his knowledge of the country and people, but resigned after a disagreement with Walker, and now that his old chief was sorely pressed he had decided to return to his aid. With these came also General Robert Chatham Wheat, who had been captured in Cuba while following Lopez, and had served several months as a prisoner in Spain. Later he had participated in a revolution in Mexico, attaining the rank of brigadier-general and becoming military governor of Vera Cruz. He had attended college with Walker's brother James at Nashville, and his desire to be with his countrymen caused him to resign his Mexican commission and go to Nicaragua. He never was able to join Walker, but lived to fight another day as colonel of the "Louisiana Tigers" during the Civil War. Colonel George B. Hall, son of a former mayor of Brooklyn, a veteran of the Mexican War, and Walker's commissary-general, was another of the detained officers, having been at home to recuperate from the fever. Still another was Captain J. Egbert Farnum, formerly of Pennsylvania, who had seen service both in the Mexican War and under Lopez. Hornsby, Norvell Walker, and Rogers, already mentioned several times in these pages, were also there. It will be seen, therefore, that Spencer had deprived Walker not only of his steamers but also of the services of some of his ablest officers.

[1] Oliphant, *Patriots and Filibusters*, 183–6.

Strange to say, these officers allowed the command of the stranded recruits at Greytown to devolve upon Lockridge, who, though given the rank of colonel, was commissioned only as a recruiting officer, and had seen no active service. It appears that as the recruits were regarded as still in transit and not yet in Walker's service, Lockridge was regarded as the proper man to take command, not by the other officers but by Harris, the agent and son-in-law of Charles Morgan, who was anxious to regain control of the Transit property and presumed to take the direction of matters into his own hands. The officers who outranked Lockridge volunteered to serve under him, and the recruits were quartered across the harbour from Greytown at Punta Arenas. The men were at once put to work patching up the old abandoned river steamer *Rescue*, which Spencer had not thought it worth while to capture, but their labours did not proceed without British interference. When in Greytown, the men were continually approached by British sailors, who gave them terrible accounts of what to expect if they persisted in going into the interior, and one morning in January Captain Cockburn came over with a boat's crew and ordered Lockridge to parade his men, stating that he intended to take away all British subjects who desired his protection. At the same time the guns of the *Cossack* were trained on the Point, and Lockridge must needs submit. When the men were drawn up, Cockburn made his offer, and some score of them stepped forward, though many of these pseudo-Britishers had a suspicious German accent instead of the expected Cockney or Irish brogue. The irrepressible Wheat, mounting a boat near by, hurled profane objurgations at John Bull and his right of search, and challenged Cockburn to a duel.[1]

In spite of such desertions, the force at Punta Arenas remained fairly intact, and perhaps was improved by the withdrawal of the faint-hearted. On February 4 the *Texas* came again, bringing

[1] Doubleday, *Reminiscences*, 178–81; Wheeler Scrapbook no. 4, 177.

the long-expected Titus and one hundred and eighty of his "border ruffians." All the men were well supplied with arms and ammunition, and the rickety steamboat was finally ready for the ascent of the river. The choice of a leader had been unfortunate. Lockridge, a tall, gaunt, stoop-shouldered Kentuckian of the Hoosier type, was anything but a soldier, and failed to win the confidence of his men or to stamp out by his authority petty jealousies and bickerings among his officers. Arriving before Hipp's Point, the Americans drove out the Costa Rican garrison with great loss and regained possession. The credit for this success lay with Anderson, Doubleday, and Wheat. Castillo Viejo was the next point of attack, and Lockridge designated the Kansas company, a fine-looking but ill-disciplined body of men, for the work. Titus, swollen with pride over the newspaper notoriety he had attained in Kansas, refused to serve under anyone else, and therefore was sent alone in the steamer with his unorganized followers, while the tried and seasoned officers remained behind. Cauty was in command of Castillo, an historic fortress of the Spanish era, sitting on a high hill and commanding the river. In the previous century it had been attacked and captured by Horatio Nelson. As Titus approached the fort Cauty hastened to save the four steamboats moored below at the head of the rapids. Two of these were carried over successfully, and the two which proved unmanageable were set on fire and destroyed. Cauty, having only thirty men in the fort and a scant supply of ammunition, abandoned the lower works as soon as Titus came in sight. The latter took possession of these and also captured the steamer *Scott*, which had been set on fire after being taken over the rapids. The fire was extinguished by the Americans and the boat was cut adrift to float out of range of the guns on the hill. Cauty then set the last of his steamers on fire and sent it drifting down on the *Scott*, but the men boarded it and tied it to the bank, though they were unable to save the craft from burning. Titus now had the Englishman at his mercy and demanded his surrender. Cauty replied that he could surrender only with the consent of his commanding officer at Fort San Carlos, and asked for a twenty-four hours' truce in order to obtain the latter's permission. Titus, who knew nothing of war or military matters, gave his consent. Cauty had already sent for reinforcements, and before the truce expired these had arrived. Titus did not even wait to ascertain the number of reinforcements, but fled down the river bank to his steamers and hastily reëmbarked. The Costa Ricans had now lost their four river steamers, but Castillo was defended more strongly than before. The Americans took up their post on San Carlos Island, some miles below Castillo Viejo, where they erected a stockade for defence against the enemy and built some rough sheds for the men's quarters. The soldiers had been exposed for weeks to the heavy rains, and were surrounded on all sides with dense tropical swamps. Fever was rife; discipline was conspicuous for its absence, and the men were in very low spirits. The return of Titus from his fiasco at Castillo increased the depression, and desertion coöperated with fever to thin the ranks. Titus was so much criticised that he gave up his command and announced his intention of going to Walker by way of Panama. Toward the middle of March one hundred and thirty fresh recruits from Texas and Louisiana arrived and brought the effective force to four hundred. The Louisiana company consisted largely of foreigners recruited in New Orleans and was not a valuable accession, but the Texans, styling themselves the Alamo Rangers, were recruited from San Antonio and were a splendid body of men. They were commanded by Marcellus French, who has left us an account of his experiences.[1]

After this reinforcement Lockridge decided to renew his attempt to take Castillo Viejo and embarked his men for the attack. They landed, only to find that the Costa Ricans since the departure of Titus had made the place well-nigh impregnable. All the under-

[1] See *Overland Monthly*, N. S., XXI., 517-23.

growth had been cleared away from around the defences, and along the slopes of the hill they had constructed an *abatis* with felled trees. Wheat, Hornsby, and Doubleday all agreed that any attack on the strengthened works would fail. Nothing remained but to reëmbark and return to Greytown, and they left Castillo in the hands of the enemy without firing a shot. On stopping at the rapids, Lockridge assembled all his able-bodied men on the hurricane deck of the *Scott* and notified them that the expedition was disbanded and that officers and men were all on the same footing. He then called for volunteers who would join him in an effort to reach Walker at any hazard, either by way of Panama or by going up the Serapiqui and cutting through Costa Rica to San Juan del Sur. Some half a dozen officers and a hundred men responded. The others were placed on board the *Rescue*, which was already carrying two hundred sick, and were sent on to Greytown. As the *Rescue*, loaded to the water's edge with sick and despondent men, pulled away down the stream, Hornsby remarked, "I have been a soldier for twenty years, and this is the saddest sight I have ever witnessed." The *Scott* followed, and on approaching Hipp's Point both the steamers were stopped, and a reconnoitering party was landed to see whether the Costa Ricans had retaken the place while Lockridge's party were up the river. Most of the men on the *Scott* went ashore, and it was lucky that they did so, for the boiler of the steamer soon thereafter exploded, killing a number and badly injuring others, among them Anderson, Marcellus French, and Doubleday. Hornsby, Wheat, and Walker's brother Norvell were among those who escaped. The injured were placed on a barge which the *Scott* had in tow, and such as could be accommodated on the *Rescue*, along with the sick already on that boat, were hurried to Greytown. Great was the disappointment of the men to learn that the *Tennessee* had left only two hours before for Aspinwall. English naval surgeons tendered their services, and as the *Tennessee* would call again at Greytown on her return to New York, Lockridge hurried back to bring the remainder of his command down the river and embark the whole force for home. Morgan had ordered the steamer to bring home any stranded fili-busters at Greytown who cared to return, and all of them had given up hope of joining Walker after the destruction of the *Scott*. As the *Rescue* returned to the harbour the men on board saw the *Tennessee* steaming out to sea and leaving them to they knew not what sort of a fate. A few moments before they had had visions of a fine steamer awaiting their arrival in order to take them back to civilization and the States. How bitter their disappointment now as they watched the hull disappear below the eastern horizon! There would not be another steamer for a month. The captain of the *Tennessee* had been urged to take all the Americans home, but would take only fifty, as he had orders to call at Key West and take on board a detachment of United States troops stationed there.

The sufferings of the poor wretches, now quartered at Punta Arenas, were terrible. Greytown was too small a village to furnish subsistence, and the sick and injured could find no accommodation there even when they chanced to have money to pay for it. The villagers even appealed to the British ships for protection against the men, many of whom were becoming desperate, and guards were stationed to prevent their entering the place without permission from the authorities. Credit, however, must be given to a few of the residents, who took into their homes some of the officers injured in the explosion of the *Scott* and nursed them to recovery without hope of any earthly reward.[1] Many of the men died from exposure and lack of food and medical care. To make matters worse, Cauty in his sole remaining river steamer came down the San Juan with a detachment of Costa Ricans, and it looked as if

---

[1] Among these good Samaritans was a Miss Roberts, a native of New York, who looked after the injuries of French and Lieutenant Sistere of Louisiana. Double-day was cared for by a family of kind-hearted Germans.

the dispirited Americans would be attacked and exterminated. The British squadron, however, quickly threw a line of small boats between the Costa Rican steamer and the Point, and hauled the *Rescue* alongside a man-of-war, thus reiterating the determination of its commander to permit no hostilities or destruction of property in Greytown harbour. The British senior officer, Captain Cockburn, now summoned Cauty and J. N. Scott, Morgan and Garrison's agent, to a conference, and announced his intention to take the men away. He asked Scott to draw on Morgan for the cost of their passage and the agent reluctantly agreed to do so. As security for the draft the Americans were required to give up their arms as well as the steamer *Rescue,* and the men to the number of 375 were then taken aboard the *Cossack* and carried to Aspinwall. Cockburn there tried to get passage on the mail steamer for the United States, but met with difficulties. In the first place the agent refused to honour Scott's draft on Morgan; Cockburn then offered to make himself individually responsible for twenty dollars a head for two hundred of the men and would raise the rest of the money by the sale of the arms given to him as security. Again there was objection: an epidemic of measles had appeared among the filibusters, and the steamer would not carry the men for any consideration. The municipal authorities refused to allow the Americans to land, declaring that they did not desire to be overrun with such vagabonds, and refused their hospital to the sick. Yea, they even refused permission to bury the dead on shore, and the sea alone seemed willing to receive their festering, vermin-ridden bodies. The survivors were finally taken to New Orleans on Her Majesty's Ship *Tartar.*[1]

Since the Transit could not be recovered, the withdrawal by Morgan and Garrison of their ocean steamers was inevitable.

---

[1] MS., Archives, Navy Department, Home Squadron, II., 27 ff.; New Orleans *Delta,* April 28, 1857; New York *Tribune,* May 7, 1857; Wheeler Scrapbook no. 4, 221.

Neither recruits nor supplies could reach Walker by way of Greytown, and passengers between New York and California could no longer be carried by the Nicaraguan route. There was nothing, therefore, for the steamship company to do but to dock its ships and leave Walker to his fate. This was done in April, 1857, and the end was then only a matter of days. Vanderbilt's man had succeeded in doing what the allied Central American States could not accomplish. It was American capitalists who set up the filibuster régime in Nicaragua, and it was an American capitalist who pulled it down.

It is worthy of note that one of Walker's officers possessed pluck enough to rejoin his chief in spite of the blockade of the river and lake. This was Rogers, the confiscator-general. Instead of following Lockridge, he embarked for Aspinwall, crossed to Panama, and finding no steamer for San Juan del Sur he hired a boat and two men, ostensibly to cross over to the Pearl Islands, some fifty miles away, but really to go the entire five hundred miles to San Juan del Sur. No boatman would have consented to make such a trip, and hence the necessity of Rogers' deception. After taking enough provisions on board for several days' journey Rogers started, and when some distance from shore he drew a brace of pistols and made the boatmen steer straight for the open sea and Walker. And so he sat, watching the men day and night, with weapons always at hand, not daring to doze even a moment, until his unwilling crew brought him safely into the harbour of San Juan del Sur. Rogers had in him the stuff of which real filibusters are made. In addition, he was an Irishman. We may condemn the wild ways of such men, but we at least must admit that the race from which they came was not degenerate. The blood in their veins flowed red.[1]

[1] Oliphant, *Patriots and Filibusters*, 226-7. Oliphant was a fellow passenger of Rogers as far as Panama, and was invited by the latter to join him in this venture. New York *Times*, March 9, 1857.

CHAPTER XIX

In the Last Ditch

About the time that Spencer began his operations on the San Juan, Walker began the concentration of his forces at Rivas. This was a small city with thick-walled adobe houses, and had already been used as a fortress by the Costa Ricans in their invasion of the preceding spring. It was well adapted for defensive operations. To the east, a league distant, lay the village of San Jorge on the shores of Lake Nicaragua. To the south lay the Transit road, to which three diverging trails led from Rivas like a fan, giving the Americans control over this highway. The total American force established here amounted on January 3, 1857, to 919, of whom 197 were reported as sick. Those detailed for duty with the commissary and other departments and those on detached services of various kinds further reduced the number available for service in the line to 518. A fortnight after the occupation of Rivas the *San Carlos* left Virgin Bay with its passengers from California, as the Americans were still ignorant of Spencer's capture of all the other steamers. As the days passed and neither of the lake steamers reappeared, the men at Rivas began to feel uneasy, but still no one dreamed that the enemy could have taken all the boats, and it was thought that one of them would surely have brought back the news if the Costa Ricans had really been seen on the river. The more optimistic therefore ascribed the delay to other causes easily imaginable in connection with the transfer of passengers to and from Greytown.

For days and days they watched and waited, but no steamer

appeared. Then one day the long expected *San Carlos* was seen coming across the lake and apparently headed for Virgin Bay, but as it drew near the landing place it failed to give the usual signals or to return those given from the shore. Instead, it only took a look at the place and then headed due north. Many of the Americans residing there immediately gathered a few belongings in their carpet-bags and started for San Juan del Sur as fast as their feet could carry them, in the hope of taking the California steamer, still waiting there to make its connection with the steamer on the Atlantic. A detachment of soldiers was hastily sent to Virgin Bay to prevent the enemy's landing. There they waited for a week, with no sign or news of the Costa Ricans, until the *San Carlos* again appeared and moored off Ometepe in full sight of the soldiers at Virgin Bay. A few mornings later they awoke to see the *Virgen* also there, and the full truth then was known.[1] Both the lake steamers and presumably all the river craft were in the hands of the enemy. It was not till the 24th of January that definite word reached Walker by way of Panama of what had actually occurred on the San Juan.[2]

Shortly before Spencer began his exploits a small schooner had been brought up the river from Greytown and was being repaired for use on the lake when the steamers appeared off Ometepe. Walker now consulted Fayssoux as to the feasibility of employing this vessel in an effort to retake the steamers. Some of the men were anxious to cross over to Ometepe in the schooner on some night when the wind was favourable and seize the steamers in the darkness. Fayssoux, however, thought it useless to make the attempt, and the schooner was burned to prevent her capture by the enemy.

General Mora made no effort to communicate with the allies at Masaya until he had brought his entire force to San Carlos and made the defence of the river secure. The allies were almost on

[1] "Experience of Samuel Absalom, Filibuster," *Atlantic Monthly*, IV., 651–65.
[2] *War in Nicaragua*, 371.

the point of abandoning the campaign when they received word of the Costa Rican successes. As these gave Mora and Cañas a preponderating influence in the counsels of the allies, Cañas became chief in command, and an immediate advance upon Walker's position was begun. Henningsen in the meantime had been putting Rivas in a state of defence. Walker still contemplated acting on the offensive but desired that the town should be put in such a condition that a small garrison could hold it and protect his military stores while he marched forth with most of his forces to give battle to the enemy. Small huts on the outskirts of the town were burned down and the dense tropical undergrowth was cleared away lest the enemy should find shelter therein. New barricades were built and old ones strengthened. Colonel Swingle set up workshops in the town and secured a small steam engine from San Juan del Sur, by means of which he was enabled to construct a foundry to make cannon balls, perhaps the first ever cast in Nicaragua. All the bells in the vicinity of Rivas were collected and cast into solid shot.

On January 26 the allies occupied the small village of Obraje, about three miles north of Rivas and fortified themselves so strongly there that Henningsen advised against attacking them in force. Two days later they moved to San Jorge on the lake, where they could communicate with Mora. This village, too, they rapidly barricaded.[1] On the 29th Henningsen and Sanders were sent to drive them out. There was jealousy, however, on the part of Sanders and other officers toward Henningsen, and the commands of the two men became separated. A number of officers, too, had imbibed too freely before going into action, and their heads were so muddled with aguardiente that they could not understand their orders or execute them correctly. The attack

[1] "The rapidity with which Central American troops throw up barricades is almost incredible, and long practice has made them more expert at such work than even a Paris mob." *War in Nicaragua*, 375.

failed, and Walker lost eighty of the four hundred men engaged. The enemy outnumbered the Americans five to one, and were so strongly intrenched that success would have been impossible unless the proportion of Americans to allies had been reversed. Owing to the jealousy of Henningsen, Walker recalled him, and on February 4 took charge himself of an attack on San Jorge, which was made at four o'clock in the morning with two hundred men. Again it proved impossible to send the men over the barricades, and again the Americans suffered losses they could ill afford — twenty-five men, including several of the best officers.

President Mora now resorted to new tactics to compass the downfall of the filibusters. A year before, when he invaded Nicaragua, he had threatened all filibusters with death who were taken with arms in their hands. This had only strengthened the Americans in their resistance, and had caused them to fight all the more fiercely. He now scattered printed proclamations in the outskirts of Rivas, promising protection and a free passport home to all who should desert Walker. No longer was he seeking to destroy all invaders, but only their leader. In 1856 he had declared war on all filibusters; in 1857 he was making war on only one. The effects of Mora's proclamation quickly appeared. Desertion became an epidemic. It was most common among the Californians, whose freer life in the West had made them less amenable to the rigours of military discipline than were the troops from the Atlantic States. Recruits came only from San Francisco, after the closure of the San Juan River, and many of these, grievously disappointed at finding conditions not at all as they had been represented, and feeling in no way bound by honour to serve what seemed to be a dying cause, went over to the enemy at the first opportunity. There were no ties to bind them to Walker like those that bound the survivors of the "original fifty-six," and other early comers.

With each repulse of the Americans the enemy grew bolder and

fought with more confidence. They now came out from their
barricades, and on March 5 appeared on the Transit road and
inflicted a severe defeat upon Walker's Rifles, commanded by
Sanders and Waters, who had been sent to drive them back to
San Jorge. This time both sides were about equal in numbers
(160 Rifles and 200 allies), and the effect of the defeat was therefore
very depressing upon the Americans. Seeing that something must
be done to revive the drooping spirits of his followers, Walker now
planned to throw his entire strength upon the enemy at San Jorge
in one final effort to dislodge them from their position. Four
hundred men were all he could muster for the purpose. Henningsen brought out all the available artillery, seven guns of various
patterns. The march on the village began at two o'clock on the
morning of March 16, and at daybreak the artillery opened the
combat. The fire drove the enemy from the plaza, and they moved
out in large numbers through the dense vegetation, so as to place
themselves in Walker's rear and prevent his return to Rivas. This
necessitated Walker's facing about and giving battle on the road
leading back to his headquarters. The allies had tried to enter
Rivas during his absence, but were held at bay by Swingle. Half
a mile from the centre of the town, however, they had erected
a barricade, and it required a day's fighting before the whole
force with its artillery and the wounded could be brought
back to the starting-point. Seventy-six of the four hundred were
killed or wounded, and the Americans had nothing to show for
the attack. The allies still held San Jorge, and were receiving
constant reinforcements, while the strongest force that could be
sent against them narrowly escaped being surrounded and wiped
out. With the affair of March 16 Walker shot his last bolt.
Henceforth he remains strictly on the defensive. While the allies
in nearly every encounter suffered much heavier losses than the
Americans, they could afford to lose five men to Walker's one and
still fight on equal terms.

On March 23, just a week later, the enemy took the offensive and attacked the Americans in Rivas just before daybreak. The allies were driven back with heavy loss and Cañas' four-pound gun, which had been handled with much skill by an Italian gunner, was captured and taken into the town. The allies also employed two antiquated twenty-four pounders of the Spanish days, which had been brought across the lake. At infrequent intervals they dropped solid shot into the plaza. Swingle took these, re-cast them into six-pound shot, and fired them back at the enemy.

A roster of the forces, sent by Walker to Edmund Randolph on the following day, shows that there were all told some eight hundred people in Rivas, of whom 332 were men fit for duty in the line and 224 were sick or wounded. The remainder consisted of ordnance, commissary and hospital employees, discharged soldiers, and citizens. Walker stated that a very slight blow would dislodge the enemy, but as he did not wish to lose men unnecessarily he would merely occupy the town and wait for something definite from Lockridge. He had sent word to the latter by way of Panama to join him at Rivas, and did not wish to evacuate the place as long as a hope remained that the Americans on the river would succeed in forcing its passage.[1]

It was now impossible for foraging parties to go very far from Rivas, as they were likely to fall into an ambush. On March 27 the besieged got their first taste of mule meat.[2] The first mules were killed secretly at night along with some oxen, and no one suspected the nature of his diet. On the next day, however, the secret was discovered, and a number refused their meat until told that they had already been eating it unawares. Along with mule meat the men received plantains and chocolate. The animals were fed on the leaves of mango trees. It was not mule meat or twenty-four-pound guns that did most to depress the men at Rivas,

---

[1] Wheeler Scrapbook no. 4, 235.
[2] Jamison, *With Walker in Nicaragua*, 154; New Orleans *Delta*, May 28, 1857.

but the constant desertions to the enemy. Some of those who deserted on Mora's promise of protection threw notes within Walker's lines notifying their comrades that the Costa Ricans were doing all for them that had been promised. These notes sometimes reached their destination and greatly increased the desertions. The last company to arrive from California, the Red Star Guards, numbered seventy when it reached Nicaragua on March 7, but early in April only twelve were left.[1]

The Americans suspected that the allies would choose the anniversary of the second battle of Rivas, April 11, for another attack on the town, and shortly before dawn on this date their suspicions were confirmed. The enemy fell upon the town at three different points, but were everywhere repulsed. A body of recruits from Guatemala, which had arrived on the previous day, went into action in entire ignorance of the range of rifles and were sent so close to the American lines that the defenders were almost moved with pity as they shot them down. Walker lost only three killed and six wounded, while the allies lost between 600 and 800. As Walker had no food for his enemy's wounded left within his lines after the attack was repulsed, he sent these back to the allies under a flag of truce. During the fighting the Americans also captured seventy uninjured prisoners. Walker proposed to exchange these for beef cattle, but the allies rejected the offer. He next proposed that the allies feed these prisoners while they were in his custody. This proposition they also declined, as the enemy had reason to doubt whether the food they sent would reach those for whom it was intended. The action of April 11 was the last engagement of the war with the allies. The fighting thereafter consisted only of desultory firing and skirmishing between advanced posts and detachments.

On the night after the attack Walker despatched Captain Han-

---

[1] The captain of this company has left an account of its short and inglorious career. See William Frank Stewart, *Last of the Filibusters*. (Sacramento, 1857.)

kins and two native boys to San Juan del Sur to get the mail from Panama. Hankins returned on the 14th riding a horse, which was a welcome addition to the food supply. This incident shows that the enemy had made no effort to invest the entire town, and that the whole force could have marched from Rivas to the Pacific coast without let or hindrance. In fact, it was this very thing that Walker had planned to do as soon as the exhaustion of his supplies made it impossible longer to hold Rivas. He remained in the town partly on account of Lockridge, whom he had ordered to join him there, and partly because he was unwilling to leave several hundred sick and wounded to fall into the hands of the allies. It was his purpose, if it became necessary to abandon Rivas, to march to San Juan del Sur and place his effective force on board the *Granada*, which was now well supplied with munitions of war. Hankins brought letters notifying Walker of the arrival of the Alamo Rangers and a Mobile company on the San Juan to reinforce Lockridge. This gave some encouragement, but he also brought letters from New York announcing that Morgan and Garrison had definitely decided to withdraw their ocean steamers from the Nicaraguan service. Even, therefore, if Lockridge's efforts should be successful, no further reinforcements from the United States could be expected until other arrangements for transportation could be effected, and it was evident that the days of the filibuster régime were numbered.

Walker attributes his abandonment by the steamship company to weakness and timidity, and declares that while he expected Morgan and Garrison to remain loyal to him only so long as their interests required it, he at least expected them to display more boldness and sagacity than they exhibited during this period of crisis.[1] As a matter of fact, however, these men showed good judgment in realizing the futility of further fighting with Vanderbilt, and as their steamers could no longer be used except to convey

[1] *War in Nicaragua*, 408-9.

recruits and supplies to Walker, now leading a forlorn hope, their withdrawal of the ships was not only necessary as a matter of business policy, but was also an act of humanity. Every additional recruit was doomed to much suffering and perhaps to death, and could be lured to the country only by deception. It was not through treachery of Morgan and Garrison that Walker's cause was lost. Their steamers remained in service on the Pacific for more than three months after the closure of the Transit, and from the Atlantic ports they also brought recruits as long as any hope remained of reopening the river.

Another actor now appeared on the scene. Early in February the United States sloop-of-war *St. Mary's*, Commander Charles H. Davis, had arrived at San Juan del Sur. Davis had received instructions on January 19, 1857, from Commodore Mervine at Panama to proceed to San Juan del Sur and take such steps as circumstances required for the protection of American citizens and their property during the unsettled state of affairs in Nicaragua.[1] Shortly after Davis's arrival the allies asked him to prevent the further landing of recruits for Walker at San Juan del Sur, alleging that such an act would be in complete conformity with the policy of the American government, which on numerous occasions had prevented the departure of expeditions from the United States. Davis replied that while the officers of his government were bound to enforce the neutrality laws within the jurisdiction of the United States, this did not mean that naval officers must enforce such laws within the territory of foreign powers. He stated further that his government recognized a condition of civil war in Nicaragua and was neutral as between the parties thereto. As a neutral he would lend his aid to neither party, but would see that the property and lives of American citizens were duly protected.

In protecting American property Davis showed commendable zeal. An American vessel, the *Narragansett*, was in the port of

[1] House Ex. Doc. 2, 35 Cong., 1 Sess. Wheeler Scrapbook no. 4, 203.

San Juan del Sur at the time of the capture of the lake steamers. Walker took possession of her boats and put them on the lake with the idea of using them to regain possession of the steamers. Davis secured their return. A band of Costa Ricans at San Juan del Sur fired on a party of sailors from Morgan and Garrison's steamer *Orizaba*. They had been sent ashore to obtain water, and one of the sailors was made a prisoner. Davis intervened and secured his release.[1] On April 24 Davis sent Lieutenant Huston and a corporal of marines into Rivas, after securing the consent of the belligerents, to remove the women and children to San Juan del Sur under the protection of the American flag.

While this was in progress a truce was declared, and the opposing forces mingled freely around the outer barricades. The natives gave the Americans aguardiente and tobacco, which were boons to those who were addicted to their use, and they probably persuaded many doubting Thomases to desert. At any rate, the desertions became even more common thereafter, and during the following week amounted to from fifteen to twenty per day. Even one of the surgeons in the hospital deserted and at night came within speaking distance of the barricades and urged all who could to join the enemy, assuring them good treatment and pledging his honour as a Mason that the enemy would not molest the sick and wounded Americans if Rivas were taken.[2] It was this last consideration which had caused numbers of filibusters still to remain loyal. The fear that the enemy would butcher their sick and wounded comrades, as the Costa Ricans had done the year before, had nerved many with a resolve to fight to the death. Titus, the "border ruffian," who after his fiasco at Castillo Viejo had joined Walker by way of Panama, Bostick, Walker's secretary of state, and Bell, major in the infantry, were among those who went over to the enemy's camp. The bad example set by the officers had its effect on the men. Some of the deserters were so inconsiderate

---

[1] Wheeler Scrapbook no. 4, 229.　　　　[2] *Ibid.*, p. 212.

as to take their horses with them, thus materially reducing the scant provisions. Titus and other deserters night after night mounted the allies' barricades and called on their comrades to come and join them, sometimes singling them out by name, and regaling the starving men with accounts of an abundance of food, tobacco and aguardiente. The Americans were not fighting for their native country; very few were fighting for aught but adventure — a cause hardly to be regarded as sacred — and it is not surprising that they availed themselves of the opportunity to escape the torments of hunger and of thirst for strong drink, which most of them possessed, and escaped during the heavy night rains to the camp of their erstwhile foe. Walker at length issued a proclamation that all who wished to leave might do so by applying to him for their passports. This would prevent their being regarded as deserters. Only five men availed themselves of this opportunity, and as they left the town they were hissed and hooted as long as they were in hearing. The courage of one of these failed him and he turned back, but Walker compelled him to go on.

On April 28 Walker visited the men at their quarters and assured them that he had received news from Lockridge, and that the latter was expected to arrive at almost any time. It was known that Walker had received letters that day, and the men hoped that what he told them was true. Nothing occurred, however, except desultory firing until the evening of the 30th, when a letter came to Walker from Commander Davis, borne by an aide of General Mora. Davis had come to the conclusion that Walker's position was no longer tenable, and had visited the allies in the capacity of mediator, proposing to end the conflict by removing the Americans from the country. Mora, who had twice been beaten back from his assault on Rivas, according to his own statement had concluded that it would cost too much blood to take the place by assault and had found the opposing force much stronger than he had been led to believe. He had just resolved

to starve Walker into surrendering when Davis intervened, and
stated that if the Americans would be spared he would compel
Walker to surrender. In return for sparing their lives, Mora was
to receive all the elements of war at Rivas and San Juan del Sur.[1]
The proposition of Davis was readily consented to by the allies,
as it achieved all they were contending for without further fighting
or expense. Davis then sent to Walker the letter just referred to.
Several messages were exchanged before negotiations were finally
undertaken. Early in the night the preliminaries were arranged,
and Walker sent Henningsen and Waters as envoys to Davis in
the camp of the allies. The naval officer told them that he had
full knowledge of Walker's situation, and that they could hold out
only a few days longer at the most. He told them also that
Lockridge had abandoned the San Juan campaign and returned to
the United States, and that no more steamers would come to San
Juan del Sur. He knew that the Americans lacked food and were
deserting in large numbers, and he proposed that the survivors
should surrender to him and that Walker and sixteen officers that
he might select should go aboard the *St. Mary's* and proceed to
Panama, while the other officers and the men were to be taken to
Panama by another route, accompanied by a United States officer
and protected by the American flag. Henningsen was inclined at
first to demur, stating that it was not yet certain that Lockridge
had abandoned the river, and that if he had Walker could easily
cut his way out of Rivas and embark at San Juan del Sur on the
Granada. Davis then announced that he would not allow the
schooner to leave the port, but intended taking possession of her
before he left San Juan del Sur. The conference lasted until two
o'clock in the morning, when Henningsen and Waters returned to
Rivas, promising to give Davis Walker's answer the next morning
at ten, if negotiations were not broken off.

[1] Mora's official report was copied in a number of American papers from the San
José *Cronica*. Wheeler Scrapbook no. 4, 215.

Davis's announcement of his determination to seize the *Granada*, thus cutting off all hope of escape, made his proposition nothing less than an ultimatum to which Walker must agree or perish. Articles of capitulation were therefore drawn up at Walker's headquarters, embodying the propositions made by Davis and containing an additional provision for the protection of Walker's native allies, about whom nothing had been said at the conference. Walker declared that he would sign no agreement that did not contain stipulations for their protection. With these articles Henningsen returned to Davis at the appointed hour. They met his approval, and Henningsen then went back to get Walker's signature. While in conference with Davis Henningsen avoided the officers of the allies, merely exchanging common courtesies with two of them and taking pains to show that he was treating only with the American commander. Waters was sent to Davis with the papers and remained until Walker notified him that he was ready to leave.

Meanwhile the arsenal and cannon were destroyed by Henningsen's orders. The engine, fan, and cupola of the foundry were demolished. Thirteen guns were made useless by breaking their trunnions and sawing through their carriages, and 1500 pounds of powder, 55,000 cartridges, and 300,000 percussion caps were thrown into wells. It was not for lack of munitions of war that the filibusters surrendered. Only the small arms and some six hundred solid shot and shell for the artillery remained undestroyed.

At five o'clock in the afternoon of May 1 Davis and Zavala entered the plaza, the latter for the purpose of acting as a personal escort of Walker and his officers through the lines of the allies. The men were drawn up in the plaza and Walker's last order (no. 59) was read to them. In this Walker stated that he had entered into the present agreement on the solemn assurance that Lockridge had abandoned efforts for their relief and returned to the United States. He then declared that he parted with them for the present and expressed his thanks to the officers and men under his command, declaring that they were reduced to their "present position by the cowardice of some, the incapacity of others, and the treachery of many," but that "the army has yet written a page of American history which it is impossible to forget or erase. From the future, if not from the present, we may expect just judgment." After this farewell address the text of the agreement between Walker and Davis was read. Henningsen then stepped forward and announced to the men that they were under the control of Commander Davis and under the protection of the American flag, and that they would be expected to yield to the naval officer the same implicit obedience that they had rendered to their commander-in-chief. Henningsen then formally turned over the garrison to Davis, and the latter also spoke to the men, asking them to assist him in carrying out his arduous labours. The sailor and the filibuster then repaired to Walker's headquarters but found them unoccupied. While the proceedings just narrated were taking place, Walker and his chosen officers had procured horses and taken the road to San Juan del Sur, accompanied by General Zavala.[1]

Walker's early departure was much resented by the rank and file, who felt that their leader was deserting them in their hour of misery and thinking of his own safety first of all. Like the captain of a sinking ship, he should have stood by till the last person was saved. Instead, he was the first to seek safety and left a third of his followers sick and wounded. That he chose to return home by a different route from theirs also aroused unfavourable comment, and some of his critics stated that he was afraid to face any but his most trusted officers after all restraint of military discipline had been removed. Walker's seeming desertion of his followers was made all the more apparent shortly after the soldiers of the allies marched into the plaza at Rivas. He had given no promise to Davis concerning the arsenal and its contents, and it is probable

[1] Wheeler Scrapbook no. 4, 202; *War in Nicaragua*, 421-7.

x

that the latter did not even suspect its existence. The allies, however, chose to regard the destruction of the arsenal as a base violation of the capitulation, and their soldiers were so enraged when they discovered what had been done that their officers had difficulty in preventing them from venting their wrath upon the now helpless filibusters.[1] The allies, however, had no cause for anger, as Walker had not surrendered to them but to the commander of an American man-of-war, who had made no stipulations as to the disposition of the armament other than that the enlisted men were to give up their arms while all the officers were to retain their side arms, and Walker and his sixteen chosen officers were to retain their pistols also. It is worthy of note, too, that the articles provided that those who had remained faithful to Walker should not be sent home in company with any who had deserted.

At the time of the capitulation the filibusters still had on hand enough food to sustain them for two or three days; namely, two oxen, two mules, and about a thousand pounds of sugar. For more than a month horse and mule meat, sugar and chocolate, had been their steady diet. A few mangoes were sometimes gathered at great risk in the outskirts of the town; but as many who intended to desert allowed themselves to be "captured" while gathering this fruit, those who desired their loyalty to be above suspicion staid away from the mango groves.

The total number who surrendered at Rivas was 463, grouped as follows: officers and enlisted men fit for duty, 164; wounded, sick, surgeons, and hospital attendants, 173; departmental employees and armed citizens, 86; native troops, 40.[2] These figures speak more eloquently than words of the extent of death, disease, and desertion during the siege of Rivas. When Walker gathered his men there for a final stand his total force amounted to

[1] Statement of General John T. McGrath. See also Wheeler Scrapbook no. 4, 215.
[2] Henningsen's report in Wheeler Scrapbook no. 4, p. 202.

919. On the 1st of February he received forty recruits from California and on the 7th of March seventy more. There were thus 1026 men shut up in Rivas; and as only 463 remained when Walker surrendered, the total number of deaths and desertions in four months amounted to 566, or 55 per cent. of the entire force. It is noteworthy that forty natives remained with Walker to the end. Their service was purely voluntary. Unlike the Central American generals, Walker never forced a native to serve in his ranks, and it was their freedom from conscription which caused the poorer classes at first to regard him as a deliverer. Opposition to the Americans in Nicaragua was for a long time confined to the upper classes, or *calzados* (those wearing shoes). It was only when the Rangers came and carried away their horses, mules, cattle, and provender that the poorer natives turned against the *filibustero*. The Rangers' visit meant impoverishment, which was worse than the hated conscription of their internecine warfare. Native commanders, it is true, had impressed supplies, but their demands were far less exacting than those of the Americans. The wants of the native soldiery were few and simple; they could fare well on plantains and tortillas in amounts that would have caused a filibuster to die of slow starvation. The American, on the other hand, demanded his beef every day, and consumed what the native would regard as an enormous quantity of food and drink. His appetite thus led to the plundering of a province.

The Nicaraguans under Walker at Rivas frequently conversed with their fellow countrymen at the opposing barricades during a lull in the firing. Some of those with the allies told their compatriots on the other side that they were *aggarados* (caught) and compelled to serve at the barricades, and Walker states that there was no firing on Rivas from the barricade at which the Leonese were stationed.[1]

Walker and his chosen staff of officers, with the exception of

[1] *War in Nicaragua*, 412.

Henningsen, took up their quarters on board the *St. Mary's* on the night following the surrender. Davis did not arrive until the following morning, when he proposed that Walker should surrender the *Granada* to him without the necessity of using force. The agreement had made no mention of the schooner, and Walker declined to surrender the vessel. Davis, however, would listen to none of his arguments and ordered his first lieutenant, Maury, to seize the craft. The officer boarded the *Granada* and ordered Fayssoux to surrender. The doughty captain replied that he would do so only in the face of a superior force. The guns of the *St. Mary's* were then turned on the schooner, and the boats of the warship were manned with armed sailors. Maury now told Walker that if he desired to avoid bloodshed he should order Fayssoux to surrender. The fallen filibuster then wrote Fayssoux this note: "Deliver the *Granada* to the United States." Soon thereafter the Nicaraguan flag came down to be replaced by that of the United States, and the Nicaraguan navy was no more. To make the filibuster cup of bitterness full, Davis on May 4, the second anniversary of the sailing of the *Vesta*, turned the vessel over to the Costa Ricans, and the officer who took charge of her was a Jamaica negro, an aide to General Cañas. Shortly thereafter the schooner was loaded with Guatemalan troops and anchor was weighed for Realejo. A storm drove the vessel ashore, and she was a total loss, though the troops were saved. Thus ended the brief career of the first Nicaraguan man-of-war.[1]

The only authority which Davis possessed for his intervention was his instructions from Mervine to protect the persons and property of American citizens. The Secretary of the Navy, however, had sent directions to Mervine to give Walker and such of his followers as were citizens of the United States an opportunity to retreat from Nicaragua, but Davis had acted before these

---

[1] Walker's letter to Buchanan in Washington *States*, June 17, 1857; *War in Nicaragua*, 428-9.

instructions were received. The Navy Department approved all that Davis had done except his seizure of the *Granada* and delivery of the vessel to one of the belligerents.[1] The survivors of the expedition, to the number of 364, were sent to Panama, where they were cared for by Mervine. The women and children, whom Davis had removed from Rivas during the hostilities, had been placed in the house of the American consul at San Juan del Sur, and the officers of the *St. Mary's* had contributed between four hundred and five hundred dollars for their maintenance. These, with the sick and wounded and the officers Walker had left behind, were taken to Greytown, where English surgeons from the *Orion* assisted in caring for the ill. The American warship *Cyane* took the entire party, numbering 142, including thirteen women and five children, to Aspinwall, where they arrived on June 16. The *Orion* preceded them and again offered its aid. Commodore Hiram Paulding, commanding the vessels stationed in Caribbean waters, endeavoured to obtain passage for them to New York on some regular steamer, but the steamship company would agree to take them only as far as New Orleans. The surgeons insisted that they should be taken to a more northerly climate, and Paulding carried them to New York on his flagship, the *Wabash*. Over half the party were sick, and all were in destitute circumstances when taken aboard the American vessels, lacking adequate clothing and infested with vermin. Their wants were supplied so far as practicable from the ship's stores. Captain Erskine, of the British fleet, offered the use of the *Tartar* to convey the survivors to the United States as soon as this vessel returned from its trip to New Orleans with Lockridge's men, but Paulding declined his offer.[2] The *Wabash* arrived in New York on June 28 with 138 refugees, four of them having died on the way.

[1] Report of the Secretary of the Navy, 1857, in House Ex. Doc. 2, 35 Cong., 1 Sess.

[2] MS., Archives Navy Dept., Home Squadron, II., 33 ff.

Meanwhile Mervine found himself greatly encumbered with more than three hundred of Walker's men; they were in great distress and a menace to the health of his own command. He sent them by rail from Panama to Aspinwall, whence they were taken to the United States.

The invasion of Nicaragua had been no holiday outing. It has been estimated that in proportion to numbers the losses of the fili-busters were about double those of the American army in the Mexican War. At Rivas, on April 11, 1856, the filibusters lost twenty-four per cent of their force engaged; at Masaya, in the second engagement on November 17, they lost thirty-five per cent; at the siege of Granada, fifty-seven per cent; in the first battle at San Jorge, twenty-three per cent; and in the last battle, eighteen per cent.[1] The total loss of the Americans from all causes has been variously estimated. M. Felix Belly, a Frenchman who visited Nicaragua shortly after Walker's downfall and has given us a very entertaining if not very accurate account of his experi-ences there, declared that fourteen thousand filibusters died in Nicaragua.[2] According to another account, seven thousand men went to Nicaragua from the Atlantic States and about half that number went from California.[3] Both statements are gross exag-gerations. Walker's effective force at no time exceeded twelve hundred, and the largest number he ever sent into an engagement was eight hundred, in his first attack on Masaya. According to a report purported to have been prepared by Walker's adjutant-general, the total enlistment up to February 24, 1857, excluding native troops, department employees, and citizen volunteers, was 2288.[4] Only seventy recruits joined the army after that date. Henningsen, who reported details with military precision, gave the total enlistment from the time of Walker's landing until the

[1] Henningsen's report. See Wheeler Scrapbook no. 4, 208.
[2] Belly, À travers l'Amérique Centrale, I., 285.   [3] Dublin Review, XLIII., 375.
[4] Peter F. Stout, Nicaragua, 209–10. (Philadelphia, 1859.)

date of his surrender as 2518. This includes the groups excluded from the report of the adjutant-general, and the two statements thus corroborate each other. Henningsen also attempts to show what became of those who enlisted. One thousand died of disease or were killed; 700 deserted; 250 were discharged; 80 were captured in garrison or on the steamers, and the remainder surrendered at Rivas, with the exception of a few score unaccounted for. Thirty-four per cent of the total force were either killed or wounded; forty per cent were killed or succumbed to disease; twenty-eight per cent deserted; ten per cent were discharged; four per cent were captured or unaccounted for; and only eighteen per cent were left to surrender at Rivas.

The estimates of the losses of the allies are only guesses, but it is a safe hazard that they were four or five times greater than those of the Americans. They had neither arms of precision nor skill to use the weapons they had, while their opponents were in large part trained marksmen. The Frenchman, M. Belly, who warmly sympathized with the allies in their struggle against Walker, portrays quite eloquently the horrors which afflicted them in their campaign. "Cholera and plague," he says, "joined with American rifles to make of every town a tomb and every march a hecatomb. . . . This was not a war; it was a butchery." [1] President Mora, too, after the battle of Rivas on April 11, 1856, declared that the Americans fought more like demons than men, but that the worst enemy of both Americans and Costa Ricans was the Nicaraguan climate, to which he attributed the loss of a thousand of his soldiers.[2] Henningsen, whose guess is as good as any, estimated the total force employed by the enemy against Walker as 17,800. Of this number 11,500 came from other States than Nicaragua. The total losses of the allies in killed and wounded he put at 5860, but attempted no estimate of the losses from

---

[1] Belly, *op. cit.*, I., 285.   [2] New York *Times*, Mar. 9, 1857.

cholera and other diseases.[1] Henningsen's estimates of the numbers and losses of the allies are much more conservative than the reports sent in by newspaper correspondents at the time of the various engagements, and while all such statements concerning the allies should be dealt with cautiously, the figures given by him are those of a trained military observer, with nothing to gain by exaggerating the enemy's strength or belittling his own, and are therefore entitled to more consideration than the blind guesses of various news writers.

There was no rejoicing in the United States over Walker's downfall, except on the part of the strenuous opponents of slavery extension. Much consolation was drawn from the fact that Walker was defeated only by American help furnished by Vanderbilt, Spencer, and Davis.[2] The ablest and most consistent opponent of filibusterism was Horace Greeley, whose journal, the New York *Tribune*, while expressing its satisfaction at the outcome, declared, "In his whole career we look in vain for a single act of wisdom or foresight. All the success he had he owed to the total exhaustion of the Nicaraguan population by civil war, and the desire for peace at any price."[3] On the other hand, *Harper's Weekly*, which had published a number of articles reflecting severely on various phases of Walker's campaign, called on the *Tribune* to show that the closing of the Transit, which followed the weakening of Walker's power, had been compensated by any corresponding advantage to commerce or civilization, and added that if Walker were invited to return to Nicaragua by any considerable portion of its people and proved wise enough to join his interests to those of the company which ruined him, his second inauguration as president would not be a matter of serious regret.[4]

---

[1] President Mora was quoted as saying that the ravages of cholera and the near approach of the rainy season would have made the dissolution of the allied army inevitable within twenty days had Walker been able to hold out during that time. Wheeler Scrapbook no. 4, 249.

[2] Wheeler Scrapbook no. 4, 239.

[3] New York *Weekly Tribune*, July 3, 1857. [4] *Harper's Weekly*, I., 530.

The British press naturally expressed much gratification that Walker was no longer a disturbing factor in Central America. Few Englishmen seemed to comprehend Walker's purposes, if their journals reflect the prevailing opinion. To them he was always a bandit, a brigand, a ruthless plunderer, and a leader of an armed rabble. The London *Times* expressed its regret that Davis intervened and prevented "an ignominious ending of their career, unless their own despair had anticipated the ultimate event." "Let the United States make war and conquer if they can find a cause and are prepared to face the responsibility; but it is a disgrace to any nation which is chary of its fair fame to constitute itself the patron — even the unavowed patron — of such bandits as these filibusters and their chief." [1] More than half a century later the idea that the Pierce and Buchanan administrations were using Walker as a tool to effect the annexation of parts of Central America still persists, and is not confined to English writers.

[1] London *Times*, June 18, 1857. Fine words, these, from a nation which owes its beginnings to buccaneering expeditions of Viking and Norman and its Eastern empire and its mastery of the seas to the buccaneers of the sixteenth and seventeenth centuries. Yea, the Jameson raid in the Transvaal is still fresh in the memories of men.

CHAPTER XX

MORE FILIBUSTERING MISHAPS

WHILE filibusterism in Nicaragua was making its last desperate stand at Rivas, attention was again directed toward Sonora, which was subjected to another invasion from California. The leader of this expedition was Henry A. Crabb, whose name has already appeared several times in these pages. Crabb was a native of Nashville, Tennessee, and had been a schoolmate of Walker's. He entered the legal profession and began the practice of law at Vicksburg. In 1848, during the presidential contest, he quarrelled at a political meeting with the editor of the Vicksburg *Sentinel*, a man named Jenkins, and the next day, when the two encountered each other on the street, the quarrel was renewed, resulting in an exchange of shots, in which Crabb was wounded and Jenkins was killed. Crabb was tried for murder and acquitted, and shortly thereafter he joined the caravan of "forty-niners" and betook himself to California. After settling at Stockton he resumed the practice of law and was soon elected city attorney. In 1852 he was a member of the lower house of the State legislature and during the next two years served in the State Senate. In 1855 he joined the Know-Nothing party and announced his candidacy for the United States Senate, but withdrew from the race when he found his chances hopeless.[1]

Disappointed in politics, Crabb began to seek elsewhere an outlet for his energies. Like Walker, he took a deep interest in

[1] H. S. Foote, *Casket of Reminiscences*, 385–7 (Washington, 1874), and *Bench and Bar of the South and Southwest*, 144 (St. Louis, 1876); O'Meara, Broderick and Gwin, 47–8; Bell, *Reminiscences of a Ranger*, 217; Hittell, *History of California*, III., 806 ff.

the schemes of the French in Sonora, and in October, 1853, he engaged passage on the brig *Caroline* from San Francisco to Guaymas to take a look at the country. He had married the daughter of a Manila Spaniard named Ainza. This family had settled in Sonora with considerable wealth, but had become impoverished by revolutions and confiscations and had finally migrated to California as refugees. By this visit Crabb apparently intended to seek some means of obtaining the restitution of the Ainza property. It so happened, however, that the *Caroline* was the very vessel Walker had engaged to convey his filibusters to Lower California, and when these heterogeneous adventurers came on board Crabb realized that the chances of his success in Mexico would be ruined if he entered Sonora in such company. He therefore ordered his baggage put ashore and postponed the Sonoran visit to a later day.[1]

Shortly thereafter Crabb visited the East, and while crossing the isthmus at Nicaragua he conceived the idea, as previously shown,[2] of bringing a force of Californians to that country to take part in the struggle between the Legitimists and the Democrats. On his return to California he was accompanied by C. C. Hornsby and Thomas F. Fisher, whom he had induced to join him in this enterprise. Through the instrumentality of Fisher a contract was negotiated with General Jerez for bringing five hundred men to Nicaragua, but when Crabb reached California he conceived an ambition to enter the United States Senate, and as he seemed to have some chance to reach this coveted goal he abandoned the idea of filibustering and again plunged into politics. The contract with Jerez he then offered to his friend Walker, but the latter preferred the grant which Cole had secured from Castellon. It was partly due to Crabb's influence that Walker and his men eventually succeeded in putting to sea in the *Vesta.*

[1] *Alta California*, Oct. 21, 1853.   [2] See above, p. 86.

His new venture in politics brought Crabb only disappointment and humiliation, and the news of Walker's success in Nicaragua caused him to suffer another attack of the filibustering fever. He could not go to Nicaragua without playing second fiddle to Walker, but Sonora was still crying for the advent of a "regenerator," and his marriage into a Sonoran family had given him a special interest in this region. Accordingly, a colonization company of about one hundred persons was organized early in 1856, consisting mainly of former Sonorans, and Crabb set out with these for Mexico. His wife and several members of her family accompanied him, an indication that this was no mere filibustering raid. When the party reached Los Angeles the prospect of a weary journey through the desert caused about half the members to withdraw, but the rest crossed the border. They found Sonora in its normal state of civil commotion; for a revolution under the leadership of Ignacio Pesquiera was then in progress against Gandara, the governor. The insurgents asked Crabb's aid and offered him a number of inducements to bring a colony into the country, declaring that they desired the annexation of Sonora to the United States, after securing its independence, and that they regarded American colonization as a means to this end.

Crabb returned to California in the autumn, cherishing an ambitious colonizing scheme, but finding the people too engrossed in the coming presidential election to give much attention to his plans, he was compelled to postpone his undertaking for several months. In the meantime the two factions in Mexico had come to an understanding and had buried the hatchet. Their previous invitation to American colonists became a source of great embarrassment to the Pesquiera faction, now that they had made their peace with the government, and they sought to atone for their former disloyalty by denouncing as *filibusteros* the men they had invited to come.[1]

[1] House Ex. Doc. 64, 35 Cong., 1 Sess.

After the political excitement in California had subsided Crabb began the organization of what he called the "Arizona Colonization Company," and many prominent California politicians joined the enterprise. In January, 1857, between fifty and sixty expeditionists assembled in the town of Sonora, Tuolumne County, and on the 20th proceeded to San Francisco, where another detachment was awaiting them. The combined force, amounting to about one hundred men, then embarked for San Pedro, where they arrived on the 24th. They next proceeded to El Monte, in Los Angeles County, and spent a week there buying animals, wagons, and provisions. On February 27 the party reached Fort Yuma, where another week was spent "recruiting animals."

The company was organized on a military basis, and during its stay at Fort Yuma had its daily routine of drill and guard mounting, and its officers endeavoured to maintain rigid discipline. Crabb was commander-in-chief; R. N. Wood, his adjutant-general, was a former member of the California legislature, and had been one of the Fillmore electors in that State; T. D. Johns, who had the rank of chief of artillery, was a West Point graduate, and had served as a lieutenant in the regular army; Dr. T. J. Oxley, the surgeon-general, had been a Whig and Know-Nothing leader and a member of the legislature; J. D. Cosby, ranking as a brigadier-general, was still a member of the State Senate; William H. McCoun, the commissary-general, was also an ex-legislator of California; and Henry P. Watkins, Walker's former law partner and co-labourer in the "regeneration" of Sonora, was quartermaster-general.

Early in March Crabb and his party left Fort Yuma and took the trail through the desert toward Sonora. On the 25th they arrived at the pueblo of Sonoyta just over the Mexican boundary line. The warden of the village at once notified the prefect of El Altar of their arrival, stating that the men were armed with daggers, pistols, and rifles, but that they paid due respect to individuals, families, and property. News of their coming had already reached the Mexican authorities and they were taking measures to resist. The prefect at El Altar had called upon the Sonorans to take up arms against "the bandits." Ignacio Pesquiera, now enjoying the title of "substitute governor of the State and commander-in-chief of the forces on the frontier," out-Heroded Herod in his efforts to prove his loyalty and his utter detestation of the men who had come to Sonora at his invitation. In a flamboyant proclamation he exclaimed: "Let us fly to chastise, with all the fury which can scarcely be restrained in hearts full of hatred of oppression, the savage filibuster who has dared in an evil hour to tread on the national territory and to provoke — Madman! — our anger. No pity, no generous sentiments for that rabble! Let them die the death of wild beasts who, trampling under foot the law of nations, and despising the civil law and all social institutions, are bold enough to invoke as their only guide the natural law, and to ask as their only help the force of brutes!" [1]

Crabb seemed very much surprised at the hostility shown by the officials, and immediately after reaching Sonoyta he went before the warden and assured him of his friendly intentions, at the same time protesting against the hostile acts and accusations made against him. He also wrote to the prefect at El Altar, stating that he and his men had come in conformity with the colonization laws of Mexico, and at the invitation of very influential citizens, "with the intention of finding most happy firesides with and among you." His present party, he said, was to be joined by nine hundred more men. They had made only "pacific proposals" and meditated no hostilities. They were well armed, it was true, but this was customary when people passed through regions infested with hostile Indians; and great was their surprise at finding

[1] House Ex. Doc. 64, 35 Cong., 1 Sess.

the officials resorting to warlike measures, threatening to poison
wells, and intriguing with Indians. He ended his letter with a
warning that "if blood is to flow, with all its horrors, on your
head be it, and not on mine." [1]

Crabb remained at Sonoyta only two days and then set out for
Caborca, a small town near Point Lobos on the Gulf of California. [2]
At about eight o'clock on the morning of April 1, when about
half a mile from this town and while moving along the road between fields of wheat in no military order, the Americans were
suddenly fired upon by Mexicans lying in ambush. They pressed
on toward the town, exchanging shots with the enemy, who had
concealed themselves on both sides of the road wherever there
was available cover. After an hour of fighting the Americans
took shelter in a row of adobe houses, while the Mexicans took
their station in a church across the street. In the skirmish two
of Crabb's men were killed and eighteen wounded, three of the
latter dying the following night. Some hours after reaching the
houses, Crabb and a squad of his men rushed across the street
with a keg of powder, intending to blow open the doors of the
church. The effort failed; several were killed, and a number,
including Crabb, were wounded. The Americans were then closely
besieged till April 6, when the roof of their building was ignited
with a burning arrow. A keg of powder was set off in the room
below the burning roof in the hope of blowing away the blazing
thatch. The plan failed, and Crabb then made overtures of peace.

Shortly before eleven o'clock at night one of the men was sent
over to the church bearing a flag of truce. He was not allowed
to return, but called to his companions that Gabilondo, the commander, had promised to send them to Altar and give them a fair
trial if they would march out of the house one by one and leave
their arms behind. Crabb then had his brother-in-law, a Spanish-
American named Cortlezon, to negotiate at long distance with

Gabilondo. The Mexican commander stood in the belfry of the church and Cortlezon in the door of the adobe house. Gabilondo promised the Americans a fair trial, and Crabb told Cortlezon to ask how the wounded would be treated. To this the Mexican replied that he had a good physician who would look after them well. On receiving these assurances Crabb decided to surrender, though some of his men were not so easily satisfied as he with Mexican promises. The Americans marched across the street one by one, leaving their arms behind them, and on entering the church they were seized and bound with ropes and conducted to the barracks. Crabb was separated from his men and not allowed to communicate with them. At one o'clock on the morning of the 7th, just two hours after their surrender, a sergeant came with orders, which he read in Spanish, and Cortlezon interpreted them as he read. The orders were to the effect that the men would be shot at sunrise.

A few hours later the sentence was carried out. The men were shot in squads of five and ten. The soldiers detailed for this work were so unnerved that their aim was bad and they wounded more of the victims at the first few volleys than they killed. The writhings of the wounded men unnerved them still more. The backs of the prisoners were then turned toward the soldiers so that they would not have to look into the faces of the men they were shooting, and this enabled them to do their work much better. Crabb was reserved for special treatment. He was tied to a post in front of the building he had occupied, with his face to the post and his hands bound high above his head. A hundred shots were said to have been fired and his limp body remained hanging by his tied hands. The head was severed, and after being exhibited for several days in the village was preserved in mescal as a ghastly trophy of victory over *los filibusteros Americanos*, and as proof of the loyalty of the Pesquieristas to the existing government. The bodies of the slain were left unburied, and the Mexicans boasted that their swine were fattened on American carcases. Gabilondo too boasted that he had promised the Americans a good physician and that he had kept his promise. The massacre was evidently done at the instigation of Pesquiera, who was now ashamed of his former relations with Crabb, and knew that dead men could tell no tales. With the Americans there was a fourteen-year-old boy by the name of Charles Edward Evans. His life was spared, and he alone was left to tell the story. Gabilondo took him to his house and treated him as a menial until the American vice-consul at Mazatlan secured his release.[1]

According to the Mexican version Crabb's men surrendered unconditionally, but even if this were true, it is no justification of the massacre of the prisoners. Granting that the men were pirates or bandits, this fact of itself would not justify their captors in shooting them on the spot. Such an act was merely a resort to lynch law, and it is strange indeed to observe an American historian seeking to condone it.[2] The shooting of Crabb and his companions aroused much feeling in the United States, especially in California, where the leader and his chief associates were well known and much respected, and where Mexicans were cordially detested. Minister Forsyth called on the Mexican government to make an investigation and punish those who were responsible for such high-handed measures, but the delays that characterize Spanish-American negotiations caused the matter to be lost in the sloughs of diplomacy.

There is of course no question that Crabb was contemplating something more than a mere colonization enterprise. He was really seeking to emulate Sam Houston in Texas and Walker in Nicaragua. The *San Joaquin Republican*, a paper published in Stockton, his old home, stated, after chronicling his death:

---

[1] House Ex. Doc. 64, 35 Cong., 1 Sess.
[2] H. H. Bancroft, *North Mexican States and Texas*, II., 694-5. (San Francisco, 1889.)

Y

"That his purposes were dishonourable or sordid will not be believed by anyone acquainted with the character of the men who led and organized the party. . . . We believe that his most inveterate enemy will admit that no man in California bears or has borne a more unsullied reputation."[1] While brave, honest, and determined, Crabb did not have in him the stuff of which real filibusters are made. Walker and Henningsen frequently found themselves in much more desperate straits than were the filibusters at Caborca — notably at the first and second battles of Rivas and at the siege of Granada — but they always managed to extricate themselves. The reliance which Crabb placed on Mexican promises speaks well for his heart, but not so for his head.

Let us now return to Walker, whom we left aboard an American man-of-war at San Juan del Sur. From that port the fallen filibuster and his staff were conveyed to Panama on the *St. Mary's*, whence they proceeded to the United States, reaching New Orleans on May 27. There they received an enthusiastic welcome. As soon as he stepped from the gang-plank Walker was lifted to the shoulders of several men and borne to his carriage. The cheering crowd formed a procession and followed him to the St. Charles Hotel, where he was compelled to make a speech from the balcony. His admirers refused to disperse and called so persistently for another speech that he entered the rotunda, mounted a table, and gave them an encore. A mass meeting was arranged for the evening of the 29th, and was held on the "neutral ground" of Canal Street.[2] Walker and his staff occupied a platform dec-

---

[1] *San Joaquin Republican*, May 17, 1857.

[2] A New Orleans lady, Mrs. V. E. W. McCord, composed a poem to Walker on his arrival in that city. The composition is devoid of literary merit, but the last of the fifteen stanzas is interesting as reflecting the idea of the average American concerning Walker's plans:

> All hail to thee, Chief! Heaven's blessings may rest
> On the battle-scarred brow of our national guest,
> And soon may our Eagle fly over the sea,
> And plant there a branch of our national tree.
>
> Major Heiss's Scrapbook.

orated with the stars and stripes and with his flag of Nicaragua.
The filibuster general spoke for two hours, giving a synopsis of
his career in Nicaragua, defending his course, and paying his
respects to those who had stood in the way of his success.[1] From
New Orleans he went to Memphis, thence to Louisville, where
he visited his sister, Mrs. Richardson, then to Cincinnati and from
there to Washington. On June 12 he paid a visit to President
Buchanan by appointment, and three days later submitted to
him in writing his case against Commander Davis, protesting
against that officer's interference, and especially against his seizure
of the *Granada*.[2]

On June 16 Walker reached New York. He was met at
Amboy by a committee of admirers and escorted up the bay to
Battery Park, where he made a speech in a shower of rain. On
the following evening he attended the Bowery Theatre with his
staff, and the next evening attended Wallack's Theatre, occupying a box with General and Mrs. Henningsen. As they entered,
the orchestra struck up "Hail, Columbia," and Walker was compelled to address the audience from his box. Curious crowds so
beset him that he had difficulty in leaving the theatre, and on
reaching his hotel he was serenaded by a brass band. No one
deprecated such publicity more than Walker himself, and for his
peace of mind he was compelled to leave the hotel and seek a
secluded place where only his intimate friends could find him.
Henningsen, who had sailed from Aspinwall direct to New York,
was welcomed even more heartily than his chief.[3]

The hero-worship of the New-Yorkers, however, was destined
to be of short duration. Walker's constant aspersion of the motives of Davis did not take very well with the average citizen,
who looked upon the naval officer as the cause of his being alive.
Moreover, the *Wabash* soon came into port, bringing its cargo of

---

[1] Wheeler Scrapbook no. 4, 208.   [2] Washington *States*, June 17, 1857.
[3] New York *Herald*, June 17–19, 1857; Wheeler Scrapbook no. 4, 202.

miserable wretches, whose terrible condition of destitution, sickness, and utter helplessness was fully depicted, and probably overdrawn, in the public prints. Many of them told tales of their leader's cruelty and indifference, which obtained additional colour when it became known that Walker did not even visit those who had suffered so much in his cause or take any steps to alleviate their distress. Instead, he ran away from them, taking a hurried departure for Charleston three days after their arrival. From Charleston Walker took his way by easy stages through Georgia to his old home in Nashville, and from there proceeded to Mobile, where preparations for another expedition to Nicaragua were already under way. In August the press described the organization of a "Central American League," with branches in all the large cities of the United States, for the purpose of organizing and equipping a second expedition on a much greater scale than the first. Walker made no secret of his intention to return, and Henningsen, on bidding farewell to Lockridge in New York, had exclaimed, "We'll meet again at Philippi." When autumn came, Henningsen in New York, Waters in Mississippi, Lockridge in Texas, and Rogers in New Orleans were all suspected of being busily engaged in securing recruits and supplies.[1]

Knowledge of these facts and rumours caused Irisarri and Molina to notify Secretary Cass of the intended expedition, the armament for which they believed was being collected in New York, and they begged the American government to prevent the landing of the expedition at any Central American port in case its departure from the United States could not be prevented.[2] Cass immediately sent a circular letter to all the United States marshals, district attorneys, and collectors of the ports of the Southern and seaboard States, notifying them of the projected expedition and urging them to be diligent in enforcing the law and

[1] New York *Herald*, Dec. 14, 1857.
[2] MS., Archives, Department of State, Notes, Central America, II.

to communicate at once to the Department any information that might come to them concerning such expeditions. The same instructions were sent by the Secretary of the Navy to the commanders of vessels in Central American waters. The officials at Mobile and New Orleans acknowledged the receipt of Cass's letter, but furnished no information of filibustering expeditions. The Federal district attorney at New Orleans, however, notified Cass that if such an expedition should depart from that port there would be no means of preventing it, as the naval force there was entirely inadequate. Cass at once communicated this to the Secretary of the Navy, Isaac Toucey, who ordered the *Fulton* to touch at Mobile and New Orleans on its way to Central American waters. This was not a very aggressive method of suppressing filibustering, but was about all that the Navy Department could do with the forces at its disposal.

On October 30 the United States attorney at Nashville notified Cass that there was no doubt that recruiting had been going on in his district and that he had brought persons supposed to have a knowledge of Walker's plans before a grand jury, but had failed to secure sufficient evidence to justify an indictment. The activities of Walker's supporters had recently abated, he said, and the expedition had evidently been abandoned or postponed. Ten days later word came from Charleston that a former captain of Walker's, J. T. Mackey, had raised a company of one hundred men in the upper part of the State, and that they would assemble at Charleston and join another company at Savannah. The district attorney at Charleston was awaiting the rendezvous in order to make arrests.[1]

When Toucey ordered the *Fulton* to call at Mobile and New Orleans on its way to the Central American coast he instructed its commander, Lieutenant John J. Almy, to report to the Department what he could learn in these cities concerning the prob-.

[1] House Ex. Doc. 24, 35 Cong., 1 Sess., 13, 14.

able departure of filibusters. Almy's instructions also included the directions given to other naval officers in the Caribbean with regard to the enforcement of the neutrality law. To every naval officer these instructions were exceedingly vague, as they were originally intended only for civil officials in American ports, and Almy before sailing wrote for a fuller explanation of his duties in carrying them out. The questions he asked must have been uppermost in the minds of all his fellow-officers stationed in the Central American ports. Since the neutrality law applied only to ports of the United States or to those under its jurisdiction, must he seize a suspicious vessel in a foreign port, he asked, or merely prevent its passengers from landing? Again, what must he do if the passengers inform him that they are travellers intending to cross the isthmus or are merely peaceable settlers? Toucey's reply was not very enlightening: naval officers must not act arbitrarily or on mere suspicion, and must be careful not to interfere with lawful commerce; but where a vessel was manifestly engaged in filibustering they must use the force at their command to prevent men and arms from being landed.[1] As a matter of fact, the stationing of American vessels in foreign ports to enforce the laws of the United States was such an anomalous proceeding that no cabinet officer could have given specific directions as to the exact procedure that should be followed.

After reaching Mobile Almy heard rumours of a filibustering expedition, but could hear of nothing sufficiently tangible to justify official action. He found public sentiment very favourable to the movement, and there was a general opinion that the Washington administration was disposed to wink at such enterprises. This impression he strove to correct, but the citizens were inclined to lay much stress on Cass's oft-repeated statement that Americans had a right at all times to emigrate and take their arms with them. While he found that the sympathies of the people

[1] Senate Doc. 13, 35 Cong., 1 Sess.

were all on the side of the filibusters, the financial distress was then so acute that the contemplated movement was seriously hampered by a lack of funds.[1] From New Orleans Almy on November 1 sent a similar report. Financial depression had caused the filibustering fever greatly to subside, and the prevailing opinion was that no expedition could leave the country for a year to come. Walker was in the city, but appeared to be comparatively quiet, and the violent filibusters, who were always airing their views in the public prints and causing excitement, were violent only with tongue and pen.[2]

The naval officer failed to read the signs aright. Even as he wrote, the preparations for Walker's return to Nicaragua were nearing completion. The Federal civil officers of the port were more alive to the situation, and on November 10 caused Walker to be arrested on an affidavit charging him with violation of the neutrality law. The arrest took place at Walker's lodgings on Custom House Street shortly before midnight, and the filibuster was taken to the St. Charles Hotel, where the district judge was waiting to take his recognizance for his appearance on the following morning. Pierre Soulé and Colonel S. F. Slatter were also there, the one to offer his services as counsel and the other to act as his bondsman. Walker was released for a hearing the next morning, with Slatter as his security in the sum of two thousand dollars. On the following morning Walker duly appeared, and was discharged to reappear for examination on the 19th. The district attorney asked the court to increase the amount of Walker's bail, but the request was refused.

Walker's arrest had been prompted in part by a telegraphic despatch from New York published in the New Orleans papers and stating that an expedition was to leave the latter city in the course of the week for Nicaragua. Few persons even knew that

[1] This was in the midst of the panic of 1857.
[2] MS., Archives, Navy Dept., Officers' Letters, Nov., 1857.

Walker was in New Orleans until they saw this statement in the press. The Federal authorities met in consultation at ten o'clock on the evening of the 10th, and decided on Walker's arrest. They were strengthened in their suspicions by the knowledge that the steamer *Fashion*, then in port, had been taking on a large cargo of provisions. The steamer had formerly been a government transport, and a few days before had been sold in New Orleans for a nominal sum to J. G. Humphries, a man supposed to be a supporter of Walker. Her scheduled departure from Mobile to Greytown as a regular packet of the Mobile and Nicaragua Steamship Company had been widely advertised, and government officers therefore had kept a close watch on the boat. When it became known that a crew had been engaged and that a cargo had been taken on board, Walker's arrest immediately followed. The *Fashion* was searched, but as nothing suspicious was found on board, no attempt was made to detain her, and a few hours after Walker's arrest she weighed anchor and proceeded down the river to Mobile. On the next afternoon Walker, in spite of the fact that he was under bail, took passage with his staff and a large number of his followers on the mail boat for Mobile, and on arriving there boarded the *Fashion*, anchored some distance down the bay. On leaving New Orleans his men made their way to the mail boat in small groups by different routes so as to arouse no suspicion.

As soon as Walker's departure from New Orleans was known, District Attorney Clack telegraphed the fact to Cass and stated that the officials would be helpless without a steamer to pursue the filibusters to their supposed rendezvous.[1] At the same time he notified the district attorney at Mobile to watch the *Fashion* in the event that she came to that port. Cass on hearing of Walker's departure telegraphed Clack to employ a steamer and take on board the marshal and a sufficient posse to overhaul the

---

[1] House Ex. Doc. 24, 35 Cong., 1 Sess., 14.

Fashion; but the message for some reason was never delivered, and the Federal activity at New Orleans was at an end. At Mobile the Federal officers were more lax. The district attorney, on receiving Clack's message, laid the matter before the collector of the port, Thaddeus Sanford, and the latter ordered an inspection of the steamer. This inspection was a farce; the cargo was found to be above suspicion, and the 270 passengers were apparently lawful emigrants. The vessel was therefore allowed to depart ✓ for Greytown, although Walker was suspected of being on board.[1] For his failure to detain the *Fashion*, Sanford was severely censured by Howell Cobb, the Secretary of the Treasury. The collector thereupon submitted a lengthy and feeble explanation, indicating a guilelessness on his part which even the angels might have envied. His chief defence was his lack of knowledge of the facts in the case until the steamer had actually departed. The vessel was anchored six miles below the city, and when the inspector left her decks she was ready for sea and was gone by the time that he delivered his report to Sanford. This lame explanation Cobb accepted, but enjoined upon the collector the necessity of preventing repetitions of the incident. The censure had its effect, for on December 16 the owner of the *Fashion* applied for a clearance for the schooner *Queen of the South*, bound for Greytown with coal and merchandise. A band of emigrants had arrived in Mobile a few days previously, and it was generally supposed that they intended to embark on the schooner. Sanford withheld a clearance, though the pressure of public opinion upon him was severe. The night after his action a public meeting was held at which an ex-governor and other prominent citizens bitterly criticised the action of the government. So strong was the popular disapproval that the collector asked the Secretary of the Treasury for a special endorsement of his action. Cobb replied that "the circumstances under which you refused the clearance

[1] House Ex. Doc. 24, 35 Cong., 1 Sess., 24–7; 39–44.

fully justify your course, and the department unhesitatingly
approves it." [1]

The escape of the *Fashion* caused the government to increase
its vigilance so as to prevent reinforcements going to Walker.
Captain J. T. Mackey, the former filibuster, for some time suspected of recruiting in South Carolina, was arrested in Charleston,
but on being allowed to leave the court room to obtain sureties
for his bond effected his escape. Cobb warned the customs officers at Galveston and New Orleans to keep a sharp lookout for
the *Fashion*, which was expected to return at once for a second
instalment of recruits for Nicaragua; and Toucey ordered the
steam frigate *Susquehanna*, stationed at Key West, to proceed at
once to Cape Gracias, Honduras, and from there cruise along the
coast to Greytown. [2]

The *Fashion* had put to sea on November 14. As soon as
she was beyond the jurisdiction of the United States, the men
were organized into a battalion of four companies. Of the men
aboard the steamer thirty had been with Walker during his previous campaign, and six had belonged to the "original fifty-six."
Hornsby, Anderson, Fayssoux, Swingle, Bruno von Natzmer, and
the ever-fighting and much-wounded Henry were among those who
were willing to face again the hardships of a tropical campaign.
John Tabor was also returning to resume his editorial duties with
El Nicaraguense. Henry, now having the rank of colonel, drilled
the men every day, giving especial attention to the details of
camp duty, such as guard mounting and the posting of sentinels,
while Swingle instructed the men in the moulding of bullets and
making of cartridges. Land was sighted on the 23d, but the
steamer, instead of making for Greytown, headed for the mouth of
the Colorado River, a southern fork of the San Juan. When this
point was reached, three boats were lowered and one of the companies, with Anderson in command, was ordered to disembark

[1] House Ex. Doc. 24, 35 Cong., 1 Sess., 44–6.   [2] *Ibid.*, 29–32; 49–56.

under arms. They rowed away up the stream in a heavy down-
pour of rain, and the *Fashion* again stood out to sea. All night
long the steamer hung along the coast, and at seven o'clock on
the morning of the 24th ran boldly into the harbour of Greytown
and headed for Punta Arenas. The vessel was brought alongside
the hulk of an old abandoned Transit boat now used as a wharf,
and the men were ashore within five minutes after the steamer
was made fast.[1]

All this took place under the very eyes of the officers on the
American sloop-of-war, *Saratoga*, which had been stationed in the
harbour to prevent just such an occurrence. It seems that Commander Chatard's suspicions were entirely lulled when the steamer
came in so boldly and passed so near him, showing only about
fifteen men on deck. He decided that the vessel was bringing a
party to reopen the Transit route.[2] Great was his chagrin when
he saw several hundred men, armed with rifles, leaping over the
gunwales to the hulk. He was now confronted with the same
problem which had puzzled Almy. He did not wish to open fire
on the vessel in a neutral port so as to stop the disembarkation,
and when the men had landed he had no jurisdiction over them.
In much perturbation he wrote to his flag officer, Commodore
Hiram Paulding, at Aspinwall, urging him to come to Greytown
at once. The British mail steamer *Dee* came into port some days
after the arrival of the filibusters, and Chatard hurried her off to
Aspinwall with his message to Paulding several hours before her
scheduled departure. Accompanying his official communication
Chatard sent Paulding a private letter bewailing his own stupidity
in allowing the filibusters to outwit him. "Somehow or other I
was spellbound, and so my officers seemed to be. . . . I beg you,
sir, in the most earnest manner, to come here and advise me. I am
in a very cruel state of mind and look gloomily to the future."[3]

---

[1] Wheeler Scrapbook no. 4, 278, 280; New York *Herald*, Dec. 14, 1857.
[2] MS., Archives, Navy Department, Home Squadron, II., 58.   [3] *Ibid.*, 58 ff.

The *Fashion* reached Aspinwall almost simultaneously with the *Dee* and brought Paulding a letter from Walker complaining that Chatard was subjecting him to petty annoyances. On the ground of protecting American property, Chatard had refused to allow the filibusters to occupy the buildings of the Transit Company on the Point; some of his officers, not in uniform, had entered Walker's camp without noticing the sentry's challenge; target practice with howitzers was carried on so close to Walker's camp that a stray shot might have caused serious trouble; and Chatard finally had notified Walker that his camp was in the way of any shot the *Saratoga* might have to fire to bring to a suspicious vessel and must be moved.[1] Walker had already moved part of his camp to avoid danger from Chatard's target practice, and paid no attention to this last demand. Piqued at being foiled by the filibusters, Chatard was venting his spite in such petty ways in the hope that he would provoke them to commit some act that would justify him in interfering and breaking up the expedition, and thus retrieving to some extent his blunder in allowing them to land. As soon as Paulding received these letters from Chatard and Walker he made ready to go to Greytown, where he arrived December 6.

After making his camp on Punta Arenas, Walker waited for reinforcements which were expected to arrive under the leadership of Henningsen, and for news from Anderson, whom he had left with a company of men at the mouth of the Colorado River. It was Anderson's purpose to capture the river steamers, so as to allow Walker and his men to proceed to the interior. He reached the junction of the Colorado and San Juan before the rest of the men had landed at Punta Arenas, and thus was enabled to prevent the news of their arrival from reaching the forts and the steamers on the river. Anderson met with success from the start. By December 1 three river steamers and the lake steamer *Virgen*

---

[1] MS., Archives, Navy Department, Home Squadron, II., 59 ff.

were in his hands, as well as Fort Castillo. Walker meanwhile waited impatiently for news from the men on the river, for their failure meant the ruin of his hopes. On December 4, when no news had arrived, he grew uneasy and sat up all night waiting for a courier from Anderson. All the next day he watched and waited, but still no news. The men began to show signs of discouragement; the Point at its best was only a dreary, desolate sand spit, and the terrific rains since their arrival had made it all the more disagreeable as a camping-ground. Late in the afternoon of this day, however, a canoe came in sight, and as it drew near one of Anderson's men was descried sitting in the stern, while the two men paddling the boat were visible evidence of Anderson's victories, being Costa Rican prisoners of war. "Huzzah for Frank Anderson!" the occupant shouted as soon as he came within hearing distance. "We have taken the fort of Castillo, the river steamers, and the lake steamer *Virgen* without the loss of a man." The messenger announced that he had come within twelve miles of Greytown in one of the captured steamers, which had run aground, and he had been sent on with the news. The drooping spirits of the men at once revived, and in the filibuster camp there were sounds of revelry by night.[1] They would soon be leaving the dreary Point for the worldly paradise of the interior.

But when morning dawned there hove in sight the magnificent new steam frigate *Wabash*, fifty guns, with the broad pennant of Commodore Paulding at her fore. She came up the bay and anchored just outside the harbour, which was too shallow for her draft, and directly opposite the filibuster camp. On the next day came the United States steamer *Fulton*, making three American men-of-war off the Point. On this day, too, came the ubiquitous Union Jack, borne by the British steam frigate *Leopard*, twenty guns, which dropped anchor close to the *Saratoga*, and the

[1] New York *Herald*, Dec. 28, 1857.

monster ship of war *Brunswick*, ninety guns, which hove to near the *Wabash*. The captains of the British vessels and the British consul dined that day with Paulding.[1]

The arrival of so many men-of-war caused the filibusters no little apprehension, but as the hours passed and nothing untoward occurred the men were assured that the American vessels were there only to watch the British and prevent any interference from that quarter. During the day several boats put out from the *Saratoga* and went up the river, but as these were supposed to be watering parties they attracted no particular attention, except from the experienced officers, who noted that the boats did not come back. Shortly after midnight Walker quietly sent Fayssoux up the river in a canoe to learn the object of the boats being there. He found that they were maintaining a blockade. This was kept from the men, but the next morning Fayssoux and Hornsby were sent to Paulding to protest. The Commodore told them that the river had been blockaded to prevent Walker's ascending it, and that he intended to make all the men prisoners and carry them back to the United States. The two filibuster officers were detained on the flagship, and preparations were made for landing a force on the Point.[2] Three hundred marines and sailors were placed aboard the *Fulton*, the smallest of the vessels, to which Paulding transferred his flag, and she was taken in to the Transit Company's wharf. Here the men were landed and were marched to the rear of Walker's position. At the same time the *Saratoga* moved in and trained her broadside on the filibusters, and small boats with howitzers in their bows were ranged close inshore directly in front of the camp. The demonstration of superior force was well managed, and Walker, familiar with the events of the previous night, was not surprised at the movement. Be-

---

[1] Rebecca Paulding Meade, *Life of Hiram Paulding, Rear-Admiral U.S.N.*, 183 ff. (New York, 1910.)

[2] New York *Herald*, Dec. 28, 1856.

fore Paulding's arrangements were completed Walker had dismissed his guard and disbanded his military organization, telling some of his more impetuous followers, who were spoiling for a fight, that resistance would be the height of folly. Paulding sent Captain Engle to Walker with a written demand for his surrender. The two met and shook hands, and Engle delivered his communication. Walker read it without changing a muscle of his face, and then remarked, "I surrender to the United States." Engle then asked him to lower his flag, and Walker ordered one of his officers to do so. After further conversation Engle remarked, "General, I am sorry to see an officer of your ability employed in such a service. Nothing would give me greater pleasure than to see you at the head of regular troops." Engle then ordered the naval forces back to their ships and returned to the *Fulton*. Several oral messages now passed between Paulding and Walker, and one of these, misunderstood by the bearer, greatly offended the Commodore. He had tried to show Walker some consideration, and sent him word that the officers and men would have separate quarters. Walker replied that he was asking no special benefits, and Paulding, regarding this as a piece of impudence, commanded his immediate embarkation upon the *Fulton*. What followed may best be told in Paulding's own words, in a letter to his wife: "Upon this [order to embark] he came to see me, and this lion-hearted devil, who had so often destroyed the lives of other men, came to me, humbled himself and wept like a child. You may suppose it made a woman of me, and I have had him in the cabin since as my guest. We laugh and talk as though nothing had happened, and you would think, to see him with the captain and myself, that he was one of us. He is a sharp fellow and requires a sharp fellow to deal with him. I have taken strong measures in forcing him from a neutral territory. It may make me President or may cost me my commission." [1]

[1] Meade, *Life of Hiram Paulding*, 183 ff.

There was something almost dramatic in the meeting of these two men for the first time, and the officers and crew could barely conceal their excitement as the filibuster stepped on the deck of the *Fulton*. The gigantic frame of the Commodore in uniform contrasted strangely with the slight figure of the General in sombre civilian garb; and observers noted that Walker's eyes were very red, an indication, as Paulding himself has testified, that his emotions had gotten the better of him.

It was the irony of fate that just as Walker surrendered to Engle, and his red-starred flag was hauled down, the belated river steamer, which had gone aground twelve miles up the stream, came in sight with twelve filibusters and thirty Costa Rican prisoners aboard. A detachment of marines seized the boat, liberated the prisoners, captured the filibusters, and placed the steamer in the keeping of the United States commercial agent at Greytown. C. J. McDonald, the agent of Morgan and Garrison, who had accompanied Walker to Nicaragua, claimed the steamer on behalf of his principals, but Paulding declined to adjudicate the matter.

When Walker surrendered, some forty of his men took to the chaparral, intending to make their way up the river and join Anderson. On the following day the marines beat around the dense undergrowth and by night had rounded up thirty-two of them. The rest had taken a boat and gone up the river. On the night after the surrender the denizens of Greytown came over and plundered the camp to their heart's content. Much that they could not take way they buried for future use. The camp stores that remained were placed aboard the *Wabash* to be turned over to the United States authorities. In the excitement incident to the surrender many of Walker's followers had destroyed their arms.

The officers and men, with the exception of Walker and John Tabor, were placed aboard the *Saratoga*, and on the 12th, less than a month after their departure from Mobile, were on their way back to the United States. Walker was not placed aboard this vessel on account of the ill-feeling between him and Commander Chatard. The *Saratoga* took the men and officers to Norfolk, while the *Wabash* returned to her station at Aspinwall.[1]

Walker gave his parole to Paulding to return to the United States on the regular mail steamer and to surrender himself on reaching New York to the United States marshal. His conduct on the *Wabash* was in complete contrast with his attitude toward the officers on the *St. Mary's* after his surrender to Davis. On the latter vessel he had been morose, insolent, and overbearing, while he was now genial and conciliatory. As he reached Aspinwall five days before the scheduled departure of the New York steamer, Paulding endeavoured to persuade him to remain on the ship, where he would have better quarters than on shore, but he declined to remain even for another meal after the vessel had cast anchor, and took a room at one of the town's indifferent hotels. Here he remained most of the time in seclusion, occupying himself with writing, but taking an occasional stroll to the railway company's workshops for recreation.

When the *Wabash* steamed away from Greytown Anderson was still up the river. The *Fulton* was sent to the mouth of the Colorado, and the *Susquehanna*, which had just arrived, was stationed at the mouth of the San Juan to prevent the escape of Anderson and his men and the landing of any reinforcements for Walker that might be on their way from the United States. On hearing of Walker's capture Anderson abandoned Castillo, spiking the guns and destroying the frame buildings, and placed his force on board the steamer *Ogden*. On December 20 he sent a letter to Captain Sands, commanding the *Susquehanna*, stating that he wished to disband his command, and inquiring whether they would be permitted to enter Greytown. Most of them, he stated, wished

---

[1] Among the "filibusters" returning on the *Saratoga* was a Mrs. Buttrick and her three children. Her husband was a captain in Walker's service.

z

to return to the United States. Sands replied that he would send back to the United States any man who would surrender to him on board his ship.[1] On the 24th Sands took his boats' crews up the river, towed by the steamer recently seized by Paulding, and captured the remnants of the filibusters on the *Ogden*. Anderson surrendered under protest. The command, numbering forty-five, were taken to Aspinwall in the *Fulton* and there transferred to the *Wabash*. Paulding put them ashore at Key West, and Walker's third filibustering expedition was a thing of the past.[2]

[1] MS., Archives Navy Department, Home Squadron, II., 67 ff.
[2] *Ibid.*, 71, 74-6; Senate Ex. Doc. 63, 35 Cong., 1 Sess.

CHAPTER XXI

The Walker-Paulding Imbroglio

WALKER arrived in New York from Aspinwall on Sunday night, December 27, by the steamer *Northern Light*, and went at once to the residence of Henningsen in Twelfth Street. His old companion in arms was in Washington at this time, but Mrs. Henningsen was on hand to give him a welcome. The following morning, in accordance with his parole, he presented himself to the United States marshal, who was none other than his great friend and admirer, Isaiah Rynders. It was Rynders who had been a moving spirit in promoting the various public meetings in New York in behalf of Walker's cause during the previous year. Walker was accompanied by his counsel, Thomas Francis Meagher, Malcolm Campbell, and General Wheat. As they entered the office Rynders grasped Walker's hand and said, "I am happy to see you, General, as Captain Rynders, but as United States marshal I cannot say that." The filibuster general quietly returned his greeting and handed him a letter from Paulding assigning Walker to the marshal's custody. As Rynders had neither a warrant nor instructions to arrest Walker, he was puzzled as to what course he should pursue. He took his prisoner aside, and after some consultation it was agreed that they should go to Washington together and lay the case before the administration. As soon as this matter was disposed of Walker met the newspaper reporters. Though it takes much to surprise men of this calling, they listened in amazement while he coolly discussed Paulding's invasion of the territory of a friendly power and his insult to its flag. It was the duty of the American government, he said, to

333

return his men to the place from which they had been forcibly removed, and to salute the flag of Nicaragua for the insult it had received.[1] He was the most composed and self-possessed person in the room, and also the most insignificant, so far as external appearances went.

Shortly after reaching Washington, Walker and Rynders called on Secretary Cass, and the marshal stated the conditions under which he held his friend as a prisoner. Cass declared that the executive department had no right to detain Walker in custody, and that regular legal proceedings would have to be instituted before he could be arrested for violating the neutrality law. The marshal then notified Walker that he was no longer in custody. Walker's release was regarded as the administration's disavowal of Paulding's act. The arrest of the filibusters by an American officer on Nicaraguan soil called forth a number of different opinions. The abolitionists naturally applauded the deed, and were fully satisfied in stating that Paulding had acted in obedience to the "higher law." On the other hand, indignation meetings were held in all the principal cities of the South, at which resolutions were adopted remarkable chiefly for their fervid language.[2] Several Southern Congressmen gave notice that they would introduce a resolution that Walker be returned to Nicaragua in a national vessel. Their leaders, however, were in a dilemma, fearing to take issue too strongly with the administration lest they endanger its support of their position on the Kansas question.[3] The decided

---

[1] New York *Herald*, Dec. 29, 1857.

[2] At a meeting in New Orleans, Dec. 31, 1857, it was resolved, "That this meeting unanimously condemns the conduct of Paulding in this proceeding as being without excuse, and without precedent in the history of any civilized country, contrary to the law of nations, and deserving the condign punishment of the United States," and "that in the opinion of this meeting it is the imperative duty of this government to restore General Walker and his captive companions to the country from which they have been so unlawfully taken by irresistible force; and also fully to indemnify them for all losses they have sustained from capture, detention and privation of liberty and property." New York *Times*, Jan. 9, 1858.

[3] See Alexander Stephens's letters to his brother Linton, in Johnston and Browne, *Life of Alexander Stephens*, 328–9. (Philadelphia, 1878.)

opposition of Buchanan and his cabinet to the Walker enterprise
had been a surprise to the entire country. It had been freely
predicted that with the outgoing of Pierce and Marcy the filibusters would find easier sailing. Buchanan, as one of the joint
authors of the Ostend Manifesto, favoured the acquisition of Cuba,
even by force if such a proceeding were essential to the internal
peace and the preservation of the Union. Moreover, he had
accepted a nomination and had been elected on a platform
which expressly sympathized with the efforts being made to
"regenerate" Central America. *"Quae te, genitor, sententia
vertit?"* was a question running in the minds of Southern
statesmen.

The first public expression of the President's real opinion of the
Walker enterprise appeared in his first annual message to Congress
on December 8, 1857, submitted shortly after the escape of the
Fashion from Mobile. Referring to this incident, he declared,
"Such enterprises can do no possible good to the country, but
have already inflicted much injury, both on its interests and its
character." He urged Congress to adopt such measures "as will
be effectual in restraining our citizens from committing such
outrages," which "the most eminent writers on public law do
not hesitate to denounce as robbery and murder." [1] Buchanan
soon had an opportunity to explain his position more fully. On
January 4, 1858, the Senate passed a resolution calling for "the
correspondence, instructions and orders to the United States
naval forces on the coast of Central America, connected with the
arrest of William Walker and his associates." [2] The transmission
of this information the President made the occasion for a special
message, in which he declared that Paulding, in landing an armed
force on Nicaraguan soil, had committed "a grave error," which
should not go unnoticed lest it be construed as a precedent. It

---

[1] *Messages and Papers of the Presidents*, V., 447–8.
[2] *Congressional Globe*, 35 Cong., 1 Sess., pt. 1, 179.

was evident, however, that the Commodore, whom he referred to as "a gallant officer," had acted "from pure and patriotic motives and in the sincere conviction that he was promoting the interest and vindicating the honour of his country." While his act was a violation of her sovereignty, Nicaragua had sustained no injury therefrom, but rather had been benefited by the removal of a hostile invader; and that State alone had any right to complain. Walker, himself an invader, could not complain of the invasion by Paulding. If the naval officer had arrested Walker at any time before he entered the port he would have been wholly justified and have performed a praiseworthy act, as the eighth section of the neutrality law empowered the President to use the land and naval forces of the United States to prevent the "carrying on" of such expeditions to their consummation after they had succeeded in leaving the country. The President then took occasion to avow his determination to enforce the law. He reiterated his belief in the "manifest destiny" of the American people to dominate the affairs of the western hemisphere, but designated Walker's enterprise as a crime, defeating the object at which it expressly aimed. "Had one half the number of American citizens who have miserably perished in the first disastrous expedition of General Walker settled in Nicaragua as peaceful emigrants, the object which we all desire would ere this have been in a great degree accomplished." It would be better, he declared, for the government itself to undertake such enterprises than to allow them to proceed under the command of irresponsible adventurers. Such lawless expeditions had the further bad effect of interfering at every step with the conduct of foreign affairs with Central American governments.[1]

No one was more surprised at the President's attitude than Walker himself. At the time of his arrest he solemnly assured Paulding that he was acting with the full sanction of the Presi-

[1] *Messages and Papers of the Presidents*, V., 466-9.

dent; but the Commodore could not make himself believe it.[1] Soon after reaching the United States and finding himself publicly proclaimed at Washington as a lawless adventurer, a robber, and a murderer, he addressed an open letter to Buchanan, protesting against the President's harsh criticism of him and his men and calling attention to the fact that many of his officers had served with distinction during the Mexican War and that one of them had been rewarded for "the first planting of your colours upon the heights of Cerro Gordo." [2] He showed that his vessel's papers were correct in every particular, and that even if his party were belligerents against a power with which the United States was at peace, they were beyond the right of the United States to interfere as soon as they reached the high seas, as "the owners of a neutral vessel had a clear right to carry warlike persons as well as contraband of war, subject only to the risk of capture by the enemy's cruisers." He concluded his letter by boldly avowing his intention to return to Nicaragua.[3]

Walker remained but a few days in Washington, and then started for the South. This was the only section to which he now could make an effective appeal. It was generally supposed in the North that he could not survive his last misfortune. The masses were inclined to regard success as a proof of a righteous cause, and two failures made the filibuster a reprobate. This idea was by no means confined to the North. A Florida news-

[1] Meade, *Life of Hiram Paulding*, 183 ff.

[2] This was Thomas Henry, sergeant of the 7th Infantry, U.S.A., 1838–47; second lieutenant in May, 1847, and breveted first lieutenant for gallant and meritorious conduct at Contreras and Cherubusco, August 20, 1847. Heitman, *Historical Register and Dictionary of the United States Army*, I., 524.

[3] "As long as there is a Central American exiled from his native land, and deprived of his property and civil rights for the services he rendered us in evil as well as good report, so long shall our time and our energies be devoted to the work of their restoration. As long as the bones of our companions in arms, murdered by a barbarous decree of the Costa Rican government, lie bleaching and unburied on the hillsides of Nicaragua, so long shall our brains contrive and our hands labour for the justice which one day we will surely obtain." Wheeler Scrapbook no. 4, 283; *Harper's Weekly*, II., 38.

paper, for instance, declared : "At first we felt inclined to bid him
Godspeed, but the belief is now fast becoming general that the
'man of destiny' has had his day, and that he will not again be
allowed an opportunity to trifle away the lives and fortunes of
his fellow citizens. With all the advantages in his favour, his
present position and that of Nicaragua fully attest that he was
not the man for the crisis. We trust the administration will
enforce our neutrality laws to the letter." [1]

In like manner at a Democratic meeting in Montgomery on
January 26 Henry W. Hilliard, a former Congressman from
Alabama and at one time *chargé d'affaires* in Belgium, declared
that even if Walker were *de jure* President of Nicaragua he would
have no right to recruit forces for his service and organize them
within the boundaries of the United States, and that it was the
duty of the American government to prevent any such violation
of the law. William L. Yancey, however, who represented the
extreme Southern wing of the Democratic party, challenged this
view. "Every American citizen," said he, "has a right to expatriate himself. If one can go a thousand can go, all with common intent, if they do not organize an armed expedition here.
The republican foundations of the State of Texas were laid and
cemented on this great American principle, and I understand that
General Walker and his compatriots have been careful to keep
within the scope and spirit of this principle. If so the President
had no right to arrest him [even] on the high seas." [2]   It is evident
that few Southerners were so confident as Yancey that Walker
was guiltless of violating the neutrality laws, or the Southern press
would not have raised such a clamour for their repeal. [3]

Walker's progress southward was more like that of a conquering
hero than of a fallen filibuster. At Richmond, Montgomery, and

[1] Apalachicola (Fla.) *Advertiser*, quoted in the New York *Herald*, Dec. 14, 1857.
[2] Montgomery *Advertiser*, Jan. 28, 1858.
[3] See, for example, the Montgomery *Advertiser* of Jan. 14, 1858.

Mobile he was dined and fêted, and prominent citizens vied in doing him honour. He announced that he was on his way to New Orleans to demand a trial for the offence for which he had been arrested on the eve of his departure. At Mobile he delivered an address purporting to be an exposure of his relations with the Buchanan administration and an explanation of its recent hostility to his enterprise. He referred to his visit to the President by special appointment the previous June, and asked why, if he were the lawless person referred to in the President's messages, he should have been received at the White House as an equal. The President and his cabinet were friendly, he said, until September, when the government's Nicaraguan policy was suddenly changed. He declared that their motives were not disinterested; that Buchanan had set his heart upon the scheme for a railway and canal across the isthmus of Tehuantepec, fostered during the summer of 1857 by Emile La Sére and Judah P. Benjamin of New Orleans; that Pierre Soulé had accompanied these gentlemen to Mexico and thrown obstacles in the way of their enterprise; and that the administration was now seeking to revenge itself upon Soulé, who was regarded as Walker's chief sponsor, by blocking further efforts to Americanize Nicaragua, where Soulé had invested considerable capital.[1] That Soulé had blocked some of the schemes of Benjamin and La Sére in Mexico is true; and that Buchanan was highly enthusiastic over the Tehuantepec scheme and resentful of any effort to thwart it is also true; but whether his resentment were sufficient to cause him to seek to strike Soulé by crippling Walker is another story. It is a question not of facts but of motives, and one upon which documents throw no light. It is certain, however, that the administration had shown its hostility before the results of the mission of Benjamin and Soulé were known at Washington, as

[1] Mobile *Mercury*, Jan. 26; Wheeler Scrapbook no. 4, 295; New York *Herald*, Feb. 2, 1858.

the Tehuantepec promoters did not return to New Orleans until October,[1] whereas Cass's circular letter enjoining vigilance on the part of the Federal officers in checking unlawful expeditions was issued on September 18. The Soulé-Benjamin episode therefore could only have given Buchanan another count at the most against the Nicaraguan filibusters, if it influenced the conduct of the administration at all.

But the foregoing was not the only disclosure which Walker made in his speech at Mobile. While the administration would kill off the Nicaraguan enterprise, it was not hostile, he said, to filibustering in another quarter, and was perfectly willing to leave Walker unmolested if he would conduct his operations according to the President's ideas. Walker claimed that John B. Floyd, the Secretary of War, had consulted with Henningsen and urged that the filibusters abandon the Nicaraguan enterprise for the present and turn their attention to Mexico. They were to enter the military service of that country and precipitate a war with Spain by some hostile act toward that nation; and as soon as hostilities began they were to seize Cuba.[2] Walker declared that the President's change of front and abuse of him in his public utterances had freed him from any further obligation to keep these facts secret, and that the public was entitled to hear both sides of the controversy. Buchanan's enthusiasm for the Tehuantepec scheme, and his views on the annexation of Cuba accorded so well with Walker's story that even many of the filibuster's opponents were inclined to give it full credit. Of the conferences between Henningsen and Secretary Floyd there can be no doubt, but whether Henningsen understood fully the nature of the Secretary's proposals and whether Floyd was authorized to speak for

---

[1] For an account of the administration's interest in the Tehuantepec project, see Pierce Butler, *Judah P. Benjamin*, 185–90.

[2] Wheeler Scrapbook no. 4, 295; New York *Herald*, Feb. 2, 1858, quoting Mobile *Mercury*, Jan. 26; New York *Times*, Feb. 2, 1858; *Edinburgh Review*, CXII., 566–7.

the President, even if he so declared to Henningsen, are matters upon which we need more information before passing final judgment upon the merits of the filibuster's "disclosures." Floyd met the story with a flat denial.[1]

In the meantime the Walker-Paulding imbroglio was having an airing in both houses of Congress. The Senate, as we have seen, had called on the President for the correspondence and instructions of naval officers on the coast of Central America concerning the arrest of Walker; and the House, on January 12, went further and called for all the information in the President's possession concerning Walker's second expedition to Nicaragua, which could be submitted without detriment to the public interest. Debate in the House had already begun eight days previously, and was to continue in both branches, with certain intervals of suspension, for five months. It is useless to go into the details of the various arguments presented. Those of the administration's critics may be briefly summarized as follows: (1) Walker was guilty of no violation of the neutrality law, as the expedition was not organized on a military basis within the jurisdiction of the United States. (2) Even if this were the case, the emigrants could not be lawfully molested once they had reached the high seas, as the laws of a nation are not in effect at a distance exceeding a marine league from its shores. (3) Neither Chatard nor Paulding, therefore, had any right to interfere with Walker in the harbour of Greytown or on the high seas,[2] and in removing Chatard for not acting and censuring Paulding for acting the administration was guilty of gross inconsistency. The act of landing an armed force would be no greater breach of Nicaraguan sovereignty than the act of forcibly preventing their landing. What would we say

---

[1] New Orleans *Picayune*, July 22, 1858.

[2] It will be recalled that Commander Davis refused to prevent the landing of recruits for Walker at San Juan del Sur, when requested to do so by the allies, on the ground that it was not his duty to enforce the laws of the United States within the territorial jurisdiction of a foreign power. See above, p. 294.

if a British officer had acted as Paulding did? There was danger now that the British would make this a precedent. (5) The fact that Nicaragua did not complain was no justification of Paulding's act. That matter was beside the point. Louis Philippe would not have complained either if an American naval officer had landed a force in France and aided him in putting down the revolution of 1848. (6) And finally, even Nicaragua's full consent to the arrest, previously obtained, would not *ipso facto* empower the President to authorize the seizure unless he had previously received such authority by an act of Congress.

It is interesting to note that many of those who held these views had little or no sympathy with Walker himself. Senator Stephen A. Douglas, for instance, who gave a very clear-cut exposition of his views, declared, "I have no fancy for this system of filibustering. I believe its tendency is to defeat the very object they have in view, to wit: the enlargement of the area of freedom and the flag." [1] Jefferson Davis expressed similar views. Even if we had had an extradition treaty with Nicaragua, we could not have done what Paulding did. Still he had, apparently, a very poor opinion of Walker. "I know nothing of him. I have no sympathy with such expeditions. I think we should execute our neutrality law within our own limits." If it is desirable to have the President order the patrol of the high seas, the law should be amended so as to permit it. [2] Senator Pugh, of Ohio, did not think much of Walker, but declared that the worst men often represent in their persons great principles, and Walker represented the right of an American to expatriate himself. Walker's chief defenders were Brown, of Mississippi, and Toombs, of Georgia, in the Senate, and Stephens, of Georgia, Clingman, of North Carolina, Warren, of Arkansas, Taylor, of Louisiana, and Quitman, of Mississippi, in the House. [3] Critics of Walker were found among

[1] *Congressional Globe*, 35 Cong., 1 Sess., 223.
[2] *Ibid.*, 217.   [3] *Ibid.*, *passim.*

both the Northern and Southern delegations. The same is true
with regard to defenders of Paulding, though the latter got only
occasional commendation from the South. Senator Mallory, of
Florida,.was one of Paulding's warmest defenders. He knew the
Commodore personally and regarded him as one of the brightest
ornaments of the service. "The instructions were vague and might
be interpreted so as to authorize this action." Mr. Zollicoffer, of
Tennessee, also was inclined to blame the author of the instructions rather than the man who tried to carry them out.[1] If Chatard could lawfully have prevented the landing in a neutral port,
Paulding could lawfully have landed a force and broken up the
expedition after it landed. Wright, of Georgia, sought to secure
consideration of a set of resolutions declaring the arrest unlawful
but in accordance with the instructions of the Secretary of the
Navy.[2] Senator Crittenden, of Kentucky, was among those who
denied that Paulding had committed a grave error. Other defenders of the naval officer were Messrs. Ritchie, of Pennsylvania,
Thompson, Pottle, and Palmer, of New York, Curtis, of Iowa,
and Montgomery, of Pennsylvania. In the Senate, Doolittle, of
Wisconsin, introduced a joint resolution directing the presentation
of a gold medal to Paulding, for his conduct in removing the
filibusters from Nicaragua. Brown, of Mississippi, immediately
moved to strike out all but the enacting clause and substitute a
resolution disavowing and condemning the officer's action.[3] Whenever this resolution came up for discussion it precipitated such a
flood of debate that its consideration would be postponed; and
it finally was talked to death.

Paulding's defenders based their arguments on the following
grounds: (1) Walker was a fugitive from justice, and an American
officer had a right to arrest him anywhere, with the consent of
the country in which he had sought an asylum. (2) This consent

---

[1] *Congressional Globe*, 35 Cong., 1 Sess., 284.
[2] *Ibid.*, Appendix, 458.   [3] *Ibid.*, 265.

had practically been given in the note of Molina and Irisarri of
September 14, when they asked that a naval force be stationed
off the coast to prevent the filibusters from landing. Neither of
these gentlemen at that time was entitled to speak officially for
Nicaragua, it is true, but on November 15, three weeks before
Walker's arrest, Irisarri had been formally received as the representative of that country. (3) Even if there were no previous
consent, the point at which Walker disembarked was an uninhabited barren waste, over which no country had ever effectively
extended its jurisdiction, and the landing of an armed force there
was no real violation of foreign territory. (4) Finally, the United
States was responsible to any friendly power for an armed invasion
of its territory by American citizens, and because of its responsibility it was justified in taking the measures necessary to break it up.

Palmer, of New York, declared that if Paulding committed "a
grave error," it was in not leaving Walker to the justice of the
country to which he had migrated.[1] Montgomery, of Pennsylvania, said that if it were an invasion to take Walker away, would
it not be another invasion to take him back, as some of his friends
were urging should be done. Still, in his own opinion, it would
be a good plan for the government to take him back and allow
him to test the affection of the Nicaraguans. If they really desired his return, he would need no military expedition to accompany
him.[2] The debate showed much conflict of opinion. The friends
of neither Walker nor Paulding accepted the viewpoint of the
administration, and consequently subjected Buchanan to severe
criticism. At the same time, many who agreed with the President in condemning both the filibuster and the Commodore
strongly disapproved the government's method of dealing with
the case. Strange to say, among the small number who sided
with the President was William H. Seward, who defended Buchanan's whole course in the matter except his allowing Walker to

[1] *Congressional Globe*, 35 Cong., 1 Sess., 300.   [2] *Ibid.*, 281.

go free when he presented himself as a prisoner at Washington. Seward evoked much laughter in the Senate in declaring that he was glad to see the President in his message championing "the higher law," a proceeding that was regarded as the New York Senator's special prerogative.

The most striking feature in the debates was the indication that Walker did not enjoy the united support of the Southern members. This has already been indicated to some extent in preceding paragraphs. Walker received no severer castigation than came from Southern tongues. Lamar, of Mississippi, said: "While I am a Southern man, thoroughly imbued with the spirit of my section, I will never consent to submit the fate of our noble institutions to the hands of marauding bands, or violate their sanctity by identifying their progress with the success of unlawful expeditions." He declared that he would consent to no new schemes of territorial acquisition until the question of the right of the South to extend her institutions into territory already within the Union had been practically and satisfactorily settled. This presented a question "before whose colossal magnitude the wrongs of Walker and the criminality of Paulding sink into insignificance."[1] Hawkins, of Florida, declared, "I have but small faith in the star of 'the grey-eyed man of destiny,' for it shines dimmed and pale, receiving or borrowing no lustre from his civic or military talents. That he possesses uncommon personal courage, force of will, and firmness under difficulties there is no doubt; but these attributes of character appear unaccompanied by the requisite knowledge of the art of war, the gift of gaining the affection of his troops, and the enforcement of a salutary discipline, save by acts of extreme and probably unnecessary severity."[2] Winslow, of North Carolina, spoke in a similar vein, declaring that such enterprises

---

[1] *Congressional Globe*, 35 Cong., 1 Sess., 279. In the appendix to the *Congressional Globe* this speech is published in revised form, and its tone is much milder.
[2] *Ibid.*, Appendix, 461.

tended to degrade the American character and alienate from us the weak powers of the continent. "If the acquisition of Nicaragua is necessary for our safety and happiness, let us acquire it in a manly and open warfare; do not let us 'set the dogs' on her." [1]

The severest arraignment, however, came from Senator Slidell, of Louisiana, regarded as the mouthpiece of the Buchanan administration. Paulding received some censure, but the denunciation of Walker was unsparing. The Commodore, by his highhanded action, had succeeded only in arousing a false sympathy for the filibuster and had given him a martyr's crown. "Pseudomartyrs have, in all ages, found devotees to worship at their shrine." He referred to Walker sarcastically as "a new William the Conqueror;" declared his election a farce, "played with the soothing accompaniment of the bayonet," and that his whole career was marked by rapine and blood. He was no soldier; he had reviled the man who had saved him from an ignominious death; his very name was mentioned with dread by the whole of Central America. Slidell defended the administration in its displacing of Chatard for not acting against the filibusters while censuring Paulding for acting. Chatard, he said, should have arrested Walker and his followers on board the *Fashion.* This was an American vessel flying the American flag, and was therefore a bit of American territory wherever it might be. The organization of an armed expedition on the decks of this steamer was therefore a violation of the neutrality law, and its voyage was illicit. As long as the filibusters were on board the *Fashion* they were subject to arrest, but once they had stepped on foreign soil they were beyond the jurisdiction of the United States.[2] This was meant to be the administration's answer to its many critics, but its chief interest lies in the fact that it was spoken by a Senator representing a region where filibustering had hitherto received its strongest support.

[1] *Congressional Globe,* 35 Cong., 1 Sess., Appendix, 504.   [2] *Ibid.,* 1538.

The reaction against Walker both North and South amply attests the truth of the old adage that "nothing succeeds like success." When Slidell made his speech in the Senate less than twelve months had passed since Lewis Cass, now Secretary of State, had declared that "the heroic effort of our countrymen in Nicaragua excites my admiration, while it engages all my solicitude. I am not to be deterred from the expression of these feelings by sneers, or reproaches, or hard words. He who does not sympathize with such an enterprise has little in common with me." [1] A few months had wrought great changes. Politicians were no longer willing to hitch their wagon to a falling star. The information transmitted to the two Houses of Congress by the President was referred in the Senate to the Committee on Foreign Affairs and to the similar committee in the House, except the part dealing with naval orders and instructions, which was referred to the Committee on Naval Affairs. The reports of these committees merely reëchoed the views expressed in the message of the President. [2]

After his censure by Buchanan, Paulding was relieved from duty and replaced by Commodore McIntosh. During the remainder of this administration he was in virtual retirement, and was made a defendant in several lawsuits brought by the thwarted filibusters. [3]

It was at least some comfort to him, however, to know that he had the gratitude of Nicaragua. Before his return to the United States General Jerez, Walker's former companion in arms and cabinet minister, visited the Commodore on the *Wabash* and thanked him very profusely for the removal of the filibusters. [4]

---

[1] New York *Times*, May 24, 1856.

[2] See Senate Report 20, and House Report 74, 35 Cong., 1 Sess. Three members of the House Committee on Naval Affairs, however, presented a minority report commending Paulding.

[3] *Congressional Globe*, 35 Cong., 1 Sess., 1539; Meade, *Life of Hiram Paulding*, 200.

[4] Senate Doc. 10, 35 Cong., 2 Sess.

2 A

A formal letter of thanks also came from the Nicaraguan Minister of Foreign Relations, who spoke in behalf of his government. Señor Irisarri also expressed to Cass the thanks of the Nicaraguan government for the conduct of Paulding.[1] The republic of Nicaragua voted Paulding a jewelled sword and twenty *caballerias* (about 670 acres) of land, and Congress in 1861 gave him permission to receive the sword but not the land, as the acceptance of the latter gift might prove a dangerous precedent.[2] While we may appreciate this officer's motives, we must agree with the administration in censuring his act, and this regardless of any question of the merits or demerits of filibustering. Paulding himself, as has been shown already, admitted in a letter to his wife that he had taken a very high hand. In his official report to the Secretary of the Navy he made no attempt to justify his conduct on the basis of his instructions, but stated that he "could not regard Walker and his followers in any other light than as outlaws who had escaped from the vigilance of the government and left our shores for the purpose of rapine and murder, and I saw no other way to vindicate the law and redeem the honour of our country than by disarming them and sending them home. In doing so I am fully sensible of the responsibility I have incurred and confidently look to the government for my justification. . . . Humanity, as well as law and justice and national honour, demanded the dispersion of these lawless men."[3] If Paulding sincerely believed that Walker was an outlaw and pirate, bent on rapine and murder, why did he address him as "General," share with him his mess and cabin, and send him all the way from Aspinwall to New York on his mere parole of honour? A number of journals ascribed Paulding's act merely to pique because his

[1] *Congressional Globe*, 35 Cong., 1 Sess., 357.

[2] MS., Archives, State Department, Notes from Department, Central America, I., 200; Notes to Department, Nicaraguan Legation (1862–67); Meade, *Life of Hiram Paulding*, 198–9.

[3] MS., Archives, Navy Department, Home Squadron, II., 61.

squadron had been outwitted, and the filibuster had dared to "talk back" to a captain in the service.[1] Others ascribed it to the influence of the two British commanders who had dined with the American commodore on the day preceding the arrest. Indeed, the commander of the *Brunswick* offered to coöperate with Paulding in removing the party from Punta Arenas, but Paulding declined his offer.[2] It has also been pointed out that Paulding was a warm friend of Commander Davis, and had been offended by Walker's criticism of that officer.[3] Among the officers in the navy there was a strong *esprit de corps*, and they were quick to resent the aspersions of an outsider. It will be recalled, also, that during the previous summer Paulding had been compelled to carry home from Aspinwall a large number of survivors of the siege of Rivas, and their sufferings and destitution were still vivid pictures in his memory. It is probable that his conduct was guided somewhat by all of these facts, and that his motives were really more complex then he would be willing to admit. At any rate, such conduct, whatever the motive, should not have gone unrebuked. In censuring Paulding the administration was only following the precedent established in the case of Commodore David N. Porter, who in 1825 landed a naval force in Porto Rico and compelled the alcalde of a village to apologize for the insults offered to an American naval officer. For this Porter was censured and suspended from service. There are times, indeed, when an officer is justified in breaking his instructions, times of great crisis when immediate action is imperative and obedience to instructions would mean disaster. Paulding was confronted by no such situation. He might, on arriving in the port and finding the filibusters landed, have cut off reinforcements and when Anderson seized the steamers and sent them down the river to convey

---

[1] Wheeler Scrapbook no. 4, 273 ; 278–9.

[2] MS., Archives Navy Department, Home Squadron, II., 61.

[3] Roche, *Byways of War*, 213–14.

the filibusters to the interior he might have seized these also in accordance with instructions to protect American property. This would have quickly reduced the filibusters to voluntary submission and prevented their being regarded as martyrs.

It is interesting to note that a little over two years before Walker's arrest William L. Marcy, then Secretary of State and no friend of the filibusters, had occasion to give an opinion on an hypothetical case very similar to that involved in Walker's third expedition. Señor Marcoleta, the minister from Nicaragua, in the summer of 1855, shortly after the departure of Walker and Kinney, addressed the State Department and asked that an American vessel be stationed in the harbour of Greytown to prevent the landing of arms and supplies for the filibusters then in his country. Marcy replied on August 11 that if an armed expedition escaped from the territories of the United States and entered the boundaries of a foreign State, it could not be pursued thither and seized when within the territory of another State. A vessel of the United States in the port of San Juan "could not, without assuming illegal power involving the rights of that State, interpose to prevent the disembarkation of arms, ammunition, or other articles to which reasonable suspicions were attached." A compliance with such a request "would be an open invasion of the sovereign rights of Nicaragua, and lead to acts toward individuals by the United States which could not be justified by any municipal or international law." [1]

It will thus be seen that Marcy in 1855 held the same views that Stephen A. Douglas and Jefferson Davis held in 1858. None of these men can be accused of leanings toward filibustering. Next it should be observed that Secretary Toucey ordered his naval officers to do the very thing that Marcy expressly declared that they had no legal right to do; namely, hold up illegal expeditions in

[1] MS., Archives, State Department, Notes from Department, Central America, I., 85–7.

Central American ports and prevent their landing. This shows a distinct step in advance by the government in repressing filibustering, and it had the full approval of Buchanan. Yet this Executive has been roundly accused many times of winking at such enterprises! It is certain that the chief of filibusters did not regard him as a friend of his enterprise. Neither did the British minister. On November 16, immediately after hearing of the sailing of the *Fashion*, Lord Napier, the British minister to the United States, wrote to Lord Clarendon: "I believe that the President and General Cass sincerely deprecate and regret the present attempt to invade the peace of Central America." [1] Coming from such a source, this, if not praise, was at least exculpation from the throne. Two months later Sir William Gore Ouseley, en route to Central America as a special commissioner of the British government, held a consultation with Buchanan. His impressions were not different from Napier's. The President assured him of his determination to put down filibustering and declared that the majority of respectable and thinking men in this country were on his side. "I have every reason," wrote Sir William, "to rely on the literal truth of the President's assurances as to his own feelings respecting filibustering; and my own observation quite confirms his Excellency's opinion as to the sense of the majority of influential men in this country, including the Southern and slave-holding States, being ready to support his acts." [2]

A year later we find Buchanan not only repudiating filibusterism but also scouting the idea of annexing any part of Central America to the United States. "What could we do with such a people?" he asked Napier. "We could not incorporate them; if we did, they would tear us asunder." Napier replied that he was fully aware of the constitutional and political impediments confronting the annexation on equal terms of any region popu-

[1] *British State Papers*, XLVII., 742.   [2] *Ibid.*, XLVIII., 632.

lated by mixed races, but that he believed some Americans contemplated the creation of colonies or dependencies of some portions of Central America. Buchanan denied the possibility of grafting such a novelty upon the institutions of the United States and repeated a statement which the British minister had often heard him make, "We can only annex vacant territory." [1] And this came from one of the authors of the Ostend Manifesto!

[1] *British State Papers*, XLVIII., 754.

CHAPTER XXII

TRANSIT TROUBLES

AFTER the removal of Walker from the isthmus in May, 1857, Generals Jerez and Martinez, the respective heads of the Democratic and Legitimist parties in Nicaragua, pronounced against the government of Patricio Rivas, which had been recognized by all the Central American republics, and put themselves at the head of a new government, thus establishing a kind of duumvirate.[1] Although revolutionary, this made possible a union of all factions among the natives. In a typically Latin-American fashion the two chieftains now banished the unlucky Rivas, at whose call the allies had marched against the filibusters, and he fled to England. A constitutional convention was subsequently called, and Martinez was chosen president without opposition. This government was no more constitutional than any that had recently preceded it, including even Walker's. The two military chieftains had no power to call a convention, and no military officer above the rank of lieutenant-colonel might legally become president while in actual service.[2]

Meanwhile the Transit remained closed, to the great detriment of American interests. The new Nicaraguan government was approached from many sources on the subject of reopening it, and this brought about complications between Nicaragua and Costa Rica. The latter had continued to hold the steamers of

[1] MS., Department of State, Bureau of Indexes and Archives, Central America, Notes to Department, II.; Nicaraguan and Costa Rican Legations, Despatches, III.
[2] MS., Department of State, Bureau of Indexes and Archives, Nicaraguan and Costa Rican Legations, Despatches, III.; Notes to Department, II.

the Transit Company after the cessation of hostilities and had
demanded that Nicaragua recognize her rights to the entire south
bank of the San Juan River. The forts of Castillo Viejo and San
Carlos were also included in the demand. Nicaragua ceded
Castillo Viejo for a period of twenty years, but refused to cede
San Carlos. As a result of this disagreement the two countries
were soon involved in a warfare of paper and ink. The dispute was
intensified by the Transit's becoming a bone of contention between
them. Costa Rica claimed certain rights over the route by virtue
of her occupation and claim to the southern bank of the river, and
she further declared her occupation a military necessity, since
Nicaragua would be unable to defend the Transit in the event of
another invasion and would allow it to become an open door to
filibusters.

Three rival groups of capitalists were now contesting for the
franchise: the original grantee, the Atlantic and Pacific Ship
Canal Company, with H. G. Stebbins as president and Joseph L.
White as chief schemer (usually referred to as the Stebbins and
White Company); the Accessory Transit Company, headed by
Cornelius Vanderbilt, who had never acknowledged the legality of
the revocation of his charter by the Rivas-Walker government;
and Morgan and Garrison, who naturally maintained that the
rights they had recently secured were still valid.

The Englishman Webster, who had assisted Spencer in planning
the operations on the San Juan, made use of his opportunity while
in San José to secure some sort of a concession from Costa Rica,
and having fallen out with Vanderbilt he joined forces with Morgan
and Garrison. It was necessary for him to secure the same concession from Nicaragua also, but this he failed to do. Meanwhile
the Stebbins and White Company began to use its influence upon
Señor Irisarri, the recently accredited minister from Nicaragua,
but not yet recognized as such at Washington, and sought to obtain
a new transit concession through him. Irisarri was completely

captivated by the blandishments of Joseph L. White, but Vanderbilt, whose influence in high political circles was supreme, endeavoured to prevent his recognition. The situation was still more complicated by a scheme of General Cañas, who had remained in Nicaragua in command of the Costa Rican forces and had conceived the idea of creating a new political organization embracing the districts of Rivas, Guanacaste, and the San Juan River. He seems to have planned a *coup d'état*, which he hoped to achieve with Vanderbilt's aid, and intended to repay the financier by granting him the Transit route. Vanderbilt advised against this plan on account of the sparse population in the region to be embraced within the new State, but urged Cañas to place the steamers in his (Vanderbilt's) possession and allow him to reopen the Transit, and assured him that he would meet with every encouragement in this step from the United States, as the administration at Washington had made known its intention to protect any government opening the Transit. After securing this object Cañas was to have himself designated as minister from both Nicaragua and Costa Rica and come to Washington to replace Irisarri, who had been made the tool of speculators. Vanderbilt also secured the services of Goicouria, who sought to undermine Irisarri in Nicaragua and aid his patron by letters to General Jerez, whom he had known when they both served under Walker in the spring of 1856.[1] Webster, whose Costa Rican concession had proved valueless, now abandoned Morgan and Garrison and returned to the service of Vanderbilt. He visited Costa Rica again in the autumn of 1857 with Vanderbilt's son-in-law, Daniel B. Allen, to secure a concession to which both the Central American republics would agree.

Irisarri, however, had already made a contract with Stebbins and White on June 27, and this had been confirmed by his gov-

[1] MS., Archives, Department of State, Central America, Notes to Department, II.

ernment in July. The Vanderbilt forces at once protested, claiming that the Accessory Transit Company still possessed exclusive rights by virtue of its original charter, and that the revocation by the filibuster government in February, 1856, was null and void. Morgan and Garrison, too, were bent on maintaining their former rights and privileges, but as they had been closely identified with the filibusters the Nicaraguan government was not disposed to heed their claims.[1]

The American government took an active interest in the reopening of the route, and sent William Carey Jones as a special agent to Nicaragua to report on conditions there. A more unfortunate choice could hardly have been made. If newspaper reports are correct, he was rarely sober and never diplomatic,[2] and was called home without having furnished any information worth while.

The anxiety of the Buchanan administration to reopen the route led to the recognition of Irisarri as minister from Nicaragua on November 16, the day following Walker's departure from Mobile on the *Fashion*. Immediately after his reception a treaty negotiated by him and Cass was submitted to their respective governments for ratification. It is probable that it had been drafted before he was recognized as Nicaraguan minister. As he had been representing Guatemala and San Salvador near the American government for several years he was able to discuss Nicaraguan affairs indirectly with Cass before presenting his credentials from the latter country. The treaty as proposed provided for an open and neutral transit through the republic of Nicaragua, and empowered the United States to employ military force, if necessary, to protect persons and property conveyed over the route.[3] It was the object of Buchanan and Cass to secure a safe and neutral highway between the oceans, open to all nations upon equal terms,

---

[1] *British State Papers*, XLVII., 710.   [2] See New York *Herald*, Jan. 1, 1858.
[3] For full text of the treaty see Senate Ex. Doc. 194, 47 Cong., 1 Sess., 117–25.

and not liable to interruption by the miserable civil wars on the isthmus. They were somewhat taken back, therefore, when immediately after the convention was signed Irisarri told Cass that the Stebbins and White Company was the only corporation in Nicaragua that had the right of transit across the isthmus.

Naturally the opponents of that company desired to prevent the ratification of the Cass-Irisarri convention, and the Vanderbilt agents in Nicaragua worked strenuously toward this end. Vanderbilt also continued to curry favour with Costa Rica — a scheme that had its advantages, as that country still held the steamers and controlled the river and lake — and he seems to have hoped to displace Irisarri at Washington with General Cañas. With the Cass-Irisarri agreement rejected in Nicaragua, he believed that the administration in its desire to revive interoceanic communication would enter into negotiations with Costa Rica, and with Cañas as minister he would achieve his full purpose.[1]

In the meantime the relations between Nicaragua and Costa Rica had become very strained. The boundary between the two countries had long been a subject of dispute, and Costa Rica thought this a favourable moment to secure her claims. Nicaragua was exhausted and incapable of effective resistance. Moreover, she was indebted to her sister State for deliverance from the filibusters. Upon the refusal of Nicaragua to surrender Fort San Carlos Colonel Cauty was sent with a force of Costa Ricans to starve the garrison into submission, and war between the two republics seemed inevitable. Thanks to Walker, however, the political situation suddenly cleared. His arrival at Punta Arenas in November, 1857, put the two States into such a panic that by mutual consent they dropped their quarrel and made common cause against the filibusters. After Paulding's arrest of Walker there was harmony on the isthmus. A treaty was negotiated between the two repub-

[1] MS., Archives, Department of State, Central America, Notes to Department, II., III.

lies on the very day of Walker's capture and provided for the settlement of the boundary dispute.[1]

The attention of Nicaragua was next directed toward the Cass-
Irisarri convention. The recent return of Walker was used as a
bugaboo by the Vanderbilt agents to prevent its ratification. President Martinez, who hated Americans, and had no desire to see the
Transit reopened, referred the measure to the assembly, feeling
confident that it would be voted down; but when, to his astonish-
ment, it was eventually ratified, he refused to sign it.[2] He did
not dare, however, to make public the withholding of his signature,
and allowed the impression to prevail that the document had been
signed. He even delivered a sealed package to the representative
of the Stebbins and White Company (who happened to be none
other than Louis Schlessinger, the coward of Santa Rosa), telling
him that it was the treaty. Schlessinger was to be the messenger
to take the treaty to the United States, and he secured from Mr.
Mirabeau B. Lamar, the new minister from the United States, a
letter to the commander of the *Fulton* at Greytown requesting him
to take Schlessinger to Aspinwall so that he could reach the United
States with the news at the earliest possible moment. Luckily, the
warship was not in the port when the messenger reached Greytown,
and the American navy was spared the indignity shown American
diplomacy.[3]

The insolent trick played upon the American minister was a
result of the arrival of a new Richmond in the field in the person
of a versatile Frenchman, M. Felix Belly. Though merely the
agent of a few obscure Parisian speculators, he had a keen eye
to the possibilities of the situation, and possessing considerable
dramatic ability, he managed to invest his mission with a kind of

[1] *British State Papers*, XLIX., 1222–24.
[2] MS., Archives, Department of State, Nicaragua and Costa Rica, Despatches,
III.
[3] New York *Herald*, May 31, 1858; Belly, *À Travers l'Amérique Centrale*, II.,
160 ff.

awe-inspiring mystery, causing a number of French and American journals to report that he was an official representative of the French Emperor. After landing at Greytown on March 14, 1858, he sent communications to Presidents Mora and Martinez, couched in mysterious language, declaring his visit connected with vast projects which he would be glad to submit to their Excellencies. "I have been devoted for several years to the cause of Central American independence and prosperity, and it will not be my fault if the triumph of this cause is not the immediate and natural result of my journey," he said. He went first to Costa Rica, and Mora on hearing of his coming ordered a guide and mules at midnight to go from the capital and meet him. Colonel Barrillier, the French Zouave, was also sent to act as one of his escorts, and he was heartily greeted in all the villages along the way. This was only a few months after both Walker and Kinney had been again in Greytown harbour, and while Vanderbilt's agents were keeping the people alarmed at possible invasions of the filibusters. The suavity of the Frenchman entirely captivated Mora, who gave a great ball in his honour. Belly denied that his mission was official, but did it in such a way as to convince the officials that the denial was made for diplomatic reasons. He declared furthermore that he had the personal assurance of the continued interest of Louis Napoleon in the canal project, and even had the effrontery to present the draft of a proposed treaty between Nicaragua and Costa Rica providing for their joint control of the canal and enjoyment of its privileges. Within a week he had persuaded Mora not only to sign the treaty but also to go with him to Rivas and persuade President Martinez to do likewise.

At this juncture this grandiose personage came near encountering complete defeat. His pocket-book became empty, and the speculators at home who promised to send him funds apparently had forgotten him. Fortunately, one of his fellow countrymen in Costa Rica came to his aid, and he was enabled to continue his game. On April 24 the two presidents met about a mile from Rivas, where twelve months before Nicaraguan and Costa Rican troops had fought side by side, and together they entered the ruined town and began their negotiations in a bullet-riddled house. Belly had things all his own way. An "international convention" was drawn up at his instigation, which gave the company to be formed by "M. Felix Belly, publiciste," the exclusive privilege of building and operating the Nicaraguan canal.

But the Frenchman did not stop at that. He succeeded also in effecting a treaty of limits between the two countries, by which Nicaragua made a remarkable cession of territory to Costa Rica, in consideration of the aid and coöperation of the latter State in the event of any controversy between Nicaragua and the United States. Costa Rica thus became a joint owner of part of the Transit route, and the Cass-Irisarri convention, even if eventually ratified, would have very little value without Costa Rica's assent thereto. Belly assured the two chiefs that France would protect the interests of their respective countries, now that a French company was to be associated with them in the construction of a canal.[1]

Belly next played what he probably regarded as his master stroke by having Mora and Martinez sign a joint declaration placing Nicaragua and Costa Rica under the protection of France, England, and Sardinia, and empowering "M. Felix Belly to request in our name the immediate assistance of all the European vessels of war that he may be able to meet with. We charge him especially to solicit the despatch to San Juan del Norte of one or two vessels from the French station of the Antilles, and we place the two republics of Costa Rica and Nicaragua in Central America entirely under the guarantee of European law and of the special enactments against pirates and buccaneers." [2] The reasons given for this

[1] MS., Archives, Department of State, Nicaragua and Costa Rica, Despatches, III.

[2] For the full text of this curious document, see British State Papers, XLVIII., 695-6, or Accounts and Papers, 1860, LXVIII., 122.

unusual action were the imminent invasion of American filibusters
and the exhaustion of Central America, which could be defended
now only with European assistance.

Along with this commission to Belly the two presidents issued
an elaborate manifesto directed against the United States and
intended for European consumption. This document stated
that a new invasion, under the patronage of the United States
government, was menacing the independence of Nicaragua and
Costa Rica; that the United States openly menaced Central
America with annexation by force unless the States surrendered
voluntarily; that all official agents of the United States in Nicaragua had acted as accomplices of the invaders; and that the
present minister had publicly boasted of presenting the ultimatum
of accepting legal annexation by the ratification of the Cass-
Irisarri treaty or a new invasion of filibusters already organized at
Mobile under the American flag. Moreover, the American government had admitted to the Costa Rican ministers its inability
to prevent the departure of filibusters or to protect the neutrality
of Central America; and inasmuch as the Central American States
were so exhausted after their recent resistance that they could not
withstand another attack, "they must succumb before a superior-
ity of numbers, unless Europe deign at least to defend them against
attempts unprecedented in the nineteenth century." Mora and
Martinez therefore placed their countries under the protection of
England, France, and Sardinia, who had caused the independence
of the Ottoman Empire to be respected, and appealed to these
powers no longer to leave the shores of Central America defenceless,
and "its rich countries at the mercy of barbarians." [1]

With an eye for dramatic effect, Belly conducted these negotiations so that the various documents described above were all
signed at Rivas on May 1, 1858, the anniversary of Walker's sur-

[1] MS., Archives, Department of State, Nicaragua and Costa Rica, Despatches,
III.

render to Davis. Deceived as to Belly's real status, Martinez
felt that with his support he could beard Minister Lamar, who had
been labouring earnestly for the ratification of the Cass-Irisarri
treaty, and defy the assembly, which had ratified it in the face of
his known opposition. When Belly took his leave to return to
Europe with his canal concession, Martinez even requested him on
reaching Greytown to make an official investigation of Kinney's
recent irruption and report the facts to Louis Napoleon.[1] History
furnishes few more striking illustrations of opera bouffe than the
transactions of Belly and the two presidents at Rivas.

Inflated with his success, the Frenchman went to Aspinwall and
thence to New York. As his vessel steamed into the American
port a press boat came down the bay bringing the latest papers,
and in a copy of the New York *Herald* he saw in flaring headlines
"Disavowal of M. Belly," and read below that the French government had declared that it had no connection with him and regarded
him as a mere adventurer. For several weeks his mysterious
doings in Central America had alarmed all American expansionists
and champions of the Monroe Doctrine and had even revived
some of the dwindling sympathy with filibusterism. It was feared
that he was the secret emissary of the French Emperor. But now
the truth was known, and the whale had shrunk to the dimensions
of a minnow. Belly had planned to play the same rôle in Washington that he had acted so well on the isthmus and seek to obtain
a good understanding between his proposed company and the
United States government. The disavowal, however, took all the
wind out of his sails, and he got no satisfaction either from Cass or
from the French minister. He took ship for home and reached
Liverpool with eighteen francs in his pocket. The secretary of
the Honduran legation lent him money to continue his journey
to Paris, and there few men of influence would even give him a
hearing. Some promoters of equivocal standing finally advanced

[1] Belly, *op. cit.*, II., 178.

him funds to return to Nicaragua and begin the survey of the proposed canal, but on his arrival he found that the Central American diplomats in Paris had issued letters of warning describing Belly's supporters as a bad lot and had distributed these liberally in Nicaragua. Funds for continuing the survey were soon withdrawn, and all of Belly's fine schemes came to naught. His chief accomplishment was the blocking of the American efforts to reopen the Transit.

The joint manifesto of Mora and Martinez vexed Cass no little. It not only accused the American government of weakness and bad faith in its conduct toward the filibusters, but also violated the Monroe Doctrine by proclaiming the establishment of a European protectorate over Central America. The Secretary of State therefore called upon Lamar to determine by a categorical inquiry whether the manifesto were authentic. If it should prove to be genuine, the United States would deal with the provocation with forbearance, though "had such a cause of offence been given by France or England or by any other nation with a well established government properly appreciating its duties toward foreign powers," all diplomatic intercourse would have been suspended forthwith. Lamar was ordered to notify the governments that if any arrangements made with Belly interfered with the rights previously acquired by American citizens, full reparation would be demanded. As to European intervention in American affairs, the United States had long ago avowed its opposition to such a proceeding and would resist it under any and every circumstance. Finally, he was to show the executives that had it not been for the neutrality law of the United States the invasion which resulted from Nicaragua's own invitation would have succeeded, and that they owed their present power to the fact that this law had been executed. In return for this fidelity to its obligations the American government had been subjected to an undignified denunciation before the world. It had yielded long enough to the weakness of

2 B

the Central American republics, and without doing them injustice it would now take care to do justice to itself. Preparatory to such action as might be necessary, a fleet would be stationed in the ports of San Juan del Sur, Realejo, and Greytown.[1]

Upon the receipt of these instructions Lamar notified the Nicaraguan government that the arrangements made with the Frenchman must not jeopardize any rights previously acquired by American citizens and inquired whether the Mora-Martinez manifesto were genuine. On the following day he received a reply stating that there was no intention of defrauding the American citizens of their rights, but ignoring entirely his question concerning the manifesto. Some days later the American minister repeated the question and asked for an immediate and direct answer. When no reply came he made the demand a third time, and even more emphatically: "Is the document genuine or not?" This brought a reply. The document was genuine, but was signed by Martinez when he was at Rivas acting as a private citizen and not in his official capacity. It was, therefore, not an official act, but merely the expression of a desire on the part of a private citizen to rid his country of filibustering.[2]

On August 8 Lamar reached San José and presented his credentials to the Costa Rican government. In a conference with Mora he was told that the manifesto had originated in mistaken conceptions, and that when it was drafted the fears of a filibuster invasion were so great that his country would have thrown itself as a colony into the arms of any nation that would give protection. On Sep-

[1] MS., Archives, Department of State, American States, Instructions, XV.

[2] MS., Archives, Department of State, Nicaragua and Costa Rica, Despatches, III. The weakness of this explanation (not to use a harsher characterization) is attested by the preamble of the manifesto, which reads: "*The supreme chiefs* of the two republics of Nicaragua and Costa Rica, assembled at Rivas, after having settled the questions which divided the republics, and having reëstablished peace and the most complete harmony between them with a common accord, and in order to secure the independence and safety of the two countries as well as of all Central America," etc. (The italics are mine.)

tember 16 Mora made further amends by a letter in which he denounced the sentiments expressed in the manifesto as groundless and expressed full confidence in the good faith and upright intentions of the President of the United States.[1] On the 25th Martinez did likewise.

With the entrance of Belly into Nicaragua the American capitalists who were competing for the transit concession did not abandon their fight. The grant which had been obtained on June 27, 1857, by Stebbins and White was revoked, at the instigation of Vanderbilt's agents, on January 28, 1858, and on the 8th of March following the concession was transferred to Vanderbilt. Stebbins and White denied the legality of the revocation, appealed to the United States for protection, and continued their preparations for inaugurating a steamship service.[2]

It soon became evident that Vanderbilt had no intention of reopening the route, but on the other hand desired the concession so as to prevent any one else from using it. It transpired that the Panama line, or Pacific Mail Company, desiring to monopolize the traffic between Panama and California, agreed to pay him a monthly subsidy of $56,000, provided that he would neither run in opposition to this company nor allow anyone else to do so.[3] He therefore made peace with Morgan and Garrison, and they retired from the field. This narrowed the contest to one between Vanderbilt and the Stebbins-White organization. The latter held on persistently; perhaps Vanderbilt thought it would never command sufficient resources to become formidable and merely tolerated its existence.

It is significant, however, that Señor Irisarri, who had championed the cause of Stebbins and White, was replaced in October, 1858, by Jerez, whom the archives of the American State Depart-

[1] MS., Archives, Department of State, Nicaragua and Costa Rica, Despatches, III.
[2] *Ibid.*
[3] *Harper's Weekly*, III., 114; New York_Herald, June_5,_1858.

ment show to have been in correspondence with Vanderbilt's agents before his appointment.[1] It is also significant that as soon as the first Stebbins-White steamer was advertised to sail for Greytown Jerez published a card over his name in the New York papers warning persons against attempting to go to California by this route, as the company had no steamers on the lake or river, and the transit would have to be made in bungoes. It was taken for granted that the minister published this at Vanderbilt's suggestion.[2] For this diplomatic indiscretion he was rebuked by Cass.[3]

The steamer *Washington*, the first boat of the Stebbins and White Company, duly sailed from New York for Greytown on November 7 with 320 passengers. On her arrival at Greytown an officer from the United States ship *Savannah* examined her in accordance with instructions and found nothing suspicious. The Nicaraguan government, however, had notified the company's agent at Greytown that the passengers would not be allowed to cross the isthmus. The agent took a river steamer and went to Granada to attempt to get the government to recede from this attitude. At San Carlos the boat was compelled to take on a file of soldiers before being allowed to proceed across the lake. The agent found the officials obdurate and learned that the California steamer which touched at San Juan del Sur had already departed. While the *Washington* was awaiting his return she was boarded by British officers and searched a second time. Being unable to send her passengers by way of Nicaragua, the *Washington* proceeded to Aspinwall and sent them to California on the steamers of the rival company. About ninety refused to continue the journey and returned to New York.[4] This was the Alpha and Omega of the transportation business of Messrs. Stebbins and White; and the Transit remained closed. The spectre of Walker and his men

[1] MS., Department of State, Central America, Notes to Department, II.
[2] Washington *Evening Star*, Nov. 4, 1858.   [3] Wheeler Scrapbook no. 4, 336.
[4] MS., Archives, Navy Department, Home Squadron, 1858–9, 129; Wheeler Scrapbook no. 4, 336.

returning to Nicaragua was a sufficient guarantee that the Transit would remain closed and that Vanderbilt would draw his subsidy for many months to come.

Finally in the autumn of 1859 Vanderbilt terminated his alliance with the Pacific Mail Company and announced his intention of reviving the Nicaraguan service. It was even rumoured that he would use the filibusters for this purpose if the Nicaraguan government proved obdurate, and one of his steamers actually took on board a cargo of arms in New York and proceeded to New Orleans, whence she attempted to clear for Aspinwall, but was prevented by the interference of the government.[1] For some reason Vanderbilt abandoned his plan before the route was reopened. Various other schemes were proposed in the following decade, but they never went beyond the stage of incubation. Finally the building of the transcontinental railways in the United States deprived the isthmus of much of its former geographical importance. The closure of the Transit was perhaps the most important result of Walker's career in Nicaragua. Before his advent some twenty thousand Americans were passing through that country each year. His acts, resulting in the turning of this traffic elsewhere, perhaps changed the destiny of Nicaragua.

[1] See the account of the detention of the steamer *Philadelphia* in the following chapter.

CHAPTER XXIII

THE FINALE OF FILIBUSTERING

It will be recalled that when Walker left New Orleans for Nicaragua in November, 1857, he was under bond on a charge of violating the neutrality law. On his return to the United States he announced his intention of going to New Orleans and demanding trial for this alleged offence, and this announcement was probably what saved his bondsman from having to pay for his forfeiture. When Walker reached Mobile he was arrested upon the request of the Federal authorities in New Orleans, but was released upon a writ of habeas corpus,[1] and after reaching the latter city was indicted, along with Anderson, for violation of the neutrality law of 1818.[2] He remained there throughout the spring, being most of the time in seclusion in his quarters at 184 Custom House Street, where he was busily engaged in the preparation of a history of his career in Nicaragua. He and Anderson were brought to trial on May 31. Pierre Soulé appeared in their defence. The government produced as witnesses Bruno von Natzmer, Julius Hesse, the agent of J. G. Humphries and secretary of the recently organized Southern Emigration Society, Messrs. Pilcher and Slatter, who had charge of the sale of Nicaraguan bonds, and Captain Chatard, formerly commander of the *Saratoga*. Damaging evidence was produced, and the charge

---

[1] *Louisiana Courier*, Jan. 26, 1858.

[2] After Anderson and his men were landed at Key West they were held for examination before a United States district judge, who refused to raise the point of the jurisdiction of the government over the high seas, but ruled that inasmuch as there was sufficient evidence to indicate a violation of the law at New Orleans the offenders should be sent there for trial.

of Judge Campbell was by no means favourable to the defendants. Walker, as in his trial in California, addressed the jury in his own defence. After deliberating for an hour and a half, the jury reported that it was unable to agree, and was discharged. Ten stood for acquittal, and two for conviction. Walker, confident of ultimate acquittal, demanded a new trial, but the district attorney entered a *nolle prosequi.*[1]

After his trial Walker remained in New Orleans. He still avowed his purpose of returning to Nicaragua, and declared that he would eat his Christmas dinner in Granada.[2] Preparations had been in progress for several months. On February 8 the legislature of Alabama incorporated the Mobile and Nicaragua Steamship Company with an authorized capital of one hundred thousand dollars.[3] About a month later the Southern Emigration Society, with branches throughout the South, but strongest in Alabama, Mississippi, and South Carolina, was formed for the purpose of "colonizing" Nicaragua. During the spring and summer Walker made a lecture tour through the cities and towns of the Lower South in an effort to arouse interest in his cause and secure funds for another attempt.[4] The steamer *Fashion* had been brought back to Mobile, and on being condemned for having sailed under a false clearance, was sold for two hundred dollars and became the property of the recently incorporated Mobile and Nicaragua Steamship Company.

Early in April Henningsen made a mysterious trip into Mexico, with which Walker had no connection, and was supposed to

[1] New Orleans *Commercial Bulletin*, June 1–3, 1858; *Louisiana Courier*, June 1–3, 1858; New Orleans *Picayune*, June 1–3, 1858.

[2] *Harper's Weekly*, II., 626, 706, 802.

[3] Acts of Ala., 1857–8, 216–9; MS., Department of State, Bureau of Indexes and Archives, Central America, Letters from Department, I., 138–9; Notes to Department, III.

[4] "General Walker could raise a million dollars in Dallas County to Americanize Central America," wrote the highly enthusiastic editor of the Selma (Alabama) *Sentinel*, just after he had heard Walker make a speech. Montgomery *Advertiser*, May 21, 1858.

have volunteered his services to General D. Santiago Vidaurri, the leader of the Liberal party then conducting a revolution in that country. Lockridge had also volunteered his services to Vidaurri on March 29 and had offered to bring men and arms for his cause on condition that when peace was made Lockridge should be allowed to organize in one of the Mexican ports on the Gulf an expedition to "liberate" Cuba. On hearing of Henningsen's visit to Monterey, the Liberal headquarters, Lockridge was very much disturbed lest the services of that distinguished soldier should be preferred to his own. He was also smarting under the criticism of Walker and Henningsen of his fiasco when leading the relief expedition on the San Juan. He therefore sought to forestall Henningsen and at the same time retaliate against him for slurs on his military capacity, and wrote Vidaurri a letter of warning, declaring that Henningsen was merely Walker's agent and was meditating some piratical project. Vidaurri in reply cited a note which Lockridge had published in a Galveston newspaper showing that the latter's motives in bringing a detachment of troops into Mexico were quite different from those which he had professed in his communications with the Mexican leaders. Henningsen, on hearing of Lockridge's communication, denied that he had come in the interests of Walker or meditated any invasion, and declared that if he took part in the revolution it would be only at Vidaurri's express invitation.[1] The effect of this falling out of the two filibusters was to make the Mexican leaders suspicious, and this proffered foreign aid was not employed.

Returning from Mexico, Henningsen stopped in New Orleans, and for a time was seen in almost daily consultation with Walker. In the autumn the government became aware that another expedition was coming to a head in Mobile. On the 8th of October the Southern Emigration Society issued from its headquarters in Mobile a circular informing all prospective emigrants that a

[1] Wheeler Scrapbook no. 4, 323.

vessel would sail from that port for Nicaragua on November 10.[1]
The American naval forces in the Caribbean were urged to vigilance, and President Buchanan, on October 30, 1858, issued a
proclamation enjoining all officers of the government to be diligent in suppressing the illegal enterprise and warning any who
might be inclined to join the undertaking that their claim to go
as peaceful immigrants could be no longer advanced.[2] Irisarri
three days before had notified Cass that no foreigner, except passengers going through to California, would be permitted to enter
the country without a passport signed by the minister or consul-
general resident in the country from which he came.[3] About the
same time Lord Napier notified Cass that any attempt of the
filibusters to land at Greytown or upon the Mosquito Coast would
be repelled by the forces of the British navy, and any attempt
to land in Nicaragua proper or Costa Rica would be repelled if
the governments of these countries so requested.[4] Malmesbury
in London also notified the American minister, George M. Dallas,
that two British ships had been ordered to Greytown to intercept
the filibusters, and asked that the American vessels in Central
American waters be ordered to coöperate.[5] A similar request was
made of the French government, which consented and also ordered a naval force to Central American points.[6]

Commodore James H. McIntosh, who had succeeded Paulding

[1] The text of this circular was reproduced in several Southern papers, for example
the Montgomery *Advertiser*, in October, 1858. See also *Gulf States Historical Magazine*, II., 184.

[2] Moore, *Works of James Buchanan*, X., 230.

[3] MS., Archives, State Department, Central America, Notes from Department, I., 148; Letters from Department, I., 147–8.

[4] MS., Archives State Department, American States, Instructions, XVI., 23 ff.;
British State Papers, XLVIII., 699.

[5] *British State Papers*, XLVIII., 711–12.

[6] MS., Archives State Department, American States, Instructions, XVI., 23 ff. It
is perhaps needless to say that Cass, with his well-known European antipathies, did
not relish these measures of England and France, and notified Lord Napier and M. de
Sartiges that such acts by their governments would arouse ill-feeling in the United
States and further complicate the existing Central American problems.

in command of the American squadron stationed in the Caribbean, was cautioned on November 17 by the Secretary of the Navy, Isaac Toucey, to be vigilant and intercept any unlawful expedition headed for Nicaragua. To avoid a repetition of the Paulding affair he was ordered to interfere only *at sea.* "You will not do this within any harbour, nor land any part of your forces for the purpose."[1] The Navy Department's stationing of warships in Central American ports to prevent the landing of filibusters and then ordering their commanders to act only on the high seas was an occasion of much bewilderment to the naval officers concerned. They addressed frequent letters to the Department asking further enlightenment as to their duties, and even setting forth hypothetical cases on which they desired the Department to prescribe a definite course of conduct. It is needless to say that Toucey was never able to explain just how a warship lying at anchor, say, in Greytown harbour, should intercept a filibuster craft before it came within a marine league of the shore. Moreover, the officers were warned that they must not act on mere suspicion and must not interfere with lawful commerce, — injunctions which still further befuddled the nautical brains.

On October 16 Thaddeus Sanford, the collector of the port of Mobile, notified Secretary Cobb that he had just received a visit from Walker, who stated that a ship would leave Mobile for Greytown about the 15th of November, and would take about three hundred peaceful emigrants, but no arms. The filibuster stated that he himself would not be one of the emigrants, if that were objected to. Cobb told Sanford that if a clearance were requested, to refer the matter directly to the Treasury Department. On November 9 a clearance was asked for the barque *Alice Tainter,* which was to convey three hundred or more passengers, and Cobb ordered the clearance withheld. A number of

[1] House Ex. Doc. 24, 35 Cong., 2 Sess.

these passengers had passports signed by Irisarri, which were at first thought to be forgeries, as Irisarri claimed to have issued only twelve passports to persons who were going on the regular steamer *Washington*, of the Stebbins and White line, on December 6. Strange to say, these passports were now in the hands of the filibusters in Mobile, though no one knew how they were secured. When the *Tainter* was detained many of the recruits for Nicaragua returned to their homes. On November 30 Walker was summoned before a grand jury in Mobile, but no bill was returned against him.[1]

At this time a number of Southern papers were openly commenting upon the preparations. The New Orleans *Crescent* stated that a company was forming in that city, and the Augusta (Georgia) *Despatch* announced the departure of Colonel A. F. Rudler, a former member of Walker's staff, for Mobile, whence he was to sail for Nicaragua.[2]

On December 4 Collector Sanford was again approached by persons implicated in filibustering expeditions and was asked for a clearance to Key West for the schooner *Susan*. Sanford denied the application as before and referred the matter to the Secretary of the Treasury. Humphries, the owner of the vessel, threatened the collector with a damage suit, and several friends of the former tried to intimidate him with threats of violence. When these tactics failed they resolved upon the desperate plan of sending the schooner off without a clearance. A hundred and twenty emigrants under the command of Anderson and Doubleday were taken on board between ten and twelve o'clock on the night of December 4, and the schooner was towed down Mobile Bay to Dog Bar, where the tug cast off and the vessel headed for Central America under its own sail. Among the officers were a number of veterans of previous campaigns: Colonels Bruno von Natzmer and Rudler, Major Hoof, and Captains McMichael,

[1] House Ex. Doc. 25, 35 Cong., 2 Sess.   [2] Wheeler Scrapbook no. 4, 336.

Rhea, and McEachern. All day of the 5th the schooner lay becalmed, and the next day, while still in the bay, was overhauled by a revenue cutter. An officer boarded the *Susan* and asked to see her papers. Captain Harry Maury, the skipper, stated that he had not cleared yet and was on his way to the fleet station down the bay to prepare for sea. The officer took Maury's explanation to his commander and soon returned, declaring the vessel a prize of the United States, and ordered an immediate return to Mobile. Maury flatly refused to obey and dropped his anchor. The commander of the cutter and six men came aboard. As their boat drew near, the filibusters lined the rail with drawn revolvers and bowie knives, and they made many threats during the parley between Maury and Anderson and the cutter's officers, declaring that they would not allow the commander to return to his ship. The latter then ordered his officer in the boat alongside to return to the cutter and open fire on the *Susan*, regardless of the commander's life. This determination of the officer seemed to cool the anger of the "passengers," and he was allowed to return unmolested. He declared as he left that if the schooner left the spot he would sink her. Unluckily, he left one of his officers on board, and Maury now had him as a hostage. Knowing that the cutter would not fire on his vessel under such circumstances, he at once weighed anchor and a merry chase began down the bay. It was useless for the cutter to try to board the schooner, as the latter's force outnumbered the government crew five to one and could easily have pitched the boarders into the sea without resorting to further violence. The revenue officer on the *Susan* was invited into the cabin, and, according to report, soon went the way of all bibulous flesh.

A heavy fog came down and the vessels lost sight of each other. The filibusters then crowded all sail and made for the Gulf, but suddenly out of the mist the cutter appeared just in front of them. They at once dropped anchor and the cutter followed suit. Parleying was resumed that night by the two skippers, with no result, and the next day Maury made an effort to slip through Grant's Pass, but turned back when the cutter cleared her decks for action. The two vessels then beat about till after dark, when Maury paid the cutter a visit and suggested that they both anchor for the night as before. This was agreed to, and when Maury returned he had the anchor chain run out of one hawse-hole and pulled back through the other. The cutter's commander, hearing the rattling of the chain and thinking that the schooner had anchored, hove to and dropped his anchor while the *Susan* sped on in the darkness, shading her binnacle light with a blanket and protected by a gathering fog. On perceiving this ruse, the cutter's skipper started in pursuit, but ran aground, and the *Susan* was many miles away when he was again afloat. The revenue officer, who was still on board the escaping vessel, on seeing the trick, ordered Maury to drop anchor and not leave the bay. Maury coolly replied that he could not think of it; and the guardian of the nation's honour accepted the situation with something of the philosophy of Omar Khayyam and returned to the wine pots of the cabin. Two days out, the *Susan* hailed a vessel for New Orleans and transferred the government officer to it. As he left the schooner the "passengers" gave him three cheers for a jolly good fellow.

Doubleday describes the men aboard the schooner as being "mostly of the class found about the wharves of Southern cities, with here and there a Northern bank cashier who had suddenly changed his vocation." [1] They had sailed with sealed orders, to be opened two days out, and these directed Anderson to land at Omoa in Honduras and seize the castle of San Fernando, a very strong fortress, which was to be a rendezvous for other expeditions to follow. In this way the war vessels at the Nicaraguan ports might be avoided. Walker felt justified in land-

[1] *Reminiscences*, 201.

ing an armed force at any point in Central America on account of
the war which all the States had undertaken against him. The
filibusters, however, came to grief before reaching their destination, as the *Susan* early on the morning of December 16 struck
a coral reef about sixty miles from Belize. After being stranded
there for three days the men were taken off and landed on a small
island, where they subsisted for a week or more on tropical fruits
and fish and some of the ship's stores which were saved from the
wreck. The schooner's single boat was taken by Maury and Anderson to Belize, where they tried, unsuccessfully, to secure another
vessel to take them to their destination. Luckily, the British
war sloop *Basilisk* was on hand, and her captain came to the
rescue. He not only took the shipwrecked filibusters on board
his ship, but offered to convey them home, regarding them not
as filibusters but as shipwrecked citizens of a friendly nation.
The *Basilisk* reached Mobile on New Year's day, and less than
a month after their departure the filibusters were back at their
starting point. As they entered the harbour they passed very
close to the revenue cutter which had caused them so much trouble,
and its commander must have looked upon their present discom-
fiture with little or no regret. The citizens of Mobile gave a
banquet in honour of the officers of the *Basilisk* and bestowed upon
them the freedom of the city in recognition of their kind treatment
of Walker's disappointed and unfortunate followers.[1]

Secretary Cobb, shortly after the return of the wrecked filibusters, ordered their prosecution, and on January 19 the principals in the *Susan* episode, Anderson, Maury, Natzmer, and
others, were hailed before a United States commissioner and held
in a bond of $2500 each for violation of the neutrality law. The
grand jury, however, would find no bill, and they were not further

[1] On the voyage and wreck of the *Susan* see *Harper's Weekly*, III., 22–39 ; Wheeler
Scrapbook no. 4, 335 ; Doubleday, *Reminiscences*, 192–216 ; *British State Papers*,
XLVIII., 756 ; Mobile *Register*, Jan. 4, 1859.

molested.[1] Julius Hesse, the agent of J. G. Humphries, who owned the *Susan, Fashion,* and *Alice Tainter,* brought suit in the State court against Sanford for $25,000 damages for his refusal to issue a clearance to the *Alice Tainter.* The collector alleged that his act was that of an officer of the United States and secured a transference of the case to the United States circuit court, whereupon Hesse gave up the fight and a *nolle prosequi* was entered.[2]

The news of Walker's intended return threw the Central Americans into a panic, in spite of the protection afforded by English, French, and American warships. On January 18 the Nicaraguan government requested the British to land marines and assist in expelling the filibusters in case they should escape the vigilance of the combined fleets and succeed in landing. Commodore McIntosh, commanding the American squadron, made overtures to the government, intimating that he would be pleased also to receive a request to land his forces if it should prove necessary.[3] The Nicaraguans were not satisfied with this protection, and professed great fear of an attack from the Pacific side, which was undefended. They pretended to fear that the filibusters, finding it impossible to land at any port on the eastern coast of Nicaragua, would go to Aspinwall, cross the isthmus, take a vessel at Panama, and land unopposed at San Juan del Sur or Realejo. At their urgent request, therefore, Sir William Gore Ouseley, then in the country to negotiate a treaty, asked the commander of the British ship *Vixen* to visit all the small ports on the Pacific and prevent any filibusters from landing there. Ouseley had gone to Nicaragua to negotiate a treaty of commerce and navigation and to relinquish the Mosquito protectorate; and the naval demonstration in the Caribbean was intended by his government ostensibly for his protection. Malmesbury had stated that so long as Ouseley remained in Central America the British war vessels

---

[1] House Ex. Doc. 25, 35 Cong., 2 Sess.; Mobile *Register,* Jan. 20 and June 2, 1859.
[2] Mobile *Register,* May 26, 1859.   [3] *British State Papers,* L., 150–1.

would repel any filibustering invasion. The diplomat thus became to Nicaragua a kind of insurance against Walker's return, and the wily officials resolved to delay their negotiations as much as possible and keep the minister on their soil as long as the British government would tolerate their procrastination. As soon as negotiations would be well under way an alarm that the filibusters were coming would be manufactured, and the treaty-making would be suspended. Some of the reports were of the silliest character imaginable. In March, for example, it was published abroad that Walker, under the assumed name of Wilson, had crossed the isthmus of Panama with one hundred and fifty of his followers on his way to California, where he would organize another expedition. It was also reported that Henningsen and a large band of followers were marching through Mexico to join Walker in California, where it was planned to embark over a thousand men for Nicaragua. Strange to say, Ouseley accepted all these reports in good faith, and doggedly persisted in his efforts to secure a treaty. Malmesbury finally intimated to him that he was being made the victim of a ruse, and that the explanations given for the delay in the negotiations were unsatisfactory. It was evident that the Nicaraguans at this time were loath to consent to the withdrawal of the protectorate over the Mosquito Coast, as it would leave their flank more exposed to filibustering invasions. In August Ouseley was called home, having accomplished very little.[1]

In September, 1859, the filibusters, who had been very quiet during the year, again began to show signs of activity. Walker had spent a good part of the summer in New York, and, it was thought, had secured the promise of more arms from George Law. At any rate, in September the steamer *Philadelphia* received a large supply of arms and ammunition and left New York for New Orleans, where filibusters appeared to be congregating.

[1] *British State Papers*, L., 147, 186, 189–90, 214–48.

On the day fixed for departure, to avoid suspicion, the men went several miles below the city and boarded the towboat *Panther*, which landed them at the Southwest Pass. Here they intended to wait for the steamer which was to pick them up after leaving the port. A clearance for Aspinwall was asked for the *Philadelphia*, but as the government officials had become suspicious of the movements among the friends of Walker, it was refused. The United States marshal secured a company of artillery from the garrison at Baton Rouge and proceeded to the Southwest Pass, where he arrested the waiting filibusters. They took their arrest good-naturedly, raising a black flag as a joke when the troops came in sight and stated that they were only taking a little fishing trip down the river. When they were taken back to New Orleans, Anderson, Maury, Fayssoux and William W. Scott, their leaders, were held in bail to the amount of three thousand dollars, but were later released, as a Federal grand jury failed to return an indictment against them.[1] The others were quartered in the barracks below the city, whence they decamped, as they were not placed under guard. The *Philadelphia* was searched, but nothing suspicious was reported by the searchers. The following night, however, the arms were thrown overboard. On hearing of this the government officers libelled the vessel. A second search revealed a concealed hatchway covered with tar so as to be indistinguishable, and with barrels placed over it as an extra precaution. This hatchway was opened, and disclosed a secret compartment filled with ammunition.[2]

[1] New Orleans *Picayune*, Oct. 18 and 25, 1859.

[2] Mobile *Register*, Oct. 5, 9, 20, 22, 26, 1859; New York *Herald*, Oct. 6, 7, 8, 10, 1859; *Harper's Weekly*, III., 663; *British Accounts and Papers*, 1860, LXVIII., 295-7. On October 7, 1859, Howell Cobb wrote to President Buchanan: "You will be gratified to learn that the Walker expedition has in all probability been frustrated by the energy of our officers. We heard that [illegible] and two hundred men were to go from New York in the *St. Louis* when I directed the proper steps to be taken there to prevent it. The *St. Louis* was accordingly refused a clearance." *The Correspondence of Robert Toombs, Alexander H. Stephens, and Howell Cobb*, 447, edited by U. B. Phillips. (In *Annual Report of the American Historical Association*, 1911, II.)

During the period in which Walker was compelled to remain quietly under the eye of the government he was not idle. Though forced to lay aside the sword, he found occasion to wield a mightier weapon, the pen, in the use of which he had acquired skill while editing newspapers. He was now engaged in the preparation of a history of his career in Nicaragua, and in the spring of 1860 the work was published in Mobile in the form of an octavo volume of 431 pages and under the title of *The War in Nicaragua*. The book contains a very full account of the filibuster's experience in Nicaragua from the sailing of the *Vesta* until his surrender to Commander Davis. His previous experience in Lower California is summarized in six pages of the first chapter, and it is evident, from the gingerly manner in which he deals with this part of his career, that he did not regard it as a very pleasant subject. Throughout the book the author always refers to himself in the third person. The style is clear, terse, and direct, and the diction is pure. His treatment of both friend and foe is remarkably dispassionate, and his pen has betrayed very little of the emotion that he must have experienced as he sat and recounted the events of his rise and fall. The facts are recorded with scrupulous accuracy, and the greatest compliment that could be paid him on this score has come from hostile Central American historians, who while impugning his motives and condemning his acts accept his version of the actual events without question.[1]

Few writers have succeeded in narrating a story in which they have played such a predominant part with so little revelation of their own personality. To the reader the author appears as the cold embodiment of an idea or purpose rather than as a being endowed with all the traits characteristic of human nature. A careful study of the work shows that the main purpose of its author was not merely to record the history of his struggle for supremacy

[1] Montúfar, for example, when confronted by conflicting statements, usually accepts Walker's version in preference to that of his own countrymen.

in Central America, but also to make an effective appeal for Southern aid and sympathy in his further efforts toward this goal. In
Chapter VIII he poses as a potential saviour of the Southern cause,
and asserts that the Nicaraguan movement offers the South a
last and only hope for the safeguarding of her existing economic
and social institutions. It is this chapter which has caused
Walker to appear in the eyes of many students of his history as
one of the chief apostles of slavery propagandism. Due regard,
however, should be given to the circumstances under which the
work was written.

It was at this time that Walker took another step that seemed
to many only further preparation for his return to Latin America.
Born and bred in a strictly Protestant atmosphere, and mani-
festing in early life a deeply religious nature, he now announced
a change of heart and became a communicant in the Roman
Catholic Church. His friends declared this a result of genuine
conversion; his enemies scoffed at his sincerity and claimed that
his purpose was to allay any prejudice which might have existed
against him in Central America on account of his Protestantism.

Shortly after the detention of the *Philadelphia*, news came from
Honduras that revived the drooping hopes of the filibusters.
For nearly a decade the disposition of certain islands off the coast
of that country had been a bone of contention between Great
Britain and the United States. In 1841 Colonel McDonald, the
British superintendent of Belize and the Warwick of the Mos-
quito Kingdom, hauled down the Honduran flag on the island of
Ruatan and raised the British flag in its stead, claiming Ruatan
as a dependency of Belize. This island had fine harbours, which
were rare on that coast, and a commanding geographical position,
so that the reasons for British encroachment were not far to seek.
The Clayton-Bulwer treaty, in 1850, according to the American
interpretation, had stipulated the restoration of this island to
Honduras. The British government, however, not only retained

its hold on Ruatan but added to it in 1852 five other islands which it designated collectively as "The Colony of Bay Islands." [1] In the United States this action evoked much resentment, and the Senate passed a resolution declaring it a violation of the Clayton-Bulwer treaty. The Dallas-Clarendon treaty of 1856 was amended in the Senate by the insertion of a clause restoring the Bay Islands to Honduras. The British government rejected this and suggested in turn that the disposition of the colony should be fixed by a treaty between Great Britain and Honduras. The American government would not concede that Honduras should dispose of any of her territory by treaty with a European power. The question remained in dispute, therefore, until November 28, 1859, when Charles Lennox Wyke, the successor of Sir William Gore Ouseley, concluded a treaty with Honduras providing for the restoration of the Bay Islands to that government.[2]

A large portion of the inhabitants of Ruatan, being British subjects, were bitterly opposed to the transfer of the island to Honduras and sent a memorial to Queen Victoria praying that the Wyke treaty be not ratified. The ratification was announced to the islanders on May 21, whereupon a public meeting was held and a declaration was adopted setting forth certain guarantees they would ask for the protection of their civil and religious liberties.[3] Reports of these proceedings in the American press gave great encouragement to the filibusters, as they seemed to foreshadow another Central American revolution.

Early in the spring of 1860 one of the discontented Bay Islanders visited New Orleans and sought to invite Walker to Ruatan to aid them in resisting the Hondurans. Walker was visiting in Louisville at the time, and the islander conferred with Fayssoux

[1] *British State Papers*, XLVI., 246 ff.
[2] Huberich, C. H., *The Trans-Isthmian Canal: A Study in American Diplomatic History*, 12. (Austin, Tex., 1904.)
[3] MS., Archives, State Department, Notes to Department, Central America, III.; Notes from Department, I., 177–196.

and left word with him for the filibuster leader to come down and help. On returning to New Orleans in April, Walker was apprized of the visit, and at once saw another opportunity of regaining his place in Nicaragua. He would put himself at the head of another body of followers, expel the Hondurans from Ruatan, and use this island as a base from which to recommence his work of "regenerating" Central America. He at once began his preparations, and on April 20 sent forward a small party to prepare the way for the others. Among these was one of his former officers, Captain West. Others followed in May and June as regular passengers on the fruit vessels, and their wants were looked after by the disaffected islanders. As the number of strange visitors increased, some of the natives grew suspicious. Many of these were negroes, and loyal Britishers assured them that they would be enslaved by the Americans.[1]

The president of Honduras at this time was none other than the Guardiola whom the American Phalanx had defeated in 1855 at Virgin Bay. As soon as he and the British authorities got word of the coming of the filibusters they agreed to postpone the transfer of the islands while the invasion was threatening. In June Rudler and Dolan, former officers of Walker's, with about twenty others, took passage on the schooner *Clifton* at New Orleans for Ruatan. This vessel carried arms and other supplies manifested in her papers as merchandise. Walker and Henry embarked on the schooner *John E. Taylor* with another section of the expedition. The *Clifton* arrived at Belize on June 14 and proceeded to discharge a portion of her cargo assigned to that port. The large number of passengers on board made the authorities suspicious, and an officer came on board and searched the vessel, finding that some of the boxes manifested as merchandise contained ammunition. These were seized as contraband, and a clearance for Ruatan was refused. The captain of the schooner then protested, hauled down his flag, and abandoned his vessel. Another

[1] New York *Herald*, July 25, Sept. 1, 1860.

schooner was chartered, however, and the men were taken to Ruatan. Off this island they met the *Taylor* with Walker and Henry and their party aboard. The entire command was now placed aboard the *Taylor* and taken to the small island of Cozumel, where the men constructed a rude shelter, as it was the rainy season, and waited for expected supplies from New Orleans. They were greatly disappointed at finding the British flag still flying over the islands and could do nothing but wait for the transfer to take place. After a week spent on the island the men were reëmbarked and cruised for about three weeks watching for the supply vessel that never came, and for the striking of the British colours that never occurred.[1]

Finally Walker resolved on the desperate plan of making an attack on the fortress at Truxillo, on the mainland in Honduras. As Honduras had made war upon him as President of Nicaragua, he easily persuaded himself that he was now justified in retaliating. The plans were very similar to those he had followed in capturing Granada five years before. They sailed past the town by night and landed in the darkness three miles up the bay. A march upon the fort was then begun, but their landing had been observed, and the people were forewarned. The filibusters reached the town just at daybreak and were fired upon from an ambush. They rushed the fort, however, which was held by only a corporal's guard, and soon had the shelter of its walls and the control of the town without losing a man, though several were wounded. The fort was a good specimen of a Spanish-American fortress, and furnished comfortable quarters for the men as well as additional ammunition, which was found in its magazine. A hospital was provided for the wounded and for two or three who had contracted fever, and supplies were obtained — we are not told how — from the town.

[1] MS., Archives, State Department, Central America, Notes to Department, III.; New York *Herald*, July 25, Aug. 18, 1860; *British State Papers*, L., 327–8.

Truxillo was captured on August 6, and on the following day Walker issued an address to the people of Honduras, giving his reasons for entering their country and assuring them that he did not make war on the people, but only on a government which stood in the way of the interests of all Central America, and that they might rely on him for the protection of their personal and property rights. The reasons he gives for the invasion are not stated with his usual clarity of expression. He was invited to Nicaragua over five years before, he says, and was promised certain rights and privileges upon rendering certain services to that State. These services were faithfully rendered, and then the Honduran government joined a coalition to expel him from Central America. The people of the Bay Islands now find themselves in a position very similar to that occupied by the Americans in Nicaragua in 1855, and the same conditions which caused Guardiola to fight the latter will cause him to drive the Bay Islanders from Honduras. A knowledge of this fact has caused some of the residents of the islands to ask "the adopted citizens of Nicaragua" to aid them in the maintenance of their rights, but no sooner had a few of these arrived than Guardiola delayed to receive the territory, thus injuring the territorial interests of Honduras and thwarting "a cardinal object of Central American policy." Moreover, the people of the islands will never submit to Honduran authority unless they receive certain concessions which Guardiola will never make, and hence they and the naturalized Nicaraguans have certain interests in common. It is now their common purpose to place in power in Honduras those who would concede the rights required by the islanders in Honduras and by the adopted citizens in Nicaragua.[1]

Walker's followers were given to understand that they might expect the aid of Cabañas. It will be recalled that Cabañas had visited Walker at Granada in November, 1855, and had then

[1] New York *Tribune*, Aug. 29, Sept. 15; *Harper's Weekly*, IV., 583.

endeavoured to secure his assistance in overthrowing the Legitimist government in Honduras. Walker's refusal had turned
both Cabañas and Jerez into avowed enemies,[1] and both had used
their influence to secure his expulsion. Cabañas was now in
exile in San Salvador, but there was no reason to believe that
he would welcome the return of the filibusters, however much he
may have hated Guardiola.

As soon as the Americans had established themselves in Truxillo they proceeded to put the fort in order, overhauling the dis-
mantled guns, remounting many of them on carriages, converting
the old military prison into a commissariat, and preparing if need
be to remain there indefinitely. Walker issued an order abolish-
ing customs duties and making Truxillo a free port, thus adding,
as the sequel showed, another to his many blunders. He was
unfortunate, a few days after his arrival, in losing the officer in
whom he placed his greatest reliance. Thomas Henry, who during the Mexican War and later in Nicaragua proved such a fighter,
receiving during the war with the allies eight wounds in about as
many months, while under the influence of liquor entered the
magazine with a lighted cigar. Always spoiling for a fight, in
battle or out, and especially so when inflamed with drink, he
attacked the officer who ordered him out of the place, and the
latter in self-defence shot Henry in the face, the bullet shattering
the jawbone. For days he lay at the point of death, and Walker
is said to have remained constantly by his side when duties did
not demand his presence elsewhere. His loss was greater than that
of fifty ordinary specimens of the genus filibuster.[2]

On the 19th of August there arrived in port H. M. S. *Icarus*,
Norvell Salmon commander.[3] From him two days later Walker
received a note stating that the customs of the port had been

---

[1] See above, p. 160–1.   [2] Jamison, *With Walker in Nicaragua*, 168 ff.
[3] The Spanish authorities in Havana also despatched a war vessel to Truxillo
on learning of Walker's landing there, but it arrived too late to be of service. *British State Papers*, LI., 1288.

mortgaged to the British government to pay a debt for which this government had made itself responsible, but that since Walker's arrival the funds in the custom-house had been seized, trade had ceased, the interests of British merchants had been seriously affected, and the presence of the invaders had deferred the completion of a treaty between Great Britain and Honduras. For these reasons, therefore, he felt it his duty to demand that Walker lay down his arms, return the funds taken from the custom-house, and reëmbark, leaving his military stores behind as a surety against further descents upon the coast. The officers, however, would be allowed to retain their side arms. Upon compliance with this demand, the safety and personal property of the men would be guaranteed by the British flag.

Walker replied at once, denying any knowledge of money being taken from the custom-house and stating that had he known the facts as given in Salmon's letter he would not have sought to modify the customs regulations of the port. His whole tone is apologetic, and quite different from that he had previously assumed in his communications with naval officers. His presence in Truxillo, he told Salmon, was "due entirely to the engagements which I consider I had in honour contracted with a people desirous of living in Central America under the ancient laws and customs of the realm, claiming with them common interests under the institutions derived from the code of Alfred. I thought it no wrong to assist them in the maintenance of the rights they had lawfully acquired." He concluded his note by saying that he deemed it no dishonour to lay down his arms to a British officer, but asked for particulars as to what Salmon would do in such an event.[1]

In reply Salmon expressed his gratification that Walker deemed it no dishonour to surrender to him and gave further reasons for making this demand. The government of Honduras did not seem "to wish the code of Alfred introduced into the country in

[1] New York *Herald*, Sept. 28, 1860.

the manner that you propose." Numerous requests for protection had come to him from the inhabitants of Truxillo and Omoa, among those at the latter place being the American consul; and he proposed to give it as he was authorized to do by international law. He would take the responsibility of giving Walker and his men the protection of the British flag, though in doing so he was liable to a reprimand from his superiors, but they must leave the country at their own expense. Two schooners were then in the harbour and terms could be made with them. The funds in the custom-house, amounting to more than three thousand dollars in coin and government paper, had been taken by some one in Walker's service, and the leader would be held responsible. Moreover, he would not recognize the right of a private individual to make war upon a recognized government, and he failed to see what political rights a people desirous of living in Central America could have lawfully acquired.[1]

This communication was received late in the afternoon, and the messenger was told to return at ten o'clock the next morning for a reply. Preparations were begun immediately for abandoning the fort. Surplus Minié rifles were broken up, and all the powder that could not be carried away was thrown into water. In the hospital were six men sick and wounded, among them the dying Henry. They were left in charge of the surgeon and the hospital steward, and at midnight the rest of the command, to the number of eighty, slipped quietly out of the fort and proceeded eastward along the coast in the direction of Cape Gracias. The men left behind in the hospital passed an anxious night, expecting at any moment a murderous incursion of the natives. Early the next morning the surgeon, Dr. E. H. Newton, notified Salmon of their predicament, and the sick and wounded men were placed under British protection before the natives were aware of Walker's departure.[2]

---

[1] New York *Herald*, Sept. 28, 1860.   [2] *Ibid.*, Sept. 16, 1860.

Native troops started in pursuit of the fleeing filibusters, and on the 23d overtook and attacked them at Cotton Tree on the Roman River. The pursuers were driven back, but Walker had one man killed and a number wounded. He himself was slightly wounded in the face. Continuing their flight and always followed by the enemy, they reached an abandoned mahogany camp called Limon (or Limas), where they were refreshed with food supplied by Carib Indians, the latter being inveterate foes of the Hondurans. Reaching the Rio Negro, they followed it to within four miles of its mouth, where they encamped at the trading post of an Englishman named Demsing.

In the meantime Salmon in the *Icarus* had reached the mouth of the Rio Negro, knowing that the filibusters would have to stop on reaching its banks, and was accompanied by a schooner bearing two hundred and fifty natives under a Honduran officer named Alvarez. The British officer on September 3 took two boats and forty men up the river and on reaching the trading post summoned Walker to a conference and demanded his surrender. Salmon in a typically bluff and pompous English fashion notified the filibuster chief that there was a large force of natives at the mouth of the river and that he should thank the British that he had a whole bone in his body. Walker twice asked to whom he surrendered, and was assured that it was to a British officer.[1]

The entire command were then put aboard the *Icarus* and taken back to Truxillo, where they were landed as prisoners. Walker and Rudler were given up unconditionally to the Honduran authorities, while the others, numbering about seventy, were held as prisoners under British protection, to be sent home as soon as possible. Salmon announced that he would hang anyone who injured any of those under his flag, and the natives showed the men great kindness, not because of Salmon's threat, but out of

[1] New York *Herald*, Oct. 4, 1860; New York *Tribune*, Oct. 4, 1860; *Harper's Weekly*, IV., 647.

sympathy with the captives, most of whom were in wretched physical condition and penniless besides.

When they reached Truxillo Walker was about the only member of his party who showed no sign of depression. To a newspaper correspondent who boarded the *Icarus*, he talked at some length and turned over to him his correspondence with Salmon, which he desired to be published. He then dictated the following protest:

> "On board the Steamer *Icarus*,
> "Sept. 5, 1860.

"I hereby protest before the civilized world that when I surrendered to the captain of Her Majesty's steamer *Icarus*, that officer expressly received my sword and pistol, as well as the arms of Colonel Rudler, and the surrender was expressly made in so many words to him, as the representative of Her Britannic Majesty.

> WILLIAM WALKER." [1]

Walker found himself a prisoner in the very fort that he had abandoned a fortnight before. The room which he had converted into a commissariat was now his dungeon. Here he was confined six days. As soon as he was incarcerated he sent for a priest and told him that he wished to prepare for death. He showed an unusual concern for his men, and begged that they should not be made to suffer, declaring that they knew nothing of his sudden resolve to reach Nicaragua by way of Truxillo, and that he alone was to blame.[2] On September 11 he was told that he was to die on the following morning, and received the news with no sign of emotion. At eight o'clock on the appointed day a detachment of soldiers escorted him from the prison to the place of execution.

---

[1] New York *Herald*, Sept. 28, 1860.

[2] This is the statement of Joaquin Miller, who received the story of Walker's last hours from the priest who was with him till his death. See *Sunset Magazine*, XVI., 564.

Accompanied by two priests, he walked erect and resolute, with the appearance of being engaged in earnest religious devotion. His whole attention seemed occupied with the consolations of the priests. A large crowd followed the procession, and faces appeared at every door and window along the street. Among the natives there seemed to be great jubilation that the terrible Walker was soon to be no more. At the ruins of an old garrison, about a quarter of a mile outside the town, the procession halted. Walker was conducted to an angle in a ruined wall, and the soldiers were drawn up on three sides of a square with the wall forming the fourth side. The priests now administered the last rites of the church and withdrew, while a squad of soldiers stepped forward and fired at the command. A second squad fired a volley at the fallen body, and a single soldier then went up, and placing his musket close to the head, fired again, mutilating the lifeless face. The troops then formed in column and marched away, leaving the corpse where it fell. The priests and several Americans secured a coffin and gave the remains a Christian burial.[1] Some time later an effort was made to secure the removal of the body for burial in Tennessee, but the Honduran authorities would not permit it.[2] Among Walker's effects was the great seal of

[1] There are several different versions of Walker's execution. None are plausible except the one here given. According to one account, Walker made a speech, stating that he died in the Roman Catholic faith; that he had done wrong in making war on the Hondurans and desired their forgiveness; that his men were not to blame, and that he was ready to die. (*Harper's Weekly*, IV., 647.) One version says that he spoke in Spanish (Jamison, *With Walker in Nicaragua*); another that a priest spoke for him. As a matter of fact he spoke to none save the ministering priests. The entire account of Walker's last expedition given by Jamison as narrated by a survivor fifty years later is erroneous and misleading. The version accepted by the author is that given by two of Walker's officers, Dolan and West (New York *Herald*, Oct. 4, 1860), immediately after their return to the United States, and while the events were still fresh in their minds. Moreover, this is substantiated from two other contemporary sources. William S. Elton, an engineer on the Panama Railway, who chanced to be in Truxillo at this time and claimed to be an eyewitness of the execution, and a filibuster deserter named Scheffe, gave accounts which correspond very closely to that given by Dolan and West. See New Orleans *Delta*, Oct. 5, 1860.

[2] *American History Magazine*, III., 219.

Nicaragua, which was returned to President Martinez, along with the sword which he had surrendered to Salmon. The latter was given to the keeping of the city of Granada, where it might be cherished as an emblem of the destruction of its destroyer.[1]

Walker was no more. The fate which he had so ruthlessly decreed against Mayorga, Corral, and Salazar had now fallen upon himself, and none can say that it was undeserved; for his attack upon the inoffensive garrison and town of Truxillo was wholly indefensible. At the same time, none can approve the means by which his death was accomplished. The action of Salmon in receiving Walker's surrender to a British officer and then delivering him to the tender mercies of the Hondurans was nothing less than treachery of the basest sort, and entirely inconsistent with the high sense of honour that has always characterized the officers in the British naval service. Had the filibuster chieftain known the real purposes of Salmon, he would undoubtedly have fought to the end and have died like a soldier rather than like a felon. Granting even that Walker was no better than a pirate, Salmon had given him an officer's word, and he tarnished his epaulets when that word was broken.

By a strange coincidence, on the very day of Walker's death, his friend Edmund Randolph, delivering an address in San Francisco in celebration of the tenth anniversary of California's admission into the Union, made a reference to Walker that was in part almost prophetic: "You cannot tell to-day which pine sings the requiem of the pioneer. Some have fallen beneath their country's flag; and longings still unsatisfied have led some to renew their adventurous career upon foreign soils. Combating for strangers whose quarrels they espoused, they fell amid the jungles of the tropics and fatted the rank soil there with right precious blood. Or, upon the sands of an accursed waste, they were bound and slaughtered by inhuman men, who lured them with

[1] Perez, *Memorias*, pt. 2, 216.

promises and repaid their coming with a most cruel assassination."[1]

It was the irony of fate that President Mora, the soul of the native resistance to American filibustering, should perish in the same month and in the same manner as Walker. He had been reëlected president of Costa Rica in May, 1859, but a conspiracy of the discontented faction in the following August drove him from power and expelled him from the country. He came to the United States, and later settled on a coffee plantation in San Salvador. Some of his former supporters and others who were disaffected toward the existing government urged him to return and regain his power. In September he landed at Punta Arenas and collected three or four hundred followers, but was attacked before beginning his march on the capital. His supporters fled incontinently, and he surrendered. Tried by a drum-head court-martial on September 30, he was condemned to die, and was shot within three hours after sentence was passed. Two days afterward his brother-in-law, General Cañas, incurred the same penalty.[2]

All of Walker's followers except Rudler were kept in the custody of the British; eleven were sent home by way of Havana, and fifty-seven of them were taken direct to New Orleans in H. M. S. *Gladiator*.[3] Rudler was sentenced to die, but at Salmon's intervention his sentence was commuted to four years' imprisonment. Later some of his friends in the United States intervened and secured his pardon.[4] After Walker's departure from the United States two detachments of reinforcements followed him. The first, consisting of thirty-five men, sailed from New Orleans on August 31, and the second, somewhat larger, sailed two weeks later. The latter passed the mail steamer bringing news of Walk-

[1] The last sentence refers to Crabb. Shuck, *Representative Men of the Pacific*, 597.
[2] Bancroft, *Central America*, III., 372-5; *Harper's Weekly*, IV., 679.
[3] London *Times*, Oct. 12, 1860; New York *Herald*, Oct. 4, 1860.
[4] Jamison, *With Walker in Nicaragua*, 176.

er's capture, but had no communication with it, and learned the facts only on arriving off Ruatan. There was nothing for these expeditionists to do but to return to New Orleans.

The news of Walker's death was received in the United States with little less than indifference. His repeated failures had caused thousands who once had wished him well to look upon his further undertakings with stern disapproval. Even in his native city of Nashville, where personally he enjoyed the highest respect as a man of education and irreproachable private life, his fellow townsmen believed that his talents should have been employed to better advantage. His home paper, in commenting upon his death, said, "There are thousands in this country who will hear of his death with regret, — as that of a man who had qualities and capacities entitling him to a better fate. Throughout his career he has shown a degree of steady courage, of unflinching tenacity of purpose under the most disheartening reverses, which would have earned for him a high position if they had been used in subordination to law and in harmony with the public good."[1] In like manner, in New Orleans, where he had thousands of sympathizers, his repeated failures shook the faith of those who once had believed in his destiny, and a paper that had hitherto been favourable declared that "The mad and unwarrantable enterprise of the great filibuster has ended in disaster and defeat. Another band of brave, but recklessly impulsive, young Americans have, it is most probable, by this time met with the fate of their predecessors in Central America."[2] With these critical estimates of the man where he was best known in the South it is interesting to compare the criticisms of the papers of New York, where Walker was best known in the North. To quote the New York *Times:* "Whatever hard things may have been said of General Walker — and

[1] Nashville *Republican Banner*, Sept. 30, 1860.
[2] New Orleans *Commerical Bulletin*, quoted by the Nashville *Republican Banner*, Sept. 16, 1860.

much, we doubt not, would have been left unsaid had his fortune been more propitious — he was at least no vulgar adventurer, either by birth, habits, or education, or the honourable purposes with which he set out in life. His parentage was unsullied, his private walk and temperance unquestioned, his learning profound, and his original aims, however subsequently misdirected by an unchastened ambition, such as commended him to success, while enlisting the esteem of numerous friends. Even those who deny him all claims to military skill or political sagacity as a leader, pay the highest compliment to his moral force and personal integrity, since without these his first failure as an adventurer must inevitably have been his last." Another New York journal attributed the outcome to Walker's failure to win the wealthy and influential citizens to his support. Instead of seeking to win friends, he manifested only a blind and foolish reliance on his own destiny. Nevertheless, it averred, "had William Walker been an Englishman, or a Frenchman, he would never have become a 'filibuster,' but would have found ample scope for the exercise of his extraordinary qualities in the legitimate service of his country." It compared the government's ban upon Walker's undertakings to the attitude of the Church of England towards Knox, Whitefield, and Wesley.[1]

In his annual message to Congress in December, 1860, President Buchanan barely missed congratulating the country upon the death of Walker. "I congratulate you upon the public sentiment which now exists against the crime of setting on foot military expeditions within the limits of the United States, to proceed from thence and make war upon the people of unoffending states with whom we are at peace. In this respect a happy change has been effected since the commencement of my administration. It surely ought to be the prayer of every Christian and patriot that such expeditions may never again receive countenance or

[1] *Harper's Weekly*, I., 200, 332.

depart from our shores." [1] Henningsen, however, voiced quite a different sentiment in a long letter in vindication of his late chieftain. "So far," said he, "from filibusterism being laid in the grave of William Walker, it may safely be predicted that from every drop of blood shed from the death wounds inflicted, as we are informed, 'amidst the cheers of the natives,' to whom he had been delivered up, bound by the infamy of Norvell Salmon, will spring another ardent filibuster." [2] But Henningsen was wrong. His dead chieftain was the last, as well as the greatest, of American filibusters. The surplus energies of the young nation, which were the fundamental cause of such enterprises, were soon to find another outlet in four years of terrible civil war; and the result of this struggle was to remove another, but only a proximate, cause of filibustering, African slavery.

Even before the death of Walker all immediate prospects of a regenerated Central America had disappeared. A region that for twenty years had been wasted by civil wars, and whose heterogeneous population had demonstrated its inability to govern itself or prevent its own political dissolution, certainly needed the introduction of a new element to set things in order. The Nicaraguan emigrants belonged to a hardy race of toiling pioneers who had conquered the western wilderness and developed in half a decade in distant California a civilization superior to that of two-thirds of Europe. To Walker therefore a splendid opportunity was given. Though he never had the support of the United States government, many of the most prominent political leaders of the nation and the leading captains of American industry interested themselves in his behalf. Yet in spite of all this he failed. He was not big enough for the task. In the space of six months he had aroused against him every force that should have been enlisted on his side. The qualities wherein he was strong

---

[1] *Messages and Papers of the Presidents*, V., 649.
[2] Nashville *Republican Banner*, Oct. 10, 1860.

proved elements of weakness. Mastered by, rather than master of, his dreams, with a blind belief in his own destiny, unable to receive advice or suggestions from others (except when it came from much stronger men who sought to make him a catspaw), sadly lacking in knowledge of human nature, greedily hastening to seize supreme power, unable to conciliate opposition, but overcoming resistance by inspiring terror, utterly wanting in tact or diplomacy, his undoing was foreordained. With some fewer gifts of intellect, but with a broader knowledge of human nature and a more liberal endowment of common sense, he might have succeeded in putting an end to anarchy and founding a tropical empire on the ruins of unhappy experiments in democracy. That his success would have inured to the benefit of civilization few, perhaps, in view of the present condition of Central America, will be so rash as to deny.

As it was, his enterprise, by reason of his failure, was productive only of evil consequences to all concerned. It was injurious to private capital in the United States; it caused enormous destruction of life and property in Nicaragua; it created a suspicion in Central America against the American people which still persists; it had an untoward effect upon the relations of Great Britain and the United States; and lastly, and apparently most important of all, it destroyed interoceanic communication by way of the San Juan River and thus delayed indefinitely that "regeneration" of Nicaragua which he always declared to be his heart's desire.

INDEX

Printed in the United States of America.

Japanese Expansion and American Policies

By J. F. ABBOTT
Of Washington University

Cloth, 12mo, $1.50

Here Professor Abbott sums up dispassionately and impartially the history of the diplomatic and social relations of Japan with the United States, and in particular gives the facts that will enable an American to form his own opinion as to the possibility of future conflicts between these two countries. The work is neither pro-Japan nor anti-Japan, but seeks, rather, to present the case justly. The author emphasizes the importance of an intelligent understanding of the subject, believing that in spite of the present lull owing to acute interest in European affairs, it is yet a problem that will periodically and persistently come to the fore until it is satisfactorily solved. Professor Abbott has given careful study to Far Eastern matters for the past fifteen years, has traveled at various times throughout the Orient and previous to the Russian War was an instructor in the Imperial Japanese Naval Academy.

THE MACMILLAN COMPANY
Publishers   64-66 Fifth Avenue   New York

Law and Order in Industry

By JULIUS HENRY COHEN

Cloth, 12mo, $1.50

A lawyer who knows the facts of the case from intimate knowledge gives in this book a comprehensive story of the " Protocol " experiences in the cloak and suit industry of New York. He describes vividly the processes and results of collective dealing between a trades union and an employers' association covering a period of five years. The solution of the apparently baffling problems furnishes lessons of great immediate and future import to all employers of labor, trades unionists, social reformers and students of political science and economics.

The Mastering of Mexico

By KATE STEPHENS

With maps and half-tone plates. Decorated cloth, 12mo, $1.50

This is a simple, close-knit story of adventure founded on eye-witness accounts of one of the sixteenth century conquerors. Verisimilitude is kept even to the use of the I form of narration. The conquest of Mexico was one of the most picturesque military exploits in all history. How the doughty Spaniards made it a community, democratic affair and how that fact insured its success, the three hundred and fifty pages of this book tell in limpid, idiomatic English.

THE MACMILLAN COMPANY

Publishers   64-66 Fifth Avenue   New York

The Diplomacy of the Great War

By ARTHUR BULLARD

Cloth, 12mo, $1.50

A book which contributes to an understanding
of the war by revealing something of the diplomatic
negotiations that preceded it. The author gives
the history of international politics in Europe since
the Congress of Berlin in 1878, and considers the
new ideals that have grown up about the function
of diplomacy during the last generation, so that the
reader is in full possession of the general trend of
diplomatic development. There is added a chapter
of constructive suggestions in respect to the probable diplomatic settlements resulting from the war,
and a consideration of the relations between the
United States and Europe.

THE MACMILLAN COMPANY

Publishers   64-66 Fifth Avenue   New York

Printed in February 2023
by Rotomail Italia S.p.A., Vignate (MI) - Italy